# VEGANOMICON

# VEGANOMICON

## THE ULTIMATE VEGAN COOKBOOK

ISA CHANDRA MOSKOWITZ & TERRY HOPE ROMERO

MARLOWE & COMPANY
NEW YORK

Veganomicon: The Ultimate Vegan Cookbook
Copyright © 2007 by Isa Chandra Moskowitz and Terry Hope Romero

The Veganomicon V was designed by Vivian Ghazarian and Matt Bouloutian

Published by
Marlowe & Company
An Imprint of Avalon Publishing Group, Incorporated
245 West 17th Street • 11th Floor
New York, NY 10011-5300

AVALON
publishing group incorporated

Cataloging-in-Publication Data is available from the Library of Congress

ISBN-13: 978-1-56924-264-3
ISBN-10: 1-56924-264-X

9  8  7  6  5  4  3  2

Designed by Pauline Neuwirth, Neuwirth & Associates, Inc.

Printed in the United States of America

# CONTENTS

# INTRODUCTION

Veganomicon. *What does it mean? Is it the economic theory of eating tofu-dogs? Maybe an all-meatless convention? Or was it from that movie . . . that book Bruce Campbell finds in the woods and accidentally reads aloud, and then his dead girlfriend is flying around laughing inside the cabin, and he suddenly has a chainsaw instead of a hand?* *

No, no, it's none of those. It's just the doorstop of a cookbook that you hold in your precious hands—over 250 of our new favorite, most-requested recipes—and a big vegan cookbook needed a big vegan name. (But just to be safe, don't read this cookbook backward at the stroke of midnight.)

This is the book that was the proverbial flax-egg before the unchicken. That is, it's the epic, master guide we've wanted to write for years, back when *Vegan Cupcakes Take Over the World* was just a twinkle in our eyes and long before *Vegan with a Vengeance* packed up her things, flew the nest, and moved away to attend community college. Our new baby, the *Veganomicon*, is a big, bold vegan cookbook that doesn't hold back any punches. But don't be scared; she's quite a softy compared to her punk-rock older sister. She's like a love song ('80s power ballad, with some light '70s rock and a touch of post-punk angst) to our favorite things about vegan cooking—its diverse, delicious flavors and limitless possibilities.

But enough with the pop-culture references; what the heck is it, really? Well, it's a good old-fashioned, all-purpose cookbook. And when we say "all-purpose" we mean it—you'll find everything from savory sauces and flaky potpies to luscious pastas and fabulous finger foods . . . there are nourishing soups; amazing salads that step way beyond mixed greens; and protein-packed entrées that make the best use of tofu, tempeh, and homemade seitan. And, even after an entire book of cupcakes, there's still plenty of dessert to go around.

Many of the recipes were written for everyday meals, in hopes that you won't even need to look at the recipe again after making it a few times. You know, the kind of chow you can whip up any night of the week with your pantry staples and some seasonal produce. But you can also trust this cookbook when you're looking for an extravagant spread to impress, say, your in-laws, or the mayor of your town when she stops by.

Besides just giving you recipes, we've included lots of basic cooking information. Maybe you already know how to roast pumpkin, soak beans, and toast millet. In that case—awesome! (Then you can just be like, "Shut up, Isa and Terry!" and move on to an adventurous casserole.) But we also wrote this book with the beginner cook in mind, or maybe just the forgetful cook who can't be bothered to memorize grain-to-water cooking ratios or the baking time for sweet potatoes. So we've included simple preparation guides for beans, grains, and veggies (see pages 24–44).

## RECIPES WE WISH WE GREW UP WITH

"How do you come up with a recipe?" is a question we get time to time. (Why nobody believes us when we mutter things about sacrificing beets under the full moon, we'll never guess.) Instead, be content in knowing that we are tireless and slightly obsessed foodies. There's not a vegetable we don't adore (except a certain so-called baby corn), nor a spice that doesn't take up precious real estate in our spice racks.

It also helps that we call the greatest city in the world our home. New York City is a supermarket of almost every flavor of ethnic cuisine. We can't help but be inspired by it. It's what we're thinking about when munching on crispy yet soft scallion pancakes or tucking into a saucy eggplant rollatini, when digging into a sub sandwich bursting with tangy barbecued seitan or scooping up that last bit of hummus with freshly baked pita bread. We get flashes of inspiration after finally putting down that huge canvas bag on the kitchen floor; the one filled with gorgeous Brussels sprouts still on the stalk, creamy yellow ears of corn, or voluptuous butternut squash from the farmers' market, all grown within a few dozen miles of the city and lugged home for a few more on the subway.

It may sound a little New Age, but we spend so much time thinking about food that ideas for recipes often strike when we're nowhere near a kitchen . . . walking down the street or running after a bus. Hang

with us for any length of time and it will probably happen to you, too (if it doesn't already).

During the course of developing recipes, we kept coming back to this phrase: *Recipes you wish you'd grown up with*. These aren't necessarily restaurant masterpieces, although we bet lots of these dishes rival the $26 entrée at many vegan eateries. These meals were not born in spotless, stainless-steel, made-for-TV kitchens. The recipes that await you in *Veganomicon* were created by two women who cook, live, and eat in real, urban kitchens. Since we're both apartment dwellers, these are lessons learned from waging wars with temperamental gas burners, moody ovens, and tiny little cabinets bursting with pots, gadgets, and groceries. This is food made while chatting with significant others, gossiping with friends, and shooing nosy pets off the countertops. In other words, this is kind of food you make and eat while life happens.

## LET THEM EAT TEMPEH

We didn't make this cookbook alone. Well, by definition, we wrote it together so already we weren't alone. What we mean is, the results are a combination of many things: years of being out there in the field, talking to, meeting, and eating a bazillion meals with vegetarians and vegans of all stripes, taught us lots. It seemed that no matter how long it's been since you've stopped eating hamburgers—be it eight months or eight years—the common question seemed to be, "What else is there for dinner/lunch/breakfast/midnight snack/Groundhog Day party?", besides tofu hot dogs or pasta and jarred sauce? Fans of *The Post Punk Kitchen* and *Vegan with a Vengeance* were hungry, and they let us know. They were starved not just for new ideas to prepare whole foods, but also for new takes on old favorites ranging from tastier tofu and tempeh, to cheeseless mac n' cheese, to what-in-the-world-do-I-do-with-all-this-zucchini?

This book owes a huge debt to our secret fleet of recipe testers scattered across the globe like poppy seeds on a bagel. Thanks to the miracle of this Internet, we've had the support of this tireless bunch of testing maniacs cooking and giving us feedback for many months during this book's development. Each recipe has been tested by several people, from new cooks to old hands, from teenagers to grad students to dads to grandmothers. Their feedback and guidance informed this cookbook every step of the way.

## VEGAN FOOD = NORMAL FOOD

And there is a larger reason why we wrote this book. Our mission in life is to prove that vegan food doesn't have to be repetitive, difficult, or inaccessible. So let us bore you for a few moments with our culinary philosophy.

People tend to think that the way we eat is the way it always has been and the way it always will be. But food is in constant flux, traveling all over the world and taking root from one continent to the next. The foods that are available to us influence our entire culinary identity, and that identity is ever-shifting. For example, we think of Italian food as loaded with tomato-y goodness, yet the tomato was not widely used in Italy until the eighteenth century, which in the grand scheme of things is a pizza throw away from present times. Just like that, our definition of what makes a complete, satisfying meal can forever change. In today's world, average folks are evolving and learning that dinner need not be defined by a big ol' chunk of meat surrounded by a few bits of overboiled vegetables.

The beauty of this culinary whippersnapper (vegan cuisine) is that it draws influences from every part of the world to create an entirely new way to eat. And we explore the dickens out of that in the *Veganomicon*: stuffing samosa filling into baked potatoes, throwing apples into green chile, tossing lemongrass into risotto. Tradition always starts somewhere, and we hope that something in these pages will inspire a few new seedlings of tradition to take root.

With love from Queens & Brooklyn,
Terry & Isa

* Movie: *Evil Dead II*. What does this have to do with vegan cooking? We'd have to grill, roast, or poach you if we told you.

# VEGANOMICON

# ABOUT THE ICONS

You might be wondering what all those cute little icons right at the beginning of each recipe mean. Behold, the mystery revealed! With just a flick of the eye muscle you'll know if a recipe is gluten free, low fat, or soy free. You'll also know whether you can just shop at Giganto-Mart or need to make an additional stop at the Organic Natural Wonderland grocery, before cooking dinner—plus an approximation of how long things will take once you've procured all your ingredients.

## SOY FREE

Recipe doesn't contain tofu, tempeh, soy milk, soy sauce, or any other soy-derived product.

## GLUTEN FREE

No wheat, vital wheat gluten, or other gluten-containing flours or grains, such as rye. We can't vouch for ingredients that might contain gluten on a very small scale (for celiacs who require a strict gluten-free diet), but all of the major gluten offenders have been accounted for in these recipes. Several recipes marked gluten-free call for soy sauce; be sure to use tamari or gluten-free soy sauce.

## LOW FAT/REDUCED FAT

Usually less than 2 tablespoons of oil in the entire recipe, so we figure it's got to be low fat (or lower fat).

## UNDER 45 MINUTES

We're experts at the 2-hour recipe, but we know that you busy types want to know how long it will take you to do something. Of course, the 45 minutes doesn't include time spent yapping on the phone and running into the living room to watch some television. Many recipes with this icon take just 30 or even 15 minutes to prepare.

## SUPERMARKET FRIENDLY

In a perfect vegan world, the local supermarket always has nutritional yeast and whole wheat pastry flour, right next to the multipack of toilet paper and giant tin of cinnamon. Until then, most of us need to make an additional trip to pick up organic or particularly "vegan" ingredients at a health food/natural grocery.

When recipes have this icon, probably no such trip is required and your regular old grocery store should do the trick. Since we live in New York City, our view on "supermarket friendly" might differ from yours, but to gauge this accurately we made sure that the supermarket closest to Isa's in-laws in rural Vermont had all the items on the shelves. So tofu and soy milk are included in this icon, but agar, for example, is not.

# STOCKING THE VEGANOMICON PANTRY

For your shopping convenience, here's a list of ingredients that feature in these recipes. We call these "pantry" items, but really what we mean is that they are ingredients that we always keep on hand; that way, there is never "nothing to eat." This isn't a list of *every* ingredient in the book, just some of the ones we can't live without. You may already have a few, or a lot, of these pantry staples already stored away on your kitchen shelves and cabinets. If you encounter an ingredient that is new to you, take advantage of the opportunity and try out a recipe or two with this new ingredient. Who knows, you might find yourself wondering how you ever cooked anything without mirin, chickpea flour, or basmati rice!

## CANNED GOODS

**Beans:** A whole dinner can start with just one can of beans. Keep a can or two of the following on hand, but don't limit yourself to: chickpeas, black beans, kidney beans, navy beans, cannellinis, black-eyed peas, and pintos.

**Coconut milk:** Nothing beats the creaminess coconut gives to bisques and curries. *Nothing.*

**Pureed Pumpkin:** We use it in a few entrée type dishes, but it's also great to have around for baked goods on the off chance that you're not in the mood for chocolate. Be sure that the only ingredient is pumpkin and that the label doesn't say "Pumpkin Pie Mix."

**Tomatoes:** Most often our recipes call for crushed tomatoes, but we also keep canned whole tomatoes and plain tomato sauce on hand. For tomato paste, we prefer the kind that comes in a tube. We usually just go for the cheapest brand we can find, unless we're cooking for company—then we buy those fire-roasted ones and deplete our hedge funds. (P.S. What's a hedge fund?)

## FRIDGE STAPLES

What is a fridge but a climate-controlled cold pantry? The following are things that any vegan fridge can't be without. Some start out in the pantry but need to be refrigerated once opened.

**Apple Sauce:** Sure, it's a nice treat to just to eat out of the jar with a spoon, but it's also a great ingredient for baked goods, especially for low fat baking.

**Capers:** The briny taste of caper berries is the secret ingredient in quite a few of our recipes. They're usually relegated to a garnish in Mediterranean cuisine, but we branch out and use them blended up in dips and salads as well.

**Dijon Mustard:** Sometimes the tangy bite of mustard is just what sauces, casseroles, and salad dressings need to make them complete. Sometimes it isn't. But for those times when it is, keep your fridge stocked with whole grain Dijon mustard.

**Jams and jellies:** We use these to add yumminess to baked goods, either in the batter or as a spread or as a filling, as in the Jelly Donut Cupcakes (page 253). And you don't need us to tell you to eat PB&Js! What flavors do we consider staples? We have at least raspberry, strawberry, and apricot in our pantry at all times.

**Margarine, Earth Balance vegan, nonhydrogenated:** Forget what you know about margarine; this brand is heaven on a butter knife. We try not to use too much of it in the *Veganomicon*, but sometimes nothing else will do. Its buttery flavor is essential in some baked goods, soups, and casseroles.

**Miso:** Everybody's favorite fermented Japanese paste. The standard kind you'll find in most American supermarkets is made from soybeans and rice, but there are dozens of other varieties out there—brown rice, chickpea, barley—all with their own unique properties and flavors ranging from sweet or winey, to earthy or fruity. We often use miso the same way vegetable broth is used—to give soups, stews, and gravies an intriguing backdrop. The recipes in this book use either white (or sweet) miso, which is a blond sort of color and has a mild, slightly sweet flavor or brown rice miso, which is rich and full bodied. Store miso in an airtight container.

**Nondairy milk:** Use whatever kind floats your boat, be it soy, rice, almond—even hazelnut. As long as it's not an overly sweetened or flavored milk, you can use any of these milks interchangeably in all recipes.

**Tempeh:** A fermented soybean patty. That doesn't sound all that appealing now does it? But trust us, when treated right—and the Veganomicon will make sure that you do treat it right—tempeh is a succulent and welcome addition to your diet. Isa's mom swears by it.

**Tofu:** Some people like to pronounce it *tofu*, we think in an effort to make it sound bad. Well nice try, haters, tofu is here to stay!

**Vegenaise:** This brand is the absolute best vegan mayonnaise; don't bother with anything else. We use it for some salads and dressings, and of course, for sandwiches.

## HERBS AND SPICES

Loosely defined for culinary purposes, an herb is the leaves of a plant (as in thyme or dill) and the spice is anything that isn't the leaf, such as the root (ginger), fruit (chile), seeds (cumin), berry (allspice), or bark (cinnamon) of a plant.

The spice rack is the heart of the vegan kitchen and getting to know your herbs and spices is a fun and magical journey. It's smart and easy to let regional cooking be the first steps in this adventure. You probably already know that Italian cooking relies on the flavors of thyme, oregano, and rosemary, whereas

Mexican cooking often uses cumin, coriander, and chile. As you familiarize yourself with the tastes and aromas of your collection, you can begin to branch out and try combinations that, while probably not unknown to man, might be unknown to you.

The recipes in this cookbook don't shy away from herbs and spices, and we hope that as you cook from it, your spice rack will become as overflowing and varied as ours are. To that end, don't worry just because you see coriander seed on a recipe list and don't happen to have any. Either try the recipe without it and get some seeds for next time, or flip to a recipe that you do have all the ingredients for and build your arsenal as you go along. Instead of obtaining your spices in expensive glass jars from the grocery store, find a source for bulk herbs and spices, which are often 75 percent cheaper than prepackaged spices are. Indian, Middle Eastern, or Chinese markets are great for this, and often health food stores have a nice bulk selection. If all else fails, you can order online from many sources, including Penzey's (www.penzeys.com). Here is a good list to get you through most *Veganomicon* recipes. Those marked with an asterisk are what we consider essentials and should be the first items you obtain. With the exception of basil, whose strength and taste are hugely different in fresh and dried forms, fresh herbs can be used interchangeably with dried in most any recipe. The basic guide to go by is 1 teaspoon dried herb/spice = 1 tablespoon finely chopped fresh herb/spice, but taste as you go, to make sure the flavoring does not overpower the recipe. For best results and flavor, use purchased ground herbs/spices within a year or by the expiration date. Please throw out that five-year-old, beat-up can of ground black pepper! The flavor just won't be there anymore, and can sometimes even make your foods taste old and dusty.

### Dried Herbs
Basil
Dill
Marjoram
Mint
Oregano*
Rosemary
Tarragon*
Thyme*

### Spices, Ground or Whole
Cardamom pods
Caraway seeds
Cayenne pepper, ground*
Celery seeds, whole
Cumin, ground* and whole seeds
Cinnamon, ground* and sticks
Cloves, ground and whole
Coriander, whole seeds
Curry powder (we like to have a variety)*
Garam masala
Fennel seed, whole*
Mustard, ground/mustard flour
Mustard, black, brown or white, whole seed
Nutmeg, whole
Paprika (Hungarian if you can find it)
Red pepper flakes
Black pepper, whole* (grind in a pepper grinder)
White pepper, ground
Saffron

## BAKING BASICS

Always having the right sugars, extracts, and powders handy means that fresh muffins and cookies are just a few mixing bowls away.

**Agar powder/flakes:** A magical seaweed that, when boiled in a liquid, forms a kick-ass vegan alternative to gelatin. We feel like we're forever talking about the wonders of agar, but that's a small price to pay for the world to know what they're missing. Fun fact: agar "gelatin" can firm up at room temperature, unlike that stuff made from animal bones (but it will cool faster if refrigerated).

Purchase agar in either powdered or flake form. The powder is a little easier to use and considerably more concentrated than the flakes. The flakes should be allowed to soak in the liquid they will be boiled in for about 10 minutes before heating. Agar can be found in well-stocked health food stores or Asian groceries.

**Agave nectar:** Agave is the majestic cactus used to make tequila of all stripes in Mexico. And it just happens that the sap (before distilling) is a tasty, syrupy stuff that's sweeter than sugar and entirely agreeable in dressings, drinks, desserts, and baked goods. Not to make any revolutionary health claims, but it seems that some people with certain sugar intolerances can handle agave nectar with ease. More and more regular supermarkets are carrying agave these days, but if yours doesn't, try a health food store.

**Baking powder and baking soda:** The wonder twins of chemical leaveners that are the key to success with vegan baked goods. Baking soda (sodium bicarbonate) is an alkali ingredient that releases leavening carbon dioxide when it is combined with moisture. Baking powder is baking soda plus an acid salt (such as cream of tartar). When double-acting baking powder is combined with an acidic ingredient (such as vinegar or lemon juice), you get the chemical reaction that makes your cakes and muffins rise, first when wet meets dry and again when the batter goes into the oven. Are you still awake? Have fresh boxes in your pantry at all times.

**Extracts:** Vanilla extract, the Cadillac of extracts, is one you'll most often be using. So it's worth spending a little extra to get the real stuff—stay away from anything labeled "artificial" or "vanillin." It's hard to imagine any baked good without a hint of vanilla; it pulls all the ingredients together and provides that bakery-fresh aroma. If you love to bake, it's recommended that you pad your baking

supplies with a few extra extracts. Others we use in this book include almond, anise, hazelnut, and coconut, but it never hurts to add other extracts to your collection, such as lemon, mint, or raspberry.

**Liqueurs:** Back to the booze again! Liqueurs have been used to flavor all kinds of food for centuries but we mostly use them when baking. Hazelnut and coffee liqueur are our hands-down favorites, the ones we use most often in our dessert recipes. Unless you live in a state where it's legal to sell hard alcohol in the supermarket, you'll find flavored liqueurs at the liquor store.

**Maple syrup:** Isa calls this "the taste of freedom" because she spends too much time in Vermont. Pure maple syrup can be expensive so we use it sparingly, not just for baking but to give a hint of sweetness where ever needed. But it isn't just for the elite. Budget-minded people like us are never fooled into buying a little expensive bottle of the "grade A" stuff. "Grade B" syrup, a little darker in color but just as flavorful, works just as fine for you, me, and true democracy. Don't forget to refrigerate after opening.

**Shortening, nonhydrogenated:** We don't use it much in our recipes, but a little bit makes piecrusts flaky and gives cookies a dense, chewy, or shortbreadlike texture. Our favorite brand is Earth Balance.

## SUGARS

Yes, we're guilty of using sugar. While we love whole wheat, sugar-free raisin bran muffins as much as the next guy, we also know that life often requires fluffy cupcakes, chocolate chip cookies, and pumpkin crumble pie. Adding sugar is also much cheaper than baking with maple syrup or agave all the time, not to mention far more predicable when it comes to getting the results you want with baked goods. Happily, lots of organic, vegan-friendly sugar options are easily obtainable these days:

**Granulated sugar:** When we call for just "sugar," we always mean granulated. We use interchangeably evaporated cane juice, such as Florida Crystals, or brands that specifically say "beet sugar" on the packaging. "Cane sugar" is typically made with the use of animal products in the form of bone char in the processing, so some vegans avoid it.

**Brown sugar:** Also called muscovado sugar when it is raw and unrefined, typical brown sugar is refined sugar with a little bit of the molasses left in or added back to it.

**Confectioners' sugar:** A combination of finely ground sugar and cornstarch, also called powdered sugar. We use confectioners' sugar to create glazes and frostings.

**Turbinado sugar:** A coarse, unrefined, steam-cleansed sugar that has bigger crystals (for example, Sugar in the Raw) We use turbinado wherever a little crunch is desired. You can also use it in place of regular sugar, but results may vary.

## FLOURS AND THICKENING STARCHES

**All-purpose flour:** You should always have a sack of unbleached all-purpose flour the size of a small child around. Even if the cupboard is bare, you'll be able to whip up some pancakes or muffins. Even though we mostly use flour for baking, we've also been known to use it to thicken sauces and make tempura.

**Arrowroot, powder/ground:** This fine white powder—ground from the roots of a tropical vine—is ideal for thickening sauces and soups, particularly if a clear, nonopaque appearance is desired. Arrowroot also helps bind and provides a crisp texture in baked goods.

**Chickpea flour:** A pale yellow flour, sometimes called garbanzo flour, made from ground chickpeas. Look for it in most health food stores and Indian grocery markets where it is called gram flour or besan). Imparts a sweet, nutty, beany (some might even call it "eggy") flavor to baked goods and sauces. It's especially good for crepes and flatbreads.

**Cornmeal:** We use it in some recipes to add a little crunch, particularly to baked goods. And having some around in case of a corn bread emergency is not a bad idea.

**Cornstarch:** Also used to thicken, at half the price of other starches. Plus, it adds crispiness and structure to baked goods.

**Tapioca flour:** Our starch of choice for thickening custards and fruit pies, available at health food stores. This is a fine powder; do not use granular or pearl tapioca as a substitute.

**Whole wheat pastry flour:** Whole wheat pastry flour (not to be confused with ordinary whole wheat flour) is just as finely milled as white flour, but not all of the bran and germ has been processed out of it, making it a healthier, more fiberific choice. It is difficult to detect a *very* significant difference between whole pastry and regular old all-purpose flours, but whole wheat pastry flour can make baked goods a bit more dense and healthier tasting, so we often do an equal mix with all-purpose.

**Vital wheat gluten:** The naturally occurring protein in wheat that makes it all happen; it's what gives wheat dough its characteristic stretch and makes seitan (sometimes called wheat meat) so toothsome. We also use it in combination with beans in several recipes to give a more chewy, meaty texture. Look for organic brands at your health food store, usually in the baking section. We recommend Arrowhead Mills brand above others if you have a choice.

## OILS

**Canola oil:** Short for "Canada oil" and formerly known as "rapeseed oil" this oil is now politically correctly named, available most everywhere, and a fine choice for multipurpose use. Mild in flavor, it's perfect for baking and cooking when a neutral-tasting oil is desired. Look for "high-heat" canola oil for use in sautéing and grilling. Canola oil also provides you with a healthy dose of essential omega-3 fatty acids.

### What Is a Fatty Acid and Why Is It Essential?

WITHOUT getting into words that we cannot pronounce, our bodies need fats, not only to store energy but to absorb vitamins and protect our vital organs from disease (unless you don't consider your brain a vital organ). We naturally produce some of the necessary fats but others need to be obtained from our diet. The very base of our existence, our cells, are largely composed of such fatty acids making these, well, essential!

**Coconut oil, refined/unrefined:** Poor coconut oil has been typecast in the role of a nutritional bad guy for too long. Nonhydrogenated

coconut oil is perfectly healthy consumed in small amounts. We like unrefined oil for its luscious coconut aroma and delicate flavor. It's a favorite of ours when cooking Indian and Southeast Asian inspired cuisine.

**Olive oil:** There's a reason people have been cultivating this stuff for thousands of years. Olive oil is so good for you, plus its rich, earthy, and fruity flavor is essential in cooking all things Mediterranean and Middle Eastern. We use extra-virgin for almost everything, but the purist might want to use cheaper virgin or blended oils for frying (even though people have been shallow-frying in good olive oils for as long as it's been made, it can be used for longer or deeper frying. The key is to use low to medium heat, never, ever high heat!).

**Grapeseed oil:** A light, nearly colorless oil made from pressed grape seeds. We love it in salad dressing because it has the thickness and body of olive oil, but a neutral taste. While it isn't an essential thing to have, it should be the first item you purchase once you've decided to broaden your oil horizons. It's a bit pricier than canola oil, but not as expensive as olive oil and it's available in most health food stores and, increasingly in regular old supermarkets.

**Peanut oil:** Another stock oil in our pantries, peanut oil is a must when cooking many things Asian, as it's often that little touch of authentic flavor that missing from homemade stir-fries and curries. Its high smoke point also makes it perfect for frying.

**Toasted sesame oil:** We don't usually use this oil to cook with, but it adds a fragrant sesame taste to finished dishes and salad dressings. Regular sesame oil can be substituted for toasted but the flavor will not be anywhere as intense.

## PANTRY SUNDRIES

Why say "other stuff" when you could say sundries?

**Dried Beans:** It's worth making a pot of beans every now and then; we keep on hand the usual suspects that are also listed in the canned section. They're incredibly economical and the flavor is superior to the canned stuff. It's helpful to buy them in bulk and store them in one-pound increments for quick and easy measuring and cooking. Quick-cooking beans such as lentils and split pea are an absolute, economical must for soups during those cold winter months when you're saving up all your money to buy a sled or pay your health insurance. (For information on specific beans, see our bean-cooking section, page 42.)

**Grains:** Ditch that dusty old box of instant rice! We keep a variety of whole grains in airtight jars in our cupboards, and use them in lots and lots of *Veganomicon* recipes. (See page 37 for how to cook some of our favorites.)

**Nutritional yeast:** Not to be confused with brewer's yeast or any other kind of yeast, "nooch" (as we call it) is great to add an umami (savory) taste to sauces or just to sprinkle on rice and beans. We don't use it in too many *Veganomicon* recipes because it's hard to find and people tend to love it or hate it. Most commonly, this mustard-colored yeast comes in flake form, and that is what we call for in our recipes. But sometimes you'll find it in powdered form, which is just ground-up flakes. If you can only find the powdered kind, reduce every ¼ cup called for by a tablespoon.

**Nuts:** Always have slivered or sliced almonds and walnuts on hand for pesto and to create texture in casseroles and sauces. Nuts are also great toasted in salads, breaded on tofu, and of course for all kinds of baked goods and desserts. If you are going to be storing them like a human-squirrel for months and months, keep them in the freezer. Other nuts we like to have around: cashews, hazelnuts, pecans, peanuts (which are actually botanical beans), and pine nuts.

**Seeds:** Any seed that goes on a bagel should also have a place in your pantry. Toasted sesame and black sesame seeds go a long way toward providing flavor to our dishes, as well as adding drama to the presentation. We also keep flaxseeds in the refrigerator, either in ground or whole form, for baking and sometimes for sprinkling onto our oatmeal.

**Pastas:** Keep a few boxes around of pastas of all shapes and sizes. We don't need to remind you what it's good for! (See our pasta section, page 188, for different types that we like.)

## WINES AND VINEGARS

A snotty person once said that you shouldn't cook with any wine you wouldn't drink. We say "Pfft!" The wines you'll find in any supermarket marked simply "cooking wine" are just fine. But whether you use the cheap stuff or a $30 Australian Riesling splurge, a shot or two of wine can elevate that sauté from just homemade to near restaurant quality. There's really nothing like wine when it comes to drawing out the flavors of seared and sautéed vegetables (particularly mushrooms), herbs, and oils. We use white wine most of the time, but red and sherry are good choices to have around, too. For the straight-edgers out there, we don't mean to alienate you. Nonalcoholic wine (and beer) or vegetable broth can be substituted in these recipes. Although deglazing a pan (page 19) just isn't the same without it, it can be done. Also included here are a few vinegars that we use often.

**Cooking wine, red and white:** Like we say, cooking wine doesn't have to be anything fancy, even that box o' wine that shows up at ironic trailer-trash parties in the hip section of town will do. Just make sure it is dry, which just means not sweet. A bottle of cooking sherry will also take you places and adds that particular sweet, mellow flavor some recipes just call out for.

**Mirin:** A Japanese rice cooking wine. It has a thick, almost syrupy texture. A little goes a long way in adding a deep, complex flavor and aroma to stir-fries, soups, stews, and marinades. It's a little pricier than most fruit-based cooking wines, but nothing quite tastes like it. We recommend steering clear of any mirin with added sugar, salt, or other flavorings.

**Apple cider vinegar:** We use apple cider vinegar in our baked goods because of its mellow taste and acidity. Apple cider vinegar not only reacts with baking soda to help things to rise, it also makes our baked goods tender.

**Balsamic vinegar:** We don't douse our foods in it, but the deep, winelike taste of balsamic vinegar works wonders in marinades or to pull together a bowl of soup.

**Brown rice vinegar:** A very mild vinegar that's great in Asian food and nice to know in salad dressings.

**Wine vinegar:** Red wine, white wine, or champagne, this is your go-to vinegar for adding tangy zing to savory foods and sauces.

## A Word about Vegetable Broth

MANY of our recipes call for vegetable broth. The store-bought stuff that comes in cartons tastes great but is ridiculously expensive, not to mention a pain for us non–weight trainers—it makes our shopping bags so heavy! We like to make our own broth (page 142) and freeze it, but this isn't always practical. Enter bouillon cubes, concentrated broth, and broth powders. Find one that you like the taste of, preferably something with low or no salt and no MSG. Add to your recipe when it is simmering, usually two cubes or a tablespoon per four cups of water, or mix it with water beforehand.

# KITCHEN EQUIPMENT

*All you really need to cook is a knife, a pot, and a big spoon. But this is the twenty-first century, after all, and we're often taken in by shiny new things, so we have way more equipment stuffed into our tiny kitchen than it can possibly handle. Rather than regale you with stories about how our lives have been changed by our two-chamber automatic ice-cream maker, we've compiled a little info about the basic tools we use every day. Gadgets are great fun, but our mango slicer mostly collects dust. We're beginning to think it might be useless.*

Here's some consumer wisdom we've had drilled into our heads: if you can't afford to buy a quality, well-made kitchen tool, you may be better off without it. Sure, you can buy a peeler for 99 cents at the everything-for-a-dollar store, but will it take the skin off a butternut squash? No. Better to save up the $8.95 you'll need for that sturdy all-purpose one the kitchen supply store sells. It'll last forever. The same goes for pots and pans and knives and mixers and whatever else. A caveat, though: more expensive does not necessarily mean better! Since this is the technological age, weed through consumer reviews on such shopping sites as Amazon.com to see which ones are best. Thrift stores and flea markets and stoop sales (or tag sales for you non-New Yorkers) are also great places to find kitchen stuff, if you don't mind the questionable provenance.

## CHOPPING AND PREP TOOLS

Because having a stove is great if you intend to cook something, but unless you plan on living on whole boiled potatoes, you're going to need just a few prep tools.

### Knives

We know it's been said many times, many ways, but the only knife you need is a good chef's knife. Period. If you're still chopping vegetables with a sad little steak knife you borrowed from your mom's cutlery tray, stop it this second and go out and buy a real knife. A good knife has a solid feel, comfortable grip, and can be sharpened when it gets dull. Dull knives are dangerous! They slip off tomato skins and cut your finger. Buy the best knife you can afford; decent knives can be purchased for under $30 at discount stores, but if

# A Few Basic Knife Skills

The more you chop, dice, and slice, the better your knife skills will get. It helps to know the correct way to hold a knife, but really it's practice and intuition that makes almost perfect. We say "almost perfect" because the skills are constantly evolving and we're always figuring out new stuff and what works for us. That said, it doesn't hurt to have a little practical guidance, and since minced garlic and diced onions are included in most all of our recipes, here are a few tips for getting them prepped quickly while keeping your fingers intact.

## Garlic

Wet your hands and your knife before beginning. That will keep the garlic from sticking to your fingers and the knife. Break off a few cloves and lay your knife blade squarely over a clove. Use the palm of your hand to give the clove a whack. That should crush the clove and loosen the skin. The papery skin should slip off easily once it's been whacked. Discard the skins and continue smashing as many cloves as you need.

Once you have skinned all the cloves, bunch them up on the cutting board. The quickest and easiest way to mince is to use a seesaw rocking motion. Use your writing hand to grasp the blade and use your other hand to rest on top of the blade to provide balance. Rock the knife back and forth steadily, stopping once in a while to bunch all the garlic up again, because it will spread out as you are mincing. When you have this method perfected you should be able to mince a whole bulb of garlic in two or three minutes.

## Onions

First, slice off the top and bottom of the onion. Then slice the onion in half lengthwise. Now the skin should come off easily. Once the skin is removed, place the onion cut side down. With your fingers safely curled in, grasp the onion at the bottom to hold it in place. Slice the onion widthwise, trying to keep the slices intact. Then turn the onion and slice lengthwise.

Isa swears that if she breathes through her mouth, she never cries from cutting up onions. Try it for yourself and see if she's lying and crazy or not.

you've had a sudden windfall of cashola it doesn't hurt to drop a Benjamin on a really spiffy one.

Now that you have a good knife, you'd better learn how to use it. You could take some classes or watch a few hundred hours of *Emeril* (say what you will, that man can *chop*!), or you can just think about how to cut something beforehand instead of hacking away willy-nilly. Let the knife do the work—it wants to!

Besides the chef's knife, we only really bother with a serrated-bladed bread knife and a little, sharp paring knife. The bread knife is great for slicing bread, of course, but it's also a miracle worker for slicing very soft tomatoes and sushi nori rolls. The little paring knife can come in handy for reckoning with sprouting potatoes or making radish roses, if for some reason you go insane and need to make those. You can go with slightly lesser quality when it comes to purchasing these guys.

## Cutting Board

We don't want to hear about those of you out there chopping on dinner plates or directly on the countertop. Any official cutting board will do . . . oh, except those

## How to Get Knife Skills Lessons for Free

HIGH-END housewares stores usually have a well-educated staff working their way through cooking school. And the wonderful part is that they are usually bored out of their minds! When you are shopping around for your expensive chef's knife, employees will gladly take the time to demonstrate the proper way to hold the knife. In fact, when they see your wobbly and awkward grasp they may even feel *compelled* to help you, like Mother Teresas of the cooking world. Often they have a green pepper or an onion hanging around for this very purpose. So go ahead and hop from store to store, gathering knowledge as you go. It's cheaper than a degree from the Culinary Institute.

glass ones; no one wants to hear a knife "clink" on glass, what a bad idea. We prefer wood over plastic, ourselves, and particularly fancy those new bamboo cutting boards.

### *tip*

## HOW TO STOP YOUR CUTTING BOARD FROM SLIDING

We've all been there. You're blasting your Neil Diamond and getting into your cooking zone, but the damn onion keeps getting away from you because the cutting board is sliding across the counter like Brian Boitano. *Veganomicon* to the rescue! Lay out a damp kitchen towel and place your cutting board on top of it; this will give you the traction you need to keep your workstation is place. Wet paper towels work for this, too.

They're *très chic*, tougher than Thelma and Louise, and totally renewable (since that bamboo grows like a weed).

## Vegetable Peelers

The truly sadomasochistic chef (or Isa's grandma) loves to peel vegetables with a paring knife. Even our copy editor says she does it with those two for one dollar knives she's had for eons. For everyone else, there are a plethora of peelers to choose from. We're partial to the Y-shaped rather than the old-fashioned straight variety, but do what makes you happy. Get the sharpest, sturdiest one you can, with a large, comfortable handle. If you are only going to purchase one, make it the serrated kind. If you skipped the opening paragraph we'll say it again: it's a good idea to spend just a little extra on these, since nothing sucks more than a dull vegetable peeler (with a teeny, miserable handle) when you've got eight pounds of apples to skin.

## Food Processor

Wonder of wonders, miracle of miracles! Saver of time, conservator of energy! So easy! So convenient! How did I ever survive without you? Every well-equipped kitchen has a food processor in it. You can't live without one, right? Sort of. You *can* do without, but when you are staring at the latkes recipe with a tear in your eye, wondering how in the world you will fit shredding five pounds of potatoes into your busy day of video games and knitting circles, you need to get yourself a food processor. If you can't afford one right now, then get married simply so you can put this on your wedding registry.

Not only will the proper attachments shred and slice everything for you, but nothing can really replace a food processor in the kitchen when it comes to transforming tofu, vegetables, beans, and so on into smooth and silky purees. The quality is rather flexible when it comes to choosing a food processor, so go for whatever fits in your budget and literally fits on your countertop. Those combination blender/food processor gadgets are kinda small but work great.

### Blender

Speaking of blenders, it's not absolutely necessary to have a standing one for the recipes in this book, but it's pretty awesome for the occasional peanut butter-banana smoothie or to puree soups and sauces.

### Immersion Blender

This little gadget is worth every penny, which is not a lot of pennies since they're surprisingly inexpensive. Often in this book we give you two choices: you can wait for your stew or soup or whatever to cool a bit and then puree half of it in a blender or food processor, then add it back to the pot, *or the much-more-appeal-ing second choice*—simply whip out your immersion blender and puree. If you want to dabble even further in immersion blender magic, look for ones that come with a selection of attachments for whisking and grinding spices or coffee.

### Graters

Box graters are a kitchen staple that attack carrots, celery, and jicama with ease. We suppose that you could also grate vegetables with that food processor, but it seems more work than necessary to clean it if you're grating just one carrot to toss into a salad. The zester on those things is mostly useless, though, which is why we recommend you get yourself a microplane grater. Then finely shredded mounds of citrus zest and freshly grated nutmeg shall be yours!

### Mandoline

Just a note about these—mandolines are ominous, human-powered contraptions that can transform a pile of carrots or pound of potatoes into slender, completely uniform shreds in mere minutes. They are also the kind of medieval instrument one might encounter should one have the terrifying experience of going to a Renaissance fair. With a mandoline it's possible to quickly grate, slice, shred, sliver (and julienne!) any firm vegetable or fruit into a plethora of perfect shapes that would take you hours of tedious work with a knife. Careful please,

because they are armed with a *deadly serious* blade that does all that work for you. Absolutely not necessary for cooking, but something to consider should you want to live off of hash browns and shredded salads.

Enough prep work. It's time to move on to the fun stuff.

## POTS AND PANS AND OTHER FOOD COOKING VEHICLES

When we were starving artists we cooked with a found rusty wok and ate off of upside down Frisbees. Times have changed.

### Skillets

A.k.a. sauté pans, a.k.a. frying pans. We're big fans of good old cast-iron for skillet cooking, not to mention that cast iron has the added benefit of being able to be popped into the oven for additional browning, making a potpie or the best corn bread you'll ever eat. A 10- or 12-inch cast-iron skillet is all you really need, but it's mighty heavy and requires proper seasoning, so you might want something lighter around, too. It's hard to beat stainless-steel pans for bombproof func-tionality; no matter what you burn in 'em, you can get it off with a little elbow grease, and none the worse for wear (except possibly your elbow). Nonstick pans are great for their nonstickiness. They cost just a little more than stainless steel, but only buy one if you can buy a nice one—and treat it gently! A good nonstick pan has a very smooth, nearly shiny surface. No metal should ever touch that pan, so while you're shopping, get a few good-quality silicone or wood utensils to use with it. If you scratch Teflon or another nonstick coat-ing it's useless (and possibly toxic), and if you get it too hot (like 500°F hot, which is really easy to do if you're forgetful) it gives off toxic fumes.

### The Great Big Soup Pot

The name says it all. Look for a large 6- to 8-quart pot that's preferably stainless steel with a good stout bottom. Accessories (like a steamer basket) are nice. The Great Big Pot and a skillet are the bare essentials, but if you've got the scratch (and space) you'll find that it's great to have a . . .

## Cast-Iron Grill Pan

For grilling! Nothing can beat it. Unless you have a Weber in your kitchen, which is a really bad idea. So go get a grill pan, they're cheap! Since you're on a shopping spree, you might as well get a . . .

## Crepe Pan

But only if you're going to make crepes. And you will make crepes (you just don't know it yet). See page 77 about our recommendations, but in general stick to steel or cast-iron varieties. Run away from any goofy, infomercial-style gadgets that expect you to dip an electrical object into runny crepe batter.

## Casserole Dish

Is it for cooking? Is it for serving? You can have it both ways! You can use a cast-iron skillet instead if it's all you got, but you'll love having a deep, enameled, cast-iron casserole dish that you can sauté your ingredients in first, top with some dough, and then shove into the oven to finish. Yeah, you can casserole your heart out with a glass or (gasp!) metal one, but the cast-iron ones are really fun to use and look pretty, too. Also good for lasagne!

## The Spray Bottle

Our good friend the spray bottle of oil can help you use less oil when cooking, so he makes a few cameo appearances throughout recipes in the book. We're not talking about that aerosol stuff that you buy in the supermarket, but an actual bottle that you fill with the oil of your choice. You can buy the pump kind, such as a Misto, where you have to pump the top with air (kind of like how a Super Soaker works), but you can also just buy a plastic spray bottle, usually available in housewares stores in the gardening section.

## More Pots and Pans!

Okay, we lied in our introductory paragraph. You can never have enough of these. If you're getting a food processor on the wedding registry plan, go ahead and throw a set of pots and pans on the list. Or just buy 'em when they go on sale. More is more! Lots of discount stores carry good-quality pots **and dishes** that will last you the rest of your life with little care. Make sure you get the heavy-bottomed variety—give 'em a knock on the bottom to make sure they're thick and solid. If they sound like a gong and feel thin, skip them. Light-bottomed pans will burn your onions and cook unevenly. We're big fans of pots that come with a few steamer baskets of assorted sizes.

## BAKING TOOLS

You can resist that castle shaped Bundt pan for as long as you like, but if you want cookies and cupcakes, you'll need a few essentials. Not that castle shaped Bundt cakes aren't essential for all you Renaissance Fair enthusiasts.

## Baking Sheets

The classic, 11 × 17-inch, slightly rimmed jelly-roll pan will serve you well roasting just about any vegetable—just line the bottom with baking parchment or aluminum foil first, or you'll never get them clean again. You can also use it for baking jelly rolls! Nonrimmed cookie sheets work for roasting, too, but you risk having the juices run off and burn to the bottom of your oven.

## Baking Tins

This is where you can go all freestyle with your bakeware collection. Large muffin tins, medium muffin tins, little bitty cutie little muffin tins . . . go crazy! Hate muffins (and don't have a soul)? Then don't get muffin tins. But maybe you fancy Bundt cakes, so go get the best Bundt cake pan you can afford. And don't forget a standard loaf pan, unless you want to live a monklike existence free of banana bread. In general, we don't care for silicone bakeware, but we understand if all those pretty colors lure you in.

We had to go and bring up baking, didn't we? Well, then you'll also need this stuff:

### Mixing Bowls

These are for more than just baking—you'll use them for everything. You might as well buy a set, since it's nigh-impossible to buy them separately, but you'll be happy you did. The stainless-steel ones are tops in our book, although plastic will do. Glass or ceramic ones are great as well but your cat will knock them onto the floor and cause disaster, so only get them if you're allergic to cats.

### Measuring Cups and Spoons

Psychic chefs can use the power of their minds to determine ⅓ cup of nutritional yeast or ¾ teaspoon of vanilla. For the rest of us, a sturdy metal or high-quality plastic set of measuring cups and spoons will do. Bonus: a stainless-steel tablespoon makes a cool MacGyver-style melon baller.

### Kitchen Timer

In our carefree youth, we would put some cookies to bake in the oven, then go call a friend, play with the cat, take a nap and watch the last fifteen minutes of the *McNeil-Lehrer News Hour*. Okay, maybe we're exaggerating about the nap but the resulting charcoal cookies would make us take note that maybe getting a kitchen timer would be a good idea. Older and wiser, we've learned to relax a little and let the timer do all the work of reminding us to do something. Nothing fancy required, as long as you keep a plastic one away from the stove so it doesn't melt. If you happen to be a cheapskate with a cell phone, most cell phones have a timer feature.

### Oven Thermometer

How much do you trust your oven? Unless you have one of those fancy top-of-the-line super expensive ovens (and even if you do), trust us, your oven is lying to you. Buy an oven thermometer, they're cheap and will save you burnt cookie heartache.

## STANDARD UTENSILS

**Spatulas:** Shop around for a thin, flexible, metal spatula that suits you, You'll use it for frying and sautéing in cast iron and aluminum, as well as for flipping pancakes and transferring cookies to cooling racks. A wooden (bamboo, preferably) spatula with an angled edge is great for stirring sauces and soups, and for sautéing in enamel or nonstick cookware.

**Tongs:** Tongs are great for flipping tofu on the grill, sautéing greens, mixing salads, and retrieving the olive oil cap that you dropped into the soup.

**Slotted Spoon:** It's the spoon that's not a spoon, because it doesn't hold anything! Maybe it sounds like the ultimate rip-off, but a slotted spoon is damn handy when fishing out ravioli from a boiling pot o' water.

**Pasta Spoon:** That really creepy looking spoon-thing with teeth is a superhero when it comes to grabbing lumps of linguine or spools of spaghetti.

**Ladles:** Sometimes ladles make you feel like your pouring out the finest French soup, sometimes they make you feel like you're in a soup kitchen. Either way, you need a ladle because that tablespoon isn't going to get that soup into the bowl anytime soon.

**Fork and Spoon:** You may laugh, but this humble dynamic duo from the cutlery drawer will come to the rescue in your darkest hours. Forks make great mini whisks in a pinch (just don't use them for stirring anything in a nonstick pan), and spoons are experts at seeding squash and portioning out flours.

## OTHER STUFF

Barely a day goes by where the salad spinner doesn't see some action. And that's not because we're eating salads every day; salad spinners are geniuses at washing leafy greens, mushrooms, berries, green beans, and any smallish, numerous fruit or vegetable. Not to mention it doubles as an extra colander and additional large bowl to hold annoyingly large vegetables and greens. Speaking of colanders, you need one. You should get a fine-mesh strainer, too, for straining stuff and sifting flour. A citrus reamer can squeeze the juice out of a lime much, much better than your hands ever will. A whisk is nice to have, also. But the bottom line is that you will cook best with the equipment you are most comfortable with. Spend as much time as you need in the housewares aisle, handling your future equipment and seeing what feels best to you. If you prefer one handle to another, don't discount this as something trivial. And if you have a hand-me-down skillet from your best friend's mother, and love cooking with it, well, then keep it and cook on.

# COOKING AND PREPPING TERMINOLOGY

*W*hen we're asking you to "sweat" some mushrooms, we're not implying that you should apply extreme emotional pressure to get the fungus to admit to some dark secret. It's just one of a few cooking terms we like to throw around here, because they're a lot easier than writing out things like "partially cover and allow to steam until tender" all the time, and also because they're fun to say. Here are a few terms to know that will have you cooking like a master chef (almost):

**Bias:** Often we say to slice something on a bias— say, carrots, for example. This mean to cut diagonally instead of straight down or across. This is usually specified when the cut makes a big difference to the texture of the food, or in situations where it will be more aesthetically pleasing. This way, instead of people barely noticing that you sliced a carrot, they will gasp in admiration of your damn fine-looking carrots.

**Blanching:** A quick boil, when you don't want to cook your veggies all the way but just get them a bit softened up, usually because they will be cooked further somewhere down the line.

**Blend:** Stirring the contents of a bowl, pot, or pan to combine all of the ingredients. Usually done at a vigorous pace and sometimes done in a blender (obviously).

**Braise:** Briefly sautéing a piece, or pieces, of food to lightly sear or brown the outside. Then a small amount of liquid is poured over the hot food; often it's a seasoned vegetable broth or alcohol but water works, also. The food is then covered and allowed to steam just enough to make the food tender. An easy way to think about braising is a cross between sautéing and steaming.

**Caramelize:** To cook, usually over moderate heat for an extended period of time, until the sugars begin to brown.

**Chop:** Cutting things up any which way. Although most recipes will give you a general size to shoot for, when we say simply to chop something rather than *dice* or *julienne* or another more specific term, it usually means that it doesn't much matter what the shape is.

**Deglaze:** After your vegetables (usually garlic and onions) are cooked, adding liquid to the hot pan to lift up anything stuck to the bottom. This is a great way to make sure that all the food and flavors are incorporated into the entire dish, rather than turning into burnt bits and getting sacrificed to the bottom of your pan. Deglazing also makes a great sizzling noise that makes you feel like a real chef.

**Dice:** Chopping vegetables or other items into uniform cubes. When we say uniform we don't mean that you should whip out a tape measure, just aim to get them as alike as you can. Typically, dicing is done in rather small pieces, about ½ inch or less.

**Fold:** Gently stirring in a single ingredient into a larger mixture or batter, usually done by stirring the bottom batter over the added ingredient with a large spoon or spatula. The idea is not to overmix the main batter or mixture, rather to evenly incorporate the new ingredient without disturbing the overall texture.

**Grate:** Scraping food along the surface of a shredder or microplane grater to yield fine shreds or particles of food.

**Grill:** Cooking marinated vegetables or proteins over a heated metal outdoor or indoor grill. The food is often turned several times to ensure it's completely cooked and the exterior lightly caramelized.

**Julienne:** We will take our carrots in matchstick form, thank you. We rarely julienne anything else, except for a cucumber here or there.

**Mince:** Using a knife, chopping vegetables or herbs into very small particles, around ⅛ inch across or even smaller.

**Process:** Basically our lazy way of saying use a food processor or blender to puree something.

**Puree:** Blending the heck of out something in a food processor or blender.

**Reduce:** Simmering a sauce or soup on a stove top until some of the water has evaporated. Usually done with the pot uncovered or partially covered. Reducing will eliminate some of the total volume of the sauce and help intensify the flavors.

**Roast:** Baking food in an oven until the exterior has browned or caramelized and the interior is fully cooked. When roasting vegetables and protein foods, it's often necessary to rub the exterior with an oil to prevent its drying out entirely.

**Roux:** A cooked paste of flour and oil. When a roux is carefully cooked and stirred it begins to brown, forming a tantalizing, full-flavored base for soups and stews. In addition to providing flavor to these dishes, it also is an effective thickening agent.

**Sauté:** Frying, while stirring occasionally, food in a skillet or pot with the addition of a fat.

**Sear:** To cook at high heat for a short period of time so that the outside of a food gets browned but the inside doesn't cook as much.

**Slurry:** A mixture of liquid and starch (usually flour, cornstarch, arrowroot powder, or tapioca starch) that's used to thicken soups and stews. The reason for making a slurry is that you can't add starch to hot things directly or it will clump up. Once the starch has been broken down in the water, it thickens a dish nice and evenly. We use this method a lot, so figured we might as well let you know the proper culinary term.

**Sweat:** In a heated skillet, partially covering a sautéed food and letting it steam until tender.

**Whisk:** Quickly stirring a liquid ingredient, or combination of ingredients, to mix and lightly beating in a little air. Usually done with a whisk, but often a dinner fork will do just as nicely.

# LOWER-FAT COOKING

First things first: this is not a diet cookbook. We love oils and nuts and avocados. They are essential for making delicious meals out of healthful foods. They are often crucial when cooking vegan, because plant foods are, in general, significantly lower in fat than animal-based foods. Flip through the pages and it will become clear that we're not shy when it comes to using olive oil or cashews and, of course, we usually leave room for dessert. Second thing: We are no strangers to diets of all kinds. We've tried many of them with some success, and some failure, over the years. Now that dozens of studies

have shown that vegans are less likely to be obese and vegan diets bring greater weight loss, one of the more interesting misconceptions about eating vegan is that you'll be instantly skinny the day after you eschew cheese or bacon. Not so true. We've encountered many vegans who struggle with weight issues just as much as their more omnivorous fellow dieters, and we're not sure of the reason, either. Maybe it's because making all this delicious food will make you want to eat more of it? Or, it could be people are a little unclear about how to eat healthy if not eating the standard American diet of meat and potatoes. French fries are vegan, right?

## Practice Low-Fat Vegan Cooking

Even if you're perfectly happy with your weight, you might want to trim some of the fat from your diet. It's been recommended by many heath impresarios and nutritionists that we should up the fiber, vegetables, and protein in our diets and keep the fat in check anyway. This might even be just the kind of cooking you flirt with a few times a week, while leaving the weekends open for occasions of full-fat desserts and fried foods.

Lucky for vegans, not only is cooking with less fat not rocket science, it isn't even seventh grade biology class. For the most part, the staples of a vegan diet—legumes, grains, vegetables, and fruit—are all naturally low in fat, as are tofu, tempeh, and seitan. The plant foods we eat that do contain significant fat, such as those aforementioned nuts and avocados, can easily be eaten in moderation. So what we need to look at are the preparation methods we use when cooking our foods. And as you've probably deduced, we're talking about oil here.

## AVOID *NO*-FAT COOKING

Way back in the '80s when people thought that "mousse for hair" was a good idea, fat of all kinds became the cold-war level threat to the country. You couldn't enter a supermarket without tripping over a fat-free cookie, salad dressing, or tortilla. So like good little dieters, we tried this fat-free business. And yes, while the pounds did come off (temporarily), we were one hell of an angry, cranky bitch the whole time. Now, in this new enlightened century, we've learned that some fats, namely high-quality, minimally processed vegetable oils, are good for you. And make you happy. Olive oil; cold-pressed nut oils; canola, safflower, and even unprocessed coconut oil are just a few of these fatty good guys. They contain lots of healthful antioxidants, help you feel full for a longer amount of time, aid in digestion, and just taste good. Cooking-wise, oils provide the necessary medium to keep vegetables moist and tender during cooking, not to mention that they "transport" the flavors of cooked foods like no other.

Now, here comes the less-than great news: you can have too much of a good thing. Yes, sopping up that fresh, crusty bread in herbed olive oil may not clog your arteries like saturated fat will, but over time it can make those jeans just a little tighter. So especially if you have weight loss in mind, keep those wonderful oils in your cupboard and in your salads, entrees, and other dishes. Just use less of them.

## SAUTÉ WITH LESS OIL

Maybe the most obvious thing in the world, but happily it's the easiest thing to do. First off, the venerable non-stick skillet is your friend here (see page 14). With your high-quality, nonstick skillet in hand, you can approach recipes with a critical eye as to how much oil is really necessary to get the approximate degree of browning and crisping. Usually if a food is just going to be browned or lightly grilled, less than a tablespoon of oil

should work. Depending on the "sticky factor" of the item, it might require more or less. A spray bottle filled with oil is a godsend here, as it will distribute only the lightest coat of oil evenly over whatever you are cooking.

For sautéing veggies, tofu, tempeh and seitan, you can substitute vegetable broth for most if not all of the oil. Our favorite method is to use a tiny amount of oil to initially lightly brown that tofu, tempeh, asparagus, and so on, then add the broth to finish the job. Technically this might be braising, except that we may or may not find it necessary to cover the pan. If you're cooking a tough vegetable that requires a longer cooking time (such as cauliflower or broccoli), then covering the pan is the way to go.

When sautéing garlic and onions as the base of a soup, stew, or sauce, you can usually get away with only a teaspoon or two of oil. Here's a little trick: Put a teaspoon or two of oil in a pool on one side of your pan, don't coat the entire pan. Now, add your onions and garlic to the oil. Sauté in that little corner of the pan, preferably using tongs. When moisture begins to release from the onions, usually after 3 minutes or so, you can spray on a little more oil. Then use broth to cook them further, if needed. Many of our soup and stew recipes call for two tablespoons of oil, which really isn't very much when divided among six to eight people, but you can use this method if you want to reduce the fat even further.

## ADD MORE VEGGIES

It's also a good idea to boost meals with more fresh vegetables in place of other calorie-dense items, whether or not you're trying to drop a few pounds. Particularly these should be of the leafy, green variety (spinach, bok choy, etc.) with the addition of red vegetables (tomatoes, red peppers, etc.) and a few other colors to that rainbow. So have that pasta, but instead of two cups of pasta with one-half cup of veggies, have one cup of pasta with two cups of veggies. See our vegetable section for a million ways prepare veggies. Well, a couple dozen at least.

# When NOT to Cook Low-Fat!

BELIEVE it or not, there are key times when you don't want to cook low-fat meals:

### Situation 1: First-Time Vegan Food-Tasters

They may not know it yet, but your flesh-eating dinner guests are going to go vegan. *Someday.* And part of your devious plan is to render them speechless with a most outrageous richly sauced seitan piccata, creamy garlic mashed potatoes, and "buttery" cookies slathered with homemade chocolate-hazelnut spread. This is where you want to pull out all the stops and smother them with tender, loving fat. Don't let their first memory of vegan eating be steamed kale and fat-free bean balls.

### Situation 2: Holidays, Birthdays, Special Occasions

Similar to Situation #1, you want to illustrate that vegan cooking does not exclude the good times. Many holidays are based in ancient beliefs celebrating that new babies continue to be born, the crops have returned, and that we didn't starve to death this winter. Save the oil-free lentil soup for an occasion other than Passover. Isn't eating matzo for eight days a trial and tribulation enough?

### Situation 3: Sad Times

Okay, maybe we're going to get into trouble with psychologists for saying this here, but there's nothing wrong with a stack of chocolate chip pancakes when you're dealing with a serious emotional crisis. Loss of family, friend, pet. The big stuff. If you're normally working hard at watching what you eat, how much you exercise, read labels, and so on, then you know what you have to do when you're ready to get back on track. And you will, since you're made of the tough stuff.

### Situation 4: Party Times

A lot like special occasions, but with potentially more people. Potlucks and picnics fall into this category. You don't want to be known by your local rotary club as "The Blanched Tofu" boy or "The Poached Spinach" lady, now do you?

## EAT LOW-GI FOODS

Choose foods that are low on what's called the "glycemic index." Don't worry, you don't need to be a nutritionist to figure out what those foods are, it simply means carbohydrates that are digested more slowly, raise your blood glucose more evenly, and keep you feeling fuller longer. Basically, you want unrefined carbohydrates, so instead of white rice choose brown rice, eat fruits rather than sugary desserts, and consume more whole grains such as quinoa and millet. Hey, this book you're holding in your hand even has some recipes for those things! For more info on the glycemic index (including where foods rank), visit www.glycemicindex.com.

## USE YOUR SPRAY BOTTLE OF OIL

See Spray Bottle (page 15) in the kitchen equipment list. It's a dieter's best friend.

# HOW TO COOK A VEGETABLE

(OR, THE ART AND SCIENCE OF TRANSFORMING EDIBLE ROOTS, SHOOTS, LEAVES, AND FRUITS OF AN ARRAY OF PLANTS WITH CRITICALLY APPLIED HEAT, OILS, AND SEASONINGS SO THAT THEY WILL BE EATEN WITH GREAT PLEASURE AND THE LEAST AMOUNT OF COMPLAINING)

*Dear Veganomicon,*

*I don't know where to begin. I've been eschewing meat and dairy products for years but I can't bring myself to eat vegetables. They are often so bland and flavorless I presume that if I ate my napkin I might acquire the same amount of fiber, without the "ick" factor of having to eat something green. But, I have heard that there are some advantages to eating these things that grow in the dirt. Whatever should I do?*

*Yours truly,*
*Cautious of Carrots*

Okay, we've never received a letter like that. However, we know that they are out there, reckless vegans and vegetarians who are pulling the green and orange blocks out of the bottom of the food pyramid and replacing them with things fried, sugary, and bready. We don't blame them. We blame society, or more exactly a society composed of limp, boiled broccoli; iceberg lettuce salads; and canned mushrooms. Don't even get us started on "baby" corn (that ain't *our* baby!). For those of you who love vegetables, this will be a tribute to everything glorious about the delicious part of the plant kingdom. At the very least, it will get you excited about roasting an extra bulb of garlic or two next time you fire up the oven. Learning how to cook vegetables so that they're flavorful, enticing, and exciting is about the best thing you can do to help spread the word about veganism, hands down. This chapter is organized according to different methods to coax the most flavor out of your veggies, to give you the skills to last a lifetime. Notice we're not a big fan of boiling (except for the occasional root vegetable, of course). It's so last century and kind of a mean thing to do to vegetables, if you think about it.

# Tools for Outdoor Grilling

**METAL TONGS:** Tongs are like an extension of our arms if there's a grill within fifty feet. Don't bother trying to turn things with a spatula; tongs are the tool of choice for flipping your veggies with precision. Simple, cheap metal ones will do, but you can get exotic with silicone-handled, heavy-duty tongs.

**SPATULA:** So you don't need a spatula for turning vegetables, but don't worry, it doesn't have to join the unemployment line just yet. Spatulas are great for flattening things out on the grill to ensure even cooking. Just be sure to get a really long-handled one for the grill, or feel free to use the little guy used for flipping pancakes if your hands are made out of asbestos.

**PASTRY BRUSHES:** Kitchen supply stores sell pastry brushes that are just a little too dainty and precious for our tastes, not to mention more expensive. So we use the kind of fat, round, nylon brush that you can find in a hardware store. Grill like a *Veganomicon* author and keep two at your side: one for brushing the grill with oil and one for brushing the veggies with oil or marinade during cooking.

**METAL SKEWERS:** For some reason, grilling vegetables in kebab form makes them 76 percent more fun to eat, according to our studies. You can also use wooden skewers, but to make sure that they don't burn: soak the wooden skewers in water beforehand for at least an hour. Get those freeloader picnic guests to assemble bite-size veggie chunks onto skewers while you make the marinades or just work on your fierce tan.

**LIDDED PLASTIC CONTAINERS:** They make for easy transport of your veggies, and you can shake them to coat your veggies in oil or marinade with no worries.

**LARGE, RESEALABLE PLASTIC BAGS:** For some vegetables, such as asparagus, it's difficult to find a container that's the right size. Hence bags.

**ALUMINUM FOIL:** You always need it for something. It's almost a mystery how aluminum foil saves many a grilling day.

**THE GRILL:** We don't live in the suburbs, so therefore we never really developed an unhealthy obsession with obtaining the perfect grill. Use any charcoal, gas-fired grill or campfire that pleases you. Generally we like the permanent, for-the-people kind you'll find in the park (a good a reason as any to leave the house on a Saturday before 11 a.m., just to lay claim on the good ones), or anything under thirty bucks. The great part about cooking veggies is that it takes a fraction of the time the meaty stuff does, so you really don't need that monster grill that costs as much as a down payment on a car.

## GRILLING VEGETABLES

Vegetarians are sometimes at a loss for what to put on the grill. It's often a sad toss-up between the oddly orange-hued tofu hotdogs or frozen disks of veggie burgers. We know this is a crazy thought but how about . . . *vegetables*?! Grilling brings out so much flavor in vegetables that you don't even need to dress them up too much. So pretty to look at and toothsome, perfectly grilled vegetables are like the Spring Break of parties in your mouth. A little olive oil and you're good to go, or if you're feeling especially inspired, some garlic and lemon juice never hurt. You don't have limit your grilling skills to the outdoors or miss out because it's snowing outside—a cast iron grill pan works wonders on the stovetop as well.

---

### The #1 Tool for Indoor Grilling

CAST aside your fears and get a cast-iron grill pan! We probably say this about ten times throughout the book, but since this section is specifically about grilling it would be remiss not to mention it here. You absolutely need to get one! Once you have procured this, the most important purchase you will ever make in your life, then you can follow these same directions for outdoor grilling, only you will be indoors. (See Grill, page 19.)

---

### Asparagus

Grilled asparagus is at once chewy and crispy, savory and sweet.

**Prep:** Remove rough end of stems. Place in a plastic bag. Add enough olive oil to coat, and a few cloves of minced garlic. Close the bag and rub all over to make sure the asparagus is coated. Let it sit for 10 minutes or a few hours—whenever you are ready to grill. When you are ready to grill, sprinkle with a little bit of coarse sea salt.

**Grill:** Turn every few minutes and brush with olive oil if it looks like it's getting dry. It's ready when the tips to turn slightly charred—but before they turn shriveled—about 5 to 7 minutes.

. . .

### Bell Peppers

The pepper of choice for the grill is the red bell pepper, for its sweetness and meatiness, but you can go with orange, yellow, or even purple if you can find it. Green bell peppers are simply not quite ripe red bell peppers, so they are a little bitter, but if that's your thing, go for it. To get the most out of your pepper, it's best to blanch it beforehand. *Blanching* is simply a fancy-pants way of saying boil for a minute or two. In the case of the pepper, blanching will get it softened up and ready to soak up the oil—plus it will make it cook faster on the grill without burning.

**Prep:** Bring a pot of water to a boil. Carve out the pepper stem with a paring knife. Remove the stem and seeds, and peel out as much of the white stuff on the inside of the skin as you can. Place the peppers in the boiling water for just a minute or two. Remove the peppers with your trusty tongs, drain the insides, and set aside to cool. Cut each pepper in half. Brush each side with olive oil.

**Grill:** Place skin side down on the grill and flatten with a spatula as much as you can. Let cook until the skin is very charred; depending on the heat of your grill this can take anywhere from 8 to 15 minutes. Once then skin is good and charred, flip the pepper over for just a few more minutes.

We like to get sneaky and cook other kinds of peppers on the grill when nobody's looking. Turn your head for just a minute and we've put whole, unpeeled jalapeños or serranos on the grill. Turn them a few times and make sure they get nicely charred and blistered, then sock them away in a covered plastic container. You'll then have roasted chiles on hand to chop up and toss into any salsa, and therefore instantly become a salsa superhero.

. . .

## Corn

We don't think it's necessary to make a case for corn on the cob, everyone loves it.

**Prep:** Pull back the husk as far as you can without ripping it off or damaging it. Pull the silk away from the corn and then close the husks back up. Soak the corn in a big pot of water for at least half an hour. The water softens the kernels as well as provides moisture that steams the corn and helps it to cook faster. Push the husks aside and brush the corn with oil and sprinkle with salt. Close the husks back up.
**Grill:** Place the whole ears on the grill and turn often for about 20 minutes. The corn is ready when the kernels are soft and release moisture if pressed.

P.S. If you're cooking with a campfire, get all outdoorsy and bury prepared, presoaked corn (make sure to keep plenty of the husk on!) in the hot ash and glowing coals of the campfire. Turn the corn once or twice. Depending on how hot your fire is, check the corn after about 10 minutes. Don't forget it or you'll have corn charcoal!

. . .

## Eggplant

We love grilled eggplant as much as the next guy, but we're the first to admit that it's been much abused by the delis and restaurants of the world in the name of "vegetarian" food. We've all been there: the only meatless thing on the menu is that grilled vegetable sandwich, usually featuring a huge blob of tasteless, rubbery "grilled" eggplant. Cast aside those fears; the eggplant grilled at home by you will banish those blues forever.

### Eggplant: To Salt or Not to Salt?

WE'VE been fence sitters on this issue for a while, but we've decided to err on the side of caution and tell you to salt the eggplant. Does salting eggplant really leach out the bitterness? Yes, even though eggplant is now bred to be less bitter. On the pro-salt side, the salt really does tenderize the eggplant, so why not take the extra time to do it? So even though we do recommend it, we aren't fascistic in our belief and you can skip this step if you feel like it.

**Prep:** Eggplant is great sliced in numerous ways; the stylish bias, completely lengthwise for huge eggplant "steaks," or the widthwise circular slice. Slices can be a little bit thicker than for summer squash, about ¾ inch. Remember to brush liberally with olive oil.
**Grill:** Grill for 5 to 7 minutes, then flip and grill for another 5 to 7. Brush often with oil as eggplant loves to drink that stuff up and tends to stick to the grill easier than do other veggies.

. . .

## Leeks

Adventurous types might enjoy throwing whole leeks on the grill. They have a great onion flavor and chewy texture that is fun and satisfying to eat.

**Prep:** Trim both ends of each leek, then slice–starting from the green end–to about halfway through the white part. Completely cover in water and allow to soak about 5 minutes, shaking to ensure than any sand or grit is washed away from the leeks. Coat liberally with olive oil.
**Grill:** Grill for 5 to 7 minutes until soft and slightly charred. Sprinkle with salt after they are grilled.

## Onions

Onions are excellent additions to your portobello burger or grilled veggie sandwich. We love using large, candy-sweet Vidalia onions but any big, preferably yellow, onion will do.

**Prep:** Slice off tops, remove the skin and cut into thick slices—a little under ½ an inch should do. Keeping each slice intact, brush with olive oil.

**Grill:** Grill for 5 to 7 minutes, until soft and slightly charred. Flip often, using the tongs to keep the rings together.

## Pineapple

PINEAPPLE is not a vegetable, you say (well, neither are tomatoes, but . . .). You haven't lived until you've tasted pineapple fresh off the grill. No, really, maybe you're a vegan zombie looking for BBQ tips or something. Anyway, to the humans out there, freshly sliced pineapple—coated with a little vegetable oil—is totally asking to be grilled, about 3 to 4 minutes each side. The sugars caramelize into a sweet heaven on the outside while the insides remain juicy. Serve warm, either with barbecue sauce–covered items or as a dessert with fresh berries and your favorite soy ice cream.

For some really good times, place a whole, peeled, unsliced pineapple on the outdoor grill. Lightly oil it and turn it occasionally to caramelize each side. This is especially a good idea if you have lots of hot, smoldering coals left over (after the main grilling) and don't want to waste them. Better than a stupid roasted marshmallow, if you ask us. It's fun to slice hot off the grill (use a big knife and pierce it with a fork so it doesn't fly off the cutting board), kind of like a big old holiday roast made just out of, you guessed it, pineapple.

## Portobello Mushrooms

Who needs burgers? Portobellos are nature's own burger, big juicy mushrooms that just beg to be grilled and placed between a bun. You could go through a whole song and dance with balsamic vinegar and soy sauce, but this is just about the basics. A little olive oil and garlic lets the mushroom flavor shine through.

**tip**

### GETTING THE STEM OFF A PORTOBELLO

NOW, this is sort of an art, as many a portobello has been ruined by untrained hands that either rip or pull too hard or crush the delicate cap. So forgive us if this is just too much detail about how to remove a stem from a mushroom (but if you had seen all the carnage that we have you would understand our precautions). Place the portobello, stem side up, on a flat surface. Place your fingers gently on the underside just outside the stem, to secure it. Using your free hand (which should be your writing hand), place your fingers at the base of the stem and gently turn the cap inward. This may take a few turns until you feel it giving; it's sort of like gently jiggling your key in a lock. When the stem gives, you should be home free and can just gently turn until the stem comes off. You don't have to do this every time; once you get a feel for the portobello you will be able to just pull a stem off in the blink of an eye.

**Prep:** Remove stem (see tip). Wipe clean with a damp towel. Brush generously with olive oil and sprinkle with salt.

**Grill:** Place on the grill gill side down. Sprinkle with a little coarse sea salt. Let the portobellos cook for about 10 minutes, then flip over and cook for another 5, brushing with olive oil if they look dry. Depending on the heat of your grill and the size of your mushrooms, you may need to cook for another 5 to 10 minutes, flipping every so often. The mushrooms are ready when they are soft and dark. The center should be tender and release moisture when you press down with a spatula.

. . .

## Tomatoes

We generally don't recommend grilling tomatoes, but we can recommend making cute little kebabs with firm, ripe cherry tomatoes and plenty of oil. These don't take very long, maybe only 2 to 3 minutes, tops, so don't go wandering over to finish off the last of the guacamole when these babies are on the grill.

. . .

## Zucchini or Summer Squash

Zucchini really takes to the grill and rewards you with those perfect grill lines you see in magazines. For best results, use young to middle-aged squash, avoiding those really huge, old zucchini that are nothing but tough skin and lots of seeds.

**Prep:** Cut off the stems. Slice on a bias (angle) into just less than ½-inch slices. The reason for cutting on a bias is so that you get nice big slices that won't fall into the grill, but it also has the added benefit of being a nicer presentation. Brush with olive oil.

**Grill:** Cook one side for about 3 to 4 minutes. Check the bottom to see if your grill marks have appeared. When they have, brush with olive oil, flip over, and cook for a few minutes more. The squash should be tender but not completely falling apart. Remove from the grill and lightly salt.

. . .

## Other Vegetables

Maybe someday you'll have the burning desire to grill a sweet potato or a rutabaga. And who are we to stop you? In general, it's helpful to keep in mind that whatever you put on the grill should ideally: (a) be completely cooked in fewer than 10 to 12 minutes, and (b) not fall

apart when put under such intense heat. Generally, it helps to keep vegetables sliced less than ¾ inch. Root vegetables should be precooked—usually by boiling—until just tender but not cooked all the way, then sliced into ½-inch-thick pieces. Same applies to winter squash; just make sure not to overcook it before putting on the grill. Use plenty of oil to protect against sticking, and have ready a spatula if anything appears to be too fragile or soft to handle with tongs.

## Kebab Advice

MAYBE you didn't ask for it, but we've got it. Our basic kebabs generally consist of: peppers, whole mushrooms, onions, and zucchini. Prep the peppers by blanching them, then cut them into inch-thick slices. Chop the zucchini and onions into ½-inch slices and leave the mushroom whole. If you need to add cherry tomatoes, fine, but make separate little skewers just for them. They cook far faster than other vegetables and will end up falling off the skewers and into the fire before the other vegetables are done.

For heartier fare, add chunks of seitan or pressed tofu. Place it all into a plastic bag or container, coat with olive oil and a few pinches of coarse sea salt, and squeeze a lemon over it. Or, use a marinade. For the professionally lazy, we'll even let you use your favorite bottled oil and vinegar dressing as a no-effort marinade. Let them sit for about 15 minutes, then place on skewers, alternating vegetables and seitan. Cook for 7 to 10 minutes, turning every few minutes and brushing with oil. Drizzle with Miso Tahini dressing (page 93) for optimal yumminess.

So now that you have the basics of grilling down, it's time to serve these babies up. If you are going the sandwich route, it's a good idea to grill the bread as well—why not? Fire is free. If not using hamburger buns, we like to use chewy peasant bread. Simply brush with oil and lightly grill each side until faint grill marks start to appear. You can also opt for garlic bread. It's simple—just puree two cloves of garlic with ½ cup of olive oil, brush onto bread, and grill. Once your bread is grilled, spread with Basil-Cilantro Pesto (page 214), pile on veggies, and enjoy!

You can also serve grilled veggies on top of a cold pasta or rice salad; the combination of hot and cold foods is the best thing in the whole world. Grill some extra vegetables and save the leftovers just for this or a dozen other reasons: to put on pizza, blend into hummus (page 67), sneak into the Roasted Eggplant and Spinach Muffuletta (page 100), finely dice and sprinkle into a bean soup, etc.

## Roasting Veggies in the Oven

Roasting simply means to cook something with indirect dry heat for a moderate amount of time. The wonderful thing about this method is that, whereas boiling leaches the flavor out of our food, roasting concentrates the flavor, as well as crisps and caramelizes the outside. Most any vegetable can be roasted and all that is needed is some oil, salt, and pepper. And of course, a little garlic never hurts. The other bonus is that the cook has to do very little work while the veggies are cooking. So, we often complete our meals with a hodgepodge of roasted veggies. This way, while the stove top might be seeing a lot of chaotic action, there is an oasis of serenity down below as our little friends do their thing and roast away.

The following are not so much recipes as guidelines for some of our favorite roasted vegetables. You'll notice, throughout the book, we demand that you serve something with roasted this or that, so we figured that it was only right that we let you know how to do it. First we give you the basic prep and cooking time, but you decide what kind of herbs and flavorings (if any) that you want to use. Go lightly with dried spices and add them before cooking. If using fresh

herbs, toss them in about 5 minutes before the veggies are done cooking. We suggest that you use a 13 × 17-inch rimmed baking sheet for all of these recipes and always cook your veggies in a single layer so that they cook evenly and perfectly.

**tip**

### HOW TO PREPARE YOUR ROASTING PAN

Baking parchment, often called "parchment paper," can be a baking sheet's best friend when roasting vegetables. It isn't completely necessary, but it does help to protect your sheet and to make sure that your veggies don't stick.

### *Asparagus*

When roasted, asparagus's rich flavors get really concentrated. The entire vegetable achieves a certain succulent texture that only happens with roasting. You'll notice, throughout the book, that we ask you to serve lots of things with roasted asparagus, and that is not because we work for the National Asparagus Council, it is just because we love it that much. (On a side note, is the NAC hiring?)

**Oven temperature:** 400°F
**Prep:** Remove the rough stem bottoms. Drizzle and coat the asparagus with olive oil, salt, and fresh black pepper. Place on a lightly greased baking sheet. If you like, add minced garlic 5 minutes before the asparagus is done, and mix it in with tongs.
**Roast:** 15 to 20 minutes, depending on the size of the asparagus. The tips should be a bit crispy and the stems should be lightly browned and crinkly.
**Complements:** Tarragon, thyme, crushed fennel seeds, rosemary, a drizzle of balsamic vinegar, or fresh lemon juice.
**Fancy it up:** Because we worry that you might not be eating enough capers, why not try tossing in

a few tablespoons of capers along with the asparagus in the roasting pan?

· · ·

## Brussels Sprouts

This is the recipe that took Isa from nose-turner-upper to fork-digger-inner. Roasting Brussels sprouts brings out their nutty flavor.

**Oven temperature:** 400°F
**Prep:** Remove the rough knobby stem; slice the sprouts in half lengthwise. Drizzle and coat with olive oil, salt, and fresh black pepper. Place cut side down on a baking sheet. If you like, add minced garlic 5 minutes before the Brussels are done and mix in with tongs.
**Roast:** 15 to 20 minutes, depending on the size of the sprouts. The cut side should be browned and crispy in places.
**Complements:** We prefer these plain and unadulterated.

· · ·

## Cauliflower

Roasting cauliflower is a popular way to serve up this vegetable in a variety of Mediterranean cuisines. Like Brussels sprouts, cauliflower has an aromatic nutty flavor when roasted, which makes sense since they are in the same family.

**Oven temperature:** 400°F
**Prep:** Slice head of cauliflower in half and remove leaves. Slice into bite-size chunks, drizzle and rub with olive oil. Sprinkle with salt and fresh black pepper. Place on a lightly greased baking sheet.
**Roast:** Roast for 15 to 20 minutes, using tongs to turn them halfway through cooking.
**Complements:** After cooking, add fresh chopped parsley and drizzle with fresh lemon juice, if you wish.
**Fancy it up:** Make a yummy Indian side dish by

adding a teaspoon each of crushed cumin and coriander seeds before cooking.

· · ·

## Eggplant

Oven-roasted eggplant is so versatile and dare we say "meaty" that you'll find a way to work it into pastas, sandwiches, curries, salads, and more. Especially nice when you're feeding a mixed crowd of meat- and plant-eaters. Simply slice the eggplant any way that you please (but keep the skin on). Cutting crosswise into ½-inch-thick rounds creates a good, all-purpose shape; ¼-inch-thick lengthwise slices rule for hero-style sandwiches and layering in casseroles. We recommend salting eggplant before cooking it (See sidebar "To Salt or Not to Salt?" on page 27).

**Oven temperature:** 350°F
**Prep:** Remove the stems. Slice as described above, or cut into ½-inch cubes for use in a soup or salad. If you want to go with salting the eggplant, rub each slice with kosher salt and place in a colander; put the colander in the sink. Let sit for 20 to 30 minutes, allowing any excess liquid to sweat out. Rinse each slice and pat dry with a kitchen towel. Whether or not you salted the eggplant, rub the slices with olive oil and sprinkle them with fresh black pepper (if you salted them, there is no need for salt here; if not, sprinkle with salt now.) Place on a baking sheet.
**Roast:** 15 to 20 minutes. You may want to spray with a little oil intermittently to prevent the eggplant from drying out. The slices should be lightly browned.
**Complements:** Tarragon, thyme, crushed fennel seeds, rosemary, oregano, a drizzle of balsamic vinegar, or fresh lemon juice. Or go in a Middle Eastern direction and sprinkle on ground cumin and paprika.
**Fancy it up:** Top roasted eggplant with lightly sautéed chopped garlic, sliced black olives, fresh parsley or dill, and drizzles of high-quality olive oil.

## Whole Eggplant

ROAST a whole eggplant in its skin? Are you mad? Mad about tender, melt-in-your-mouth eggplant, maybe. Take a small to medium-size eggplant, prick little holes all over it with a fork, place it in a "cradle" of foil on a baking sheet, and bake it at 400°F for 25 to 35 minutes, until it's collapsed and easily pierced with a fork. The resulting interior (don't eat the charred skin) is creamy, delicate, and delicious scooped away from the exterior and mashed with a little olive oil, lemon, salt, and a touch of cumin. Use as a dip with toasted pita triangles, cucumbers, and carrot spears.

## Green Beans

If roasting a green bean sounds weird to you, then get ready to question everything you thought you knew and bite into a crisp 'n' chewy, yet tender 'n' roasty green bean. These are especially lovely tossed into a pasta or potato salad.

**Oven temperature:** 400°F
**Prep:** Trim the tops. Drizzle and coat with olive oil, salt, and fresh black pepper. Place on a lightly greased baking sheet. If you like, add minced garlic 5 minutes before the beans are done, and mix it in with tongs.
**Roast:** 12 to 15 minutes
**Complements:** We prefer these plain and unadulterated.

. . .

## Roasting Garlic

SOME articles from the '80s, such as stirrup pants and banana hair clips, are best left to lame theme parties and annoying "You know you're a child of . . ." e-mail spam. However, the wonderful roasted garlic was everywhere during that decade is here to stay, if we have anything to say about it. It's so mellow, sweet, and simple to make. There's no excuse not to work roasted garlic into everything from salad dressings to hummus.

If you can tease up some "mall hair," then you can make roasted garlic. Take one or more whole, unpeeled, and unseparated bulbs of garlic. With a heavy, sharp knife, slice off approximately ½ inch of the entire top of the bulb, exposing the insides of the garlic cloves. Drizzle about 1 tablespoon of olive oil onto the top of the bulb, making sure the cut cloves are covered with oil and some oil sneaks into the spaces between the cloves. Wrap tightly in foil and bake at 375°F for 20 to 30 minutes, until the cloves are very soft and turned a deep golden color. For slightly caramelized cloves, unwrap the tops of the bulbs and let them roast for 8 to 10 additional minutes.

It may seem like a big waste to heat up the oven just to roast a few cloves of garlic. Sometimes we use our toaster ovens. Other times, if we know we're going to have the oven fired up for an hour or more (when making a casserole or roasting other veggies), we'll wrap up some garlic and sneak it into the oven even if we have no particular roasted garlic in mind, just to have it on hand. Roasted garlic, if stored in a tightly sealed container, should keep for about a week.

## Peppers

Roasting peppers at home will make you feel like you're on a cooking show. A show so fabulous that you can film in your pajamas and nobody will say anything because you're famous for your breathtaking roasted peppers.

Also, roasted peppers are particularly perfect for placing on pizzas (say that 5 times fast).

### How to Roast a Pepper on the Stove Top

SOMETIMES you want just one roasted pepper. And you want it fast. The best way to go about this is roasting a whole, unsliced pepper directly on top of the stove, on a gas burner over high heat (DON'T use an electric burner; if that's all you have, use the oven method instead). Go ahead, the pepper can take it. Use tongs to rotate the pepper as its skin starts to blacken and blister. When about 75 percent of the pepper is done roasting, pick it up with the tongs and drop it into a paper bag or a large, heatproof bowl. Crimp the top of the bag or tightly cover the bowl with a dish or some plastic wrap. Allow the pepper to sit for at least 10 to 15 minutes. This step not only lets it cool enough to be handled but also allows the steam escaping from the pepper to loosen its skin. After it's cooled for a while, gently peel away as much of the skin as possible. It's okay if bits of charred skin remain on the pepper; they're full of flavor and have that exciting barbecued look. Slice, seed, and proceed as usual.

**Oven temperature:** 425°F
**Prep:** Cut the peppers in half lengthwise and remove the stem and seeds. Coat lightly with olive oil (a spray bottle works great for this) and place on a lightly greased baking sheet.
**Roast:** 20 to 25 minutes, until skin is dark brown in spots.

**Note:** Most of the time people remove the skin before eating, but that isn't exactly necessary if your peppers aren't charred beyond belief. We actually like the way the burnt parts taste. If you would like to remove the skin, place the peppers in a paper or plastic bag the moment you remove them from the oven. Close the bag, and this will steam the peppers. When they have cooled for about 30 minutes, the skins can be peeled away easily.

· · ·

## Potatoes

When in doubt about what to eat for dinner or brunch, there's always roasted potatoes. Leave the skin on for taste and texture.

**Oven temperature:** 425°F
**Prep:** Cut into ¾-inch chunks. Drizzle and coat with olive oil. Sprinkle with salt and fresh black pepper. Place on a lightly greased baking sheet.
**Roast:** 45 to 55 minutes, turning occasionally. If you like, add minced garlic 5 minutes before the potatoes are done cooking and mix it in using tongs.
**Optional complements:** Potatoes go well with just about any herb you can think of: paprika, rosemary, thyme, sage, and on and on down the spice rack.
**Fancy it up:** What's even better than roasted potatoes? Roasted french fries, also known as "French Bakes" by maybe fifteen people. Cut potatoes into fry shapes (about ½ inch wide and ¼ inch thick); toss with a little oil, salt, and spices of choice. Lightly grease a baking sheet with oil. Spread out your fries in a single layer, and leave a little space between them. This will ensure that the fries properly roast and get crunchy instead of steaming. Bake at 425°F for 15 minutes, flip, and

bake for another 8 to 10 minutes, until they are slightly puffed, brown and crisp. Eat ASAP, dipped in ketchup, vegan mayo with a little Dijon mustard blended in, or BBQ sauce, as they get a little bit tough when they start to cool.

. . .

## Root Veggies and Tubers

Carrots, beets, turnips, sweet potatoes, parsnips—you name it, bring it on! Your oven can take these rock-hard roots and tubers and transform them into candy-sweet, tender nuggets in lovely shades of orange, magenta, and cream.

**Oven temperature:** 400°F

**Prep:** Peel the veggies and slice off their stems. The shapes you cut are pretty much up to you, although ¾ inch across in any direction is a pretty good size to aim for. Drizzle and coat with olive oil, sprinkle with salt. Place on a lightly greased baking sheet. You can also slice into ¼-inch slices for chips, in which case you should reduce the cooking time by 10 minutes.

**Roast:** 35 to 45 minutes, flipping once about halfway through cooking. The roots should be tender and easily pierced with a fork, the outsides should be browned and even lightly caramelized.

**Complements:** Rosemary and thyme or sweet spices such as cinnamon, nutmeg, and allspice.

**Fancy it up:** Add a light coating of maple syrup and minced ginger before cooking, for a hint of sweetness.

. . .

## Tomatoes

Roasting tomatoes brings out all their flavor and sweetness. Save your beautiful vine-ripened type tomatoes for a sandwich or salad, but when you have tomatoes that aren't as juicy, like plum tomatoes, then roasting is the way to go. An added bonus is that they make your kitchen smell like the most inviting restaurant in Little Italy. Roasted tomatoes in sandwiches,

along with a portobello (page 112) would be nice, or use them as the base for sauces and soups.

**Oven temperature:** 350°F

**Prep:** Remove the stems. Slice into ½-inch slices. Place on a lightly oiled baking sheet, sprinkle with salt.

**Roast:** 50 minutes to an hour, until the skin is a bit crinkled

**Complements:** Oregano, thyme, or really any herb you might find in a Simon and Garfunkel song.

. . .

## Winter Squash

Although steaming may be more convenient, roasting most winter squashes and pumpkins brings out their sweet flavor as no other cooking method can. You can roast squash whole, in its skin, and serve it in large luscious pieces, or cut it into small caramelized pieces, so we will give you directions for both ways.

### For big pieces of whole roasted squash

**Oven temperature:** 400°F

**Prep:** Remove the stem. Split the squash in half lengthwise. Remove the seeds and use a spoon to scrape out any stringy bits. Place cut side down on a lightly greased baking sheet.

**Roast:** 45 minutes to an hour, depending on the size. The outside peel of the squash should be easily pierced with a fork when it's done cooking. Slice into more manageable (but still large) pieces to serve. Leave the skins on for a more dramatic presentation; if the skin is not edible, just peel it off while eating.

### For smaller, caramelized pieces

**Oven temperature:** 400°F

**Prep:** Remove stem. Peel off skin. Split squash in half lengthwise. Remove seeds and use a spoon to scrape out stringy buts. Cut into ¾ inch pieces. Drizzle and coat with olive oil and salt. Place on lightly greased baking sheet.

**Roast:** 25 to 30 minutes, turning twice during cooking. Squash should be tender, browned, and lightly caramelized on the edges.

### For both methods

**Complements:** Rosemary, sage, thyme, or sweet spices such as cinnamon, allspice, and nutmeg.

**Fancy it up:** Before cooking, add a light coating of maple syrup. Sprinkle with crushed coriander seeds and minced ginger.

IF you're (God forbid) tired of mashed potatoes or just in need of a sweet change, use our whole-roasting method for winter squash and make mashed squash instead. Just remove the skin, and mash or puree with a little maple syrup, salt, and cinnamon.

## Zucchini or Summer Squash

"*Oy gevalt!* I've got *ferkakte* zucchini up to *mayn kepele*!" How many times have you uttered these words, amazed at your newfound grasp of Yiddish? Roasting to the rescue, once again. Get ready for succulent summer squash that will rock your *tuchus*.

**Oven temperature:** 425°F

**Prep:** Remove the stem. Cut widthwise into ½-inch pieces, try to slice at a diagonal for a nice presentation. Drizzle and coat with olive oil, salt, and fresh black pepper. Place on a lightly greased baking sheet. If you like, add minced garlic 5 minutes before the zucchini is done.

**Roast:** 25 to 30 minutes, turning once halfway through cooking.

**Complements:** Dill, rosemary, thyme, tarragon, or parsley. Drizzle with balsamic vinegar or fresh lemon once done cooking.

## SIMPLE STEAMING

Steaming should be thought of as boiling for the new century. No longer will we tolerate flaccid, drab-green vegetables when they should be crisp, flavorful, and their truer shades of brilliant greens. Steaming is also really easy; you can easily steam any vegetable without fancy equipment. A large soup pot with a lid is the all the bare-bones gear you need. If you do have a steamer basket, though, then great! (There are recipes in this book where it will come in handy.) There is definitely no need to clutter up the kitchen counter with special plug-in electric steamers or other food-steaming contraptions.

We're not too crazy about dried herbs on steamed veggies, but adding fresh herbs about 3 minutes before the veggies are done steaming is never a bad idea. Try parsley, dill, thyme, oregano, or tarragon on any of these veggies. You can also drizzle them with any of our sauces in the sauce chapter (pages 203–216).

### Shocking!

IT might not be apparent, but even after you've turned off the heat, vegetables will continue to cook. The steam that's working its way out of the vegetables will still continue the cooking process, and if you're not careful it might turn those perfectly steamed asparagus spears to mush. If you're not planning on serving vegetables immediately, or plan on serving them cold or at room temperature, quickly run them under cold water for about a minute. This is called "shocking" the vegetable, which sounds pretty cool. Transfer to a colander and allow to drain.

### Directions for preparing a steamer pot for any kind of veggies

Fill a large soup pot with 2 to 3 inches of cold water, fit your steamer basket into the pot, cover, and bring to a boil. Once the water is boiling, place the veggies in the steamer and cover. If you don't have a steamer basket, no worries, just fill the pot with 2 to 3 inches of water, cover, and bring to a boil. Once the water is boiling, place the veggies directly into the boiling water and cover. We call this boil/steaming, or stoiling—but no one else does, so never say the word aloud.

. . .

## Asparagus

What's better than crisp-tender asparagus in the height of spring? Okay, maybe there are a few other things but shhhh . . . we're totally grooving on steamed asparagus right now.

**Prep:** Remove rough stems.
**Steam:** 8 to 14 minutes, depending on thickness. Asparagus should be bright green and still crisp.
**To serve:** Drizzle with Dill-Tahini (page 215) or Cheezy Sauce (page 214).

. . .

## Broccoli and Cauliflower

Since this is what everyone thinks vegans live on, why not prove them right?

**Prep:** Cut into medium-size florets.
**Steam:** 10 to 12 minutes, tossing with tongs a few times.
**To serve:** We love these with Dill-Tahini Sauce (page 215).

## Dark, Leafy Greens

A little bit of boiling water is really the best, lazy way to cook up quickly a bunch of collards or kale. It makes you feel really healthy, too, and levels you up in the vegan echelon.

**Prep:** Wash and chop the greens into bite-size pieces.
**Steam:** 10 to 14 minutes. Toss the greens with tongs as they start to wilt. In the South, it's popular to keep on boiling these greens to form the famous delicacy of "pot liquor"; but being north of the Mason-Dixon Line, we just like 'em bright green and with a little bit of crunch left in them.
**To serve:** A simple and old-school hippie restaurant way to enjoy steamed greens is sprinkled with plenty of sesame salt (known as gomasio, which is just a blend of crushed, roasted sesame seeds and sea salt), with maybe a touch of lemon juice or a sprinkle of malt vinegar. We also like them with Citrus-Date-Sesame Sauce (page 215).

. . .

## Green Beans

Nothing scares a green bean more than being boiled to death and canned. Fortunately, we grew up on gently steamed green beans before they were the "in" thing.

**Prep:** Trim off ends.
**Steam:** 8 to 10 minutes, depending on size, tossing with tongs a few times.
**To serve:** Sprinkle with coarse salt and enjoy. Or try with Mustard Sauce (page 204).

# HOW TO COOK
# A GRAIN

*There's a reason that grains were found in the tombs of the Egyptian pyramids as well as at the base of our food pyramid: they're packed with so many nutrients, vitamins, minerals, fiber, and even protein, all while being low in fat. But grains aren't just life-giving sustenance. They're also a culinary jewel, adding notes of nuttiness, earthiness, and sometimes even floral hints to round our meals out. And their affordability will make you wanna do an infomercial about them. Following is by no means a comprehensive list of grains. There are hundreds of edible ones worldwide; these are just some that*

we consider essential and that are easy enough to find. We give you the simplest preparation methods to serve four people, but feel free to double the quantities; however, anything more than double, you will have to adjust the amount of water used. A good rule of thumb is to remove one-quarter cup of water for every multiple increment above doubling. So if you are quadrupling the recipe, subtract one-half cup of water. You'll notice that some of these preparation methods are simply to boil and simmer the water and grain together, whereas some are steamed by pouring the water over the grain and covering tightly. Still others benefit most from being toasted and then boiled. Like we said, these are the simplest preparation methods for grains meant to be served as side dishes, but of course we include all of these grains in more adventurous recipes throughout this book. An easy way to punch up the flavor and get the most out of your grains is to use vegetable broth instead of water or

throw a bouillon cube into the mix. A two-quart pot is just right for all of these recipes. The most economical way to purchase grains is to buy from the bulk bins of health food stores or co-ops, but all of the varieties listed also come in boxes or bags at well-stocked grocery stores. Store grains in airtight jars and keep out of direct sunlight, and they will stay fresh for years—an important thing to remember for when the revolution comes. With the exception of oats and couscous, you'll want to rinse everything on this list before cooking. To rinse, place in a very large bowl and cover with lukewarm water. Swish around with your hands, drain in a fine-mesh strainer, and repeat until the water is no longer cloudy. Drain very well following your last rinse.

## Bulgur

A parboiled grain made from wheat, thus it has a very pure wheat taste. It's wonderful in Middle Eastern and Mediterranean meals. Like couscous, it's steamed, but it's a whole food that's full of fiber. We especially love bulgur chilled and used in salads.

Cooking time: 30 to 35 minutes

To serve 4: 1 cup rinsed and drained bulgur, ¼ teaspoon salt, 1⅓ cups water

Cook: Place the bulgur and salt in a pot with a tightly fitting lid. Bring about 2 cups water to a boil in a teapot. Measure out 1⅓ cups of water and pour over the bulgur. Cover and let sit for about 30 minutes. The bulgur should be tender but chewy. Fluff with a fork and serve.

. . .

## Couscous

Although couscous has a culinary role similar to that of a grain and it is derived from grain, it definitely is not one unto itself; it's actually more similar to pasta. It's made by rolling moist wheat and flour in a wide, shallow bowl until the characteristic pebblelike couscous shape is formed. Because it's so filling, cooks so fast, and tastes so yummers, this African staple has become a permanent fixture in the American diet. Its neutral taste and fluffy texture makes it extremely versatile for any meal, sweet or savory. There are lots of different flavors of couscous on the market, such as pesto or sundried tomato, but we prefer regular or whole wheat.

Cooking time: 10 minutes

To serve 4: 1 cup couscous, ¼ teaspoon salt, 1 cup water

Cook: Place the couscous and salt in a pot with a tightly fitting lid. Bring about 1½ cups water to a boil in a teapot. Measure out 1 cup of water and pour over the couscous. Cover and let sit for about 5 minutes. The couscous should be soft. Fluff with a fork and serve.

. . .

## Kasha

Favored in Eastern European recipes for centuries, kasha is the whole, toasted kernels (also known as groats) of the buckwheat plant. In its untoasted form, buckwheat is also used to make soba noodles in Asian cuisine. But when toasted, buckwheat groats are strictly called kasha. Kasha has an intense earthy taste that may remind some of the smell of wet autumn leaves, but we savor its complex, hearty flavor and deep color. It goes well with other savory earthy foods, such as mushrooms and beets, and you'll feel like a Russian princess if you eat it covered in mushroom gravy. Also look for silky buckwheat flour, great in pancakes and essential for Buckwheat Blini (page 58) and Buckwheat Crepes (page 77).

Cooking time: 20 to 25 minutes

To serve 4: 2¼ cups water, 1 cup kasha, ¼ teaspoon salt

Cook: Bring water and salt to a boil in a heavy-bottomed pot. Turn the heat down very low, add the kasha, cover, and simmer for about 20 minutes. Kasha should be tender but chewy and all the water should be absorbed.

. . .

## Millet

Nothing says "health food" like millet. It's one of the more flexible grains. Lightly boiled, it makes for a nice, fluffy dish, as in Mexican Millet (page 118), and when boiled even further you get a soft dough that can be molded like polenta. One of the oldest cereal crops there is, some variety of millet exists on almost every continent and has been popular on and off for thousands of years—maybe its time has come again, and you can say you were eating it before it sold out! It has a slightly sweet, mellow taste that goes well with any meal that brown rice would complement, so add it to your grain rotation toot sweet. Millet doesn't have to be dry-toasted first, but the flavor and texture really benefit from it, so we give you those directions here.

Cooking time: 30 to 45 minutes

To serve 4: 1 cup millet, 2 cups water, ¼ teaspoon salt

**Cook:** Preheat a heavy-bottomed skillet over medium heat. Put in the millet and toast for about 10 minutes, stirring very often, until the millet has turned a few shades darker and smells toasty. Transfer the millet to a pot with a lid, add the water and salt, cover, and bring to a boil. Once boiling, turn the heat very low and simmer for 20 to 25 minutes, until soft. Fluff with a fork and serve.

. . .

## Oats

Of course, you're familiar with oats. We prefer what's called "quick-cooking" or "rolled" oats, which are different than the magic stuff that's been sweetened and flavored beyond recognition and cooked with a little boiling water and a snap of your fingers. Quick-cooking oats are whole oats that have been cut smaller so that they, you guessed it, cook quicker! Not just for breakfast, we use oats in baked goods and to add bulk to things like veggie burgers. Since you wouldn't serve oats as a side dish, we'll just give you directions for making simple morning oatmeal.

**Cooking time:** 5 to 10 minutes
**To serve 4:** 2 cups water, 1 cup rolled oats, 1/4 teaspoon salt. Optional: pinch of cinnamon and a handful raisins or other chopped dried fruit, maple syrup, soy milk
**Cook:** Bring the water to a boil in a lidded pot and add the oats, salt, and cinnamon and fruits if using. Turn down the heat to low and cook uncovered for about 5 minutes, stirring often, until the oats are creamy. Remove from the heat, cover, and let sit for a few minutes. Add a touch of maple syrup and soy milk if desired.

. . .

## Polenta

Polenta has been called many things, each more insulting than the last: cornmeal mush, grits, porridge. But it got a new lease on life in the '90s when foodies started referring to it by its proper name and charging twenty dollars a plate for it. Polenta can be served soft, as a comforting addition to soups and stews, and molded into fancy shapes and grilled or broiled. Or, serve it alongside your scrambled tofu for breakfast— we won't pretend to be above that. This recipe is for soft and creamy polenta to serve a side dish, not the kind that you mold.

**Cooking time:** 35 minutes
**To serve 4:** 5 cups water, 1/2 teaspoon salt, 1 cup polenta
**Cook:** Bring the water and salt to a boil in a pot with a lid. Pour the polenta in very slowly, stirring with a whisk as you pour. Lower the heat to a simmer and cook for 12 to 15 more minutes, stirring often. Turn off the heat and cover for 10 minutes, stirring occasionally.

. . .

## Quinoa

Cultivated by the Inca for hundreds of years, the mystique of quinoa (pronounced "keen-wah") has been taken down a few notches by its placement alongside Uncle Ben's at many American supermarkets. Quinoa comes in red and brown varieties (which taste exactly the same to us) and has a slightly bitter, nutty taste. We use it often in pilafs, salads, and the occasional muffin. It's especially attractive when cooked; the individual grains look a bit like couscous but the germ forms a pretty translucent ring around each one. Adorable. Quinoa is also a complete protein, which has recently made it something of a darling to the vegan community and health-conscious foodies.

**Cooking time:** 20 to 25 minutes
**To serve 4:** 2 cups water, 1 cup rinsed and drained quinoa, 1/4 teaspoon salt
**Cook:** Place all ingredients in a heavy-bottomed pot, cover, and bring to a boil. Once the mixture is boiling, turn down the heat to very low and simmer for about 15 minutes. The quinoa should be

translucent and the germ ring should be visible. Fluff with a fork and serve.

## Complete Proteins

EVERYONE has heard the term "complete protein" but we're willing to wager that vegans hear it more than the rest of the world. Next time people ask you the million-dollar question, "But where do you get your protein?" ask them which essential amino acid they are most concerned about. Most likely they will have no idea what an amino acid is, essential or otherwise, but you will. Proteins are made up of amino acids, many of which our body produces all on its own. Essential amino acids are the ones that our body can not synthesize without the help of the food we eat. So when we refer to proteins as "complete proteins," it just means that all ten of the essential amino acids are present.

## Rice

With the exception of the frozen continents, rice has been a staple food for every culture, each with its own laws about how it should be cooked and served, so no matter what directions we give you, someone somewhere will think we're wrong. If you have your own rice-cooking method handed down to you from your great-grandmother and handed down to her directly from God, please don't let our silly instructions to stand in your way. We don't have rice cookers because every inch of our counter space is precious real estate, so we give you directions for stove top cooking here. The secret to not burning the rice is very, very, *very* low heat.

The difference between brown and white rice is that brown rice has not had the bran removed from it, so it is much healthier— more fiber, more vitamins, and more necessary fatty acids. Brown rice has a nuttier flavor and chewier texture, which is often desirable,

but in some dishes where a more neutral flavor (read: less healthy rice) is desired, we use white rice. White rice also cooks much faster and is softer and fluffier.Rice is often labeled as long or short grain. Long grain not only refers to the shape of the rice, but to the stickiness of the starch content. Long grain rice is less sticky and often used in fried rice and pilafs. Medium grained rice is relatively sticky and used in paella and risotto. Short grain rice is the stickiest kind, and used for sushi. Sometimes short grained rice is called "glutinous" rice, but the reason for the "quotes" is that they actually don't contain any gluten, they're just super sticky. The brown varieties of this rice will always be less sticky than the white.

Dozens of rice varieties are available to us these days, such as black rice and red rice (both unmilled and unpolished rice with the bran intact), but here are a few of the basics that we keep on hand for any rice situation that comes our way. As with other grains, remember to rinse your rice before cooking.

**Arborio rice:** The favorite rice of Italy, Arborio rice is what gives risotto its succulent creaminess. We love to experiment with different herbs and vegetables to create all manners of risotto, but we don't suggest serving it alone as a side dish because the effort of all that stirring isn't worth the return if you're just cooking it plain, so try our risotto recipes on pages 198 and 199.

**Basmati and jasmine rice:** We like using both brown and white versions of these two fragrant long-grained rice. If you've never made either jasmine or basmati, you'll marvel at the wonderful buttery, popcornlike aroma both produce when cooking. The real beauty of these rices is that they make you feel like you actually put some thought and effort into dinner, when really all you did was turn on the faucet and the burner. They're perfect for Indian and Thai meals, but we like them with most anything that's a little bit sweet and fragrant, including BBQ and Mexican food.

### For brown varieties

Cooking time: 45 to 50 minutes

To serve 4: 2 cups water, 1 cup rice, ¼ teaspoon salt

Cook: Place all the ingredients in a heavy-bottomed pot, cover, and bring to a boil. Once the mixture is boiling, turn down the heat to very low and simmer for 40 to 45 minutes. Fluff with a fork and serve.

### For white varieties

To serve 4: 1½ cups water, 1 cup rice, ¼ teaspoon salt

Cook: Place all the ingredients in a heavy-bottomed pot, cover, and bring to a boil. Once the mixture is boiling, turn down the heat to very low and simmer for 15 to 20 minutes. Fluff with a fork and serve.

. . .

## Brown Rice, Short-Grained

The healthy stuff. Nutty and slightly sweet, short-grained brown rice is a nutritious staple and will make you feel like you're eating macrobiotic even if you've never touched a piece of seaweed in your whole life. It also makes nice brown-rice sushi.

Cooking time: 45 to 50 minutes

To serve 4: 2 cups water, 1 cup rice, ¼ teaspoon salt

Cook: Place all the ingredients in a heavy-bottomed pot, cover, and bring to a boil. Once the mixture is boiling, turn down the heat to very low and simmer for 40 to 45 minutes. Fluff with a fork and serve.

. . .

## Wild Rice

All-American and not really a rice, wild rice is actually a delicious grain from a marsh grass. The rice is long and a sleek black color and the textured is deliciously chewy. Its earthy flavor and pairs wonderfully with mushrooms and autumnal dishes.

Cooking time: 55 to 60 minutes

To serve 4: 2½ cups water, 1 cup rice, ¼ teaspoon salt

Cook: Place all the ingredients in a heavy-bottomed pot, cover, and bring to a boil. Once the mixture is boiling, turn down the heat to very low and simmer for 55 to 60 minutes. Fluff with a fork and serve.

. . .

## White Rice, Plain Old

Because sometimes you just want plain old white rice. These directions are of the everyday long-grained kind.

Cooking time: 15 to 20 minutes

To serve 4: 1 cup water, 1 cup rice, ¼ teaspoon salt

Cook: Place all the ingredients in a heavy-bottomed pot, cover, and bring to a boil. Once the mixture is boiling, turn down the heat to very low and simmer for 15 to 20 minutes. Fluff with a fork and serve.

# HOW TO COOK A BEAN

You can't beat canned beans when it comes to convenience, especially when you have tiny kitchens like we do. But dried beans are way, way cheaper, and there's a certain amount of satisfaction that comes from doing it the old-fashioned way. Some say the flavor of homemade beans is far more delicate and always lower in sodium (or sodium free) than the canned stuff is. Dried beans can be substituted for canned in any of our recipes, but be ye warned: preparation is everything! Dried beans (except for lentils and split peas) need to be soaked overnight before cooking! Sure, you could boil then simmer then rest

then boil again the day of, but your beans won't taste as good and overnight soaking helps dissolve the starches that are the primary source of beans' musical properties. So soak 'em! Put your dried beans in a pot with plenty of water (the water should come up two or three inches above the beans), cover, and stash in the fridge until tomorrow. Or, if you're set on cooking beans that night, why not set them to soak that morning, before you run out the door to catch the train to work?

After the beans have soaked, drain the water, then replace with fresh, cold water (roughly three cups of water to every cup of soaked beans, better too much than too little) and bring to a boil in a pot with a lid. Once the beans are boiling, reduce to a simmer—if you leave them at a boil, they will turn to mush—and cook with the pot's lid slightly ajar so that steam can escape. How long will depend on the bean; see our guidelines but note that different factors, such as how old the bean is and how dry it is, will affect cooking

times. Add a teaspoon of salt to the pot about 20 minutes before the beans are done (don't do this earlier or they'll toughen up). Once the beans are nice and tender, drain and use as called for in the recipe. One cup of dried beans will give you roughly three cups cooked (results may vary).

As a resource to you, dear reader, we've compiled this mini encyclopedia of beans and their common uses. We recommend cooking a pound of beans at a time, storing in the fridge, and using that week. To help you out, we list a few recipes where the given bean is called for. Bean on!

## Adzuki

Sometimes called aduki, sometimes called azuki, besides being incredibly fun to say, these little, deep red beans are fast cooking, low in fat, and nutritious. A popular bean in Japan and China, they have a delicate flavor that's both sweet and nutty. They're used in both savory dishes and sweet desserts (even ice cream). They also come in black, for your inner goth.

Cooking time: 1 hour
Recipes: Butternut Adzuki Coconut-Crusted Croquettes; Acorn Squash, Pear, and Adzuki Soup with Sautéed Shiitakes

. . .

## Black Beans

Billions of burritos can't be wrong. Black beans may very well be the most popular bean in vegetarian cooking. Very popular in many Latin American and Caribbean countries, but a true workhorse of a bean, good in just about everything from breakfast to dinner. These dense and meaty beans are also known as turtle beans, don't ask us why.

Cooking time: 1½ hours
Recipes: Black Bean Vegetable Soup, Acorn Squash and Black Bean Empanadas, Black Bean Burgers, Quinoa Salad with Mango and Black Beans, Grilled Yucca Tortillas (Black Bean variation)

. . .

## Black-Eyed Peas

These beans got soul. Tasty and cute, they're cream-colored beans with their namesake black spot that watches your every move. We like them worked into barbecue-themed foods and anything particularly saucy and/or spicy in American Southern, Caribbean, and African cuisines.

Cooking time: 1 hour
Recipes: Black-Eyed Pea–Collard Rolls

. . .

## Chickpeas (a.k.a. Garbanzos)

Gar-BON-zooooooooooooooo! Almost as much fun to say as *adzuki*. These are also known as ceci beans (Italy) and chana dal (India). Responsible for the miracle that is hummus, and also falafel and too many

curries to mention. Also makes an amazing flour when ground up that's great in baked goods (especially if baking gluten free is your goal). These adorable, round, pale beige beans have a rich, "full," and nutty taste that never fails to satisfy.

Cooking time: 1½ hours
Recipes: Chickpea Cutlets, Chickpea Quinoa Pilaf, Chickpea Noodle Soup, Fresh Dill–Basmati Rice Pilaf with Chard and Chickpeas, Tomato and Roasted Eggplant Stew with Chickpeas, Hummus

. . .

## Great Northern Beans (a.k.a. White Beans)

See also navy beans. We can't really discern a difference between great northern and navy beans, except that great northerns are a bit bigger. Both are nondescript in a good way, in that they work in most anything where a bean is needed, are dependable, and take on the flavor of whatever sauce or vegetables they're cooked with. They're both wonderful beans to blend into dips and spreads.

Cooking time: 1½ hours
Recipes: Escarole with Capers and White Beans, Rustic White Beans with Mushrooms, White Bean Aioli, Asparagus Quiche topped with Tomatoes and Tarragon, Sun-dried Tomato Dip, Manzana Chili Verde

. . .

## Kidney

A large, tender bean that's ideal stewed (such as in gumbo or jambalaya) or served up at room temperature in salads. They're a natural, protein-rich addition to vegetable and pasta soups, too. Cannellini beans are a variety of white kidney bean, all the rage in Italian dishes.

Cooking time: 1 hour
Recipes: Jamaican Yucca Shepherd's Pie with Sweet Potato, Kidney Beans and Plantains, Seitan

Jambalaya with White and Red Kidney Beans, Spaghetti and Beanballs, Bulgur, Arugula and Cannellini Salad

· · ·

## Navy (a.k.a. White Beans)

This little white bean is the star of a most American of bean dishes, baked beans. More or less all-purpose and very utilitarian, in that military kind of way. See also Great Northern Beans.

Cooking time: 1 hour
Recipes: Cheater Baked Beans, Tomato-Rice Soup with Roasted Garlic and Navy Beans, as well as any of the great northern bean recipes.

## Pinto

The backbone of Native American cuisine (along with corn) in many parts of the New World, this pale pink bean works well served whole or pureed. It takes well to rich, complex seasonings and the addition of vegetables. Tex-Mex cuisine just wouldn't be the same without a creamy side of refried pintos.

Cooking time: 1½ hours
Recipes: Plantain and Pinto Stew with Parsnip Chips, Unfried Refried

# THE
# RECIPES

# SNACKS, APPETIZERS, LITTLE MEALS, DIPS, AND SPREADS

"WHO REALLY MAKES appetizers at home?" we asked ourselves, in the midst of creating the following recipes. Everyday cooking usually doesn't require a little extra snack to precede a weeknight dinner or weekend brunch. But, sometimes you might just crave an appetizer as your meal—small on size but big on flavor—and who are we to argue with that?

Of course, there could be the chance occasion when you're planning on eating dinner in something other than a T-shirt and flip-flops and to have guests over who are unaccustomed to seeing you in such finery. That's where appetizers step in. Keep hungry stomachs at bay with a few Spicy Tempeh Nori Rolls or Walnut-Mushroom Pâté while you slave away in the kitchen preparing the main event. For a casual and fun evening meal, serve a spread of four or more appetizers for friends and family to nosh, in cocktail-party style. And certainly you don't need an excuse to craft a batch of grilled tortillas stuffed with creamy yuca filling or a platter of dainty Broccoli-Millet Croquettes, even if it's just for yourself.

## SPICY TEMPEH NORI ROLLS

MAKES 4 ROLLS

Ⓖ Ⓕ

**TIME:** 40 MINUTES

*Here's our recipe for the sushi rolls that starred on the very first episode of* The Post Punk Kitchen. *Since then, it's also been a featured guest at many parties and potlucks, and in lunchboxes, and will become a super celebrity in your kitchen, too. Like any celeb worth her soy sauce, these nori rolls are highly photogenic and will win the love and admiration of friends and rivals, minus the trash talk on Page Six (of tabloid fame, not this book). Enough with the chitty-chat; let's roll!*

*P.S. This sushi is just fierce enough to accessorize with completely different fillings at a moment's notice. Don't miss out on the luscious variations, or mix it up and serve two or more at your next sushi soirée.*

**tip**

➤ You'll need some extra equipment to make nori rolls. The bare essentials include: wasabi powder or prepared wasabi, shoyu (Japanese soy sauce) in small bowls for dipping, pickled sliced ginger, a bamboo sushi rolling mat, and chopsticks, of course!

➤ Sushi rice is different from regular rice. It's a short-grain rice that is rather sticky, and comes in white and brown varieties. Use either type for this sushi.

➤ For the most flavorful nori, hold each sheet with metal tongs and toast very carefully over a medium flame for 30 seconds on each side, or until sheet turns from green to deep brownish-green.

### For the sushi rice:

- 1 cup sushi rice
- 2 tablespoons rice vinegar (do not use regular white vinegar)
- 1 teaspoon sugar

### Spicy tempeh filling:

- ½ (4-ounce) package tempeh
- 2 tablespoons prepared vegan mayonnaise or Silken Mayo Dressing (page 103)
- ½–1 teaspoon hot chile-sesame oil
- 4 sheets nori seaweed
- 1 scallion, white part discarded, sliced lengthwise into narrow strips
- 1 ripe avocado, peeled, seeded, and sliced into ¼-inch-wide strips
- 1 tablespoon toasted or black sesame seeds if used inside the roll, or ¼ cup if used as a coating for inside-out rolls

IN A heavy-bottomed, 2-quart pot or saucepan with a cover, combine the rice plus 1¼ cups cold water. Turn the heat to high, bring the water to a boil, and stir the rice just once. Lower the heat to low, cover the pot, and steam the rice for 20 to 22 minutes, until it is tender and the excess liquid has been absorbed. Or, prepare the rice according to the package instructions. Cook until the rice is tender but slightly firm, and remove from the heat.

Empty the hot rice into a large glass or plastic bowl. Sprinkle with the rice vinegar and sugar, folding in the rice gently with a large spoon or rice paddle to mix thoroughly. The rice should be moist and have a very mild vinegar flavor. Cover with plastic wrap and let cool for 10 to 15 minutes. When the rice is slightly warmer than room temperature (but not completely cold), it's ready to work with.

While the rice is cooling, prepare the filling by steaming the tempeh. Allow the tempeh to cool for 10 minutes, chop into small cubes, and place in a medium-size bowl. Add the mayonnaise and chile-sesame oil and mash until chunky; taste and add more chile-sesame oil if desired.

## To assemble:

Fill a shallow cup with about ⅓ cup of water and a tablespoon of rice vinegar, and keep near your sushi workstation. Follow these steps to the perfect nori roll:

1. Place the nori sheet on the bamboo mat. With wet hands, take a snowball-shaped handful of rice, about a cup's worth. Gently pat onto the bottom two-thirds or so of your nori sheet. The layer of rice should be less than ⅓ inch thick.
2. Place a small amount of the fillings across the center of your rice. Lay or spread them horizontally to each side of the nori to create a straight line of filling—the less filling, the easier the sushi will be to roll. Aim for about 1½ tablespoons of Spicy Tempeh, three strips of avocado, and some scallion strips. You'll figure it out.
3. Using the mat, gently roll up that sushi starting from the rice-topped end; try to keep your grip relatively tight, for a firm roll. When you've reached the seaweed-only end, pat gently with a little bit of vinegar water to seal the roll.
4. Slice your roll into 1-inch pieces with a sharp, serrated knife. That's it! Make a hundred of 'em.

## Variation:

Pear and Tempeh Roll: Substitute ½ recipe (about 1½ cups) of Creamy Asian Pear and Tempeh Salad (page 90) for the spicy tempeh filling.

## Other Fillings, Made Simple and Snappy:

Here are a few alternative fillings that have been a hit with our veggie sushi fans everywhere. It's so easy to prepare one or more of these when whipping up a batch of Spicy Tempeh Nori Rolls, you've no excuses not to serve one or more of these sassy rolls.

Elephant Roll: Stuff the sushi rolls with 2 tablespoons of roasted peanuts and a few slices of ripe avocado per roll.

"Yamroom" Roll: For each roll, fill with 2 tablespoons of mashed sweet potato (page 111), 1 to 2 dried or fresh shiitake mushrooms simmered in ½ cup water, 2 tablespoons of soy sauce and a dash of mirin. Sprinkle the filling with sesame seeds before rolling.

Spinach Sesame: Lightly steam ½ pound of well-washed, fresh spinach, squeeze to remove any excess water, and chop finely. Toss with 1 teaspoon of toasted sesame oil, 1 tablespoon of sesame seeds, and a dash of rice vinegar. Fill and roll as directed for the Spicy Tempeh Nori Rolls.

## Inside Out Rolls

MAYBE you've been rolling your own for a while, or you just need to look like a master sushi chef right now! Then inside-out rolled nori rolls will get you the attention you so deserve, and with way less stress than you might expect.

Simply prepare your nori roll as directed, spreading the seasoned rice onto about two-thirds of the toasted nori sheet. Place a sheet of plastic wrap on top, gently slid your hand underneath the bamboo mat and rest your other hand on top of the plastic wrap. Then in one quick motion . . . flip everthing upside down. Remove the bamboo mat from underneath and place on your countertop. Place the nori and rice—plastic wrap side down—on the mat. Place fillings as usual on the edge without the rice underneath it. Then, carefully roll everything up, using the bamboo mat to firmly push everything together and being careful to peel away the plastic wrap as you go.

For best results, roll your spiffy inside-out rolls in fun things like toasted sesame seeds, black sesame seeds, toasted nori flakes or Japanese ground up red pepper. Terry recommends you just pour whatever it is you're rolling your sushi in into a shallow large dish and just drop your inside-out rolls into it as you work.

# GRILLED YUCA TORTILLAS

SERVES 4 TO 6

TIME: 40 MINUTES

Somewhere between a panini and a quesadilla, sans the queso, these hearty grilled sandwiches are bursting with creamy, garlicky mashed yuca. The basic filling takes readily to tasty additions such as roasted red peppers or sautéed corn kernels, and we've also included two of our favorite extra-special variations featuring fresh spinach or sweet potatoes and black beans. Try throwing these uniquely stuffed tortillas on the outdoor grill in the summertime for a tasty addition to standard BBQ fare. These are best served with Tropical Avocado Salsa Fresca (page 178) or any kind of salsa, fresh pico de gallo and of course, guacamole.

The filling can be made a day in advance, or even better, have a container of filling and some tortillas on hand for quick suppers or filling, nutritious snacks.

**tip**

➤ Yuca (pronounced "yoo-ka") is also known as cassava or manioc root; you may have already met it in the form of tapioca. It grows exclusively in the tropics but can be found in most any Latino market or a supermarket that carries tropical produce. Yuca a totally different plant from yucca, a cousin of agave that is used in foamy beverages, but chances are, if what you see is in chunks, it's yuca, however it's been spelled. While you're at it, check out the freezer case for prepeeled, sliced, frozen chunks of yuca, to shave off some prep time. Prepare according to the package directions and proceed as with cooked yuca.

**Yuca filling:**

- 1 pound yuca, peeled, chopped into 4-inch chunks, and each chunk quartered
- 3 tablespoons olive oil
- 6 cloves garlic, chopped coarsely
- 1 small yellow bell pepper, seeded and cut into small dice (about 1 cup)
- 1 jalapeño, roasted or raw, seeded and minced
- 2 teaspoons lime juice
- ½ teaspoon salt, or to taste
- Pinch of ground white pepper

**Optional additional fillings—
1/2 cup of one or more:**

- Sautéed corn kernels
- Diced roasted red pepper
- Sautéed mushroom
- Sliced black olives
- 4–6 (8-inch) flour or whole wheat tortillas

BOIL 3 quarts of water in a large, lidded pot. Add the yuca and cook for 20 to 25 minutes, until the yuca is tender and flakes easily when pierced with a fork. Drain and allow to cool. When the yuca is cool enough to touch, remove any thick, rubbery skin from the outside of the roots and/or fibrous core from the center, if present. Gently mash with your fingers and set aside.

Place the oil and garlic in a cold cast-iron skillet. Cook over medium heat, stirring constantly, for 2 minutes, or until sizzling and fragrant. Add the bell and jalapeño peppers and cook, stirring occasionally, until the peppers are very soft, 6 to 8 minutes. Remove from the heat, cool for a few minutes, then pour over the mashed yuca. Stir in the lime juice, salt, and white pepper, mashing the mixture even more, until everything is combined (using your hands is okay). If making any of the variations (below), add those ingredients and mix thoroughly. Taste the mixture and adjust the salt content to taste.

### To assemble:

Heat a griddle or cast-iron skillet over medium heat. Brush a tortilla lightly with olive oil and spread with a generous ½ cup of filling, covering half the tortilla all the way to the edges. Fold in half, gently pressing the tortilla together, and brush each side with a little olive oil. Place in the heated skillet and grill—flipping once—pressing down on the tortilla with a spatula until the outsides are nicely toasted and filling is piping hot. Remove from the heat, cut in half, and serve with salsa and guacamole.

### Variations:

**Sweet Potato–Black Bean:** ½ cup of mashed sweet potato (about 1 very small sweet potato, peeled and boiled), ½ cup of cooked black beans, ½ teaspoon of ground cumin.

**Spinach-Cilantro:** ½ cup of cooked, chopped spinach, squeezed to remove excess water (half a 10-ounce package of frozen chopped spinach is perfect), ¼ cup of chopped fresh cilantro leaves, ½ teaspoon of ground coriander.

## BUTTERNUT SQUASH AND PUMPKIN SEED RICE PAPER ROLLS

MAKES 12 ROLLS

Ⓢ Ⓖ Ⓕ

**TIME:** 1 HOUR 15 MINUTES

*Rice noodles make the perfect canvas for velvety butternut squash, crunchy pumpkin seeds, and fresh herbs. Don't be intimidated by working with rice paper wrappers; it's easy once you get the hang of it, and rolling fresh spring rolls is a skill that will last a lifetime. Before you begin, you will want to lay a very clean, slightly damp kitchen towel (or a layer of paper towels) on your counter; rice paper wrappers can be slippery and the towel makes a great work surface. Rice paper wrappers can be found in the "ethnic" section of any well-stocked supermarket, at health food stores, or at an Asian grocery.*

*We've included a simple soy dipping sauce recipe, but for a sublime and really fall-y experience pair these with Cranberry–Chili Dipping Sauce (page 213).*

**tip**

➤ Roasting the squash in cubes gives them a nice caramelized crunch on the outside that you wouldn't get if you just roasted the squash whole.

➤ If a wrapper rips a bit at the edges, don't worry; once it's rolled, you won't be able to tell.

### Rolls:

- **1 pound butternut squash, peeled, seeded, and cut into ¼-inch cubes**
- **2–3 teaspoons olive oil**
- **12 (8-inch) round rice paper wrappers**
- **4 ounces vermicelli rice noodles or rice sticks**
- **1 cup fresh cilantro, torn into bite-size pieces (Thai basil makes a nice variation)**
- **⅓ cup roasted, salted pumpkin seeds, chopped coarsely**

### Dipping sauce *contains soy:

- **2 tablespoons soy sauce**
- **3 tablespoons rice vinegar**
- **1 tablespoon Asian hot chile oil (or more to taste)**
- **2 teaspoons toasted sesame oil**
- **2 tablespoons sugar**

### Prepare the squash:

Preheat the oven to 400°F. Place the butternut cubes on a baking sheet and rub them all over with the oil; drizzle on another teaspoon if you need to.

Arrange the cubes in a single layer and roast for 15 minutes. Remove from the oven, toss, and cook for 10 more minutes or until tender and slightly caramelized. Transfer the squash to a plate to cool.

While the squash is cooking, prepare the noodles. There are usually directions on the package, but just in case: Boil a large pot of water. Once it is boiling, turn off the heat, add the noodles, and cook for 10 minutes, stirring occasionally. Drain in a colander and run cold water over them to prevent further cooking. Set aside until ready to use.

## To Assemble:

Fill a large pie plate or bowl with very warm water; tap water works just fine. Place two rice paper wrappers in the water at a time, completely submerged and let sit for about a minute, until they have softened.

Handle each wrapper gently as you place it on your work surface. Place about ¼ cup of rice noodles in the lower third of the wrapper, leaving about 1½ inches of margin from the far edges on either side (you'll be folding those in). Place a layer of butternut squash above the noodles. Sprinkle with the cilantro and pumpkin seeds. If some of the seeds get stuck to your fingers, just dip them in the water. To roll, snugly fold the left and right sides of the wrapper over the filling. Lift the bottom of the wrapper over the filling and tuck it underneath the filling, then roll firmly but gently. Place the rolls seam side down on a plate and cut in half when ready to serve. Mix the dipping sauce ingredients together and stir rigorously to dissolve the sugar. Serve with the rolls.

## BROCCOLI-MILLET CROQUETTES

MAKES 16 CROQUETTES

TIME: 2 HOURS, LOTS OF IT INACTIVE

*Somehow, forming anything into a croquette makes a meal very impressive, even though it is an easy thing to do. Millet and broccoli are cooked together with garlic, tarragon, and red pepper, formed into squat little cushions, and lightly panfried. These make a great vehicle for the White Bean Aioli (page 62) or Dill-Tahini Sauce (page 215). They are delicately flavored, so definitely include a sauce when you serve. Round out the meal with roasted asparagus and red peppers (page 26).*

## Make ahead:

Prepare the millet and broccoli a day in advance. Then you only need about 20 minutes to finish preparing this dish.

1 tablespoon olive oil, plus extra for panfrying

2 cloves garlic, minced

1 teaspoon dried tarragon

½ teaspoon red pepper flakes

Several pinches of freshly ground black pepper

½ teaspoon salt

1 cup millet

2 ½ cups vegetable broth

4 cups broccoli, tops and stalks, chopped very finely into pea-size or smaller pieces

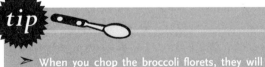

> When you chop the broccoli florets, they will probably crumble a lot. That is fine; just throw the crumbled tiny bits in with the rest of the broccoli.

PREHEAT A small pot over medium heat. Sauté the garlic in the oil for about 30 seconds. Add the tarragon, red pepper flakes, black pepper, and salt, and mix for a few seconds. Add the millet and stir constantly for about 3 minutes to toast it. It should turn a shade darker. If it doesn't, don't sweat it too bad, just proceed with the recipe. Better that than you burn the garlic.

Add the vegetable broth and cover; bring to a boil. Once the mixture is boiling, lower the heat to a simmer, cover, and cook for 10 minutes.

Mix in the chopped broccoli, cover, and cook for about 7 more minutes. Uncover and cook for another 10 minutes, stirring often. Once the water is mostly absorbed, turn off the heat but leave the pot on the stove, covered, to continue to cook for another 10 to 15 minutes. At that point, all of the water should be absorbed and the millet should be mushy if you push down on it with a spoon. It's very important that the millet be well cooked or the croquettes could fall apart, so if it doesn't seem fully cooked, let it sit for an additional 5 or 10 minutes. You are looking for a polenta-like consistency.

Transfer to a mixing bowl and let cool for about 10 minutes, then move the bowl to the fridge to cool the rest of the way, for about 45 minutes or so. Give it a stir now and again to speed up the cooling process. Don't skip or skimp on this cooling step or your croquettes will turn to millet mush in the skillet.

Once cooled, tightly form the millet into golf ball–size balls. Press them down in your hands to flatten just a bit, then roll the sides between your hands to form tire-shaped croquettes.

Heat a thin layer of olive oil in a large nonstick or cast-iron skillet over medium heat. Cook the croquettes in batches for 3 to 4 minutes on each side. They should be golden brown with a few darker spots.

Serve immediately.

## GREEK-STYLE TOMATO-ZUCCHINI FRITTERS WITH FRESH HERBS

SERVES 4-6

**TIME:** 45 MINUTES

*Just as enticing but way cheaper than a vacation on Santorini Island, these dairy-free Greek-inspired fritters are bursting with chunks of fresh tomato, dill, and mint. The addition of zucchini creates a tender and light texture. These are absolutely sublime served along with Mediterranean-Style Cashew-Cucumber Dip (page 66). You can easily make this lovely summertime appetizer into a meal by serving with salad greens dressed with olive oil and fresh lemon juice. For the fry-o-phobe, we give you alternative baking instructions as well.*

1 (1-pound) package firm tofu, squeezed to remove extra water, then crumbled
¼ cup ground walnuts
1 clove garlic, crushed
3 tablespoons fresh lemon juice
1 tablespoon tomato paste
1 teaspoon dried oregano
1 teaspoon salt
Generous pinch of ground black pepper
½ cup bread crumbs, plus an additional ⅓ cup for coating
1 tablespoon chopped fresh dill
1 tablespoon chopped fresh mint
½ pound zucchini, grated and squeezed to remove excess water (about 1 cup)
1 pound seeded, finely chopped tomatoes (about 1 heaping cup), drained to remove excess liquid
Olive oil for frying

HAVE READY layers of paper towels or a large, clean paper grocery bag for absorbing the oil after frying.

In a food processor, blend together the tofu,

ground walnuts, garlic, lemon juice, tomato paste, oregano, salt, and pepper until almost smooth (some small lumps are okay). Taste and add more salt and pepper if necessary. Scrape the tofu mixture into a large bowl, using a spatula, and mix in the bread crumbs, dill, and mint. Your mixture should have the consistency of a thick cookie dough; if it's too moist, add more bread crumbs (by the tablespoon). Gently fold in the grated zucchini and chopped tomatoes.

Heat a ¼-inch layer of olive oil in a large, heavy-bottomed skillet (preferably cast iron) over medium heat. To test the oil, sprinkle a pinch of bread crumbs into the pan. If bubbles form rapidly around them, then the oil is ready.

Using 2 heaping tablespoons of mixture per fritter, drop each fritter into the bread crumbs and roll gently to coat. Flatten to about 1 inch thick. Fry the tomato fritters for 4 to 6 minutes on each side until golden brown, turning very carefully (these are delicate, so a thin spatula works well for this). Drain on paper towels and let cool for about 5 minutes before serving.

Serve sprinkled with more fresh dill or dusted with a little dried oregano.

### Alternative baking option:

Instead of frying, you can also bake these fritters in a preheated 350°F oven for 35 minutes. Rub a large cookie sheet with olive oil, arrange the fritters on it so that they do not touch, and spray or brush generously with olive oil. Flip them over halfway through baking; spray or brush other side with oil.

## AUTUMN LATKES

MAKES ABOUT 24

**TIME:** 40 MINUTES

*These are like potato pancakes, but instead of making them with the traditional potato we make them perfectly autumnal by using beets, carrots, and sweet potatoes. It's pure fall harvest gluttony! You're going to want a food processor to shred all these vegetables or else autumn will be over by the time you're done prepping. Serve with apple sauce or Horseradish-Dill Sour Cream (page 208), or both.*

> 2 cups peeled, shredded beets
>   (about 3 average-size beets)
> 1 cup peeled, shredded carrot
>   (about 1 average-size carrot)
> 1 cup peeled, shredded sweet potato
>   (you guessed it, 1 average-size sweet potato)
> 1 shallot, chopped finely (about ¼ cup)
> ½ cup all-purpose flour
> ¼ cup cornstarch
> ½ teaspoon salt
> Several dashes of freshly ground black pepper
> 1 teaspoon fennel seeds, chopped
> ¼ cup water
> Olive oil for panfrying

HAVE READY layers of paper towels or a large, clean paper grocery bag for absorbing the oil after frying.

Combine the shredded veggies in a large mixing bowl. Add the shallot, flour, cornstarch, salt, black pepper, and fennel seeds. Use a wooden spoon to mix everything well; the flour mixture should evenly coat all the veggies. Add the water and stir again, until all the flour is dissolved.

Preheat a heavy-bottomed nonstick or cast-iron skillet over medium-high heat. Pour a ¼-inch layer of oil into the pan. Let the oil heat for about 2 minutes.

Form the beet mixture into balls the diameter of a quarter, then flatten into 1½-inch medallions. Fry the medallions in batches for 5 minutes; turn over and flatten them a bit with a spatula. Fry for another 3 to 4 minutes. Transfer to paper towels to drain. Serve ASAP.

## POTATO LATKES

MAKES ABOUT 18

PREP TIME: 15 MINUTES WITH A FOOD PROCESSOR, A LOT LONGER WITHOUT
COOKING TIME: 1 HOUR

*This is the perfect recipe for the traditional Jewish fried potato pancake. Crispy on the outside and tender on the inside, these guys are sure to please everyone at the Hanukkah table. Because they are made with matzo meal, they're good for Passover as well. If you non-Jews among us are like "Hannuwha?" and "Passwhatover?" don't worry about it, just make up a batch the next time a need for fried potato-y goodness arises. Serve with applesauce and Horseradish-Dill Sour Cream (page 208). The recipe doubles perfectly, so make enough for the meshpuchah and then some.*

2 ½ pounds white potatoes, peeled
    (Russet, Idaho, et al.)
1 small yellow onion, peeled

¼ cup potato starch or cornstarch
½ teaspoon salt
½ teaspoon ground black pepper
2 cups matzo meal
Lots of vegetable oil for frying

HAVE READY a brown paper shopping bags or paper towels for draining the oil from the latkes. You may also want to have the oven on at 200°F to keep the latkes warm until you're ready to serve. If serving immediately, just have a baking pan covered with aluminum foil ready to keep the finished ones warm after they've been drained.

If using a food processor, use the grating blade to shred the potatoes and the onion. If shredding by hand, use a grater to shred all the potatoes. Dice the onion as finely as possible.

In a large mixing bowl, using a wooden spoon or your hands (We use our hands, it's faster), mix the potatoes and onions with the potato starch until the potatoes have released some moisture and the starch is dissolved, about 2 minutes. Add the salt and pepper, and stir. Add the matzo meal and mix well. Set aside for about 10 minutes. The mixture should become liquidy but sticky.

In the meantime, preheat a large, preferably cast-iron but definitely nonstick skillet over medium heat, a little bit on the high side. Pour a ¼-inch layer of vegetable oil into the pan. The oil is hot enough when you throw a bit of batter in and bubbles rapidly form around it. If it immediately smokes, the heat is too high and you should lower it a bit. If the bubbles are really lazy, give the oil a few more minutes or raise the heat a bit.

IN Brooklyn we pronounce latke *lat-kuh,* but in other parts of the country we've heard *lat-key,* which sounds really cute. Both pronunciations are correct, so go with whatever suits you.

With wet hands (so that the mixture doesn't stick), roll the batter into golf ball–size balls. Flatten into thin, round patties. Fry about four to six at a time; just be careful not to crowd the pan. Fry on one side for about 4 minutes, until golden brown. Flip over and fry for another 3 minutes.

Transfer to the paper towels and proceed with the remaining latkes. Once latkes have drained on both sides, place in a baking pan and keep at 200°F or cover with aluminum foil, to keep warm.

# ACORN SQUASH AND BLACK BEAN EMPANADAS

MAKES 12 EMPANADAS

**TIME:** 2 HOURS 30 MINUTES, LOTS OF IT INACTIVE

*Most Latin American and Spanish-speaking countries have their own variation of empanadas, but they are all basically a savory stuffed pastry. We make our empanadas into triangles as a matter of efficiency, because we hate cutting circles and then having scraps to reroll. If you want to do circles, more power to you! The flaky crust has a hint of cornmeal, which makes this empanada dough especially tasty. Plus, the nutty flavor of acorn squash goes great with black beans. Serve these with Tropical Avocado Salsa Fresca (page 213), Guacamole (page 69), or Sour Cilantro Cream (page 209).*

Pastry:

2 cups all-purpose flour

¼ cup cornmeal

2 tablespoons sugar

1 teaspoon salt

½ teaspoon baking powder

½ cup cold nonhydrogenated vegan shortening

½–¾ cup very cold water

2 teaspoons apple cider vinegar

Filling:

1 acorn squash (about 1½ pounds)

2 tablespoons olive oil

1 average-size red onion, sliced into 1-inch pieces

2 jalapeños, sliced thinly (seeds removed if you don't want these too hot)

2 teaspoons coriander seeds, smashed (see help for crushing on page 112)

2 cloves garlic, minced

1 teaspoon ground cumin

½ teaspoon salt

About 2 tablespoons water

1 cup cooked black beans, drained and rinsed

2 tablespoons fresh lime or lemon juice

2 teaspoons pure maple syrup

*tip*

➤ If you don't have a pastry cutter, use two butter knives tightly held together to cut the shortening into the flour.

THE cooking time sounds like forever but if you roast the squash and prep your ingredients while the dough is chilling, it should take about 2½ hours from start to finish, with lots of doing nothing in between. You can also prepare the dough and roast the squash a day ahead, and then all you have to do is prepare the filling and bake, so you can have them ready in less than an hour.

PREHEAT THE oven to 400°F.

Prepare the pastry: Combine the flour, cornmeal, sugar, salt, and baking powder in a large mixing bowl. Add the shortening by the teaspoon, but you don't need to be precise about this. You just want to add it in small chunks. We add the shortening in three batches and then cut it into flour with each addition. Cut in the shortening until the dough is crumbly and pebbly, as if you are making a piecrust.

Combine the vinegar with ½ cup water. Add to the dough in three batches, gently mixing it in with a fork, until the dough holds together when pinched. If need be, add up to ¼ cup more water.

Gather the dough into a ball and knead very gently a few times until it holds together. Sprinkle a clean work surface with flour, then roll out the dough into a rectangle about 8 inches long and 5 inches wide.

Place baking parchment on a cutting board (Make sure the parchment is bigger than the cutting board because you are going to use it to roll out the dough later). Gently lift the dough onto it. Cover with plastic wrap and refrigerate for at least an hour.

Meanwhile, roast the squash: Cut it in half lengthwise and use a tablespoon to scoop out the seeds and stringy parts. Place face down on a greased baking sheet and bake for about 50 minutes, until it is easily pierced with a fork. When the squash is cooked, remove it from the oven and place on a plate, cut side up, to cool. Keep the oven at 400°F if you are making the empanadas now. In the meantime, begin making the filling.

Preheat a large skillet over medium-high heat. Sauté the onions and the jalapeños in the olive oil for 5 to 7 minutes, until softened. Meanwhile, peel the skin from the squash and cut the squash into ¾-inch chunks.

Add the coriander seeds and garlic to the pan and sauté for a minute more. Add the cumin, salt, and a few splashes of water (about 2 tablespoons). Add the squash and cook for about 5 minutes, stirring often to coat. It's okay if the squash doesn't retain its shape perfectly. Add the black beans and heat through. If the mixture looks dry, add a few more splashes of water. Lastly, add the lemon juice and the maple syrup, and stir. Turn off the heat and prepare the empanada dough.

Grease a baking sheet and set it aside. Now grab your dough from the fridge and remove the plastic wrap. Slide the dough off the cutting board, keeping the paper underneath it. Roll out the dough into a 9 × 12-inch rectangle. Trim the edges to make it an even rectangle. Slice the dough into 3-inch squares—four cuts across and two cuts lengthwise.

Take a square and roll it out a bit more, to about 6 inches square (but you don't have to be precise about it). Arrange it so that a corner is pointing toward you. Place about 2 tablespoons of filling in the lower half of the dough, leaving about ½ inch of space at the bottom point. Fold over the dough so that it is in the shape of a triangle. You may need to pull it a little bit, just do so carefully so as not to rip it. Pinch together the seams with a fork or your fingertips and place on your baking sheet. Continue forming the rest of the empanadas.

Bake for 25 to 30 minutes, until golden brown. Serve warm!

## PANKO-STUFFED MUSHROOMS

MAKES ABOUT 20

**TIME:** 45 MINUTES

*These little guys are different from your run-of-the-mill Italian-style stuffed mushrooms since they're flavored with Asian-y stuff: sesame, mirin, and scallions. Panko is a Japanese bread crumb that stays crispier than the kind we usually use. Daikon provides a little crunch but you can sub water chestnuts or maybe celery if you roll that way. We like the way DIY-toasted sesame seeds look on these because they provide some color contrast, but you can buy them toasted if you prefer. Black sesame seeds would look cool as well.*

22 big mushrooms (they sometimes are called "stuffing mushrooms"), washed and patted dry
1 tablespoon peanut oil
3 cloves garlic, minced

- **1 cup finely diced daikon**
- **3 tablespoons mirin**
- **½ teaspoon salt**
- **½ teaspoon ground white pepper**
- **1 ½ cups panko**
- **1 tablespoon toasted sesame oil, plus extra for greasing the pan and garnish**
- **2–4 tablespoons water**
- **½ cup finely chopped scallions, plus extra for garnish**
- **3 tablespoons toasted sesame seeds**

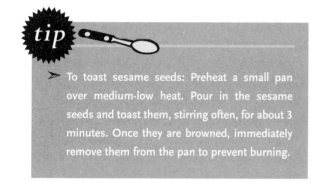

*tip*

➤ To toast sesame seeds: Preheat a small pan over medium-low heat. Pour in the sesame seeds and toast them, stirring often, for about 3 minutes. Once they are browned, immediately remove them from the pan to prevent burning.

PREHEAT THE oven to 350°F.

First, remove the stems from the mushrooms. An easy way to do this is to cup one in your writing hand, stem up, and gently but firmly twist and pry the stem out. Then use a small spoon to remove any remaining stem. Do not discard the stems; chop them up small and set them aside. It's common to break a mushroom or two, which is why the recipe calls for twenty-two mushrooms but stuffs twenty. If one breaks and can't be used, just chop it up along with the stems. If you have a mushroom stem–removing talent and manage not to break any, then finely chop the two extras anyway.

Preheat a large skillet over medium heat. Pour in the peanut oil and sauté the chopped mushroom for about 3 minutes, until some moisture has released. Add the diced daikon and cook for 5 more minutes, stirring often. Add the garlic and cook for a minute longer.

At this point, lots of moisture should be released from the mushrooms. Add the mirin, salt, and white pepper, and cook for about 2 minutes.

Turn off the heat and add the panko in ½-cup batches and stir, alternately adding the sesame oil and splashes of water (up to 4 tablespoons) until all the bread crumbs are moist. The mixture should be crumbly but, when you press some between your fingers, it should hold together. Mix in the scallions and adjust the salt to taste.

Grease a baking sheet with a little sesame oil. Stuff each mushroom with the filling and place on the baking sheet. To stuff them, place a little of the filling into the mushroom crevice and then add another tablespoon on top of that, pressing firmly to form a mound.

Bake for 20 minutes. To serve, sprinkle the toasted sesame seeds over the mushrooms and drizzle with a little sesame oil, if desired. Garnish with extra chopped scallions. If you are going for a fancy plating, place a few mushrooms on a handful of raw spinach leaves.

## BUCKWHEAT BLINI

**MAKES ABOUT 36 BLINI**
**TIME:** 1 HOUR 30 MINUTES, LOTS OF IT INACTIVE

*Blini are light, savory, yeasted pancakes with a real Eastern European feel to them. They are small and bite-sized, similar to silver dollar pancakes and make a great appetizer. This recipe is a little time consuming because you have to make the pancakes in small batches, so you may only want to serve it for special occasions. But it's really worth the trouble, we promise. Serve with thick Mushroom Gravy (page 211) and Horseradish-Dill Sour Cream (page 208) and top with fresh chopped parsley.*

1½ cups soy milk, at room temperature

2 teaspoons apple cider vinegar

½ cup warm water

1 tablespoon sugar

1 (¼-ounce) envelope active dry yeast

1 tablespoon ground flaxseeds

½ cup buckwheat flour

½ cup chickpea flour

½ teaspoon salt

2 tablespoons olive oil

Nonstick cooking spray or spray-on olive oil

**tip**

➤ Use an ice-cream scoop to efficiently pour the blini batter. Measure a tablespoon and a half of batter into it once to get an idea of how much batter that is, and then just eyeball it for the rest of the blini.

➤ Use the thinnest spatula you can to flip the blini. Since you'll be using a nonstick pan, a very thin, flexible heatproof rubber spatula makes all the difference in the world. Of course, you can still get by using any spatula you've got.

MEASURE THE soy milk into a measuring cup and add the vinegar to it; set aside to curdle.

Mix the sugar and water in a large glass or plastic mixing bowl. Add the yeast and stir briefly. Leave the bowl in a warm place and let the yeast foam up; it usually takes about 3 minutes.

Meanwhile, add the ground flaxseeds to the soy milk and stir well.

In a separate large mixing bowl, combine the remaining ingredients. Pour in the soy milk mixture and mix until smooth. Add this batter to the yeast and mix again until smooth. Place a towel over the batter and leave it in a warm, draft-free place for about an hour.

Preheat a large nonstick skillet over medium heat. Give the batter a stir—it shouldn't be bubbling over the bowl, just slightly bubbly. When the pan is hot, spray with nonstick cooking spray. Carefully **pour** about 1½ tablespoons of batter into the pan to form a blin (pancake); you can usually fit about five at a time, but take care not to overcrowd; if you can only fit four, then so be it.

The tops of the blini should bubble up and set within 90 seconds (if they do not, then either the heat is not high enough or the pan hasn't had time **to heat** up properly). Flip each blini and cook for another 90 seconds. Both sides should be a dark, flecked golden brown.

If you are serving them within 30 minutes, you can place them on a plate covered with aluminum foil. If they are for later on, place on a baking pan in a 200°F oven until ready to serve.

# EVERYDAY CHIPOTLE-VEGETABLE TAMALES

SERVES 6-8

**TIME:** 1 HOUR 25 MINUTES FOR ASSEMBLING AND STEAMING

*We were originally going to call these "fiesta-something" tamales, but then were worried that people might wait until the Cinco de Mayo or some distant holiday before ever giving these morsels a shot. And that would be a crime. Although preparing the dough and filling is simple, tamale assembly can be tedious work, so enlist the help of a friend or two.*

*This tamale recipe is as flexible as you want it to be; add roasted corn kernels, chopped chiles, or scallions to the dough if you feel like it. Small bits of seasonal vegetables such as zucchini, pumpkin, poblano chiles, and even sautéed seitan would make perfect additions, too. You need a large steamer basket for this recipe, so don't proceed any further until you go out and procure one. Well, okay, you could use a little steamer basket, but then you'll have to make these in two batches and it will take you a little longer. So be sure to have lots of chips, salsa, and guacamole on hand to keep ravenous tamale-seekers at bay.*

**2 6-ounce packages corn husks**

Tamale dough:

**4 cups masa harina corn flour**

**4 cups vegetable broth or equivalent prepared vegetable bouillon, warmed**

**2 teaspoons baking powder**

**⅓ cup olive or good-quality, unrefined corn oil**

Chipotle bean filling:

**2 tablespoons olive oil**

**1 large onion, diced small**

**1 clove garlic, minced**

**1 red bell pepper, seeded and diced**

**1 small carrot, peeled and diced**

**1 (15-ounce) can pinto or black beans, drained and rinsed**

**1 cup frozen corn kernels**

**¼ cup vegetable broth**

**2 chipotle peppers in adobo sauce, minced, plus 2 tablespoons of adobo sauce (use a 7-ounce can of chipotles in adobo sauce for this)**

**3 tablespoons tomato paste**

**1 teaspoon ground cumin**

**½ teaspoon salt, or to taste**

*tip*

➤ Canned chipotles in adobo sauce, corn husks, and masa harina can be found nowadays in most large groceries with an "ethnic" section. Larger Latin American groceries may have everything in broth, too, as well as gourmet stores. Be sure to get masa harina mix (ground corn flour specially treated with lime water); don't substitute cornmeal. Its mysterious properties are not the same and it will not work! Listen to us!

➤ Tamales freeze well after steaming; just wrap tightly in paper and pack in freezer bags. To reheat: steam again in a steamer basket or microwave, loosely wrapped, for 2 to 3 minutes on high. It might be worth your while to double the recipe and you'll always have fresh tamales on hand.

PLACE THE corn husks in a large pot (no need to separate them just yet). Cover them completely with warm water and allow to soak for at least 20 minutes until husks are soft and pliable. Keep covered in water the entire time the recipe is prepared, until ready to use.

Prepare the tamale dough: In a large bowl, combine the masa harina, broth, salt, baking powder, and oil. With an electric hand mixer, beat until a dense, moist, fluffy dough forms and the side of the bowls are clean. Cover the bowl containing the dough with plastic wrap or a damp towel and set aside.

Prepare the filling: In a large heavy-bottomed skillet, heat the olive oil over medium-high heat. Sauté the onions and garlic for 5 minutes, until softened. Add the pepper and carrot, and sauté for 3 minutes, then add beans, corn, broth, chipotles (the more chipotles and sauce the hotter) and adobo sauce, tomato paste, and cumin. Sauté and simmer until most of the liquid evaporates, about 5-7 minutes. Salt to taste and allow to cool before assembling tamales.

*To assemble:*

Depending the size of the corn husks, you will need to use 1 to 2 husks per tamale. There are a billion ways to wrap a tamale; we like this way since it's simple and makes super-cute traditional tamale shapes.

Take a corn husk and lay it flat; spread about 2 tablespoons of dough off center, leaving a 1½-inch margin from the top and bottom of the husk. Spread a heaping tablespoon of filling in the center of the dough, then top with about 1 tablespoon more of dough. Carefully roll up the tamale, making sure to completely encase the filling in the corn husk. Tie both ends securely with either heavy-duty kitchen string (maybe try different colors for different flavors), or simply tear a corn husk lengthwise into thin strips and use that.

Loosely pack the tamales into a large steamer basket. Steam for 35 to 40 minutes. The tamales will expand and feel firm to the touch when done. Remove from the heat and allow to cool slightly before serving (they will be really hot when unwrapped!). Serve with your favorite salsa and guacamole or make a whole extra-steamy affair out of it and serve with sides of rice and beans.

# SAMOSA STUFFED BAKED POTATOES

MAKES 8 POTATO HALVES

**TIME:** 20 MINUTES, ONCE POTATOES ARE BAKED

*When you want all the spicy goodness of a samosa but don't want to go through the trouble of making a dough, enter Samosa Stuffed Baked Potatoes. Serve these as a precursor to the Red Lentil–Cauliflower Curry (page 186) or really any Indian dish. You can also have two halves for an entrée and serve with Sautéed Spinach and Tomatoes (page 106). Top with 5-Minute Mango Chutney (page 212) and you've got yourself a meal!*

**TO** bake a potato, in case you don't know how: Preheat the oven to 400°F. Poke the potato with a fork about eight times and wrap in aluminum foil. Bake for about an hour, until easily pierced with a fork. When done, unwrap and let cool.

**4 large Russet potatoes, scrubbed, baked, and cooled**

**¼ cup unsweetened soy milk or vegetable broth, or water**

**3 tablespoons peanut oil**

**1 teaspoon yellow mustard seeds (or whatever kind you've got)**

**1 teaspoon coriander seeds, crushed**

**1 small yellow onion, cut into small dice (about a cup)**

**1 medium-size carrot, cut into small dice (about ¾ cup)**

**2 cloves garlic, minced**

**2 teaspoons grated fresh ginger**

**2 teaspoons ground cumin**

**½ teaspoon turmeric**

**½ teaspoon salt**

**½ cup frozen peas, rinsed**

**Juice of ½ lemon**

**Extra oil for brushing or spraying the potatoes**

SLICE THE cooled baked potatoes in half lengthwise and scoop out the insides, leaving about ¼ inch of potato in the skin. The easiest way is to hold the potato in the palm of your nonwriting hand and use a teaspoon to scoop the potato into a bowl. Go slowly and carefully so as not to break the potato, but you don't have to be a perfectionist about it. Mash the potatoes up with the soy milk and set aside the skins.

Preheat the oven to 400°F.

Heat the peanut oil in a large skillet over medium-high heat. Add the mustard and coriander seeds. The mustard seeds should begin to pop; if they don't pop in a minute or two, turn the heat up. Let the seeds pop for about a minute (put a lid on them so you don't get splattered), add the onions and carrots, and sauté for 7 to 10 minutes, until the onions begin to brown.

Add the garlic and ginger, and sauté for a minute more. Add the cumin, turmeric, and salt with a splash of water, stir well, then add the potatoes, mixing everything well. Add a little extra water if it looks too dry. Cook until the potatoes are heated through, then add the peas and cook until those are heated through. Add the lemon juice to taste and stir to incorporate.

Brush the inside of the potato skins with a little bit of oil. Then scoop the filling into the skin, pressing gently to hold the filling in place.

Line the potato halves on a baking sheet and bake for 20 minutes. You can garnish with some chopped fresh cilantro, if you are so inclined, and serve.


## CREOLE STUFFED PEPPERS

SERVES 8 AS A SIDE DISH OR 4 AS A MAIN

Ⓢ Ⓖ Ⓕ ⊡

TIME: 55 MINUTES

*These peppers are stuffed with a mildly spicy mixture of black-eyed peas and veggies. We don't know that much about Southern cooking besides what we've gleaned from too many hours of watching the Food Network, but we used the basic herbs and spices from Creole*

*cooking—paprika, oregano, and thyme—so we think these earn the right to be called Creole. Choose peppers that aren't oddly shaped and that look like they would be good for cutting in half and stuffing. Serve with Messy Rice (page 118) and Hot Sauce–Glazed Tempeh (page 129). They also go well with mashed potatoes and Jalapeño-Corn Gravy (page 216).*

4 large bell peppers

2 tablespoons olive oil

1 medium-size yellow onion, chopped finely

2 jalapeños, cut in half, seeded (if you don't want too much heat), and sliced finely

1 cup finely diced carrots

4 cloves garlic, chopped finely

2 dried bay leaves

1 teaspoon dried oregano

1 teaspoon dried basil

2 teaspoons paprika (smoked paprika if you've got it)

3 sprigs fresh thyme

1 teaspoon salt

1 (15-ounce) can diced tomatoes

2 (15-ounce) cans black-eyed peas, drained and rinsed (about 4 cups)

¼ cup chopped fresh parsley

PREHEAT THE oven to 350°F and grease a 9 × 13-inch casserole dish with a little olive oil. Bring a large pot of water to a boil.

Cut the peppers in half lengthwise through the stem end. For aesthetic purposes, try to leave the stem intact on one side; if you can't manage it, no love lost. Remove the seeds and membranes. Submerge the peppers in the boiling water and cover. Let them boil for 5 minutes, then drain them immediately and rinse with cold water to cool them down a bit.

Meanwhile, heat the oil in a large skillet over medium-high heat. Sauté the onions, jalapeños, and carrots for about 10 minutes. You want the veggies to brown, especially the carrots. If it looks like they are steaming rather than browning, then raise the heat a bit. Add the garlic about 5 minutes into the cooking process.

Add the bay leaves, the other herbs and spices, and the salt; sauté for 1 more minute. Add the tomatoes and peas, stir and cover, and cook for 10 minutes. If it seems too liquidy then remove the cover and cook long enough to reduce some of the liquid. Mix in the parsley.

Remove the bay leaves and thyme sprigs. The mixture will be hot, so we find it's easier to just remove the herbs while filling the peppers; just be on the lookout for them.

Spoon a little less than ½ cup of the veggie mixture into each pepper half. Again, the filling will be hot, so be careful while you are handling it. Place the pepper halves in the casserole dish and bake for about 25 minutes.

## CURRIED CARROT DIP

MAKES 2 CUPS

🌀 🅖 🆖 ▭

**TIME:** 25 MINUTES, PLUS CHILL TIME

*Don't let the simple ingredients fool you—this is a delicious, full-flavored dip, perfect for spreading on crackers or pita bread. We use only a touch of garlic here because raw garlic tends to overpower things, so taste first before deciding there isn't enough.*

> 1 pound carrots, peeled and cut into ½-inch chunks
> ¼ cup roasted sunflower seeds (salted are okay, just add less salt)
> 2 teaspoons grapeseed or other vegetable oil
> ½ teaspoon minced garlic
> 1 teaspoon curry powder
> ½ teaspoon ground cumin
> ¼ teaspoon salt
> 1 tablespoon fresh lemon juice

BRING A small pot of water to a boil. Boil the carrots for 7 to 10 minutes, until soft. Drain and let cool just until they are no longer steaming.

Place the sunflower seeds in a blender or food processor and process into crumbs. Add all remaining ingredients and blend until smooth, scraping down the sides of the processor as you go.

Taste for salt and adjust the spices and lemon. Transfer to a covered container and refrigerate until ready to use (at least 30 minutes).

### Variation:

Caraway-Parsley-Carrot Dip: Omit the curry and cumin. Place ½ teaspoon of caraway seeds in the food processor along with the sunflower seeds. Add ½ cup of loosely packed fresh parsley after everything has been blended, and pulse until it is chopped finely.

## WHITE BEAN AIOLI

MAKES 1½ CUPS

🌀 🅖 🆖 ▭

**TIME:** 10 MINUTES

*Traditionally, aioli is a garlicky mayonnaise, but we love this version made of white beans, olive oil, fresh lemon juice, and lots and lots of garlic. It's great for serving with grilled or roasted vegetables; for spreading on sandwiches, bruschetta, or pitas; or as a creamy topping on burgers. The garlic flavor is very strong, so a little goes a long way.*

> 1 (15-ounce) can navy or great northern beans, drained and rinsed
> 2 tablespoons lemon juice (juice from ½ lemon, depending on your lemon)
> ¼ teaspoon salt
> Several pinches of freshly ground black pepper
> ¼ cup olive oil
> 6 cloves garlic, chopped

COMBINE THE beans, lemon juice, salt, and pepper in a blender or food processor and puree until smooth, scraping down the sides of the bowl to get everything.

Preheat a small pan over low heat. Cook the garlic in the olive oil for about 3 minutes. You want just to gently heat it, not brown it.

Add the garlic and oil to the mixture in the blender and puree. Taste for salt, pepper, and lemon, and adjust to your liking.

Transfer to a container, cover, and refrigerate until ready to use.

## CHESTNUT-LENTIL PÂTÉ

MAKES OVER 2 CUPS

🌀 🄖 🍽️

TIME: 50 MINUTES (MOSTLY INACTIVE), PLUS CHILL TIME

*For dip sophisticates, this pâté has a deep, complex flavor, made woodsy and slightly sweet from the roasted chestnuts. This dip tastes especially good on melba toast or some such type of cracker. Make a few extra roasted chestnuts just for nibbling on, because you're going to want to.*

1 pound whole chestnuts

½ cup French lentils, sorted, rinsed, and drained

2 cloves garlic, crushed, crushed

2½ cups water (for the lentils), plus ¾ to 1 cup (for blending)

¼ cup grapeseed oil

¾ teaspoon salt

2 tablespoons chopped fresh parsley leaves

½ whole nutmeg, or ¼ teaspoon ground

TO ROAST the chestnuts: Preheat the oven to 425°F. Slice a little slit in the shell of each chestnut to prevent them from exploding in the heat. Place the chestnuts on a rimmed baking sheet and roast for 25 minutes. Remove from the oven and place in a kitchen towel. Let cool a bit and then bunch the edges of the towel together, tightly wrapping the chestnuts and crushing them to loosen their shells. Open the towel and peel the shells from chestnuts.

Meanwhile, prepare the lentils: Place them in a small pot with the 2½ cups of water and the crushed garlic. Cover, bring to a boil, then lower the heat to a simmer. Simmer for 30 minutes, until all or most of the water is absorbed and the lentils are very tender.

Remove as much of the garlic as you can from the lentils. Place the lentils in the food processor or blender, along with the chestnuts. Blend a bit, adding ½ cup of water until relatively smooth. Add the oil, salt, and parsley, and blend again. If the mixture seems too thick, add up to another ½ cup of water. It should be thicker than the consistency of hummus, but not by much.

Place in a covered bowl and chill for at least an hour.

Serving suggestions: Toast thin slices of French bread. Spread with a few tablespoons of pâté, then place a slice of tomato on top. Sprinkle very lightly with salt and garnish with parsley.

## CREAMY KALAMATA SPREAD

MAKES 2 CUPS

🄖 🄕 🔢 🍽️

TIME: 25 MINUTES, PLUS CHILL TIME

*Piquant cold as a spread for sammiches or as a dip for veggies and pitas. This spread is very potent and olive-y, so for serious olive lovers only.*

1 tablespoon olive oil

½ cup onion, chopped coarsely

3 cloves garlic, chopped

¼ teaspoon red pepper flakes

1 cup tightly packed pitted kalamata olives, chopped coarsely

¼ cup dry red wine

½ pound soft (not silken) tofu

2– 4 tablespoons water

PREHEAT A small saucepan over medium-high heat. Sauté the onions in the oil for 5 minutes, until lightly browned. Add the garlic and red pepper flakes; cook for 1 more minute. Add the olives and red wine, and cook until the wine has reduced, about 5 more minutes. Remove from the heat and let cool to room temperature.

Crumble the tofu into a blender and puree with just enough water to get things going (no more than 4 tablespoons). Add the olive mixture and puree until very smooth, scraping down the sides of the blender with a spatula. The dip should be the consistency of Vegenaise.

Place in a tightly sealed container and chill for at least half an hour or until ready to use.

## WALNUT-MUSHROOM PÂTÉ

MAKES OVER 2½ CUPS

**TIME:** 30 MINUTES, PLUS CHILLING TIME

*Our friend Paula brought this classy pâté to a New Year's Eve party and we seriously couldn't stop freaking out due to its lush texture and complex, savory flavor. It's delightfully rich and satisfying spread on thick, crusty bread or crisp wheat crackers. This dip is elegant enough to serve piled high in fancy dish for a cocktail party, or just tucked into pita with salad greens for a fantastic lunch or light dinner during warm summer nights.*

3 tablespoons olive oil
1 cup diced yellow onion
3 cloves garlic
1 teaspoon dried thyme
1 teaspoon dried tarragon
¾ teaspoon salt
Freshly ground black pepper
1 pound cremini mushrooms, chopped

1 cup lightly toasted walnuts
¾ cup cooked cannellini beans
1 teaspoon balsamic vinegar
Up to ¼ cup cold vegetable broth

HEAT 2 tablespoons of the olive oil in a large skillet over medium heat. Add the onions and sauté for 3 to 5 minutes until translucent, then add the garlic, thyme, tarragon, salt, and pepper, and cook for another minute. Next, add the mushrooms and cook for 7 to 10 minutes until they are very soft, lowering the heat if necessary to prevent them from burning.

While the mushrooms are cooking, place the walnuts in a food processor or blender and process until very fine.

Add the cooked mushroom mixture to the walnuts in the food processor, along with the balsamic vinegar, beans, and remaining tablespoon of olive oil. Process until smooth, adding the vegetable broth 1 tablespoon at a time as needed. Continue to puree the ingredients until the pâté resembles a smooth, thick, and spreadable paste. Scrap mixture into an airtight container and chill for at least an hour before serving, to allow the flavors to meld.

## SUN-DRIED TOMATO DIP

MAKES ABOUT 3 CUPS

**TIME:** 25 MINUTES, PLUS CHILL TIME

*A tangy, hummus-like dip that is great on a grilled veggie sandwich or on pita with a few cucumbers and sprouts.*

2 cups sun-dried tomatoes (dry ones, not the kind packed in oil)
2 cups boiling water
½ cup slivered or sliced almonds
½ cup cooked white beans, drained (navy beans are good)

**2 cloves garlic, chopped coarsely**

**¼ cup olive oil**

**2 tablespoons lemon juice**

**⅛ teaspoon salt**

**Several pinches of freshly ground black pepper**

PLACE THE tomatoes in a bowl and pour 2 cups of boiling water over them. Cover with a plate and let soak for about 15 minutes.

In a blender or food processor, grind the almonds to a powder. Use a slotted spoon or tongs to remove the tomatoes from the water (don't discard the water) and add them to the almonds. Add the remaining ingredients and puree, adding up to ¼ cup of the tomato water and scraping down the sides often until smooth.

Cover and chill for at least an hour.

### Variations:

**Sun-dried Tomato Basil Dip:** Add ½ cup of fresh basil leaves at the end and pulse a few times so that the leaves are chopped and dispersed but not pureed.

**Sun-dried Tomato and Roasted Garlic Dip:** Use an entire roasted garlic bulb instead of the fresh garlic.

## SWEET BASIL PESTO TAPENADE

SERVES 6 TO 8

**TIME:** 10 MINUTES

*A unique, spreadable basil pesto that's thickened with extra walnuts and lightly sweetened with maple syrup. Instead of putting this on pasta—which can dilute the intense flavors—try this on hot, crusty bread, alongside hummus and olives on an appetizer tray. It's an absolute must on fresh tomato pizza or slathered on roasted squash.*

**3 cups tightly packed fresh basil leaves**

**1 cup walnut pieces or halves**

**2–4 cloves garlic (roasted garlic is great here!)**

**⅓ cup extra-virgin olive oil**

**¼ cup walnut oil (or just use more olive oil)**

**⅓ cup pure maple syrup**

**1 teaspoon grated fresh lemon zest**

**1½ teaspoons salt, or to taste**

**Black pepper**

> ➤ This is a good way to use up that end-of-season basil from the garden that might taste a little too bitter all on its own. The sweetness of the maple syrup helps tone down any harsh flavors.

> ➤ If you can find it, roasted walnut oil is wonderful in place of regular walnut oil. The smoky flavor pairs nicely with the basil and maple syrup.

CHOP THE basil, walnuts, and garlic in a food processor until chunky. Use a rubber spatula to scrape the sides of the processor bowl frequently. Add the oils, maple syrup, and lemon zest, and process until thick and creamy. Season with salt and pepper. Store in a glass jar with a thin layer of olive oil on the surface, and keep refrigerated until ready to serve.

## MEDITERRANEAN-STYLE CASHEW-CUCUMBER DIP

SERVES 6 TO 8

Ⓢ Ⓖ ㊺

TIME: 15 MINUTES

*This dip is one of our favorites (but don't tell the others). So thick and fresh tasting, this is a dairy-free variation on the classic Greek cucumber yogurt dip tzatziki, something that for too long has been missing from typical vegan fare. It's perfect alongside Greek-Style Tomato-Zucchini Fritters (page 52), but there's nothing stopping you from serving as a stand-alone appetizer on warm pita bread lightly brushed with olive oil.*

**1 pound seedless cucumber, peeled and grated (about 1⅔ cup, loosely packed)**

**1 cup raw cashews (5 ounces)**

**2 large cloves garlic**

**1 tablespoon olive oil**

**1 teaspoon dried oregano**

**½ teaspoon salt**

**3 tablespoons lemon juice**

**Pinch of ground white pepper**

**1 tablespoon chopped fresh dill (optional)**

**A few kalamata olives, for garnish**

SQUEEZE HANDFULS of grated cucumber over a medium-size bowl to remove as much juice as possible. You can do this also by wrapping grated cucumber in a cheesecloth or heavy-duty paper towel. Set aside the juice and place the squeezed cucumber in a large bowl.

Combine the cashews, lemon juice, half the grated cucumber, garlic, olive oil, oregano, salt, and pepper in a food processor. Blend until creamy, scraping the sides of the processor bowl frequently. Add 1 to 3 tablespoons of reserved cucumber juice to the sauce. The final consistency should resemble a not-too-thick hummus. Scrape into a medium-size bowl and stir in the remaining grated cucumber and chopped dill.

Cover and chill until ready to use. If serving alone, garnish with a drizzle of olive oil and a few kalamata olives, if desired.

## ASPARAGUS-SPINACH DIP

MAKES ABOUT 3 CUPS

Ⓢ Ⓖ ㊺ ▱

TIME: 20 MINUTES, PLUS CHILL TIME

*A creamy, emerald dip that tickles your taste buds with the fresh tastes of springtime and a tangy kick from capers. Perfect for tank-top weather out on the porch, with a cold beer and some crackers. If we only had porches.*

**1 tablespoon olive oil**

**4 cloves garlic, chopped**

**1 pound asparagus, rough ends removed, cut into 2-inch lengths**

**1 pound spinach (about 2 bunches), washed well, stems removed, chopped coarsely**

**⅓ cup water**

**1 cup raw cashews**

**3 tablespoons capers, with brine**

**salt to taste**

**Several pinches of freshly ground black pepper**

**1 tablespoon fresh lemon juice (from ½ lemon)**

PREHEAT A large pan over medium heat. Sauté the garlic in the oil for about a minute, until fragrant, stirring to keep it from burning. Add the asparagus and water, cover, and bring to a boil. Let boil for about 5 minutes, until the asparagus is bright green. Lower the heat to medium. Add the spinach in batches, letting the leaves wilt so that there's room in the pan for more. Cover the pan to make the wilting go faster; it should take about 3 minutes. Once all the spinach has been added, cook uncovered for about 5 minutes.

Meanwhile, put the cashews, capers, salt, and pepper in a food processor or blender and blend until the cashews are small, coarse crumbs. Scrape down the sides to make sure you get everything.

When the spinach is done cooking, add to the food processor and puree until relatively smooth. Try to get as much of the garlic from the pan as possible, and any remaining water. Add the lemon juice, adjust salt and pepper if necessary, and transfer to a container. Cover and chill for at least an hour.

## A HUMMUS RECIPE

SERVES 4

**TIME:** 10 MINUTES , PLUS CHILL TIME

*Hummus is to vegetarians and vegans what air is to the rest of humanity. Or at least for most of us living in New York City, this ubiquitous chickpea puree can be found at most any party, appetizer spread, tucked in a sandwich, or neatly stowed away in a little plastic container (alongside some pita and carrot sticks) for a light, portable lunch or snack at one's desk.*

*Serve with practically any kind of bread or crisp vegetable.We especially love it paired with Sweet Basil Pesto Tapenade (page 65) and an assortment of breads and raw vegetables, for an exquisite summertime meal. Try one of the flavor variations for something different and fun. Be sure to try some "hummus for bagels" (just thick enough for shmearing) if you've never heard of such a combination before!*

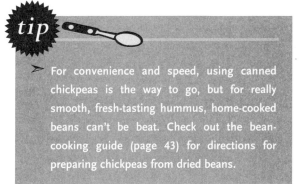

> For convenience and speed, using canned chickpeas is the way to go, but for really smooth, fresh-tasting hummus, home-cooked beans can't be beat. Check out the bean-cooking guide (page 43) for directions for preparing chickpeas from dried beans.

THE secret to really creamy hummus is to make it in a blender. It takes a little more work than using a food processor does, but the results are a smoother puree that resembles the good stuff served in Middle Eastern restaurants. Usually we find it helps to add more liquid (by the tablespoon), so take frequent breaks when blending to add a little more liquid and push the hummus around with a rubber spatula each time that you do. The break also allows you to taste and adjust the lemon juice, garlic, and salt as you prepare the hummus.

2 (15-ounce) cans chickpeas, drained and rinsed
⅓ cup olive oil
¼ cup fresh lemon juice
3 tablespoons sesame tahini
2–3 cloves garlic, crushed
¼ cup water, more or less for desired thickness
Pinch of ground cumin or ground coriander (optional)
Salt and pepper
Paprika (preferably Hungarian smoked paprika, if you can find it)

PLACE half the chickpeas and olive oil in a blender or food processor. Pulse several times, stopping to stir with a rubber spatula. When the mixture is almost pureed and creamy, add the remaining chickpeas and oil, lemon juice, tahini, garlic, cumin, and a little salt. Pulse, stopping to stir several times, until the mixture is very creamy. Season with salt and pepper; add more lemon juice to taste if necessary.

Transfer to an airtight container and chill for 30 minutes before serving.

*To serve:*

Spread into a shallow bowl, dust with paprika, and drizzle a tablespoon of olive oil on top.

Serve with pita, crackers, crostini, vegetable crudités, etc.

*Variations:*

Fold in after pureeing ½ to 1 cup of the following: caramelized onions or shallots, roasted garlic, roasted carrots, roasted beets, roasted red peppers.

Herbed Hummus: Add 2 to 3 tablespoons of the following: chopped fresh dill, fresh parsley.

Olive Hummus: Add ¼ cup black or green olives and pulse in after pureeing.

## Hummus for Bagels

HERE in NYC we love our bagels, but a longtime dilemma for vegans has been what to put on them. Sometimes tofu cream cheese is just too heavy, too fake-tasting, or just not available, so hummus has been a traditional standby. Along with a thin slice of tomato and onion, a zesty shmear of hummus is often just what a sesame or "everything" bagel really craves.

If making hummus just for bagels, a thicker consistency is desired. Reduce the olive oil to ¼ cup, up the tahini to ¼ cup, and cut the garlic down to just 1 clove. Omit the water or use just a few tablespoons. This hummus should be easily spreadable with a knife and not "wet" in texture; the grainier consistency lends itself better to spreading on to your bagel in thick layers.

# LOWER-FAT CAULIFLOWER HUMMUS

MAKES ABOUT 4 CUPS

Ⓖ Ⓕ ㊺ ⬛

TIME: 30 MINUTES, PLUS CHILL TIME

*Cauliflower joins forces with chickpeas in this low-fat, high-fiber version of hummus. If you've ever watched a movie while mindlessly munching on a few veggies and hummus and then rued the day after realizing just how much fat and calories you consumed, this is a great alternative.*

1 smallish head cauliflower (2 pounds or so),
   chopped into largish pieces
2–3 cloves garlic, chopped
1½ cups cooked chickpeas, washed and drained,
   cooking liquid reserved
2 tablespoons tahini
1 tablespoon olive oil
¼ cup chopped scallions
¼ cup loosely packed fresh parsley
½ teaspoon salt
2 teaspoons ground cumin
¼ teaspoon paprika
2–3 tablespoons fresh lemon juice
3 tablespoons or so reserved chickpea cooking liquid

BRING A pot of water to a boil. Add the cauliflower and cover. Boil for 12 to 15 minutes, until you can easily pierce it with a fork.

Drain and let cool just a bit, then place in a food processor or blender while still warm and puree a bit (a food processor works best; a cheap blender might not work unless you chop the cauliflower smaller and add some of the liquid ingredients).

Add the remaining ingredients and puree until relatively smooth. Taste and adjust the ingredients if necessary; you may want to add more cumin, salt, or lemon juice. Use the reserved cooking liquid to thin the hummus if you need to (we usually need to).

Transfer to a container, cover, and chill for about an hour. Serve cold with veggies and pita.

## GUACAMOLE

MAKES 1¼ CUPS

🄢 🄖 🄸 🄪

**TIME:** 10 MINUTES OR LESS

*We feel a little silly putting a guacamole recipe in a cookbook, but just in case you've been living under a rock here it is, the vegan's best dippable friend. It goes great with lots of things, not just Mexican food. Terry is a guacamole purist and likes to keep it as simple as can be. Isa likes to put all kinds of junk in her guac, but the kids love it anyway. So, here's a bare bones recipe that's made faster than you can say "aquacate!" that's ready for mix-ins. Like any guac, this should be made to order and served immediately. One avocado can make enough to serve two people or just one hungry avocado enthusiast, so just double, triple, or quadruple the ingredients to serve more. Make only as much as you need, though, because leftover guacamole doesn't keep!*

**THE key to great guacamole is a great avocado. There's a sweet spot in the ripening cycle of this magical fruit that is ideal: the outside of the avocado should just start to give when very gently pressed. It should never be too firm or rock hard; don't manhandle avocados or you'll be sorry. Very soft, bruised avocados will have brownish, slightly stringy flesh, and might taste bitter. Not that we've never made guacamole with these, but they don't make truly awesome guacamole.**

**Basic guacamole:**

> 1 ripe avocado
> Juice of 1 lime
> 1 small onion, minced (about ¼ cup)
> Kosher salt
> Freshly cracked pepper

**Optional—add one or more of the following:**

> 3 tablespoons chopped fresh cilantro
> 1 ripe tomato, seeded and chopped
> Pinch of ground cumin
> 1 jalapeño chile, fresh or roasted, seeded and minced
> 1 clove garlic, minced

RUN A knife lengthwide all along the middle of the avocado. Firmly grasp each half and twist to separate the halves. Remove the pit by gently but firmly hacking the knife into the pit, gently twisting the knife, and pulling it away from the avocado. Separate the peel from the avocado halves and place the flesh in a medium-size bowl. Drizzle with lime juice, and sprinkle with minced onion, salt, and pepper. Mash it all up with a fork to the desired consistency. Add the other stuff if you really think you need it. Serve immediately!

# BRUNCH

WHY DO WE love brunch so much? Maybe because the word is a most delicious-sounding portmanteau. Possibly because it's usually reserved for long, leisurely weekends so it has a holiday feel to it. Or perhaps because it's the only time it's socially acceptable to drink before noon (Bloody Marys and Mimosas, anyone?). Make it at home and you get to sip Bloody Marys *and* hang out with rollers in your hair.

We like our brunch fare hearty and savory. Our eggless Benedict (page 74) takes a vacation to the Greek islands with creamy dill-infused sauce, roasted red peppers, and plenty of kalamata olives. Try something different in the morning with a pretty baked strata (page 72), layered casserole of bread, herbed mushrooms, and fresh spinach held together with melt-in-your-mouth dairy-free custard. Or, for something quick and easy, a tasty, down-home hash of blue potatoes and tempeh (page 73) will have you ready for a day on the organic farm (or just sitting on the sofa watching interesting documentaries about people working on an organic farm).

And what would brunch be without something you can pour plenty of real maple syrup all over? Two fluffy waffle recipes await you. Take your pick from banana nut (page 75) or devilishly rich chocolate "brownie" waffles studded with chocolate chips (page 74).

Did we mention crepes? Crepes are awesome. They really should be made for dinner, breakfast, second breakfast, and any meal of the day. But we realize you might want to eat something else at some point, so we've tucked these (page 77) into Brunch.

Eating a filling meal for brunch frees up your day from planning dinner so you can do fun stuff instead, like thrift store shopping, playing with the cats, or going back to bed. Just put off the dishes until Monday morning.

## DINER HOME FRIES

SERVES 4 TO 6

**TIME:** 50 MINUTES

*This is how we do it in Brooklyn: boiled and lightly fried potatoes with green peppers and onions. It's pretty bare bones but no breakfast would be complete without them. We prefer not to spice these up because we're usually serving them with other flavorful foods and we don't want them to overpower the others. But for some Irish flair, drizzle a little malt vinegar over these spuds.*

**tip**

➤ For nicely browned and evenly cooked home fries, use your biggest pan to avoid over-crowding.

➤ To makes things faster: If you know in advance you are preparing these for breakfast, boil the potatoes the night before, drain them, and chill them in a sealed container overnight. Bring them to room temperature before cooking.

2 pounds Yukon gold potatoes (4–6 potatoes), cut in half lengthwise, sliced ⅓ inch thick or so
3 tablespoons vegetable oil
1 green bell pepper, seeded, cut into ½-inch-wide, inch-long pieces
1 medium-size onion, cut into ½-inch-wide, inch-long pieces
¾ teaspoon salt
½ teaspoon ground black pepper

PLACE THE sliced potatoes in a pot and cover with cold water. Cover the pot and bring to a boil. Once the potatoes are boiling, lower the heat to medium and cook for about 15 more minutes, until the potatoes are easily pierced with a fork but still firm. Drain and set aside.

Heat 2 tablespoons of the oil in a large, heavy-bottomed skillet over medium-high heat. Add the potatoes and flip them around with a spatula to coat them in oil. Cook undisturbed for 5 to 7 minutes; they should be lightly browned. If they are not, bring the heat up a bit. Cook for 10 more minutes, stirring and tossing occasionally to brown all sides. They won't all get browned and crispy; just do your best.

Add the peppers, onions, salt, and pepper, and another tablespoon of oil, and cook for 5 to 7 more minutes, stirring often, until the onions and peppers are lightly browned. Cover to keep warm until ready to serve.

## TOFU FLORENTINE

SERVES 4
TIME: 1 HOUR

*Crispy on the outside, creamy in the inside, serve Tofu Florentine over a layer of Diner Home Fries (page 71) or, if you want to go all traditional, on a toasted, buttered English muffin. Smother it all in Cheezy Sauce (page 214) and be prepared to blow those sleepy taste buds away. Don't let the simple ingredients fool you; their combination and the cooking methods come together spectacularly (not to be conceited). If you crave a hearty, savory dish for brunch, this is the perfect recipe for you. And it wouldn't make a bad dinner, either.*

### tip

TIP FOR MANAGING YOUR TIME: Follow this guide and everything should be finished at about the same time.

1. Press your tofu and boil the potatoes first; meanwhile, prep all your other ingredients.
2. Prep the garlic for the Cheezy Sauce and for the Broiled Tofu at the same time.
3. Start cooking Cheezy Sauce and preheat the broiler, the potatoes should be boiled by this point.
4. Start cooking the home fries.
5. Broil the tofu.
6. Cook the spinach while the tofu is broiling (about 10 minutes in).

1 pound spinach (about 2 bunches), washed well and stems trimmed
1 pound firm or extra-firm tofu
1 tablespoon olive oil

Braising sauce:
¼ cup water

2 cloves garlic, minced
3 tablespoons fresh lemon juice (juice of 1 lemon)
2 tablespoons soy sauce
Chopped tomato, for garnish
1 recipe Broiled Tofu (page 126)
1 recipe Cheezy Sauce (page 214)
1 recipe Diner Home Fries (page 71), or 4 English muffins

WHILE the tofu is broiling for the first 10 minutes, prepare the spinach: Preheat a large pan over medium-high heat. While the spinach is still wet from being washed, add half to the pan. The extra moisture helps to steam the spinach. Use tongs to toss it around. Once it is wilted, add another batch of spinach. After all the spinach is cooked, cover to keep warm.

*To serve:*

If using home fries, put about one cup's worth in the middle of each plate. If using an English muffin, toast it and place both pieces face up on the plate. Cover with a layer of spinach followed by four pieces of tofu. Ladle Cheezy Sauce over everything and top with a little chopped tomato, just to give it some color. Serve immediately.

## MUSHROOM AND SPINACH STRATA

SERVES 6–8

TIME: 1 HOUR 30 MINUTES (LOTS OF IT INACTIVE)

*A strata is a layered bread casserole that traditionally is covered with an eggy custard and baked until puffy and golden. Our old friend tofu plays a starring role in this tasty veganized version, lavishly flavored with plenty of Italian herbs and shallots.*

*For simplicity, bake it in the same cast-iron skillet that you sauté the vegetables in. If you don't have an oven-safe skillet, a 9 x 13-inch pan should also work, although the strata will come out a bit thinner. Serve with home fries (page 71) or a simple green salad. Cheezy Sauce (page 214) is great on this, too.*

**tip**

➤ This recipe requires stale bread. If you are one of the few people in the world who doesn't have a sad-looking half loaf of bread on your countertop, don't worry—just lightly toast your bread before proceeding with this recipe.

6 slices stale or lightly toasted bread, cut into 2-inch pieces

1½ cups thinly sliced shallots (5 or 6 shallots)

3 tablespoons olive oil

8 ounces cremini mushrooms, sliced thinly (about 3½ cups)

3 cloves garlic, minced

2 teaspoons dried thyme

1 teaspoon dried rosemary

1 teaspoon dried oregano

½ teaspoon crushed red pepper

Several pinches of freshly ground black pepper

1 teaspoon salt

10 ounces well-washed, chopped spinach (about 8 cups)

**Custard:**

1 pound soft tofu

2 tablespoons fresh lemon juice

2 teaspoons prepared yellow mustard

1 tablespoon cornstarch

½ cup vegetable broth or water

¼ teaspoon salt, if using water or sodium-free vegetable broth

PREHEAT THE oven to 350°F.

Sauté the shallots in 2 tablespoons of the olive oil in a large, oven-safe skillet, preferably cast iron, over

medium heat for about 5 minutes. Add the mushrooms and sauté for 7 more minutes, until the mushrooms are tender.

Meanwhile, prepare the custard: Place all custard ingredients in a blender or food processor. Crumble the tofu as you add it. Puree until completely smooth, scraping down the sides to make sure you get everything. Set aside until ready to use.

To the pan with the shallots and mushrooms, add the garlic, herbs, peppers, and salt. Sauté for another minute. Add a handful of spinach and use tongs to mix with the mushrooms and shallots. Continue adding spinach by the handful as the previous bunch wilts and makes more room in the pan. This should take about 5 minutes.

Turn off the heat, move vegetables to the side of the pan, and add the remaining tablespoon of oil. Just try to get as much oil as you can to cover the bottom of the pan to keep things from sticking. Toss in the sliced bread and mix to distribute.

Pour the tofu custard over everything. Use a spatula to smush the tofu into the veggies and bread. You want to get things as coated as you can without outright mixing it up.

Place in the preheated oven and bake for 55 to 60 minutes. The strata should be firmed and lightly browned. Let cool for 10 minutes, slice into eight pieces, and serve.

## BLUE FLANNEL HASH

SERVES 4

**TIME:** 40 MINUTES

*An all-American favorite gets a makeover with the unusual and earthy-tasting blue potato. Although blue potatoes have been cultivated in South America for hundreds of years, it's only recently that they've become widely available in the United States. Simple seasoning* and gentle cooking bring out the best flavors in these precious blue tubers. Craving a real sausage flavor? Toss in some crushed fennel seeds along with the tempeh. Sometimes purple potatoes are also called blue potatoes, but either kind will work here.

2 tablespoons olive oil

1½ pounds blue potatoes, cut into ½-inch dice

1 (8-ounce) package tempeh, cut into ½-inch dice

½ teaspoon red pepper flakes

1 medium onion, cut into ½-inch dice

2 tablespoons soy sauce

PREHEAT A large, heavy-bottomed pan (cast iron would be ideal) over medium-high heat.

Pour in the oil and let it heat up. Add the potatoes and tempeh, and mix. Cover and let cook for about 15 minutes, stirring every now and again.

Add the red pepper flakes and onion, and mix. Cover and cook for another 10 minutes, stirring whenever you feel like it.

Add the soy sauce and cook for another 3 minutes. Cover to keep warm until ready to serve.

## GREEK TOFU BENEDICT

MAKES 4 SERVINGS

TIME: ABOUT AN HOUR

*This rustic, charming brunch specialty performs all kinds of feats. Roasted red peppers stand in for salmon and Dill-Tahini Sauce for the hollandaise in a luscious Mediterranean take on the classic Benedict. Serve over Diner Home Fries (page 71) or an English muffin. You can also opt to go Greek all the way and serve over sliced, toasted pita.*

**Note:** The tofu method is the same as for the Tofu Florentine (page 72), but you can also use Grilled Italian Tofu (page 128), if you prefer.

1 recipe Broiled Tofu (page 126)

1 recipe Dill-Tahini Sauce (page 215)

2 roasted red peppers (page 33)

Olive oil in a spray bottle

⅓ cup kalamata olives

Dried oregano, for garnish

THIS is basically a conglomeration of other recipes, but don't be intimidated! Follow this list for time management and you'll be all set.

1. Press your tofu and boil the potatoes first; meanwhile, prep all your other ingredients.
2. Prepare the Dill-Tahini Sauce.
3. Start roasting the red peppers.
4. Cook the home fries.
5. Broil the tofu.

*To assemble:*

Place the home fries, English muffin, pita, or other side dish on the plate. Layer with two pieces of red pepper and four pieces of tofu. If you are serving with extra vegetables, place those around your tofu stack. Ladle on the tahini sauce, scatter with kalamata olives, sprinkle dried oregano hither and fro, and serve immediately.

## CHOCOLATE CHIP BROWNIE WAFFLES

MAKES 14 TO 16 WAFFLES

TIME: 30 MINUTES

*Are they brownies or are they waffles? Okay, anyone over the age of three won't mistake them for the former, yet these fluffy waffles with crunchy pecans baked into them could just be the perfect way to get more chocolate into your mornings. Sweet but not overly so, these are suitable for breakfast or brunch when served with maple syrup, fresh berries, and sliced bananas. Even better, throw a waffle party and serve these up like an ice-cream sundae—top with your favorite vegan ice cream, chocolate syrup, crushed pineapple, walnuts, sliced bananas, sprinkles, and more.*

- **2 cups all-purpose flour**
- **⅔ cup unsweetened cocoa powder**
- **1 tablespoon baking powder**
- **½ teaspoon baking soda**
- **½ teaspoon ground cinnamon**
- **½ teaspoon salt**
- **1¾ cups soy milk**
- **¼ cup water**
- **½ cup vanilla or plain soy yogurt**
- **⅓ cup canola oil**
- **⅔ cup sugar**
- **1½ teaspoons vanilla extract**
- **1 cup vegan semisweet chocolate chips, chopped coarsely**
- **⅔ cup chopped pecans, chopped coarsely**
- **Nonstick cooking spray**

> **tip**
>
> ➤ For best results, use a Belgian-style waffle maker, especially one that has temperature control to ensure perfectly cooked waffles. If you're using a regular waffle iron, you might need to use slightly less batter per waffle.

PREHEAT YOUR waffle iron according to the manufacturer's directions. Have a heat-proof silicone spatula on hand to help remove the hot waffles when ready.

Sift together the flour, cocoa powder, baking powder, baking soda, cinnamon, and salt into a large bowl. Form a well in the center of the sifted ingredients. In a separate bowl, whisk together the soy milk, water, soy yogurt, canola oil, sugar, and vanilla.

Pour the wet ingredients into the well of the dry

ingredients. Use a wire whisk to combine all the ingredients. Just before everything is fully blended, fold in the chopped chocolate chips and pecans. Combine until the ingredients are just moistened; do not overmix.

When the waffle maker is heated and ready to go, spray its cooking surfaces with cooking spray. Follow the manufacturer's directions regarding how much batter to use (for most square, Belgian-style waffle makers, about ½ cup batter per waffle works). Bake according to the waffle iron directions; the waffles should be lightly browned. Use a spatula to carefully lift the waffles onto a cutting board. Separate with a knife and serve immediately.

## BANANA-NUT WAFFLES

MAKES 14 TO 16 WAFFLES

**TIME:** 30 MINUTES

*With lots of bananas and walnuts, even the biggest morning-haters will roll out of bed for these. Sliced fresh strawberries and bananas on top make these bad boys really sing.*

- **1¾ cups soy milk**
- **¼ cup water**
- **2 teaspoons apple cider vinegar**
- **2 average-size bananas**
- **3 tablespoons canola oil**
- **3 tablespoons pure maple syrup or agave syrup**
- **1 teaspoon vanilla extract**
- **2¼ cups all-purpose flour**
- **1 teaspoon baking powder**
- **1 teaspoon baking soda**
- **½ teaspoon salt**
- **¼ teaspoon ground nutmeg**
- **1 cup walnuts, chopped finely**
- **Nonstick cooking spray**

PREHEAT YOUR waffle iron. Pour the soy milk, water, and vinegar into a measuring cup and set aside to curdle.

Mash the bananas very well in a large mixing bowl. Add the soy milk mixture, oil, syrup, and vanilla, and stir.

Add the flour, baking powder, baking soda, salt, and nutmeg. Use a fork to combine. Don't overmix, just mix until there are minimal lumps left. Fold in the chopped walnuts.

Spray the cooking surfaces of your waffle iron with nonstick cooking spray and cook the waffles according to the manufacturer's directions. Serve with sliced strawberries and bananas and plenty of maple syrup.

# BLUEBERRY CORN PANCAKES

MAKES 8 TO 10 PANCAKES

*The perfect summer pancake, with blueberries and a hint of lemon. Cormeal give the pancakes a little crunch and wonderful "mouthfeel" (we hate that word, but just had to use it here.)*

**¾ cup all purpose flour**
**½ cup cornmeal**
**2 teaspoon baking powder**
**½ teaspoon salt**
**2 tablespoons canola oil (any mild tasting veg oil will do)**
**1¼ cup plain soy milk**
**⅓ cup water**
**1 teaspoon vanilla**
**2 Tablespoons pure maple syrup**
**2 teaspoon grated lemon zest**

**1 cup fresh blueberries**
**Cooking spray or a little oil for greasing the pan**

PREHEAT a large non-stick pan on medium high heat.

Sift together flour, cornmeal, baking powder and salt. In a separate bowl, combine all other ingredients. Add wet to dry, mix until just combined, then fold in the blueberries. Do not over mix or pancakes will be tough, a couple of lumps is ok.

Spray pan with cooking spray. Use a ¼ cup measuring cup or an ice cream to pour out batter into pan. Cook pancakes until brown on bottom and bubbles form on top, about 4 minutes. Flip pancakes over with a thin spatula and cook until bottoms are brown and pancakes are barely firm to touch. Transfer to plates. Repeat with remaining batter, adding more oil to the pan as needed.

## CREPES: SAVORY AND SWEET, BUCKWHEAT OR WHEAT

MAKES 8 TO 10 CREPES

TIME: 35 MINUTES, PLUS CHILLING TIME FOR BATTER

*These classic, delicate, thin pancakes can be yours with just a little bit of technique and determination. Though perfect for just eating as is, crepes are commonly served rolled with filling inside, since everything seems a little more special wrapped up in a golden pancake.*

*Fillings for entrée crepes often consist of lightly sautéed vegetables, such as asparagus, mushrooms, onions, or leeks. Try draping savory crepes with Mushroom Gravy (page 211), Mustard Sauce (page 204), or Cheezy Sauce (page 214), or top cooked vegetable fillings with a little Silken Aioli Dressing (page 93) before rolling.*

*Breakfast crepes are typically humbler affairs. Often a tablespoon of your favorite jam is the perfect filling. Try adding slices of banana, strawberries, raspberries, sautéed apples, even curls of shaved chocolate wrapped in a hot, right-off-the-skillet crepe. Drizzle with warmed maple syrup or your favorite chocolate syrup or fruit syrup. Try this simple yet delicious variation: just sprinkle hot crepes with a little fresh lemon juice and dusting of confectioners' sugar.*

*Or, enjoy deviously delicious dessert crepes slathered with the homemade, hazelnut-chocolaty goodness of Not-Tella (page 262) and plenty of fresh fruit.*

*We've included two versions: the classic, all-purpose wheat crepe and a buckwheat crepe, a hearty specialty of Brittany, to impress your gourmet pals with. Either will take well to fillings and toppings both sweet and savory. Just remember that practice makes perfect when it comes to making crepes, so don't be discouraged if your first few (or the whole batch) don't look so pretty.*

### Crepe Pans

IF you find you really love making crepes (and once you get the hang of it, it's no big deal to make a batch when the mood strikes), we highly recommend investing a good crepe pan. The very best varieties are French made, usually of black steel or thin cast iron. Like steel woks and cast-iron pots, these pans need to be seasoned (follow the manufacturer's directions), but will repay your efforts with a lifetime of perfectly cooked crepes with the minimal use of cooking fat.

We're not as fond of nonstick crepe pans, but if you must, go for a high-quality brand and baby it (never, ever use a metal spatula!). Avoid at all costs any weird, electric "crepe machines" that require dipping some kind of contraption into crepe batter.

**Savory wheat crepes:**

1½ cups soy or rice milk

¼ cup water

¾ cup all-purpose flour

¼ cup chickpea flour

1 tablespoon arrowroot flour

½ teaspoon salt

**Buckwheat crepes:**

1½ cups plus 2 tablespoons soy milk

¼ cup water

½ cup buckwheat flour

¼ cup all-purpose flour

¼ cup chickpea flour

1 tablespoon arrowroot flour

½ teaspoon salt

Nonstick cooking spray

Softened nonhydrogenated vegan margarine

COMBINE THE soy milk, water, flour(s), arrowroot, and salt in a food processor or blender. If making sweet crepes or any of the variations, then add sugar and flavorings, too. Blend for a few seconds, scraping the sides of the blender once, until everything is smooth. The batter will be very thin. Pour into an airtight container, cover, and chill in the refrigerator for at least an hour, or as long as overnight. When ready to cook the crepes, briefly stir the batter if the ingredients have separated.

Over medium-high heat, heat a 9- to 10-inch crepe pan or a heavy skillet. The pan is ready when a few drops of water flicked into it sizzle. Spray with nonstick cooking spray, dab a silicone brush into softened margarine, and brush along the bottom and sides of pan.

Ladle ⅓ to ½ cup (use the bigger amount for a bigger pan) into the center of the pan. The batter should sizzle when it hits the pan. Holding the pan firmly by the handle, use your wrist to tilt the pan in a circular motion so that the batter spreads in a thin layer across the bottom. Continue to tilt the pan until the batter is fully spread and then sets.

Cook until the top of the crepe is dry, the center is bubbling, and the edges appear firm and lightly browned when gently lifted with the spatula, 1 to 1½ minutes. Gently run the spatula under the crepe to loosen it, then carefully flip and cook on the other side for 30 seconds. Slide the crepe onto a regular-size dinner plate.

Brush a little more margarine onto the crepe pan for the next crepe; if the crepes start to stick to the pan, give it another spray of nonstick cooking spray. If bits of batter collect on the pan, or the pan seems too oily, quickly swirl a crumpled paper towel across the surface of the pan to remove the crumbs. Cook the rest of crepes, stacking one on top of another (often it's easiest just to slide the flipped crepe directly onto the stack). If not serving immediately, cover the entire batch with plastic wrap and store in the refrigerator.

*Variations:*

**Sweet Crepes:** Add 2 tablespoons sugar.

**Sweet Orange or Lemon Crepes:** Add 1 teaspoon of finely grated orange or lemon zest and 2 tablespoons of sugar.

**Whole Wheat Crepes:** Substitute ½ cup of whole wheat pastry flour for ½ cup of the all-purpose flour, to add extra fiber and nutrients.

**tip**

➤ A few items that will make your crepe-making experience all the easier: a silicone basting brush (that can withstand contact with a hot pan), nonstick cooking spray, a crumpled paper towel for wiping the crepe pan or skillet, and a long, thin spatula (like the kind used to frost cakes).

➤ The buckwheat crepe batter is somewhat more viscous and difficult to work with than the wheat batter is. We recommend making the wheat crepes a few times and getting the hang of 'em before trying your hand at the buckwheat batter.

➤ Once cooked and stacked, a batch of well-wrapped crepes can keep in the fridge for a little over a week. Have some on hand for fun weekday breakfasts or simple, fun, quick dinners. To reheat cooked crepes, simply heat your crepe pan, brush with a little margarine or a spray of nonstick cooking spray, and cook the crepes for about 30 seconds each side. Flip just once.

# POTATO-MUSHROOM BLINTZES

MAKES 8 TO 10 BLINTZES

(45)

**TIME: 45** MINUTES, NOT INCLUDING MAKING CREPES

*Blintzes are plump little packets of folded crepes stuffed with a sweet or savory filling. For your brunching pleasure, we present a hearty potato-mushroom filling, wrapped in your choice of a wheat or buckwheat crepe. Serve with any sauce you'd use for crepes, such as Mushroom Gravy (page 211) or any natural applesauce. These blintzes are also an exceptional choice for dinner served alongside a simple green salad. Assemble the blintzes the day before and they'll sauté up crisp in mere minutes for a fun and filling meal.*

**1 recipe** Savory Wheat or Buckwheat Crepes (page 77)
**Softened** nonhydrogenated vegan margarine for frying

### Filling:

½ **pound** Yukon gold or other waxy potato (about 2 medium-size potatoes)
2 tablespoons canola oil
1 small onion, diced finely
1 teaspoon caraway seeds (optional)
½ pound mushrooms, any variety, sliced thinly
Plenty of freshly ground pepper
**Salt**

### Optional sauces for garnish:

**Mushroom** Gravy, Mustard Sauce, Dill-Tahini Sauce, **all**-natural unsweetened apple sauce, store-bought **soy** sour cream

FIRST, PREPARE the crepes (see page 77). Stack them, one on top the other, on a dinner plate. Cover the plate with plastic wrap and set aside.

Peel and coarsely chop the potatoes. Place them in a medium-size pot, add enough cold water to cover by 1 inch, and boil for 20 to 25 minutes until easily pierced with a fork and tender. Drain, place the potatoes in a large bowl, and mash coarsely.

In a heavy skillet over medium heat, heat the oil and add the onion. Stir and fry the onion until it's golden-brown and very soft, about 15 minutes. Add the caraway seeds and mushrooms. Sauté until the mushrooms are very tender and most of the liquid has been absorbed, about 7 minutes.

Fold the cooked mushroom mixture into mashed potatoes and season to taste with salt and plenty of ground black pepper.

To assemble each blintz, place 3 to 4 tablespoons of the filling in the center of the crepe. Pat the filling to shape it into an oblong. Fold two opposite sides of the crepe over the filling, then fold the remaining two sides over those. The resulting blintz should be a rectangular little bundle. Stack the assembled blintzes on a plate, seam side down.

Heat a heavy skillet or crepe pan over medium heat. The pan will be ready when a few droplets of water flicked onto its surface sizzle. Using a silicone brush, brush the bottom of skillet with the softened margarine. Place two or three blintzes, seam side down, onto the skillet and cook on each side for 3 to 4 minutes, until their pan-side surface is crisped and browned. Use a small, firm spatula to turn once. Serve the hot blintzes immediately.

*Variation:*

**Potato-Spinach Blintzes:** Substitute 1 pound of cooked, chopped fresh spinach for the mushrooms.

# SALADS AND DRESSINGS

WE HAVE NOTHING personal against salads. Some have suspected that we do, just because they don't feature prominently in *Vegan with a Vengeance*. It's just that, all too often, salads are assumed to be the staple of vegetarians everywhere, and lots of times they end up being just that. It's because we sympathize with the eleven-year-old vegetarian who ends up eating a sprig of parsley and a slice of limp, pink tomato while the rest of her family chows down on hamburgers that we've often paid attention to heartier, cooked fare, rather than a handful of leaves and olive oil.

But salad lovers everywhere can now rejoice that we've come to terms with all of those issues. Time well spent on the couch has allowed us to reexperience the subtle joys of arugula, spinach, fresh fruits and herbs, piquant vinegars, and oils. We lean toward substantial salads these days, so you'll notice lots of tender grains, beans, roasted vegetables, and mushrooms adding plenty of depth and flavor to the medley of traditional leafy greens.

Most of these salads can be served as entrées with a couple of add-ons. Salads deserve to hang out all year round—not just during those steamy summer days—therefore, we proudly present a salad for most any occasion and season. So dust off those salad tongs and rev up the salad spinner. And don't forget the parsley.

# CAESAR SALAD WITH ROASTED GARLIC CROUTONS

SERVES 4 TO 6 AS A SIDE, 2 TO 3 AS A ENTRÉE

**TIME:** 30 MINUTES, PLUS TIME TO CHILL

*Creamy, bold, garlicky—this is the classic salad that eats like a meal. In our version of a Caesar, ground almonds provide a texture similar to that of grated hard cheese, and capers bring on that essential briny flavor. Fresh, homemade croutons bathed in roasted garlic and olive oil really make this and are super-easy, so don't substitute lame store-bought ones if you can help it. (Be sure to roast a bulb of garlic in advance so that you can get on with the crouton recipe—see page 32.) Be generous when applying the Caesar dressing to the salad, as this dressing recipe makes a lot.*

> *tip*
>
> ➢ Leftover salad, dressing, and grilled tempeh or tofu make an amazing filling for homemade Caesar salad wraps. Just tuck and roll up filling ingredients into your favorite flatbread and eat ASAP.

## Caesar dressing:

⅓ cup slivered or sliced blanched almonds

3–4 cloves garlic, peeled and crushed

¾ pound silken tofu (preferably fresh, not vacuum-packed)

¼ cup olive oil

3 tablespoons fresh lemon juice

1 heaping tablespoon capers

4 teaspoons caper brine

1 teaspoon sugar

½ teaspoon mustard powder

Salt

## Croutons:

¼ cup olive oil

4 cloves roasted garlic (page 32)

1 tablespoon fresh lemon juice

1 medium-size loaf French or Italian bread (little less than 1 pound), stale and torn or sliced into bite-size pieces

¼ teaspoon salt

## Salad:

1 large head romaine lettuce, chopped

Freshly cracked black pepper

Handful or two of spinach and arugula, torn into bite-size pieces

PREPARE THE dressing: Pulse the sliced almonds in a food processor or blender until crumbly. Empty the ground almonds into an airtight container that you'll be using to store the finished dressing. Blend the garlic, tofu, and oil in the food processor or blender until creamy. Add the lemon juice, capers, caper brine, sugar, and mustard powder, and pulse until blended. Adjust the lemon juice and salt to taste. Pour into the container with the ground almonds and whisk to combine. Cover and allow the dressing to chill in the refrigerator for a minimum 30 minutes, optimally 1 to 1½ hours.

WE like to add a little spinach and arugula to this Caesar salad—the rich dressing contrasts perfectly with these bitter greens—but it's not essential. Make an entrée out of it by tossing cubed, grilled tempeh or tofu (page 97) and grilled mushrooms, asparagus, or leeks. Other optional add-ins include roasted red peppers (pages 26–28), shredded red cabbage, shredded carrot, steamed or roasted green beans, or slivered toasted almonds.

While dressing is chilling, prepare the croutons: Preheat the oven to 400°F. Combine the olive oil, roasted garlic, and lemon juice in a large bowl. With a fork or immersion blender, mash or blend the mixture until creamy. Add the torn bread and toss to coat each piece with the oil mixture. Spread onto a rimmed baking sheet, sprinkle with salt, if desired, and bake for 12 to 14 minutes until golden brown. Toss the croutons twice during the baking process. Remove from the oven and cool the croutons on the baking sheet.

To assemble the salad, place in a large bowl 2 to 3 cups of lettuce/greens per individual serving (amount depending on whether it's a side or entrée). If using, add vegetables, tempeh, and so on. Ladle on ⅓ cup of the dressing (or more or less to taste), and use kitchen tongs to toss the greens and coat them with dressing. Add the warm croutons, toss again, and transfer to a serving dish. Sprinkle with a little freshly cracked pepper. If not serving right away, warm croutons in 300°F oven for 5 to 8 minutes before adding to the salad.

## CORN AND EDAMAME-SESAME SALAD

SERVES 4 TO 6

Ⓖ Ⓕ ㊺ ⊟

**TIME:** 45 MINUTES

*This salad is ridiculously simple yet so satisfying—it's nutty, salty, fresh tasting, and crisp. We like to munch on it as a snack throughout the day but it's also a perfect accompaniment to an Asian-inspired meal. Try it alongside Butternut Squash Rolls (page 50) for a delicious cold summer dinner. If you like, serve over a bed of baby greens. For an even heartier salad, add two thinly sliced avocado halves right before serving.*

### Dressing:

   2 tablespoons toasted sesame oil
   1 tablespoon rice vinegar (regular vinegar works, too)
   2 teaspoons tamari or soy sauce

### Salad:

   2 cups frozen, shelled edamame
   1 cup fresh corn (1 or 2 ears, depending on the size) or partially thawed frozen corn
   2 tablespoons toasted sesame seeds
   Generous pinch of salt

BRING A big pot of water to a boil. Meanwhile, whisk all the dressing ingredients in a medium-size mixing bowl.

Boil the edamame for 3 minutes. Add the corn and boil for another 2 minutes. Drain into a colander and run under cold water until cool enough to touch. Add the edamame and corn to the dressing and toss to combine. Add the sesame seeds and toss again. Salt to taste. Cover and chill for at least 15 minutes.

*tip*

➤ If you don't have rice vinegar on hand, you can use a different kind, but nothing too strong—stick to something mild, such as red wine vinegar. If you have brown rice vinegar, not regular rice vinegar, that's fine, too. You can also use partially thawed frozen corn instead of fresh, but don't use canned.

   Although we like the taste of Bragg's in lots of things, we advise against using it in salad dressings because of its distinctive, um, well, "hippy" taste. Instead use good quality tamari or soy sauce.

➤ Make a super-cute hors d'oeuvre of this salad by placing it in radicchio cups (see photo insert). Just slice off the bottom of a head of radicchio, carefully peel off the leaves, and voilà! Cup!

➤ Make a more dramatic-looking presentation by using black sesame seeds instead of regular toasted ones.

# JICAMA-WATERCRESS-AVOCADO SALAD WITH SPICY CITRUS VINAIGRETTE

Serves 6 to 8

**TIME:** 30 MINUTES (IF YOU HAVE A FOOD PROCESSOR)

*Jicama, sometimes referred to as the Mexican turnip, is like a dream come true; it's as if an apple decided to become a root vegetable. This salad is our attempt to re-create the Thai fusion that is so popular with the kids these days, using ingredients that aren't too difficult to find. The dressing has a spicy kick from the hot chile oil but the heat isn't intense, so don't let that scare you off. The avocado and peanuts make it a meal on its own, filling enough to serve as a refreshing summer lunch or dinner.*

## Dressing:

¼ cup rice wine vinegar

½ cup fresh orange juice (juice of 1 navel orange)

2 tablespoons lime juice (juice of 1 lime)

2 tablespoons peanut oil

2 tablespoons hot chile oil

2 tablespoons soy sauce

3 tablespoons sugar

1 teaspoon sesame oil

## Salad:

1 medium-size jicama, peeled and shredded thinly (about 6 cups)

½ bunch watercress, roots removed

1 ripe avocado, peeled, cut in half, pitted, and sliced thinly

½ small red onion, sliced thinly

½ cup roasted unsalted peanuts, chopped coarsely

## Optional garnishes:

Shredded carrots

Sprigs of mint or cilantro

**tip**

➤ Use a serrated peeler to peel the jicama, or alternatively, use a paring knife to slice off the skin in sheets. If you don't have a food processor to shred the jicama, just slice it matchstick thin.

COMBINE ALL dressing ingredients and mix vigorously. If you have a small plastic bowl with a secure lid, you can mix it in there and shake it up. Let the dressing sit at room temperature for at least 10 minutes so that the sugar dissolves. Mix or shake again when you are ready to use it.

Place the shredded jicama in a large bowl. Reserve ⅓ cup of the dressing and pour the rest over the jicama; mix to coat.

Arrange a small bunch of watercress on an individual salad plate. It looks pretty if you keep it as bunched together as possible and if some of the leaves are hanging off the side, looking sort of like the long arm of a clock (stems in the middle and leaves facing outward). Drizzle a little reserved dressing over the leaves.

Place a pile of jicama (a cup or so) on the stems of the watercress to secure it. Sprinkle a little shredded carrot (if using) as well as a few half-moons of onion on top of the jicama. Add a few avocado slices either on top or along the sides. Sprinkle with peanuts. Drizzle with a little dressing and garnish with cilantro or mint. Continue with the remaining plates.

## QUINOA SALAD WITH BLACK BEANS AND MANGO

SERVES 4 TO 6

**TIME:** 35 MINUTES; 15 MINUTES IF THE QUINOA IS ALREADY COOKED

*Top secret: It isn't rocket science—you can make a salad like this with any leftover grains, beans, and fruit you have around. It is a really straightforward salad that uses simple, fresh ingredients. Each bite will bring new flavors to the table—mango, scallions, cilantro, red peppers . . . you never know what you're gonna get! Best of all, it takes practically no time if you have some leftover quinoa at hand.*

**tip**

> If you don't have any leftover quinoa, don't sweat it; it's easy and fast to prepare. Bring 1 cup of dried quinoa and 2 cups of water to a boil in a small pot. Once the mixture is boiling, lower the heat to a simmer and cook for 15 minutes, until all the water has been absorbed. Then remove from the heat and fluff with a fork. Set aside to cool, and once it has cooled you can prepare this salad.

1 mango, peeled and cut into small dice
1 red bell pepper, seeded and diced as small as you can get it
1 cup chopped scallions
1 cup chopped fresh cilantro
2 tablespoons red wine vinegar
2 tablespoons grapeseed oil
¼ teaspoon salt
2 cups cooked quinoa, cooled
1 (15-ounce) can black beans, drained and rinsed
A few leaves of lettuce for garnish

COMBINE the mango, red bell pepper, scallions, and cilantro in a mixing bowl. Add the red wine vinegar, grapeseed oil, and salt, and stir to combine. Add the quinoa and stir until everything is well incorporated. Fold in the black beans. You can serve immediately or let it sit for a bit for the flavors to meld. To serve, place a few leaves of lettuce on a plate and scoop some salad on top. This tastes good chilled and is even better at room temperature.

## LENTIL SALAD

SERVES 4

**TIME:** 55 MINUTES (MOSTLY INACTIVE)

*Thyme, tarragon, and garlic flavor this easy-to-prepare and hearty lentil salad. Serve over red leaf lettuce (or whatever kind of fancy-shmancy lettuce you can get your hands on) with oil and vinegar on the side. Having some warmed pita bread on hand wouldn't hurt, either. For a cute hors d'oeuvre idea, spoon small scoops of salad into endive leaves.*

4 cups vegetable broth
2 or 3 sprigs thyme
2 bay leaves
2 cloves garlic, crushed
½ teaspoon dried tarragon
¼ teaspoon salt
1 cup uncooked French lentils
1 small red onion, chopped very finely (about ⅓ cup)
1 small tomato, seeded and diced (about ½ cup)
2 radishes, grated (about ⅓ cup)
1 small carrot, grated
Several pinches of freshly ground black pepper

**Dressing:**

2–4 tablespoons olive oil
1 tablespoon balsamic vinegar

1 tablespoon Dijon mustard

1 tablespoon fresh lemon juice (about ½ lemon)

1 clove garlic, minced

BRING THE broth, thyme, bay leaves, garlic cloves, tarragon, and salt to a boil in a medium-size saucepan. Add the lentils and bring again to a low boil. Cover the pot with the lid tilted, allowing a little room for steam to escape. Let cook for 20 to 25 minutes. The lentils should be soft enough to eat but still firm enough to not lose their shape.

While the lentils cook, stir together all the dressing ingredients in a mixing bowl.

Drain the lentils in a mesh colander (so that the lentils don't fall out the holes). Let cool, giving the colander a few shakes every couple of minutes so that they drain and cool faster. Once the lentils are luke-warm (about 15 minutes), remove the bay leaves, chunks of garlic, and thyme sprigs. Add the lentils to the dressing along with onions, tomato, and radishes, and toss to combine. Season with salt and pepper to taste, cover, and chill for at least half an hour.

When chilled, serve over lettuce with oil and vinegar on the side.

## BULGUR, ARUGULA, AND CANNELLINI SALAD

MAKES ABOUT 8 SERVINGS

TIME: 35 MINUTES, PLUS AN HOUR TO CHILL

*Peppery arugula adds a nice crisp bite to this rustic and wholesome salad. Bulgur is a great choice for a grain-based summer salad because it cooks quickly and you don't need to stand over the stove and tend to it. It's really delicious the way the bulgur, mushrooms, and beans get all tangy and succulent when they absorb the flavors of the dressing. A small amount of oregano adds fragrance, while paprika ties everything together and*

*spices things up just a bit. You can use a different white bean, whatever is available, or even garbanzos or red kidney beans.*

**tip**

> It's a good idea to let this chill for as long as possible before digging in; it's one of those things that's even better the day after it's made and even better still the day after that.

1 cup bulgur (cracked wheat)

2 cups thinly sliced cremini mushrooms

1½ cups cooked cannellini beans, drained and rinsed

1 small red onion, quartered and sliced thinly

2 cups lightly packed arugula leaves

### Dressing

¼ cup olive oil

¼ cup red wine vinegar

1 tablespoon balsamic vinegar

2 cloves garlic, minced really well or pressed

1 teaspoon paprika

½ teaspoon dried oregano

¾ teaspoon salt

Several pinches of freshly ground black pepper

TO STEAM the bulgur: Place the bulgur in a small pot or container that has a tightly fitting lid. Boil a pot of water and measure out 1⅓ cups. Pour the water over the bulgur and cover the pot. Let sit for 30 minutes. Bulgur should be tender but chewy.

Prepare the dressing: While the bulgur is steaming, mix all the dressing ingredients together in a large mixing bowl. Stir well and add the mushrooms, beans, and onion, and let them marinate. Stir occasionally.

When the bulgur is ready, add it and any water remaining in the pot to the dressing while it's still warm. Toss to coat. Tear up the arugula leaves into bite-size pieces and add them to the salad. Mix well. Cover and refrigerate until completely chilled, preferably overnight. Once the salad is chilled, you can adjust the salt and pepper to taste.

## PEAR AND ENDIVE SALAD WITH MAPLE CANDIED PECANS

SERVES 4

🌀 🌀 🌀 🌀

**TIME:** 45 MINUTES

*Candied pecans give this salad a yummy crunch, while the sweetness of the pear rounds out the delicate bitterness of the endive. It's a simple recipe but a smorgasbord of flavor and texture. We know grapeseed oil isn't a common oil to have around but we insist you get it because it makes the best simple dressing for any salad. If you need to sub the vinegar, use red wine vinegar, not regular balsamic.*

**Maple candied pecans:**

½ cup pecan halves
About 2 teaspoons vegetable oil
Scant ¼ teaspoon salt
¼ cup pure maple syrup

**Salad**

3 Belgian endives, sliced widthwise into ½-inch slices
1 very ripe Anjou (or other soft) pear, thinly sliced into bite-size pieces
3 tablespoons grapeseed oil
2 teaspoons white balsamic vinegar

HAVE ready a flat plate lined with baking parchment.

Preheat a heavy-bottomed pan (preferably cast iron) over medium-low heat. Toast the pecans for about 5 minutes, tossing them frequently after the first 2 minutes. Sprinkle the vegetable oil and salt over the pecans, and toss to coat. Add the maple syrup and toss to coat, heating until the maple syrup begins to bubble. Let bubble for about 30 seconds, tossing the entire time. Transfer to the parchment-lined plate and allow to cool completely. You can speed up the process by placing the pecans in the fridge once they've cooled down a bit. Once they have cooled, break apart the pieces and they are ready to serve.

Use tongs to toss together all the remaining ingredients in a large bowl, making sure that the endive and pears are coated with the oil and vinegar. Divide among four plates and garnish with the candied pecans.

## ROASTED FENNEL AND HAZELNUT SALAD WITH SHALLOT DRESSING

SERVES 4 TO 6

🌀 🌀 🌀

**TIME:** 1 HOUR 30 MINUTES, MOSTLY INACTIVE

*This salad wins prizes for prettiness, taste, and longest name in this book. We couldn't help ourselves here; every component in this salad comes together to create a party in your mouth and therefore deserves a mention. The complex licorice flavor of roasted fennel along with the crunch of roasted hazelnuts and chewy tang of dried cranberries stars in this festive salad that's great for any special fall, winter, or everyday occasion. Make sure to allow the fennel and shallots adequate roasting time to ensure that their deep, sweet flavors really develop.*

**Roasted vegetables:**

2 heads fennel, sliced into ¼-inch-thick chunks
3 large shallots, peeled and sliced in half
2 tablespoons olive oil
Salt
Several pinches freshly ground black pepper

**Salad:**

1 small head of chicory, washed and torn into bite-size pieces

¾ cup hazelnuts, roasted, skins removed (see tip page 263) and chopped coarsely

¾ cup dried cranberries

**Dressing:**

¼ cup olive oil

2 tablespoons hazelnut oil, walnut oil, or more olive oil

¼ cup champagne vinegar or white wine vinegar

2 tablespoons pure maple syrup

½ teaspoon dried tarragon

½ teaspoon dried thyme

Pinch of freshly grated nutmeg

1 teaspoon salt

**tip**

➤ Just like spinach, chicory can be quite sandy, so be sure to wash thoroughly.

PREHEAT THE oven to 375°F. Place the sliced fennel on large baking sheet, rub with 2 tablespoons of the olive oil, a pinch of salt, and some ground black pepper. Rub the shallots with a little extra oil and place in the corner of the baking sheet. Bake the vegetables for 20 to 25 minutes until the edges of the fennel are browned and the shallot is starting to caramelize. Remove from the oven and set aside to cool.

To make the dressing: In a food processor, combine the roasted shallots, olive oil, hazelnut oil, vinegar, maple syrup, tarragon, thyme, nutmeg, and salt. Blend until creamy, pour into a container, cover, and chill until ready to use.

Assemble the salad by placing the chicory, roasted fennel, hazelnuts, and cranberries in a large bowl. Pour in the dressing, add a twist of freshly ground pepper, and toss with salad tongs until everything is completely coated. Serve immediately.

# PORTOBELLO SALAD WITH SPICY MUSTARD DRESSING

SERVES 4 AS A MAIN OR 8 AS A SIDE SALAD

TIME: 45 MINUTES, INCLUDING MUSHROOM COOKING TIME

*This is a staple salad at Isa headquarters. It's got everything a vegan needs to feel healthy and happy: chickpeas, greens, avocado, and mushrooms. The mustard makes the dressing nice and creamy with just a little kick. The roasted portobello recipe is for two mushrooms, but like we say in those directions, you can make four for a more elegant presentation if you're trying to impress someone. You can also add other salad-y things to this; a few sprouts never hurt anyone . . . yet.*

**Dressing:**

¼ cup prepared spicy, smooth mustard

3 tablespoons grapeseed oil

¼ cup red wine vinegar

2 tablespoons pure maple syrup

**Salad:**

8 cups mixed greens (whatever you like—we prefer crunchy things like radicchio and romaine; throw in some arugula scraps for good measure)

1 avocado, peeled, halved, pitted, and sliced thinly

1 small red onion, sliced into very thin half-moons

1 (15-ounce) can chickpeas, drained and rinsed

1 recipe Roasted Portobellos (2 mushrooms) (page 112)

*Prepare the dressing:*

Whisk all ingredients together in a small bowl. Done.

*Prepare the salad:*

Throw together all the ingredients except the portobellos, in a large mixing bowl. Pour on the dressing and use tongs to toss.

When ready to serve, place the dressed greens on plate and add the sliced, warm portobellos. That's all there is to it!

## AUTUMN ROOT SALAD WITH WARM MAPLE-FIG DRESSING

SERVES 4

🕙 Ⓖ 🖥

TIME: 1 HOUR 30 MINUTES, MOSTLY INACTIVE

*This is a classy start to an autumn dinner. You'll love the combination of earthy beets and purple potatoes, creamy sweet potatoes, and the tart sweetness of Maple-Fig Dressing. The field greens add a fresh touch and we like the texture they get as they wilt from the dressing. There are several steps, but the recipe isn't difficult and the active cooking time is minimal. Roast the beets first and, about twenty minutes before they are done cooking, prepare the yams and blue potatoes.*

### Vegetables

3 small loose beets (1 pound)
3 small sweet potatoes (1 pound), peeled
3 small purple potatoes (1 pound), peeled
A little olive or grapeseed oil
About 6 cups of field greens

*tip*

➤ To have this salad on the table in no time, prepare the beets and potatoes a day in advance and keep wrapped up in the fridge.

### Dressing:

1 tablespoon olive oil
2 cloves garlic, chopped
½ cup shallots, chopped coarsely
1 cup chopped dried mission figs
¼ cup white cooking wine
¼ teaspoon salt
½ cup water
¼ cup pure maple syrup
1 tablespoon Dijon mustard
2 teaspoons white balsamic vinegar (regular balsamic is okay, too, but try the white stuff—you'll be hooked)

*Prepare the beets:*

Preheat the oven to 425°F. Scrub the beets well and wrap in aluminum foil. Roast until tender, about 75 to 80 minutes. To make sure they're ready, unwrap one beet and stick a butter knife through the top. It should slice through the beet with no problem. Unwrap the beets and let them sit until cool to the touch, then refrigerate. Once chilled, slice into ½-inch-thick slices.

*Prepare the yams and purple potatoes:*

Slice the yams and potatoes widthwise at an angle into ½-inch-thick pieces. Place in a large, broad, lidded pan (not a pot) and cover with cold water and a sprinkle of salt. Cover the pan and bring to a boil, then simmer until the yams and potatoes are tender but still firm, 8 to 10 minutes. Use tongs to flip them once. When they are ready, drain them in a large colander and spread them out on a large plate to cool. Sprinkle with a little grapeseed or olive oil, then wrap and place in the refrigerator to chill.

*Prepare the dressing:*

Preheat a small saucepan over medium-low heat. Sauté the garlic and shallots in the oil for about 3 minutes. Add the figs and wine, cover, and bring to a simmer. When the wine has mostly evaporated (about 3 minutes), add the salt, water, and maple syrup. Cover and simmer for another 3 minutes. Turn off the heat and mix in the mustard and vinegar. Let it sit for a few minutes, stirring occasionally, then transfer the dressing to a blender and puree it until smooth. You may need to add a few tablespoons of water if it is too thick to puree; it depends on how much of the water evaporated. Serve warm, or refrigerate and reheat when ready to serve. To heat it, gently warm in a saucepan over low heat, adding a few splashes of water if necessary.

*To serve:*

In a large bowl, use tongs to mix the greens with about half of the dressing. Reserve the rest to dollop on the vegetables after they have been arranged.

On each plate, make a circle with slices of the vegetables. It looks nice using 3 or 4 beets, then 3 or 4 yams, then 3 or 4 blue potatoes. You can also alternate the vegetables. Drizzle the reserved dressing over the vegetables. Place the greens on top in the center, leaving the beets, yams, and potatoes peeking out from underneath.

## SHREDDED PARSNIP AND BEET SALAD IN PINEAPPLE VINAIGRETTE

SERVES 6

**TIME:** 50 MINUTES

*This salad is magical. At first blush, the ingredients look a little insane, but once it comes together it is out-of-control delicious; earthy, sweet, and fragrant. Oh, and it's raw! People like raw. You can serve it as a little accompaniment to a sammich, the same way you might serve coleslaw, or by itself as a dinner by placing it over a handful of mixed salad greens: drizzle the greens with some of the dressing and then plop a mound of the salad*

*over that. If you would like to make it a meal, add Tangerine Baked Tofu or tempeh.*

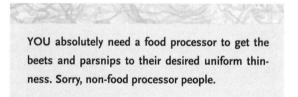

**YOU** absolutely need a food processor to get the beets and parsnips to their desired uniform thinness. Sorry, non-food processor people.

**Pineapple dressing:**

> 2 cups pineapple juice
> ⅓ cup red wine vinegar
> ¼ cup grapeseed oil
> 2 tablespoons pure maple syrup or agave nectar (you can also dissolve 2 tablespoons sugar into it if you have neither ingredient)
> 1 clove garlic, grated with a microplane grater or very well minced
> ¼ teaspoon salt

**Salad:**

> 1 pound beets, peeled and shredded (about 3 average size)
> 1 pound parsnips, peeled and shredded (about 2 average size)
> ½ cup coarsely chopped fresh mint

WHISK together all the dressing ingredients in a large mixing bowl.

Add the shredded beets and parsnips, using tongs to thoroughly mix them into the dressing. Let the veggies sit and macerate for about 15 minutes. Add the mint and mix again. Cover and refrigerate for at least 30 minutes until ready to eat.

## CREAMY ASIAN PEAR AND TEMPEH SALAD WITH WASABI DRESSING

SERVES 4

TIME: 35 MINUTES, PLUS CHILLING TIME

*Light, refreshing, a little sweet, and piquant, this is an excellent salad during the dog days of summer. Asian pears (also called Korean pears) are very large, round, sand-colored pears with a unique, snappy crunch and a hint of fruity, white winelike flavor. Any pear can be substituted, but do try to make this just once with Asian pears. Look for them wherever Asian produce or groceries are sold. Serve with rice crackers or rice cakes.*

**tip**

➤ Not all wasabi powders are created equal. Some are more flavorful than others; use a reliable brand (ask your Asian grocer which brand he or she recommends) or you might have to add quite a bit to properly season the dressing. Purists might also want to avoid brands that contain green artificial coloring.

➤ We like the flavor of Silken Mayo Dressing for this salad, but you can also use you favorite commercially prepared vegan mayo. We've suggested using less of the prepared kind because it tends to be very rich. If you find it so, try watering it down it a little bit of soy milk or soy creamer before adding to the other dressing ingredients.

1 (8-ounce) package tempeh, diced
½ cup small, sweet fresh or frozen green peas
2 teaspoons soy sauce

1 scallion, sliced very thinly
1 Asian pear or other firm, crisp pear, pitted and cut into ½-inch dice (about 2 cups)
1 cup Silken Mayo Dressing (page 92), or ⅔ cup commercially prepared vegan mayo
1½–2 teaspoons wasabi powder
2 teaspoons lime juice

IN A steamer basket, steam the tempeh for 10 minutes. Add the peas and steam for another 3 to 4 minutes, until the peas are bright green and tender. Remove from the steamer, sprinkle with soy sauce, and toss into a large bowl with the scallion. Allow to cool for a few minutes. Crush the cubes of tempeh a little with your hands and toss in the diced pear.

In a small bowl, whisk together the Silken Mayo Dressing or mayonnaise, wasabi powder, and lime juice. Taste and adjust the spice level with more wasabi if necessary.

Pour the dressing over the tempeh mixture, stir to combine everything, and place in an airtight container. Chill for at least 30 minutes or overnight, to allow the flavors to blend.

## PROSPECT PARK POTATO SALAD

MAKES A BOATLOAD

TIME: 50 MINUTES, PLUS TIME TO CHILL

*The perfect potato salad for any family reunion or general food fight. The mustard gives it a cool yellow color, with little bits of green dill. We love how the cucumbers taste like pickles when the salad has been sitting around for awhile. This recipe really does make a lot, so if not taking to a picnic or family reunion, you might want to halve it.*

5 pounds white potatoes, peeled and washed
1 seedless cucumber, sliced into small, thin pieces

1 cup Vegenaise

¼ cup Dijon mustard (whole-grain is best)

¼ cup olive oil

⅓ cup distilled white vinegar

2 tablespoons sugar

1 tablespoon dried dill

1 teaspoon turmeric

1½ teaspoons salt, or to taste

1 teaspoon ground black pepper, or to taste

1 large carrot, peeled

SLICE THE potatoes so that they are somewhere between ¼ and ½ inch thick. If very large potatoes, cut them into thirds lengthwise, then slice. If smaller ones, just cut them in half and slice. But it's nice to have different sizes because small bits fall apart and become part of the dressing, while most maintain their shape.

Place the potatoes in a very large pot and fill with water, about 4 inches or so above the tops of the potatoes. Boil for about 15 minutes, keeping an eye on them. Check that you can pierce one easily with a fork, but be careful not to overcook them; you want them to be tender but still firm and not falling apart.

Meanwhile, prepare the dressing: In a very large mixing bowl (big enough to add the potatoes later on), mix the vegan mayonnaise, mustard, olive oil, sugar, vinegar, dill, turmeric, salt, and pepper. Whisk briskly. Add the cucumber and place in the fridge until the potatoes are ready.

When the potatoes are done, drain them into a colander and give them a quick rinse under cold water. Shake the colander so that all the potatoes are rinsed. Let them cool for about 15 minutes.

Add the potatoes to the dressing and use a wooden spoon to mix and coat them. Grate the carrot directly into the salad and mix. Carrots are an essential ingredient because they add sweetness, so don't leave them out and don't chop them; they have to be grated. Taste for salt and pepper, and refrigerate until chilled.

Once good and cold, taste for seasoning one last time, and serve.

# BROOKLYN DELI MACARONI SALAD

SERVES 8 TO 10

TIME: 30 MINUTES, PLUS CHILLING TIME

*This is another classic salad that would be great for any picnic or barbecue situation. It is prepared how we like it, but people tend to be very particular about their macaroni salad, so make it once this way and then see if you want to add any extra veggies or use more Vegenaise.*

tip

> To quickly thaw your peas, run them under hot water for about 30 seconds.

### Dressing:

¾ cups Vegenaise

¼ cup white vinegar

1 tablespoon sugar

¾ teaspoon salt

Several pinches of freshly ground black pepper

### Salad:

½ cup frozen peas, thawed

2 average-size red radishes, grated

2 average-size carrots, peeled and grated

1 (1-pound) package elbow macaroni (about 3 cups)

*Prepare the dressing:*

Combine all the dressing ingredients in a large mixing bowl. Mix with a fork until completely blended.

Add the radishes, carrots, and peas, and set aside while you cook the macaroni.

Boil the macaroni in salted water. Drain and rinse under cold water until the macaroni is still warm but not too hot to the touch. Transfer the macaroni to the salad bowl that contains the dressed vegetables and toss to coat. Cover and refrigerate. Wait until the salad is cold to see if it needs more salt or pepper. Stir the salad a few times when it is in the fridge to make sure that the dressing coats everything.

# DRESSINGS

DRESSING are to salads what arm warmers are to t-shirts. Unless you hate arm warmers. What would a chapter about salads be without a note on dressings?

When it comes to salad dressings we like to keep it simple:

1. Make them fresh.
2. Make just enough for what is needed at the moment.
3. Use the best possible oils, vinegars, and herbs.
4. Season with salt and pepper to taste.

The best way to serve the following dressings is to place the greens and other vegetables in a large bowl, pour on the dressing, and use tongs to toss for at least a minute. This method ensures all the salad is evenly coated and is way better than leaving a pool of dressing on top with none below.

We love the light texture and neutral flavor of grapeseed oil in most of these salad dressings. Other great oils to use are avocado, almond, walnut, and hazelnut. Use olive oil only when the strong olive flavor is desirable. With the exception of Silken Mayo Dressing, we make these to order and use them up immediately.

## SILKEN MAYO DRESSING

MAKES APPROXIMATELY 1½ CUPS

**TIME:** 10 MINUTES, PLUS CHILLING TIME

*This is a simple, creamy, go-to basic salad dressing that's receptive to dozens of variations. It's thinner than commercially prepared vegan mayonnaise but still can be used on sandwiches, as a dip for fresh veggies, on steamed veggies, or as a base for many dressings.*

> This dressing really needs to be chilled for at least 30 minutes before using, to allow the flavors to meld. Also, homemade mayonnaise doesn't keep for very long; use within 3 days.

> For best results, use fresh, refrigerated silken tofu. Avoid the vacuum box–packed variety when making this recipe.

1 pound fresh silken tofu (not the vacuum-packed kind)
3 tablespoons brown rice vinegar or other mild white vinegar
3 tablespoons grapeseed, avocado, or almond oil
2 tablespoons agave nectar or pure maple syrup

**2 teaspoons salt, or to taste**

**¼ teaspoon ground white pepper**

**¼ teaspoon mustard powder**

BLEND ALL the ingredients in a blender until creamy, scraping down the sides with a rubber spatula to make sure you get everything. Taste to adjust the salt and spices. Chill for at least 30 minutes before using. Keep in a tightly covered container in the refrigerator.

*Variations:*

Silken Aioli Dressing: Use extra-virgin olive oil in place of grapeseed oil and fresh lemon juice in place of the vinegar, and blend in 3 to 4 garlic cloves until smooth.

Silken Tarragon-Lemon Dressing: From the aioli above, reduce the garlic to 1 clove and add 2 tablespoons of finely chopped tarragon

Dijonaisse: Add 2 tablespoons of Dijon mustard.

Thousand Island Dressing: Add 2 tablespoons of ketchup plus 1 tablespoon of pickle relish.

Creamy Pesto: Add 2 to 3 tablespoons of basil pesto.

Creamy Olive Dressing: Add ¼ cup of pitted black or kalamata olives.

Herbed Dressing: Add 2 to 3 tablespoons of any fresh herb: chopped cilantro, chives, parsley, mint, or dill.

# SUPER-SIMPLE DRESSINGS

THE following dressings are simple oil-based dressings that can service two to four servings of salad. (Think two if it's a dinner salad and four if it's a side.) Make them on the spot and use them right away.

## MAPLE-MUSTARD DRESSING

SERVES 2 TO 4

**TIME:** LESS THAN 10 MINUTES

**3 tablespoons pure maple syrup**

**2 tablespoons apple cider vinegar**

**2 tablespoons Dijon or whole grain prepared mustard**

**3 tablespoons grapeseed or nut oil**

**½ teaspoon mustard powder**

**Salt and freshly ground pepper**

WHISK ALL the ingredients together and store in an airtight container. Keep refrigerated until ready to use.

## MISO TAHINI DRESSING

SERVES 2 TO 4

**TIME:** LESS THAN 10 MINUTES

*How can just two ingredients and a little water taste so amazing? This dressing is based on an old standby that Terry used to whip up in her chef days long gone. It's perfect not just on fresh crisp greens but pored on steamed veggies, any grain or simply seasoned and baked tofu.*

*It's really good as is, but if you're feeling experimental a clove of chopped garlic, a little lemon juice or a twist of freshly ground black pepper can jazz things up a bit.*

¼ cup white, sweet miso

¼ cup tahini

⅓ cup or more warm water

IN A medium bowl with a large spoon, blend miso and tahini together to form a creamy paste. Slowly pour in warm water, gently whisking a little a time till a creamy dressing forms. If thinner dressing is desired, dribble in a little more water. The dressing will thicken if allowed to sit a while. Keep refrigerated until ready to use.

## MEDITERRANEAN OLIVE OIL AND LEMON VINAIGRETTE

SERVES 2 TO 4

TIME: 10 MINUTES

⅓ cup olive oil

¼ cup fresh lemon juice

3 cloves garlic, pressed or minced finely

1 teaspoon dried oregano

1 teaspoon dried thyme

1 teaspoon dried basil

½ teaspoon salt

Freshly ground pepper

WHISK ALL the ingredients together and store in an airtight container. Keep refrigerated until ready to use.

## SESAME DRESSING

SERVES 2 TO 4

TIME: LESS THAN 10 MINUTES

*A nice all-purpose dressing for Asian-themed green salads.*

3 tablespoons rice vinegar

¼ cup grapeseed or other light-flavored oil

1 tablespoon mirin or rice wine

2 teaspoons toasted sesame oil

1 tablespoon soy sauce

2 teaspoons sugar

1 tablespoon crushed sesame seeds

WHISK ALL the ingredients together and store in an airtight container. Keep refrigerated until ready to use.

## RASPBERRY-LIME VINAIGRETTE

SERVES 2 TO 4

TIME: 10 MINUTES

*A pretty, brilliant magenta dressing with a fresh and bold fruity flavor. Serve with the most tender, young salad greens you can find, or with chunks of ripe mango on a bed of arugula.*

12 ounces frozen raspberries, thawed

¼ cup grapeseed oil or nut oil

3 tablespoons lime juice

1½ teaspoons sugar

½ teaspoon salt

Pinch of grated lime zest

Ground white pepper

USE A large spoon to press the thawed raspberries in several batches through a large sieve into a medium-size bowl. Discard the seeds. Add the remaining ingredients, whisk to combine, and pour into an airtight container if not using immediately.

# SAMMICHES

OTHERWISE KNOWN BY most people as "sandwiches," sammiches are the miracle of modern food technology. They are simultaneously a finger food and a whole meal, loved by the young, old, and in between. We take them most seriously here in the *Veganomicon* and we're not afraid to pile on the good stuff, such as roasted vegetables, seared seitan, crunchy salads, and only the best bread we can get our hands on. These might take a little more work than your average PB&J, but they're no big cyclopean (huge, ancient, and made out of stone) effort.

# BAJA-STYLE GRILLED TEMPEH TACOS

SERVES 4 TO 6

**TIME:** 80 MINUTES, LOTS OF IT INACTIVE

*If we ever decided to drop out of cookbook-writing society completely and become surfer dudettes, we would eat these amazing tacos every single day, without even bothering to change out of our wet suits first. Beer and chile–marinated tempeh is first slapped onto the grill (or fried in a cast-iron pan), then lovingly stuffed into steamy corn tortillas, topped with a bright and tangy mayo-free coleslaw, and drenched with luscious lime crema dressing. It's a perfect, light, summer meal, or even if you just want to pretend it's summer. Best served with an ice-cold Mexican beer.*

## tip

➤ There are a few components to this recipe that need to marinate for about an hour each—half hour if you're desperate—but putting these together is a snap. Better yet, make the slaw (save some time and look for preshredded cabbage in the produce aisle) and marinate the tempeh overnight for best results. More than likely, you'll have marinade and slaw to spare, so why not marinate an additional batch of steamed tempeh while you're at it?

➤ Use Sour Cilantro Cream (page 209) in place of the lime crema. Thin it out slightly with additional lime juice or soy milk so that it's the consistency of a thick salad dressing.

➤ Leftover tempeh, lime crema, and garnishes make an amazing "taco" salad served with salad greens and crunchy tortilla chip strips.

### Taco slaw:

3 heaping cups finely shredded purple or white cabbage (10–12 ounces), or a mix of both

1 carrot, shredded finely

¼ cup apple cider vinegar

2 pickled jalapeños, diced finely

1 teaspoon salt

A few twists of freshly ground black pepper

### For the Lime Crema:

¾ cup plain soy yogurt

3 tablespoons lime juice

2 tablespoons grapeseed oil or avocado oil

⅓ cup lightly packed fresh cilantro leaves

½ teaspoon salt

### Chile-Beer Marinade:

¾ cup beer, pilsner or ale style (Mexican preferred)

2 cloves garlic, crushed

2 tablespoons peanut oil

2 tablespoons soy sauce

2 tablespoons lime juice

2–3 teaspoons chile powder (premixed or mix your own with ancho, poblano or chipotle powders)

½ teaspoon ground cumin

1 (8-ounce) package tempeh

12–16 soft, white corn tortillas

### Garnishes (use one or more):

Red radishes, sliced paper thin

Fresh tomato, seeded and diced

Pickled jalapeños, sliced

Your favorite Mexican-style hot sauce

Avocado, sliced or diced

PREPARE THE slaw first: Mix all the ingredients well in a large glass or plastic bowl; don't use metal. Either leave in the bowl or transfer to narrower, cylindrical container, such as a 1-pint plastic takeout container. Cover the top of the container loosely with plastic wrap, press it down on top of slaw, and place in fridge.

Weight down the slaw with something heavy, such as cans of beans or a full pickle jar. Allow the slaw to press for minimum an hour. Slaw improves the longer it's allowed to mellow. When ready to use, squeeze out handfuls to release any excess juice.

## Make the lime crema:

Blend all ingredients in a blender until creamy and smooth. Add more salt or limejuice to taste, if desired. Pour into an airtight container and chill for an hour.

## Make the marinade:

Whisk all the ingredients together and pour into a glass pie plate or casserole dish.

## Prepare the tempeh:

Bring a 2-quart pot of water to a boil. Slice the tempeh into three pieces lengthwise, then slice each in half horizontally through the middle. When the water is boiling, add the tempeh, lower heat and simmer for 10 minutes. Use tongs to remove the tempeh and then immediately place the pieces in the marinade dish. Marinate for 1 hour, flipping them every now and again to cover every surface.

Preheat the oven to 200°F. Preheat a greased grill pan (brush well with peanut oil or use a high-heat grill spray) over medium-high heat. Or, prepare a heavy skillet with enough peanut oil to lightly coat its surface, and preheat it.

Grill or fry each side of the tempeh pieces for 5 minutes. When each side is almost done, spoon some of the marinade over the tempeh and let it cook for 30 more seconds. Remove the tempeh from the heat and slice into thin strips. Keep warm, covered in foil in the oven while preparing and assembling tacos. Continue to heat your cast-iron grill or heavy skillet once the tempeh is done. Use a new cast iron skillet if your cast iron is too sticky, or wipe it down with a paper towel to continue.

## To assemble the tacos:

Create a taco assembly line: tortillas, lime crema, slaw, sliced grilled tempeh, and garnishes. Heat a corn tortilla on the grill for 30 seconds, then flip the tortilla over and heat until it has become soft and pliable. Repeat with a second tortilla and arrange both, slightly overlapping, on a serving dish. We like to use two tortillas per taco (helps with piling on the fillings), but you can make smaller tacos using just one tortilla. If not serving immediately, stack the hot tortillas, wrap them tightly in foil, and keep them warm in the oven. Then, spread a little lime crema down the center of the tortillas, pile on some slaw, and top with the tempeh and then with any garnish you like. Drizzle on extra lime crema and hot sauce, if desired. Fold and eat.

## BLACK BEAN BURGERS

MAKES 6

TIME: 30 MINUTES

*Here's a nice, wholesome Southwestern black bean burger. Everything's been kept fairly simple so that you can top it with all sorts of things—cilantro sour cream (page 209), tropical salsa, guacamole, or all of the above. Plain old ketchup is fine, too. Also include your good friends lettuce, tomato, and red onion. Did we mention that these freeze well, too? Once cooked, pack them in a resealable plastic bag with sheets of waxed paper to separate them, then reheat in the oven at 350°F for about 25 to 30 minutes.*

2 cups cooked or 1 (15-ounce) can black beans, drained and rinsed

½ cup vital wheat gluten

½ cup plain whole wheat bread crumbs

1 teaspoon chile powder

½ teaspoon cumin

¼ cup water

1 tablespoon tomato paste (or ketchup)

¼ cup finely chopped cilantro (optional)

2 cloves garlic

½ small onion

About 2 tablespoons olive oil plus olive oil spray

Whole wheat buns

MASH THE beans with a fork in a mixing bowl. You don't want to puree them; just get them mashed so that no whole beans are left, but you should leave some half beans.

Add the wheat gluten, bread crumbs, chile powder, cumin, water, and tomato paste (and cilantro, if using), but don't mix yet. Use a microplane grater to grate the garlic in. (A garlic press or very well minced garlic works, too.) Use the large holes on a box grater to grate in the onion.

Mix everything together with a fork, and then proceed to knead with your hands, until the mixture is firm and uniformly mixed (about a minute).

Preheat a heavy-bottomed pan over medium heat.

Divide the burger mixture into six equal pieces. Roll each piece into a firm ball. Use your palm to press the ball down on a clean surface to form a patty that is about 1½ inch thick. Press so that the patty is flat on both sides. Make six patties.

Pour a thin layer of olive oil into the pan. Cook the patties three at a time for 5 minutes on each side, gently but firmly pressing down on them with a spatula. Spray with olive oil before turning over, for uniform browning. Once cooked, the patties should be very firm when you press down on them.

Serve warm on burger buns.

## SNOBBY JOES

SERVES 4 TO 6

TIME: 60 MINUTES

*Every vegan cookbook needs a sloppy joe recipe with the name changed around a bit, right? Well, this is ours: those sloppy joes we loved as a child, but made with lentils. Snobby Joe thinks he's better than all the other Joes because he doesn't have any meat.*

1 cup uncooked lentils

4 cups water

1 tablespoon olive oil

1 medium-size yellow onion, cut into small dice

1 green bell pepper, seeded and cut into small dice

2 cloves garlic, minced

3 tablespoons chile powder

2 teaspoons dried oregano

1 teaspoon salt

1 (8-ounce) can tomato sauce

¼ cup tomato paste

2–3 tablespoons maple syrup

1 tablespoon prepared yellow mustard

4–6 kaiser rolls or sesame buns, sliced in half horizontally

POUR THE lentils and water into a small saucepan. Cover and bring to a boil. Once the mixture is boiling, lower the heat and simmer for about 20 minutes, until the lentils are soft. Drain and set aside.

About 10 minutes before the lentils are done, preheat a medium-size saucepan over medium heat. Sauté the onion and pepper in the oil for about 7 minutes, until softened. Add the garlic and sauté for a minute more.

Stir in the cooked lentils, chile powder, oregano, and salt. Add the tomato sauce and tomato paste. Cook for about 10 minutes. Add the maple syrup to taste and the mustard, and heat through.

Turn off the heat and let the pot sit for about 10 minutes, so that the flavors can meld, or go ahead and eat immediately if you can't wait. We like to serve these open faced, a scoop of Snobby Joe on each slice of bun.

## BEANBALL SUB

MAKES 4

TIME: 40 MINUTES

*This is a conglomeration of a few recipes from the cookbook that also would make great use of leftover Beanballs (page 189). We throw in a handful of spinach just for posterity; you need not be so healthy if you don't feel like it. Also, if you don't want to make the Pine Nut Cream (page 164) and just want to use soy cheese, we won't judge you. These would be perfect for a Super Bowl party, or since you are vegan and hate football, a Nobel Prize party. Ooh, we can't wait to see who wins for physics this year!*

1 recipe Beanballs (page 189)

1 recipe (4 cups) Marinara Sauce, or any of the variations (page 205)

1 recipe Pine Nut Cream (page 164)

4 hoagie rolls, split open

2 cups fresh spinach leaves, well washed

PREPARE THE recipes of the first three components. Preheat oven to 350° F. Place Beanballs on a tray and top with about 1 cup of marinara and all of the pine nut cream. Bake for 20 to 25 minutes, until pine nut cream is lightly browned. Spread more marinara sauce on one side of each roll and distribute the Beanballs evenly among the sammiches, layering the spinach leaves over them. Top liberally with more marinara sauce. Close your sammiches, slice in half on the diagonal, and serve.

## CHILE CORNMEAL-CRUSTED TOFU PO' BOY

SERVES 4

*This is another sammich that uses various recipes from this cookbook. Crusted tofu and creamy coleslaw meet a spicy chipotle mayo and a pickle. We know that po' boys usually don't have pickles, so save your e-mails! We just can't resist them.*

1 recipe Chile Cornmeal-Crusted Tofu (page 125)

1 recipe Creamy Coleslaw (page 102)

Chipotle Mayo (page 101)

Sandwich pickles

2 (12-inch) loaves of French bread, sliced in half and split open

PREPARE THE recipes of the components. Spread mayo on the bottom halves of the bread and place the tofu, then the coleslaw, then the pickles on the bread. Spread some mayo onto the top half of the bread, close the sammiches, slice in half on the diagonal, and serve.

## ROASTED EGGPLANT AND SPINACH MUFFULETTA SANDWICH

SERVES 4

**TIME:** 45 MINUTES, PLUS 3 HOURS MARINATING TIME

*Only olive lovers need apply! This monster-size, New Orleans classic sandwich is drenched in a luscious multi-olive "salad" that—thanks to a long steep in the fridge—penetrates every succulent inch. The original is a medley of meat products; our version is stuffed to near-bursting with roasted eggplant, sweet peppers, and fresh sweet spinach. Take this sturdy sandwich along to your next picnic or the beach, or drop (wrapped very tightly) into a backpack for a long bike ride. The longer it sits in a chilled environment, the better it will taste. It's really a meal in of itself but would be really nice with a little sangria and veggie crudités.*

**Mixed Olive Salad Relish:**

> 1 cup pitted kalamata olives
> 1 cup pitted green olives
> ½ cup coarsely chopped Italian parsley
> 4 cloves pickled garlic
> ½ cup sun-dried tomatoes, oil-packed or dried and reconstituted (about 10 tomatoes)
> 4 teaspoons red wine or white balsamic vinegar
> 1 teaspoon dried, crumbled rosemary
> 1 teaspoon dried, crumbled thyme
> 1 teaspoon celery seed
> 1 teaspoon dried, crumbled oregano
> 1 teaspoon dried, crumbled basil
> ½ cup extra-virgin olive oil

**Sandwiches:**

> 1 smallish eggplant (less than 1 pound)
> 3 tablespoons extra-virgin olive oil
> 1 tablespoon red wine vinegar
> 3 cups fresh spinach leaves, washed and spun dry

> 2 roasted red or yellow peppers, from a jar or homemade
> 1 (9- to 10-inch) round peasant-style loaf (about 1– 1½ pounds)

Preheat the oven to 375°F degrees. Lightly grease a rimmed baking sheet. Cut the eggplant widthwise into ¼-inch slices and rub each slice with kosher salt. Allow to drain in a colander for half an hour.

*Prepare the relish while the eggplant is draining:*

Place the olives, parsley, garlic, and sun-dried tomatoes in a large bowl. Toss with the vinegar and dried herbs. With a food processor, chop the mixture in 2 or 3 batches, adding some of the olive oil with each batch and pouring into the processor bowl. Process only enough to chop up the olives and tomatoes; stop often and use a rubber spatula to move the stuff around. The idea is to create not a paste of olives but a chunky mixture. Scrape the relish, along with the remaining olive oil, into an airtight container.

Place the spinach leaves in a large bowl (you can use the one that once held the olives). Sprinkle with 1 tablespoon red wine vinegar.

**tip**

> ➤ Use only high-quality, peasant-style bread with a thick, crisp crust. Anything less than that will disintegrate. Sourdough is particularly yummy choice for this sandwich.

> ➤ Use garlic-stuffed green olives to eliminate the additional pickled garlic. Try adding a tablespoon of capers or a few cut-up hot pickled peppers, too.

> ➤ Leftover olive relish is dynamite on pizza.

*Roast the eggplant slices:*

Rinse the salted slices with cold water, rub with olive oil, and lay in a baking sheet (some overlapping is okay). Roast in the preheated oven for 20 to 22 minutes, flipping once, until the eggplant is browned and tender. Place the hot eggplant slices on top of the spinach and toss to combine (the hot eggplant will slightly wilt the spinach leaves).

*Assemble the sandwich:*

Insert a thin, sharp knife into the side of the round loaf at a slightly downward angle. Cut the loaf in half, working the knife on the angle to create a shallow bread "bowl." Remove some of the bread from the bottom and top interior of the loaf to deepen the bowl (save the bread guts for crumbs or use it to nosh on leftover olive relish).

Spread the olive relish very thickly on each side of the loaf, making sure to get lots of the oil and juices onto the bread. Drizzle on a little extra olive oil if the relish looks a little dry. Layer the bottom with eggplant, spinach, roasted red peppers, more eggplant, and top with last of spinach. Replace top of the loaf and press down very firmly with your body weight on the entire sandwich; don't be afraid to smush it down. Wrap tightly in foil, then wrap again in plastic wrap or a few resealable plastic bags. Refrigerate, putting a few heavy items on top of the sandwich to help press it down even further (one or two unopened boxes of soy milk work nicely). For maximum flavor, allow to sit at least 3 hours—or even better—overnight. To serve, hold the sandwich firmly and cut in half with a sharp serrated knife, then slice again into four wedges.

**tip**

➤ To make chipotle mayo, add 1 canned chipotle along with a little of its sauce to ¼ cup of veganaise and mash well with a fork.

# VIETNAMESE SEITAN BAGUETTE WITH SAVORY BROTH DIP

SERVES 4

**TIME:** 30 MINUTES
(NOT INCLUDING PREPARING SEITAN)

*We are proud to present this whimsical marriage of the traditional Vietnamese sandwich, bánh mì, and the American classic "French Dip" sandwich. While both sandwiches are traditionally a parade of meat products, our meatless version still delivers a savory bite with grilled Seitan Cutlets (page 132). The sharp fresh flavors of cucumber and cilantro then team up with a spicy dipping broth that really satisfies. How to eat? Select a corner of your sandwich; dip in broth, bite, yum, repeat, yum.*

**Dipping broth:**

2½ cups broth from the preparation of Seitan Cutlets (page 132)

4 cloves garlic, left whole with peel but gently crushed

1-inch piece ginger root, sliced into ⅛-inch pieces and gently crushed

½ teaspoon five-spice powder

1 teaspoon red pepper flakes

1½ teaspoons sugar

2 tablespoons lime juice

**Sandwiches:**

4–8 Seitan Cutlets (page 132), grilled, baked or fried, cut into thin slices

4 (6-inch) French baguette, or individual mini-baguettes

Several sprigs fresh cilantro

Red onion rings, sliced thinly

Cucumber (seedless is best), peeled and sliced into long, thin strips

Prepared vegan mayonnaise or Silken Mayo (page 92), several tablespoons per sandwich or to taste

*Prepare the broth dip first:*

In a 2-quart saucepan, combine the broth, garlic, ginger, five-spice powder, and pepper flakes. Don't cover the pan. Bring to a boil and boil for 5 minutes, then turn down heat to medium-low and simmer for another 10 minutes. Turn off the heat, stir in the sugar and lime juice, and cover the broth to keep it warm until ready to serve. You may strain the broth before serving; it's easily done by ladling individual servings through a mesh strainer into serving bowls.

*To assemble the sandwiches:*

Warm the seitan slices in a pan or keep warm in the oven until ready to use. Slice each baguette in half. Keeping one long side intact, open up and lightly toast. Spread mayonnaise on each half of the baguette and layer one side with cucumber, onion rings, and seitan slices; top with the cilantro. Close the sandwiches and press down on top to smush down a little. Holding it firmly, slice each sandwich in half on the diagonal. Serve with a small cup of hot broth.

**tip**

➤ Use a good-quality French bread for this sandwich, the kind with a crunchy, shiny crust and a chewy interior. Avoid the generic, soft, thin-crusted bread typically found in grocery store chains. It will disintegrate when the sandwich is dipped into the broth.

➤ Preparing sandwiches for a crowd? Tuck the sliced seitan into split baguettes, wrap in foil, and keep warm in the oven until showtime.

➤ Don't have any leftover broth from making seitan? Just use ready-made veggie broth plus 2 tablespoons soy sauce. Proceed as directed for making dipping broth.

# BBQ SEITAN AND CRISPY COLESLAW SANDWICH

SERVES 4

**45**

**TIME:** 45 MINUTES (NOT INCLUDING MAKING SEITAN)

*Serve this luscious and saucy sandwich to any vegan food naysayer and it will whip that bad attitude right into shape. Nobody can resist this rich and savory grilled seitan served up BBQ style with cool coleslaw and stuffed into a hearty sandwich. We were inspired to create this recipe after tasting a similar sandwich at the delightful S'nice café in Manhattan. Use any kind of sandwich roll you like, except too-soft hamburger-style buns. The recipe is designed for use with a cast-iron grill pan, but you can also use a regular cast-iron pan. Or, try an outdoor grill; just be sure to use a high-heat-sustainable nonstick spray, as the seitan has a tendency to stick on the grill. This BBQ sandwich is delightful served with thick-cut potato chips or crisp, chilled baby carrots.*

**Slaw:**

¾ cup Silken Mayo Dressing (page 92) or slaw dressing (recipe follows)

3 cups finely shredded purple or white cabbage (or a combination of both)

1 carrot, peeled and shredded finely

Pinch of dried dill (optional)

**Slaw dressing:**

¼ cup prepared vegan mayonnaise

2 tablespoons plain soy milk

1 tablespoon lemon juice

Pinch of white pepper, or to taste

Pinch of mustard powder, or to taste

1 recipe Simple Seitan (page 131), sliced into ½-inch-thick strips

1½–2 cups Backyard BBQ Sauce (page 207) or your favorite prepared BBQ sauce

**Peanut oil for grilling**

**4 large, hearty sandwich rolls or sliced baguettes**

**Vegan mayonnaise (optional)**

FIRST, PREPARE the slaw. If also creating slaw dressing, whisk together the dressing ingredients in a large plastic bowl. If using Silken Mayo Dressing, pour directly into the bowl. Add the shredded cabbage, carrot, and dill. Toss to combine with dressing, cover tightly with plastic wrap, and refrigerate until ready to use.

Pour the BBQ sauce in a pie plate or medium-size shallow bowl and keep near the stove. Heat a cast-iron grill pan over medium heat and brush generously with peanut oil. Place a layer of sliced seitan on the grill, brush with more peanut oil, and grill on each side for about 3 minutes until browned and sizzling. Use metal tongs to turn the seitan; grill in two batches. When cooked, toss the seitan in the BBQ sauce to coat.

Brush the grill with a little extra peanut oil and grill the sauce-covered seitan in two batches, turning strips once. The strips should be slightly browned and some of the edges just beginning to crisp when it's ready to remove from the pan. Place the seitan back in pie plate or bowl; if not serving right away, cover with aluminum foil and keep warm in the oven.

*To assemble the sandwiches:*

Slice the rolls in half horizontally, spread with mayonnaise, and drizzle a little extra BBQ sauce if desired. Pile the slaw generously on the bottom half of the rolls, top with seitan, and press down top half of rolls. Cut in half and serve.

# MIX
# AND MATCH

VEGETABLES • GRAINS • BEANS • TOFU, TEMPEH, AND SEITAN

IN THE BEGINNING, Cro-Veganon man (and woman) subsisted primarily on extra helpings of side dishes (potatoes, corn niblets, frozen peas, etc.) while eschewing the meat in the center of his or her plate. This was called dinner. Then, he/she evolved, developing taste buds and culinary skills (even some of the Cro-Veganon's more carnivorous brethren started to get the drift that eating meat ain't cool). More and more palatable and interesting faux meat options began to appear. The former empty spot in the middle of that dinner dish could once again be claimed by these wondrous, newfangled delights. Suddenly the great plains of the supermarket and grocery store were flooded with herds of veggies burgers, tofu dogs, dairy-free cheeses, and soy kielbasa (yes, it's out there if you want it). And all was good.

Well, sort of. While we are happy that all of this stuff exists these days, we found ourselves really wanting just good, home-cooked food that didn't start its life in a factory or mystery vat of chemicals. So the answer became clear: bring the side dishes back from the sidelines and make them the main event in a meal! It's easy, fun, and completely delicious to make a nutritious meal out of a balanced arrangement of grains, beans, vegetables, and the "holy trinity" of tofu, tempeh, and homemade seitan.

Simply select a vegetable side and a grain side, and then choose between a bean or any member of the holy trinity to complete the meal.

For your ease and convenience, we've divided this chapter into four sections. "Vegetables" features recipes for all vegetables green, red, orange, and leafy. "Grains" are the traditional sides, sometimes with less common but still delicious grains, which provide the necessary balance and heartiness that meatless meals often require. "Beans" is all about this basic, protein-rich, filling, and economical staple. Lastly, we give essential recipes for making great tofu, tempeh, and fabulous homemade seitan ("meat" made out of wheat gluten).

# VEGETABLES

## BABY BOK CHOY WITH CRISPY SHALLOTS AND SESAME SEEDS

SERVES 4

*We can't deny that baby bok choy is our favorite Asian veggie. It looks like a cute little vase made of green leaves, and the flavor and texture is that of a very sweet, juicy white cabbage. We try to find reasons to eat as much of it as possible, not just a piece or two tossed in a stir-fry. So with that in mind, this is our favorite way to quickly prepare bok choy on a weeknight: lightly braised, topped with crispy brown shallots and a little bit of sesame. Perfect alongside a mound of Wasabi Mashed Potatoes (page 110).*

1 pound baby bok choy (smaller the better)

2 small shallots, peeled and sliced into very thin rings

½-inch cube fresh ginger, peeled and grated

2 tablespoons peanut oil

1 tablespoon mirin or apple juice

1 tablespoon soy sauce

1 tablespoon roasted sesame seeds

SLICE OFF the stubby base of the bok choy from the white, thick bottoms. If the bok choy is longer than 3 to 4 inches, slice the stems once or twice into large chunks. Place the bok choy in a large bowl or salad spinner, fill the bowl with water, and slosh the bok choy around to clean (it can be a little sandy, so do this a few times). Drain and shake off any excess water (if using salad spinner, give it a spin). Set aside.

Heat the peanut oil in a large, nonstick skillet over medium heat. Add the sliced shallots, separating them

*tip*

➤ If using regular "adult" bok choy: slice the white stems away from the leafy tops. Chop the stems into 2- to 3-inch chunks. When ready to cook the bok choy, place the chunks in the pan first and sauté them for 2 to 3 minutes, then add the green leafy parts and continue as directed.

in the pan with a slotted spatula. Fry gently in oil for 5 to 6 minutes until they're deep golden brown and crisp (it will take a while to get past the soft fried stage, then all of a sudden the shallots will start to crisp, so watch carefully so as not to burn them). Remove the shallots from the pan with a spatula or spoon and set aside onto a plate (it's okay if a few bits remain in the pan). If no oil remains in the pan, drizzle in a little extra oil.

Quickly sauté the grated ginger for 15 seconds. Add the bok choy and stir to coat with oil and ginger. Stir-fry for about 2 minutes until the green leaves start to wilt. Add the mirin and soy sauce, stir briefly, and cover the pan. Steam for 2 minutes, then remove the lid. Stir for about 30 seconds more and remove from the heat. Transfer the bok choy to a serving plate, top with the fried shallots, sprinkle with roasted sesame seeds, and serve immediately.

## SAUTÉED COLLARDS

SERVES 4

🅕 ㊺ 🖳

**TIME:** 15 MINUTES

*These collards use up the leftover marinade from the Smoky Grilled Tempeh (page 130), so make them together. You can also just replace the marinade with vegetable broth and a teaspoon each of liquid smoke and soy sauce. These greens are awesome because they aren't too oily and the marinade cooks them just right, tender enough to chew but not falling apart in your mouth. Well, that's how we like them, anyway. Use tongs to sauté everything; they are the best tool for throwing greens around in a skillet.*

    1 pound collards, pulled off the stem (see tip above)
    4 cloves garlic, minced
    1 tablespoon olive oil
    ½ cup leftover marinade from Smoky Grilled Tempeh

*tip*

> This is our favorite way to prep collards: To get rid of the tough stem without having to sit there cutting it, you can actually easily tear the leaves from the stem with your hands. Fill the sink with water, pull off the leaves, rip them into large pieces (collards are tough, they can take it), and put the leaves into the water to rinse them. No need to drain, just give them a shake before adding to the pan.

PREHEAT A large skillet over medium heat. Sauté the garlic in the olive oil for about a minute, being careful not to burn it. Add the collards and sauté for about 2 minutes. Add the marinade and cook for another 10 minutes, until the collards are tender and a deep green. If after 5 minutes they haven't shrunk considerably, then your heat is too low. Serve immediately!

## SAUTÉED SPINACH AND TOMATOES

SERVES 4

Ⓢ Ⓖ 🅕 ㊺ 🖳

**TIME:** 15 MINUTES

*This basic sautéed spinach recipe complements any Asian or Indian meal; it's perfectly yummy with Samosa Stuffed Baked Potatoes (page 60). You can also easily make this an Italian side by omitting the ginger, adding toasted pine nuts, and using olive oil instead of peanut oil.*

    1 bunch spinach, roots discarded, washed well
       (about 6 cups, loosely packed)
    2 tablespoons peanut oil
    1 small onion, chopped finely
    3 cloves garlic, minced (or more if you like!)

2 teaspoons grated fresh ginger

½ teaspoon salt, or more to taste

2 plum tomatoes, seeded and cut into a little less than ½-inch dice

Juice of ½ lemon or lime

PREHEAT A large skillet over medium-high heat. Sauté the onions in the oil for about 2 minutes. Add the garlic, ginger, and salt. Sauté for another 30 seconds or so. Add the tomatoes and sauté until moisture begins to release, about 2 minutes. Add the spinach and cook until the spinach is wilted. Add splashes of water to make the spinach cook faster without burning. Sprinkle with lemon juice and serve.

## ESCAROLE WITH CAPERS AND WHITE BEANS

SERVES 4 AS A SIDE OR 2 AS A MAIN COURSE

TIME: 20 MINUTES

*Raw escarole looks more like a lettuce than the leafy dark greens you might usually prepare, but once sautéed it has a delicate flavor and a great texture that's a nice balance between soggy and crisp. And we use "soggy" in a positive way. Serve with grilled tofu and mashed potatoes or rice, but it's hearty enough to stand as a meal on its own. We also like to sprinkle nooch (nutritional yeast, to you), but that is top secret.*

1 head escarole

1 tablespoon olive oil

6 cloves garlic, chopped

¼ teaspoon red pepper flakes

⅓ cup capers with some brine

Salt

1 cup cooked small white beans (navy or great northern are a-ok)

Lemon wedges for serving

PREHEAT A large pan over medium heat. Sauté the garlic in the olive oil for about 3 minutes, until just starting to brown. Add the red pepper flakes and cook just long enough to soften (a few seconds). Add the escarole and salt to taste, and use tongs to toss until it begins to wilt and release moisture. Add the capers and beans, and cook just until heated through, about 3 more minutes. Serve with lemon wedges.

## CORNMEAL-MASALA ROASTED BRUSSELS SPROUTS

SERVES 4–6

TIME: 50 MINUTES

*The secret behind absolutely mouthwatering Brussels sprouts is out: roasting is the only way to go. Now if "mouthwatering" and that certain vegetable don't necessarily go together in your head, then this is the technique to master. In this recipe, roasted sprouts get a huge flavor boost by dressing them up in an Indian-spiced crumbly cornmeal–chickpea flour coating. Rich and filling, these can make a meal served with Spiced Yogurt Sauce (page 212), but they also sing alongside a chickpea curry and basmati rice.*

8 tablespoons peanut oil

1–1½ pounds Brussels sprouts

⅔ cup cornmeal

3 tablespoons chickpea flour

1 teaspoon salt

1 teaspoon garam masala

½ teaspoon ground coriander

¼ teaspoon ground cumin

¼ teaspoon ground cinnamon

Pinch of cayenne

Lemon wedges (optional)

PREHEAT THE oven to 400°F. Prepare a large baking pan by pouring 2 tablespoons of peanut oil into it and spread it around the bottom of the pan.

**tip**

➤ For best results, purchase sprouts still attached to the stem; with these you'll get a delightful assortment of sprout sizes from tiny to large, and they'll be fresher, too. If you've never seen this before (looks a little like some kind of huge medieval clubbing weapon), search you local farmers' market. If using prepacked supermarket sprouts, use up to 2 pounds, cutting any really big sprouts in half.

Trim and wash the Brussels sprouts, shake off any excess water, and pat dry lightly with a clean dish towel. Slice any really huge sprouts into two pieces. Place the sprouts in a large bowl, sprinkle with a little salt, and dust with 1 tablespoon of chickpea flour, tossing to coat every sprout.

In a small bowl, mix together the cornmeal, remaining chickpea flour, salt, garam masala, coriander, cumin, and cayenne. Pour in 6 tablespoons of the peanut oil and mix together with your fingers to form crumbs. Add the Brussels sprouts, toss to coat with the oiled crumbs, and press as much of the crumb mixture as possible onto them. It's okay if some of the coating doesn't stick to the sprouts. You'll still have plenty of crumb mixture left over that will toast up brown and crisp during the baking.

Pour the coated sprouts and crumbs into the prepared pan and roll them around in the oil. Bake for 25 to 30 minutes, until the sprouts are browned and tender. Every 10 minutes or so while baking, turn the sprouts and crumbs with a wooden spoon or spatula, moving any overly browned crumbs on the edges of the pan toward the center to prevent burning.

*To serve:*

Pile the sprouts on a plate, heap a spoonful or two of crumbles on top, and squeeze a lemon wedge over the sprouts.

**Variation:**

Masala Roasted Okra: Substitute whole, fresh okra pods for the Brussels sprouts. Proceed as directed, roasting the okra until golden and tender.

## HERB-SCALLOPED POTATOES

SERVES 4

  if using yeast   if using flour

**TIME:** 60 MINUTES

*Garlic and herbs flavor these baked potato slices in a creamy sauce, perfect for serving with grilled tofu, tempeh, or seitan, or really anywhere mashed potatoes would fit in. If you absolutely hate nutritional yeast, use 3 tablespoons of flour in place of it. You can use any regular-size white potatoes, or even Yukon golds.*

**tip**

➤ If you find yourself without aluminum foil, place a baking sheet over the casserole to cover it.

➤ If you like your scalloped potatoes crispier, instead of baking in the oven for the last 15 minutes, turn on the broiler and broil them for 5 to 10 minutes, until the top is browned to your liking.

**2 pounds white potatoes (3 average-size), scrubbed, sliced into ⅛-inch-thick disks**
**¾ cups vegetable broth**

½ cup unsweetened soy milk

1 tablespoon olive oil

3 cloves garlic, minced

3 tablespoons nutritional yeast or flour

½ teaspoon dried thyme

½ teaspoon dried basil

¼ teaspoon dried rosemary

¼ teaspoon paprika

½ teaspoon salt

Several pinches of freshly ground black pepper

PREHEAT THE oven to 400°F. Lightly grease a 9 × 13-inch glass baking dish or ceramic casserole pan. If you don't have one, a metal one lined with baking parchment is fine, too.

Layer the potatoes in the pan, allowing them to slightly overlap. Lay them across the short way first, overlapping a little less than half of each potato slice. In each subsequent row, overlap the potatoes by about one-quarter of each potato slice.

Pour most of the vegetable broth over the potatoes, reserving a about 3 tablespoons (no need to be exact.) Pour the soy milk and drizzle the olive oil over potatoes, making sure to coat each one. If you need to use a little more than 1 tablespoon, that is okay.

Scatter the minced garlic over everything, then sprinkle 2 tablespoons of the nutritional yeast over all the potatoes. Drizzle with the remaining vegetable broth— try not to wash all the nutritional yeast off the potatoes; you just want to get it moist, so drizzle slowly. Then sprinkle with the last tablespoon of nutritional yeast, the herbs, and the salt.

Cover loosely with aluminum foil and bake for 35 minutes. Uncover and bake for an additional 15 minutes. Serve!

## LEMONY ROASTED POTATOES

SERVES 4 TO 6

**TIME:** ABOUT 55 MINUTES

*These are just like the tender, lemony and saucy potatoes beloved by Greek restaurant-goers everywhere. Serve alongside any Mediterranean-themed meal, Chickpea Cutlets (page 133), or seitan entrées. They're also excellent served with steamed greens laced with olive oil and lemon juice.*

2½ pounds Russet potatoes (medium to small potatoes work best)

⅓ cup olive oil

6 cloves garlic, chopped finely

½ cup freshly squeezed lemon juice

1 cup vegetable broth

2 teaspoons dried oregano

2 teaspoons salt

1 teaspoon tomato paste

Freshly ground black pepper

Chopped fresh parsley or dried oregano (optional)

PREHEAT THE oven to 375°F degrees. Peel the potatoes, slice in half lengthwise, and slice each half into wedges no more than ¾-inch thick.

In a large, deep baking pan or casserole dish (at least 10 × 17-inches or bigger), combine the olive oil, garlic, lemon juice, vegetable broth, oregano, salt, and tomato paste. Add the peeled, sliced potatoes. Sprinkle with freshly ground black pepper and toss the potatoes to cover with the sauce. Cover the pan tightly with foil (or use lid of casserole dish), place in the oven, and bake for 30 to 35 minutes until the potatoes are almost done. Several times during the baking process, remove the pan from the oven, uncover, stir the potatoes, place the cover back, and return the pan to the oven.

Uncover the pan one last time, stir the potatoes again, and bake, uncovered, for an additional 15 to 20 minutes, until most of the sauce has evaporated and some of the potatoes have just started to brown on their edges. Sprinkle with chopped fresh parsley and/or more dried oregano before serving.

## MASHED POTATOES WITH VARIATIONS

SERVES 4-6

TIME: 30 MINUTES

*A classic recipe that will never let you down. We've included tasty variations that happily mix and match with practically any cuisine you feel like cooking up tonight.*

SURE, use any potato you like, but different potatoes will yield different results. For light, fluffy mashed potatoes use a starchy, pebbly-skinned "baking" variety such as Idaho. A dense, creamy mash can be obtained from waxy, thin skinned potatoes such as red or Yukon Gold (which make awesome buttery-hued mashed potatoes). Sometimes we peel our potatoes, sometimes we leave the skins on for the ever-so-hip variation of "smashed" potatoes (mostly when using waxy potatoes).

2 pounds potatoes
2-3 tablespoons margarine
1/2 cup soy, rice or oat milk (for best results used unsweetened milk)
2 teaspoons salt
ground white pepper or black pepper

FILL a large pot with water, leaving enough room for the potatoes. Add the salt to the water.

Wash your potatoes and peel them (or don't), cut them into 1-inch chunks, and add them to the water. Bring the whole thing to a boil, then reduce to simmer, until the potatoes are soft (15-20 minutes). Drain.

Put the drained potatoes back in the pot or in a bowl, add the margarine, and mash with a potato masher or heavy-duty spoon. Add the soy milk or potato-cooking water and mash till desired consistency. Taste and add a little more margarine or soy milk if desired. Salt and pepper to taste. Serve!

*Variations:*

Add 2-3 tablespoons of the following along with the margarine: pesto, finely chopped chives, parsley, roasted garlic

Whisk into the soymilk (before adding to potatoes): 1-2 teaspoon wasabi powder or curry powder

*tip*

➤ Low fat mashed potatoes you ask? Reduce margarine to 1 tablespoon (or omit entirely), and replace half or all of the soymilk with warm, reserved potato-cooking liquid.

➤ For really smooth, creamy mashed potatoes try using this old fashioned gadget, the potato ricer. Looks a little like a giant garlic press, the potato ricer (and your biceps) transforms chunks of cooked potatoes into a fluffy, creamy mass. Best for use with starchy potatoes. If you use one we recommend first pressing hot, cooked potatoes first, then adding in margarine and soymilk.

## RUTABAGA PUREE

SERVES 4 TO 6

TIME: 30 MINUTES

*Rutabaga is the unsung hero of the root vegetable world, unless you live in Sweden (then you're probably like, "Enough with the rutabaga already!"). Fortunately, we're in NYC where the rutabaga is always a nice surprise. They taste like a slightly sweeter turnip, and in this recipe rutabaga is pureed with a little coconut milk, lime juice, and just a tiny hint of agave, for a Thai twist. Also, try our variation for cilantro-pureed rutabaga. It would go wonderfully with the Tamarind Lentils (page 123).*

### tip

➤ Since you use very little coconut milk for this, make sure to cook some other recipe that calls for a full can. Most recipes won't miss the ¼ cup (you can just add ¼ cup of water to make up for it).

➤ Turnips work well with this recipe, too!

2½ pounds rutabaga, peeled, cut into ¾-inch chunks
2 tablespoons fresh lime juice
¼ cup coconut milk
2 teaspoons agave syrup
½ teaspoon salt

PLACE the rutabaga in a medium-size lidded saucepan and cover with water. Put on the lid and bring to a boil. Once the water is boiling, lower the heat to a simmer and cook for about 20 minutes, until the rutabaga is tender.

Drain and transfer to a food processor. Add the remaining ingredients and puree until smooth. Serve immediately, while still warm.

*Variation:*

Cilantro-Pureed Rutabaga: Add 2 loosely packed cups of chopped fresh cilantro to the food processor and blend until the rutabaga is bright green.

## MASHED SPICED SWEET POTATOES

SERVES 6

TIME: 1 HOUR

*Everyone has a recipe like this, but this is the best one. Mashed sweet potatoes spiked with pumpkin pie–type spices, are wonderful alongside collards (see page 123) and grilled tofu.*

3 pounds sweet potatoes
½ teaspoon salt
½ teaspoon ground cinnamon
⅛ teaspoon ground allspice
¼ teaspoon ground nutmeg
¼ teaspoon ground ginger
2 tablespoons pure maple syrup
1 tablespoon grapeseed oil or other light vegetable oil (but not olive oil)

PREHEAT THE oven to 400°F.

Place the sweet potatoes directly on an oven rack (no tray is needed and no need to poke holes in them). Depending on the size of the sweet potatoes, the cooking time will vary. An average-size sweet potato takes about 45 minutes but large ones can take longer, sometimes up to 75 minutes if they are the giant kind.

Once you can easily poke through the potatoes in the center, they are done. Remove from the oven and split them lengthwise; leave them opened to speed up cooling.

When still warm but not too hot to handle, scoop out the sweet potatoes with a spoon and place in a large bowl. Discard the skins.

Add the remaining ingredients and mash everything with a strong fork. Serve warm.

> You can also bake the sweet potatoes on the top rack of the oven if you have other things baking at the same time. If the oven is at a lower temperature, that's okay. Just bake a little longer.

> Most ovens bake unevenly. Occasionally change the positions of the sweet potatoes so that they bake at the same rate.

## ROASTED BUTTERNUT SQUASH WITH CORIANDER SEEDS

SERVES 6 TO 8 AS A SIDE DISH

TIME: 50 MINUTES

*Here's a very simple way to serve butternut squash. Feel free to try it with different spices or even without any spices at all; the butternut will be able to stand on its own. To smash the coriander seeds easily, place them in a small plastic sandwich bag. Place a few layers of newspaper on top of the seeds and then have at it with a hammer or a mallet. You can also place them in a coffee grinder and pulse a few times (use caution, you don't want to reduce them to a powder).*

2 medium-size butternut squash, peeled, seeded, and cut into ¾-inch chunks
2 tablespoons olive oil
2 tablespoons coriander seeds, smashed
¼ teaspoon salt

PREHEAT the oven to 375°F.

Combine all ingredients on a rimmed baking sheet (the "rimmed" part is essential, since you don't want the oil dripping off into the oven and causing a fire. Or *do* you?). Make sure that all the squash pieces are coated in oil and seeds, and spread into a single layer. Cook for about 35 minutes, tossing occasionally, until the squash is tender and slightly caramelized.

## ROASTED PORTOBELLOS

SERVES 2 AS A MAIN, 4 AS A SIDE

*These multipurpose succulent mushrooms are perfect for salads, in sammiches, or just as a veggie side for pretty much any type of savory meal, even brunch. You get enough marinade for four small caps or two huge ones, but your mileage may vary depending on the size of your caps. You can marinate and roast these in a glass pie plate or use a small casserole dish. Any pan greater than eight inches across would spread the marinade too thinly. The ingredients are really simple, but you can add dried herbs, such as oregano, thyme, and basil, if you think it will go with whatever else you are eating. Using herbs is an especially good idea if you are going to make this into a portobello sammich.*

Marinade:
½ cup cooking wine
1 tablespoon olive oil
2 tablespoons soy sauce
2 tablespoons balsamic vinegar
2 cloves garlic, minced
2 large or up to 4 small portobello caps

COMBINE all ingredients for the marinade in a glass pie plate or small casserole. Place the mushrooms upside down in the marinade and spoon a lot of the marinade into each cap to form a small pool. Preheat the oven to 400°F and marinate for about 20 minutes.

Cover with aluminum foil and bake for 30 minutes. Remove the foil, use tongs to flip the caps over, and cook, uncovered, for another 10 minutes. If you're using your portobello as a burger, just put that puppy between a bun with some lettuce, tomato, Vegenaise, and avocado, and call it a day. If using for a salad, let it cool a bit and then slice the mushrooms very thinly on the diagonal to make nice meaty slices.

## EASY STIR-FRIED LEAFY GREENS

SERVES 4 6

TIME: 20 minutes

*Eating enough green, leafy vegetables through the week can be a challenge for even the most dedicated vegan or vegetarian. While we're repeat customers when it comes to spinach, collards, and kale, there's a whole world of Asian and other greens that pack nutrition and flavor yet all too often don't get enough face-time on our dinner plates.*

*Spicy mustard greens, crisp Chinese broccoli, sweet chard, and others really cook up quickly and easily when stir-fried with a touch of ginger, garlic, and soy sauce. There's no sticky, overly sweet sauce in this recipe, just clean flavors and bright, crunchy greens that cook in less time than it takes to steam rice or fry a main-dish protein.*

1 pound dark, leafy greens, such as: mustard greens, Chinese broccoli, large bok choy, chard, water spinach, dandelion greens (use 2 pounds), watercress (use 2 pounds), green choy sum, etc.

2 tablespoons peanut oil

3 cloves garlic, minced finely

½-inch cube ginger, grated

1 tablespoon rice cooking wine, cooking sherry, or mirin

2 teaspoons soy sauce

Pinch of sugar

1 teaspoon toasted sesame oil or chile-sesame oil (optional)

HOLDING THE greens together in bunches, slice into 1- or 2-inch-wide sections. If the greens have any thick stems or bottoms, remove and place the stems in a bowl separate from the leafy green tops. Wash and dry both bowls of greens, and shake off any excess water.

In a large, nonstick skillet or wok, heat the peanut oil over medium-high heat. Add the garlic and ginger; cook, stirring constantly, for 30 seconds. Add the thick stems and stir-fry for about 1 to 2 minutes until stems begin to soften.

*tip*

➤ Any leafy green can be prepared this way, so if you see something new and interesting at the farmers' market, don't hesitate to experiment with this recipe. Also, asparagus and green beans can be prepared in this manner. Just trim any overly tough stems and allow a slightly longer cooking time, depending on your desired degree of crispness.

➤ We've included instructions on preparing greens with thick, juicy stems. This is not necessary when cooking thin-stemmed vegetables such as water spinach, watercress, or dandelion, so skip the step of separating stems from leaves.

➤ Tongs are the ideal tool to use when sautéing leafy greens.

Add the leafy tops, stirring constantly for another 2 to 3 minutes, until the tops begin to wilt and soften. Sprinkle with cooking wine, soy sauce, sugar, and chile-sesame oil. If the leaves are very large and piled high in the pan, cover the pan for 1 to 2 minutes to sweat and wilt them so that they can be easily stir-fried. Stir to combine all the ingredients. Stir-fry until the vegetables are bright green and the stems are tender but still slightly crisp. Remove from the heat and serve immediately.

# GRAINS

## BROCCOLI POLENTA

SERVES 4 TO 6

**TIME:** 70 MINUTES

*Broccoli gives polenta a great texture. It just makes it, like, "RAR!" That's the only way we can describe it. We're giving you several options for molding and serving the polenta once it is prepped; try them all and see what you like best. You can serve this as a main dish with any of the marinara sauces or pesto, or serve it as a base for either the Braised Seitan with Brussels (page 182) or the Sautéed Seitan with Mushrooms and Spinach (page 187). If you don't want to think about the various molding and cooking methods, then just do the muffin tin and broiling method, because it's cute. If you're short on time, you can even skip the molding step and just serve this as is after boiling.*

> 3½ cups vegetable broth or water
> ½ teaspoon salt (you may need more depending on how salty your veggie broth is)
> 1 cup polenta corn grits (polenta)
> 2 tablespoons olive oil
> 4 cups very well-chopped broccoli, stalks and tops (pieces should be no larger than ¼ inch)

BRING THE water and salt to a boil in a medium saucepan. Add the polenta in a slow, steady stream, mixing with a whisk as you pour it. Add the broccoli and olive oil, and lower the heat to low. Cover and let simmer for 15 minutes, stirring often. Turn off the heat, cover, and let sit for 10 more minutes, stirring occasionally.

*Molding Methods:*

**Tin Can:** Grease two empty 20-ounce cans (tomato cans, for example) with olive oil. Spoon the polenta into the cans and place in the fridge for about 2 hours. Use a butter knife to help coax them out of the mold, slice into inch-wide pieces and proceed to Cooking Methods. This method of molding takes longer to chill because of the volume in each mold.

**Muffin Tin:** Grease a muffin tin with olive oil. Spoon the polenta into the tin, almost all the way to the top of the compartments. Smooth the tops with the back of the spoon. Refrigerate for about an hour. Use a fork to pry the polenta out of the tins and proceed to Cooking Methods. This method works best when you broil the polenta.

**Square Pan:** Grease an 8-inch square (slightly bigger or smaller is okay) food storage container, casserole, or brownie pan. Spoon in the polenta and spread it out evenly. Refrigerate for about an hour. Cut into squares and proceed to Cooking Methods.

### Cooking Methods:

**Broil:** Preheat the broiler. Grease a rimmed baking sheet with olive oil. Place the polenta slices on baking sheet and broil 3 to 4 inches away from the flame, for about 7 minutes, or until lightly browned. If using the muffin tin molding method, place them upside down on the baking sheet so that the rough tops are at the bottom.

**Panfry:** (Note: This doesn't really work with the muffin tin mold molding method.) Preheat a nonstick pan over medium heat. Pour a very thin layer of olive oil into the pan. Place the polenta slices in the pan and cook on both sides for about 5 minutes each, until lightly browned.

## SOFT POPPY-SEED POLENTA

SERVES 4 TO 6

**TIME:** 30 MINUTES

*This is mushy comfort food at its best: a simple, creamy polenta that goes great with strongly flavored savory dishes, such as Tomato and Roasted Eggplant Stew (page 179). The poppy seeds make the usually humble polenta really aesthetically pleasing.*

**5 cups vegetable broth or water**
**½ teaspoon salt**
**1 cup polenta corn grits (polenta)**
**2 tablespoons olive oil**
**2 teaspoons poppy seeds**

BRING THE water and salt to a boil in a medium-size saucepan. Add the polenta in a slow steady stream,

mixing as you pour it. Add the poppy seeds and olive oil, and lower the heat to a simmer. Cook for 12 minutes, stirring often. Turn off the heat and cover. Let sit for 10 more minutes, stirring occasionally.

## CHICKPEA-QUINOA PILAF

SERVES 4 TO 6 AS A SIDE

**TIME:** 40 MINUTES

*Nothing fancy, just a nice basic and versatile pilaf with quinoa—the grain of the Aztecs. You can come up with all sorts of variations here—use different beans and different spices and what-not. We like to cook quinoa this way, rather than flavoring it after it's cooked, because it absorbs all the spices so well. Don't forget that cooking with quinoa at least once a week will elevate you to level 7 vegan in no time.*

**2 tablespoons olive oil**
**1 small yellow onion, chopped finely (about 1 cup)**
**2 cloves garlic, minced**
**½ teaspoon ground cumin**
**1 tablespoon coriander seeds, crushed**
**Several pinches of freshly ground black pepper**
**½ teaspoon salt**
**1 tablespoon tomato paste**
**1 cup quinoa**
**2 cups cooked or 1 (15-ounce) can chickpeas, drained and rinsed**
**2 cups vegetable broth or reconstituted bouillon**

IN A small stockpot over medium heat, sauté the onions in olive oil for about 7 minutes. Add the garlic and sauté for 2 more minutes.

Add the tomato paste, coriander, cumin, black pepper, and salt; sauté for another minute.

Add the quinoa and sauté for 2 minutes.

Add the chickpeas and broth; cover and bring to a

boil. Once the mixture is boiling, lower the heat to very low, cover, and cook for about 18 minutes, or until the quinoa has absorbed all the water; stir occasionally. Fluff with a fork and serve.

## FRESH DILL–BASMATI RICE WITH CHARD AND CHICKPEAS

SERVES 4 TO 6

TIME: ABOUT 65 MINUTES

*Fresh spinach and dill paired with chickpeas and basmati rice makes a complete meal. But we won't hold anything against you if you'd rather pair this alongside any vegetable side and Spiced Yogurt Sauce (page 212). It's best prepared in a heavy-bottomed cast-iron pot (such as a Dutch oven), but the combined ingredients can be finished in a rice cooker (follow the manufacturer's instructions).*

### tip

> We like to soak the basmati rice before cooking because it makes the rice exceptionally fluffy. It's totally optional, so if you can't be bothered, skip this step—just rinse the rice and go!

2 cups basmati rice

2 shallots, minced

1 small onion, cut into fine dice

2 tablespoons peanut oil

½ teaspoon cumin seeds

1 teaspoon garam masala

1 bunch fresh dill, large stems removed, chopped finely (about ¾ cup)

1 pound chard, washed and any thick stems removed

1 (15-ounce) can chickpeas, drained and rinsed

2 cups water or vegetable stock

1½–2 teaspoon salt (use less if using a salty vegetable stock)

1 teaspoon freshly grated lemon zest

Freshly ground pepper

Pinch of cayenne

Juice of 1 lemon

1–2 lemons, sliced into wedges (optional)

IN A medium-size bowl, rinse the basmati rice with a few changes of water, then cover with at least 2 inches of water. Set aside while preparing the other ingredients, allowing the rice to soak in the water for at least 20 minutes. When ready to use, carefully drain the rice with a fine-mesh strainer.

Steam the chard either in a steamer or a large, covered pot filled with about 2 inches of boiling water. When the chard is limp and bright green, transfer it to a bowl to cool and squeeze as much water as possible from the it. Roll tightly into bunches and chop finely.

In a large, lidded, heavy-bottomed 4-quart pot, heat the peanut oil over medium heat. Add the cumin seeds, fry for 15 seconds, then add the shallots and onion. Sprinkle with the garam masala and sauté the mixture until the onions and shallots are soft, 6 to 8 minutes. Add the drained rice, folding to coat the grains with spiced oil mixture. Add the chopped dill, chard, chickpeas, veggie stock, salt, lemon zest, pepper, and cayenne. Cover and increase the heat to bring to a boil, then quickly lower the heat to medium-low and tightly cover. Cook for 25 to 30 minutes, until liquid is absorbed and rice is fluffy, watching carefully as not to burn.

Remove from the heat, sprinkle with the lemon juice, fluff the rice with a fork, and cover again. Allow to sit another 10 minutes before serving. with lemon wedges.

## ISRAELI COUSCOUS WITH PISTACHIOS AND APRICOTS

SERVES 4

**TIME:** 40 MINUTES

*Israeli couscous is bigger and more fun than your average couscous. You could say they are the beach balls of the couscous world. This is a Turkish-inspired dish, or at least we think it is; it's fragrantly spiced and would be perfect to serve with roasted or grilled veggies (page 26–35)—try using it to complement sweet potatoes, Brussels sprouts, and/or red peppers.*

**tip**

➤ Toasting the couscous before steaming it gives it a firmer texture and a deeper flavor.

2 tablespoons vegetable oil

3 cloves garlic, minced

2 cups Israeli couscous

2½ cups water

1 cinnamon stick

1 teaspoon ground cumin

¼ teaspoon ground cardamom

Several pinches of freshly ground black pepper

½ teaspoon salt

Zest from 1 lime

¼ cup chopped fresh mint

½ cup chopped dried apricots, chopped to the size of raisins

½ cup shelled pistachios

Juice from ½ lime

PREHEAT A large heavy-bottomed skillet over medium-low heat. Place the garlic and oil in the pan and sauté for 1 minute. Add the couscous, raise the heat to medium, and stir pretty constantly for 4 or 5 minutes; the couscous should start to toast.

Add the water, cinnamon stick, cumin, cardamom, pepper, salt, and lime zest. Raise the heat and bring to a boil. Once the mixture is boiling, lower the heat again to as low as possible and cover. (We know, lot's of raising and lowering the heat but that's cooking for you.) In about 10 minutes, most of the water should have been absorbed. Add 2 tablespoons of the mint, and the apricots, pistachios, and lime juice. Stir, cover again, and cook for 5 more minutes. At this point, the water should be thoroughly absorbed.

Remove the cinnamon stick, fluff the couscous with a fork, garnish with the remaining mint, and serve.

## TOMATO COUSCOUS WITH CAPERS

SERVES 4 TO 6

**TIME:** 25 MINUTES

*With just a few more ingredients, regular old couscous transforms into a pretty pilaf that goes perfectly with any French, Spanish, or Italian main dish. Try it alongside Rustic White Beans (page 120) or any kind of savory protein dish. After all of the ingredients measured and prepped, this side dish can be put together in less than 15 minutes.*

1 (28-ounce) can diced tomatoes

1½ cups uncooked whole wheat or regular couscous

2 tablespoons olive oil

½ teaspoon salt

1 teaspoon oregano

¼ teaspoon ground cloves (optional)

Generous pinch of ground cayenne

2 tablespoons small capers, drained of brine (if using large capers, chop coarsely)

IN A medium-size bowl, strain the juice from the diced tomatoes to measure 1½ cups of juice, squeezing the diced tomatoes as much as possible to remove their excess liquid. Discard any remaining juice; if not enough juice is available to total 1½ cups, add either vegetable broth or water. Gently crush any large chunks of diced tomatoes and set aside.

Combine the juice, olive oil, and oregano in a medium-size saucepan. Cover and heat to medium-high, to bring to a boil. Stir continuously as you pour in the couscous in a steady stream. Quickly stir in the salt, cayenne, and cloves. Stir to combine, turn off heat, cover the pan, and allow it to sit for 5 minutes, or until the liquid is completely absorbed. Fold in the reserved diced tomatoes and capers, cover again, and allow to sit for 2 to 3 minutes to warm the tomatoes.

## MEXICAN MILLET

SERVES 4

🌀 Ⓖ Ⓕ ㊺

TIME: 45 MINUTES

*You might be tempted to call this recipe "Meximillet" or "Mexican Mullet," but after one taste we'll think you'll pronounce this "que yum"! It's a twist on the classic Mexican/Spanish side known as (surprise!) "Spanish Rice", made instead with millet, which is soft and crunchy at the same time. Serve alongside any Mexican, Tex-Mex, or Latino-themed meal, or break all the rules and eat it for breakfast.*

2 tablespoons peanut or vegetable oil

1 clove garlic, minced

1 cup millet

1 small yellow onion, diced finely

1 jalapeño, seeded and minced

2 cups vegetable broth

3 tablespoons tomato paste

½ teaspoon salt, or to taste

¼ teaspoon ground cumin

⅓ cup finely diced tomato (about 1 medium-size, firm, ripe tomato, seeded), plus extra for garnish

2 tablespoons finely chopped cilantro

Freshly squeezed lime juice, for garnish

HEAT THE peanut oil and garlic in a medium-size, heavy-bottomed saucepan over medium heat. When the garlic begins to sizzle, add the onion and jalapeño, and fry, stirring occasionally, until the onion is soft and slightly golden, 6 to 8 minutes. Add the millet, stir to coat, and sauté for 4 to 6 minutes, until the millet is lightly golden. Pour in the vegetable broth and add the tomato paste, salt, cumin, and diced fresh tomato.

Bring the mixture to a boil, stir once, and cover. Lower the heat to low and cook for 25 to 30 minutes, until all liquid is absorbed.

Remove from the heat and allow to sit, covered, for 10 minutes, then sprinkle with chopped cilantro and fluff the millet with fork. Garnish each serving with a little fresh lime juice and diced tomato, if desired.

## MESSY RICE

SERVES 4

🌀 Ⓖ Ⓕ ▱

TIME: 1 HOUR

*This is supposed to be like dirty rice, but the dirt is from crushed coriander seeds, not whatever gross stuff they traditionally put in dirty rice. The ingredients are simple but the rice is deceptively flavorful and scrumptious. Serve with Hot Sauce–Glazed Tempeh (page 129) and Creole Stuffed Peppers (page 61) for a down-home meal. Don't sub with commercially prepared coriander powder; it won't do this rice justice.*

1 tablespoon vegetable oil

¼ cup finely chopped yellow onion

2 teaspoons whole coriander seeds, crushed

2 cloves garlic, minced

2 tablespoons tomato paste

½ teaspoon salt

Several pinches of freshly ground black pepper

1 cup jasmine rice (plain old white rice works, too, but we love the flavor jasmine lends it)

1 ½ cups water

PREHEAT A medium-size saucepan over medium heat. Sauté the onions in the oil for about 5 minutes, until softened and lightly browned. Add the crushed coriander and garlic, and sauté for 2 more minutes. Add the tomato paste and stir it around for about a minute to get it well distributed. Add the salt, pepper, rice, and water, and stir. Cover and bring to a boil.

Once the mixture is boiling, give it another stir and lower the heat immediately to as low as it will go (to prevent sticking). Cover and cook for 35 to 40 minutes, until the rice is thoroughly cooked. Then, fluff with a fork and serve.

## SAFFRON-GARLIC RICE

SERVES 4

**TIME:** 45 MINUTES

*This tasty, golden-hued rice is infused with subtle saffron and gently sautéed garlic. It's easy to cook on a back burner while preparing a main-dish protein or vegetables, and tasty enough that you'll never ever want to go back to those rice pilafs out of a cardboard box. Serve this simple rice side with any Spanish or Middle Eastern entrée or perfectly steamed asparagus paired with your favorite sauce. We like the way bouillon tastes here but if you would rather use vegetable broth be our guest.*

1¾ cup water

1 vegetable bouillon cube

Pinch of saffron threads (5–6 threads)

2 tablespoons olive oil

5 cloves garlic, minced finely

1 small yellow onion, diced finely

1 cup long-grain white rice, such as jasmine or basmati, rinsed and drained

Pinch of ground coriander

Salt and ground white pepper

⅓ cup toasted, sliced almonds (optional)

*tip*

➤ The saffron threads can be drained and used once more in another dish. The easiest way to do this is to place the threads in a small cup and pour in ¼ cup or less of the hot, prepared bouillon. Allow the threads to steep for at least 10 minutes. Using a small fine-mesh strainer (the kind used for straining tea leaves), pour the steeped broth back into the rest of the vegetable broth. Set the strainer aside, over the cup or on a dish, and allow the saffron to dry completely. Gently shake or tap strainer to remove the dried saffron threads, and store in an airtight container.

IN A medium-size saucepan boil the water, add the bouillon cube, and stir until the cube has dissolved. Turn off the heat, add the saffron threads, and stir. Cover and set aside until ready to use.

Preheat a medium-size pot over medium heat. Sauté the garlic in oil until it has softened and is just starting to turn golden, 3 to 4 minutes. Add the onion and continue to sauté until the onion turns translucent, 5 to 6 minutes. Add the rice and stir to combine. Sauté the rice for about 1 minute. Pour in the warm vegetable broth and stir in the coriander. Cover and bring to a boil, stir the rice just once, and lower the heat to low. Cover and let the rice simmer for 20 to 25 minutes, until the liquid has been absorbed and the rice is tender.

Remove from the heat and allow the rice to stand for 10 minutes. Fluff with a fork, add the toasted almonds, and season with salt and ground white pepper, if desired.

# BEANS

## RUSTIC WHITE BEANS AND MUSHROOMS

SERVES 6 TO 8

**TIME:** ABOUT 65 MINUTES (NOT INCLUDING BEAN-SOAKING TIME)

*These are simple, homey, French-inspired, stick-to-your-ribs beans for early autumn days. The tarragon and leeks really shine through the mild white beans, and the mushrooms add a chewy bite. Tomato Couscous with Capers (page 117) rounds out this meal. This recipe is made with dried beans; canned beans can't be substituted, so plan accordingly and soak the beans overnight or in the morning before you leave to work, if indeed you have a job and don't just sit at home cooking all day.*

*For a real treat, prepare the casserole-style variation that follows: a delectable layer of buttery, herbed bread crumbs tops the beans and then the whole thing is baked to golden-brown perfection.*

> **2 cups dried white beans, soaked for at least 8 hours**
> **1 small onion, peeled and sliced in half**
> **1 stalk celery, cut into two pieces**
> **1 small carrot, sliced in half lengthwise**
> **1 teaspoon dried thyme**
> **2 teaspoons dried tarragon, or 2 tablespoons fresh**
> **¼ cup olive oil**
> **2 large cloves garlic, peeled and minced**
> **1 large leek, sliced thinly**
> **½ pound (about 2 generous cups) mushrooms, either cremini, shiitake, or oyster, or a combination, rinsed and sliced thinly**
> **1½ teaspoon salt, or more to taste**
> **Freshly ground pepper**

DRAIN AND rinse the beans and transfer them to a stockpot. Add 4 cups of cold water, cover, and bring to a boil. Boil for about 3 minutes. Skim off any white foam from the top. Cover the pot and lower the heat to medium; add the onion, celery, carrot, thyme, and tarragon.

Simmer for about 45 minutes, until the beans are very tender. Remove the onion, carrot, and celery (either discard or use in a stock). Lower the heat to low and continue to simmer while preparing the remaining vegetables. The beans should resemble a very thick stew, not a soup. If there's too much liquid, leave the pot uncovered and stir occasionally.

About 10 minutes before the beans are done, place the garlic and 2 tablespoons of olive oil in a cold skillet. Heat the skillet over medium heat, allowing garlic to sizzle for about 30 seconds. Add the chopped leek and sauté until soft, 1 to 2 minutes. Scrape the leeks into beans. Add the remaining 2 tablespoons of oil to the pan, allow it to warm for about 30 seconds, and add the mushrooms. Sprinkle the mushrooms lightly with ½ teaspoon salt and sauté until most of the mushroom liquid has evaporated, anywhere from 8 to 12 minutes depending on the kind of mushroom. When most of the excess liquid is gone, add the mushrooms to beans. Turn off the heat and season the beans with the remaining salt (or more, if desired) and freshly ground black pepper. Allow the beans to stand for about 10 minutes before serving.

### Variation:

Crumb-Topped Casserole: Preheat the oven to 350°F. Spread the cooked bean mixture into a 2-quart casserole dish. Top with the Sage Bread Crumbs from the Pumpkin Baked Ziti (page 194), and bake for 20 to 25 minutes, until the bread crumbs are golden and the beans are bubbling.

## MEDITERRANEAN-STYLE BAKED LIMA BEANS

SERVES 6-8

**TIME:** 1 HOUR 30 MINUTES (NOT INCLUDING BEAN-SOAKING TIME)

*You may have lima bean baggage but this recipe will help you work though it. Please set your issues aside and for a moment imagine large, mild, tender beans with a creamy interior and a slightly chewy exterior, all of it lovingly smothered in a tangy tomato sauce. (If you must, you can substitute navy or cannellini beans for the limas. But be sure to try it at least once with large lima beans.) This is a delightful spin-off of a traditional Greek home-style dish and is hearty meal alongside rice, potatoes, and steamed greens. Or, serve them the traditional Mediterranean way, just slightly warmed, as part of a meze spread with olives, hummus, Cashew-Cucumber Dip (page 66), pickles, pita, and the like.*

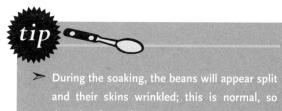

**tip**

> During the soaking, the beans will appear split and their skins wrinkled; this is normal, so don't be alarmed.

**Beans:**

- 1 pound dried, large lima beans, soaked for at least 8 hours
- 2 quarts water
- 2 bay leaves

**Sauce:**

- 1 vegetable bouillon cube
- ¼ cup olive oil
- 4 cloves garlic, minced
- 1 medium yellow onion, chopped finely
- 1 small carrot, shredded

- 1 (28-ounce) can diced or crushed tomatoes
- 2 teaspoons red wine vinegar
- 2 tablespoons tomato paste
- 1 tablespoon pure maple syrup or agave nectar
- 1 tablespoon dried oregano
- 2 teaspoons dried thyme
- 1½ teaspoons salt
- Pinch of ground nutmeg
- Black pepper
- ¼ cup finely chopped fresh parsley
- 3 tablespoons finely chopped fresh mint

DRAIN AND rinse the beans and place them in a large pot with the 2 quarts of cold water and the bay leaves. Cover, bring to a boil, then lower the heat to medium. Simmer the beans for 30 minutes, until tender but not fully cooked (the interior of the beans will still be grainy). Skim off any foam that may collect while beans are cooking. Drain the beans, reserving 1 cup of bean liquid, and set aside (leave the bay leaves with beans). Dissolve the vegetable bouillon cube in the reserved 1 cup of hot bean liquid; set aside.

While the beans are cooking, preheat the oven to 375°F. Lightly oil a 4-quart Dutch oven or casserole dish (you can also prepare the beans in two batches in two 2-quart casseroles or Dutch ovens).

Prepare the sauce in either the prepared Dutch oven, if using, or a separate large saucepan. Heat the garlic and olive oil over medium heat until the garlic starts to sizzle. Add the onion and stir until translucent and softened, 3 to 4 minutes. Add the carrot, stir and cook for another minute, and add the tomatoes, reserved veggie bouillon, red wine vinegar, tomato paste, maple syrup, oregano, thyme, salt, and nutmeg. Stir and bring to a boil, then lower the heat and cook for 10 to 12 minutes, to reduce the sauce a little. Taste the sauce and season with black pepper and more salt if necessary. Stir in the beans, parsley, and mint.

Place in the prepared casserole dish (if not already using the Dutch oven), cover the dish, and bake the beans, stirring occasionally, for 30 minutes, until they are tender and the interior of the beans is creamy.

Uncover and bake for an additional 10 to 15 minutes, to reduce the sauce a little bit and give the beans a slightly dry finish. Remove from the oven, remove the bay leaves, and allow to cool for 10 minutes before serving.

## BLACK BEANS IN CHIPOTLE ADOBO SAUCE

SERVES 4

TIME: ABOUT 50 MINUTES

*Feeling lazy, but not so lazy that you'll only open up that takeout menu? Then you might like transforming ordinary canned black beans into simple, savory side or main dish with just an onion and some time. A simple adobo sauce—featuring smoky chipotles—drizzled on top makes these beans special, but you can serve them without if your prefer. Pair it up with Mexican Millet (page 118) or rice and a green salad.*

Beans:

2 (15-ounce) cans black beans, drained and rinsed

1 bay leaf

3 cups cold water

1 large onion, peeled and halved

Salt and freshly ground pepper

Chipotle adobo sauce:

1 large onion, cut into small dice

4 cloves garlic, minced

3 tablespoons olive oil

2 chipotle peppers in adobo, minced

2 tablespoons adobo sauce from the chipotles

COMBINE THE beans, onion, bay leaf, and water in a large saucepan. Bring to a boil, then let boil for 1 minute. Lower the heat to medium and simmer, uncovered, for 40 minutes, until the beans are very tender and about half of the water has evaporated. Remove the bay leaf and onion before serving.

While the beans are cooking, prepare the chipotle adobo sauce: In a heavy-bottomed skillet over medium heat, sauté the onion and garlic in the olive oil until the onion is very soft, 10 to 12 minutes. Stir in the chipotles and adobo sauce, cook for 30 seconds, and remove from the heat.

Allow to cool a few minutes, empty the sauce into a food processor bowl, and briefly pulse until a chunky sauce forms. You may also use an immersion blender to do this. Serve the sauce drizzled over individual servings of beans.

## CHEATER BAKED BEANS

SERVES 6

TIME: 75 MINUTES

*These are "cheater" because the recipe uses canned beans—perfect for when you have some visitors from Boston drop by without any warning. We like these better than just using baked beans from a can because they aren't cloyingly sweet. Serve with Smoky Grilled Tempeh (page 130) and collards (page 106). Or, slice up tofu dogs and throw 'em in, see if we care.*

2 tablespoons olive oil

1 medium-size yellow onion, diced as small as you can

3 cloves garlic, minced

1 (15-ounce) can tomato sauce

½ cup light molasses (not blackstrap)

2 teaspoons mustard powder

1 teaspoon salt

¼ teaspoon ground allspice

1 bay leaf

2 (15-ounce) cans small white beans (about 4 cups), drained and rinsed

PREHEAT THE oven to 350°F.

Preheat a medium-size oven-safe pot over medium heat. Sauté the onions in the oil for about 10 minutes; you want them to be a little bit browned, but definitely not burnt, just a little caramelized. Add the garlic and sauté for one more minute. Add the tomato sauce, molasses, mustard, salt, allspice, and bay leaf, and cook for about 5 minutes.

Add the beans, then cover the pot and transfer it to the oven for an hour. Give it a stir just once, about 30 minutes into the baking process. The sauce should thicken and sweeten. Keep warm until ready to serve.

## TAMARIND LENTILS

SERVES 4–6

TIME: 45 MINUTES

*Savory, tangy, and sweet, these Indian-inspired lentils are simple to prepare while cooking any basmati-type rice and vegetable side dish. We like them served over basmati rice with Poppy-Seed Cornmeal Roti (page 221).*

> **tip**
>
> ➤ For best results, use a small lentil that keeps its shape during cooking, such as black or green lentils. Brown lentils can be used but tend to get a little mushy, which isn't a bad thing but we just thought we'd let you know.

**3 tablespoons coconut or peanut oil**
**3 cloves garlic, minced**
**½-inch-cube fresh ginger, peeled and minced**
**1 large onion, diced**
**1 teaspoon garam masala**
**½ teaspoon whole cumin seeds**

**Generous pinch of cayenne**
**1 cup dried lentils, picked over and rinsed**
**2 cups vegetable broth or water**
**2 teaspoons concentrated tamarind syrup or paste**
**1 tablespoon pure maple syrup or agave nectar**
**2 tablespoons tomato paste**
**½ teaspoon salt**

IN A heavy-bottomed medium-size pot with a lid, melt the coconut oil over medium heat. Add the garlic and ginger, and let sizzle for 30 seconds. Add the onion and fry until translucent and soft, 2 to 3 minutes. Stir in the garam masala, cumin seeds, and cayenne, and stir for another 30 seconds until the spices smell fragrant. Add the lentils and vegetable broth, increase the heat to high, and bring the mixture to a boil. Stir and lower the heat to medium-low. Partially cover and simmer for 25 to 30 minutes, stirring occasionally, until the lentils have absorbed most of the liquid and are very tender. The lentils will be very thick; add a few tablespoons of water if a thinner consistency is desired.

In a small cup or bowl, combine the tamarind, maple syrup, tomato paste, and salt. Use a rubber spatula to scrape all of the mixture into the lentils; stir to completely dissolve the flavorings. Simmer the mixture for another 4 to 6 minutes, stirring occasionally. Adjust the salt to taste and serve immediately.

## CHICKPEAS ROMESCO

SERVES 4 TO 6

COOKING TIME: 50 MINUTES

*If these chickpeas could talk, they'd probably be a little fresh and need at least a PG-13 rating due to extreme sauciness. (On the other hand, if chickpeas could talk they probably wouldn't be vegan anymore.) Yet these delicious chickpeas—gently simmered in a savory tomato sauce with roasted red peppers and ground almonds—make a great family dinner or potluck dish nonetheless. Pair this Spanish-style entrée with Saffron-Garlic Rice (page 119) and your favorite steamed green vegetable or simple salad.*

⅓ cup sliced almonds

1 (28-ounce) can diced tomatoes (fire-roasted are especially good here)

2 roasted red bell peppers, homemade (page 33) or store-bought

3 tablespoons olive oil

3 cloves garlic, minced finely

2 shallots, minced finely

1 red serrano chile, seeded and minced finely (leave some seeds if more heat is desired)

¼ cup white wine or vegetable broth

2 teaspoons red wine vinegar

2 teaspoons sugar

1 teaspoon dried thyme

½ teaspoon dried rosemary, crumbled

2 (15-ounce) cans chickpeas, drained and rinsed

½ teaspoon salt, or to taste

Freshly ground pepper

USING A food processor (or an immersion blender with a food processor attachment), grind the almonds into very fine, almost powdery crumbs. Empty into a small bowl and set aside.

Working in two or more batches, puree the tomatoes and roasted peppers together until until smooth. Pour the tomato mixture into a large bowl and set aside.

Preheat a medium-size heavy-bottomed saucepan over medium heat. Sauté the garlic, shallots and chile in oil until the shallots are turning golden, 4 to 5 minutes. Pour in the white wine and stir to dissolve any browned bits of garlic from the bottom of the pot; simmer for 1 minute. Add the tomato puree, vinegar, sugar, thyme, and rosemary. Turn the heat to medium-high and bring to a near boil. Lower the heat to medium-low and simmer for about 10 minutes, stirring occasionally.

Add the ground almonds and stir the mixture until they are completely combined. Fold in the chickpeas and simmer, uncovered, for 20 to 25 minutes, until the sauce is slightly reduced and the chickpeas are very tender. Remove from the heat, season with salt and pepper, and allow to cool for 5 to 10 minutes before serving.

## CHILE CORNMEAL-CRUSTED TOFU

SERVES 4

TIME: 20 MINUTES,
NOT INCLUDING PRESSING TOFU

*A light coating of cornmeal, spices, and lime zest turns humble tofu into something we can get excited about. You can fry or bake these bad boys, so fry them up when you want to impress Paula Deen fans. Bake them when you're having a nice vegan night in, writing checks to Farm Sanctuary, and kicking back and reading the latest issue of* Herbivore *magazine. Be sure to check out the Po' Boys (page 99) that feature this tofu or serve with Southwestern Corn Pudding (page 151) and Green Pumpkin-Seed Mole (page 210).*

Corn or vegetable oil for frying
1 pound extra-firm tofu, drained and pressed
1 cup soy or rice milk
2 tablespoons cornstarch
1 cup cornmeal
2 tablespoons chile powder
1 teaspoon ground cumin
¼ teaspoon cayenne
1 tablespoon grated lime zest
1½ teaspoons salt

SLICE THE tofu widthwise into eight slices, then cut each of those slices in half diagonally—from the upper left corner to the lower right corner—so that you have sixteen long triangles. Set aside.

Combine the soy milk and cornstarch in a wide, shallow bowl. Mix vigorously with a fork until the cornstarch is mostly dissolved.

In another shallow bowl, toss together the cornmeal, spices, lime zest, and salt.

*Frying Directions:*

Heat about ¼ inch of oil in a large skillet, preferably cast iron, over medium heat. To test if the oil is ready, sprinkle in a pinch of batter. When the batter sizzles and bubbles form rapidly around it, you're good to go.

Dip each individual tofu slice in the soy milk mixture. Drop it into the cornmeal with your dry hand and use your other hand to dredge it in the mixture, so that it's coated on all sides. Transfer the tofu to the skillet in two batches so as not to crowd the pan. Fry tofu for 3 minutes on one side, use tongs to flip over each piece, and fry for 2 more minutes. Drain the fried tofu on a clean paper bag or paper towels.

*tip*

➤ You need a wet hand and a dry hand when dredging stuff in batter, otherwise the batter will clump up all over your hands and make you unhappy. So use your left hand to soak the tofu and to drop it in the cornmeal. Then, use your right hand to do the rest of the dirty work.

➤ For baking breaded things, ideally, you need a spray can of oil, and not the kind you buy in the supermarket (although that would work in a pinch). Use the kind that you fill yourself with oil. So try to get one—if you are doing lots of low-fat cooking, it will be indispensable. If you don't have a spray bottle of oil, then just use a paper towel to spread a very thin coating of oil in the pan.

*Baking Directions:*

Preheat the oven to 350°F. Line a baking sheet with baking parchment. Place the coated tofu on the baking sheet in a single layer. Spray with oil until lightly coated. Flip over and spray the other side. Bake for 12 minutes on each side.

## BASIC BROILED TOFU

SERVES 4

**TIME:** 25 MINUTES

*Broiling tofu gives it a nice, dark, crusty skin. Intense heat concentrates and elevates the simple flavors of the ingredients—garlic, lemon juice, a little soy sauce. What we are saying is we like this method: it's fast, super easy, and pretty hard to mess up. Using the broiler does require that you spend a few minutes at your oven on guard, making sure what you're cooking doesn't burn. But get to know your broiler and it's sure to be the beginning of a lasting relationship.*

*We use this tofu in several of our brunch recipes, including Tofu Florentine (page 72) and Greek Tofu Benedict (page 74), but you can also stuff it into a pita with lettuce, onion, and tomato and pour Dill-Tahini Sauce (page 215) over it, or just serve as a simple dinner with some sautéed veggies.*

**1 pound extra-firm tofu**

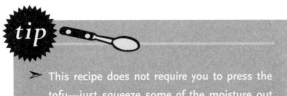

> This recipe does not require you to press the tofu—just squeeze some of the moisture out with your hands. But if you do prefer to press it, go right ahead!

**Braising sauce:**

**¼ cup water**

**2 cloves garlic, minced**

**3 tablespoons fresh lemon juice (juice of 1 lemon)**

**2 tablespoons soy sauce**

**A spray bottle of olive oil or 1 scant teaspoon olive oil**

PREHEAT THE oven to broil.

Cut the tofu into triangles, like so: Slice widthwise into four equal slices. Cut each of those slices in half, widthwise, so that you have eight squares. Lastly, cut each of those squares in half diagonally to make sixteen triangles.

Mix all the ingredients for the braising sauce together in a small bowl.

When the broiler is good and hot, spray a thin layer of olive oil on the bottom of an oven-safe pan (cast iron works great) or small rimmed baking sheet. If you don't have a spray bottle of oil, then just use a paper towel to spread a very thin coating of oil in the pan.

Dip each piece of tofu in the braising liquid and place in the pan. Put the pan in the broiler and cook for about 10 minutes, until the tofu is lightly browned. Remove the pan and pour a few spoonfuls of braising liquid over the tofu (no need to turn it). Put back in the oven for 3 more minutes, then repeat with the remaining braising liquid. Cook for about 3 more minutes—at this point the tofu should be golden brown. Remove from the oven and serve.

## TANGERINE BAKED TOFU

SERVES 4

**TIME:** 1 HOUR, PLUS TOFU PRESSING TIME

*Tofu bakes up chewy and saucy when marinated in bright citrus juices and a healthy dash of rum. A nice 'fu that's ideal for Caribbean-themed meals, or anything Latin really. Try it topped on Quinoa Salad with*

*Black Beans and Mango (page 84) or alongside Black Beans with Chipotle Adobo Sauce (page 122) and rice.*

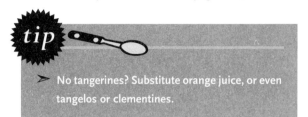

**tip**

➤ No tangerines? Substitute orange juice, or even tangelos or clementines.

1 pound extra-firm tofu, pressed and sliced width-wise into eighths

Marinade:

1 heaping teaspoon tangerine zest

⅓ cup freshly squeezed tangerine juice (from 2–3 tangerines)

3 tablespoons lime juice

2 tablespoons soy sauce

1 tablespoon agave nectar or pure maple syrup

1 tablespoon peanut oil

¼ teaspoon ground cumin

⅛ teaspoon ground allspice

Freshly ground pepper

2 tablespoons dark rum

PREHEAT THE oven to 425°F.

In a shallow 11 × 7-inch glass baking dish, whisk together all of the marinade ingredients. Place the tofu cutlets in marinade. Using a fork, carefully poke a few holes into the cutlets, flip them over, and do the same on the other side.

Bake the tofu for 45 minutes, flipping several times, about every 15 minutes or so. The tofu is ready when most of the marinade has reduced. Spoon any remaining marinade over the cutlets before serving.

## CURRIED TOFU

SERVES 2 TO 4

*Enjoy this flavorful tofu either baked or grilled. It's the perfect compliment to any Indian meal or even on a sammich with curried mayo (just add 2 teaspoons curry powder to ¼ cup veganaise). We love it with basmati rice and tamarind lentils. As always, reserve the marinade for the next time you make a stir fry.*

1 pound extra firm tofu, pressed and sliced into 8 equal pieces

For the marinade:

1/2 cup vegetable broth

3 tablespoons rice vinegar

2 tablespoons olive oil

2 tablespoons soy sauce

¼ cup curry powder

1 teaspoon cumin seeds

optional: 2 tablespoons mirin

IN a large mixing bowl, combine all marinade ingredients and wisk together.

*For Grilled Tofu:*

See page 128.

*For Baked Tofu:*

See page 129.

## BAKED BBQ TOFU

SERVES 4

**TIME:** 1 HOUR, NOT INCLUDING TOFU-PRESSING TIME

*Forget digging up a barbecue pit in your backyard. This chewy and succulent barbecue comes straight outta the oven. Serve with rice or mashed potatoes and steamed broccoli.*

> 1 recipe Backyard BBQ Sauce or Apricot BBQ Sauce (page 207)
> 1 pound tofu, drained and pressed, cut widthwise into eighths
> 2 tablespoons peanut oil
> 1 tablespoon soy sauce

PREHEAT THE oven to 350°F. In a 9 × 18-inch (preferably glass or ceramic) baking pan, dredge the tofu in the peanut oil and tamari to coat on both sides. Bake for 15 minutes, then flip the slices and bake for 15 more minutes. Meanwhile, prepare whichever sauce you're using.

When the tofu is done baking, pour the sauce over it, smothering it all over. Return to the oven and bake for 15 more minutes. Remove from the oven and serve.

## MARINATED ITALIAN TOFU

SERVES 4

**TIME:** 1 HOUR 20 MINUTES, NOT INCLUDING TOFU-PRESSING TIME

*Why mess with perfection? This recipe and the following one are two basic tofu marinades from* Vegan with a *Vengeance—simple recipes that go well with just about anything, either grilled or baked.*

> Since these cook so fast, a little advance planning will make your dinner a snap to prepare. Press your tofu the day before and prepare your marinades and refrigerate overnight. The next morning, slice up your tofu, drop into your marinade of choice, and refrigerate. When you get home, you should be able to have dinner on the table—or on your lap in front of the computer—in about 30 minutes.

> 1 pound extra-firm tofu, drained and pressed
> ½ cup white cooking wine
> 2 tablespoons olive oil
> 2 tablespoons balsamic vinegar
> 2 tablespoons Bragg Liquid Aminos or tamari
> 2 tablespoons fresh lemon juice
> 2 cloves garlic, smashed
> A big pinch of dried basil
> A big pinch of marjoram
> A big pinch of thyme

PREPARE THE marinade: Combine all the marinade ingredients in a wide shallow bowl.

### For Grilled Tofu:

Cut the tofu widthwise into four equal pieces. Marinate for an hour, flipping over after 30 minutes.

Grease a stove-top grill pan (preferably cast iron) with vegetable oil. Preheat over a high flame for about 3 minutes. Use tongs to distribute the tofu slabs evenly onto the grill. Gently use the tongs to press the tofu into the grill ridges, to get nice dark lines. Cook for 3 minutes on one side without lifting, then turn the slabs 90 degrees to create a crosshatched pattern on the bottom of the tofu. Cook for 2 minutes, then flip over and cook for another 2 minutes. Move to a cutting board and cut each piece diagonally across into two triangles with a sharp knife.

*For Baked Tofu:*

Preheat the oven to 400°F.

Cut the tofu widthwise into eight equal pieces. Marinate for an hour, flipping after 30 minutes.

Place the tofu on a baking sheet and bake for 20 minutes. Flip over and bake for another 10 minutes. Place in the broiler for about 3 more minutes for extra chewiness.

## MARINATED ASIAN TOFU

SERVES 4

**TIME:** 1 HOUR 20 MINUTES, NOT INCLUDING TOFU-PRESSING TIME

*This tofu goes great with Wasabi Mashed Potatoes (page 110) and asparagus. It's also perfect to top off the Corn and Edamame Salad (page 82).*

1 pound extra-firm tofu, drained and pressed
½ cup mirin
3 tablespoons tamari
2 tablespoons rice wine vinegar
1 tablespoon sesame oil
2 teaspoons Asian chile sauce
1-inch chunk of ginger, peeled and chopped coarsely
2 cloves garlic, smashed

PREPARE THE marinade: Combine all the marinade ingredients in a wide shallow bowl.

*For Grilled Tofu:*

Cut the tofu widthwise into four equal pieces. Marinate for an hour, flipping over after 30 minutes.

Grease a stove-top grill pan (preferably cast iron) with vegetable oil. Preheat over a high flame for about 3 minutes. Use tongs to distribute the tofu slabs evenly onto the grill. Gently use the tongs to press the tofu into the grill ridges, to get nice dark lines. Cook for 3 minutes on one side without lifting, then turn the slabs 90 degrees to create a crosshatched pattern on the bottom of the tofu. Cook for 2 minutes, then flip over and cook for another 2 minutes. Move to a cutting board and cut each piece diagonally across into two triangles with a sharp knife.

*For Baked Tofu:*

Preheat the oven to 400°F.

Cut the tofu widthwise into eight equal pieces. Marinate for an hour, flipping after 30 minutes.

Place the tofu on a baking sheet and bake for 20 minutes. Flip over and bake for another 10 minutes. Place in the broiler for about 3 more minutes for extra chewiness.

## HOT SAUCE–GLAZED TEMPEH

SERVES 4 AS A SIDE, 2 AS A MAIN

**TIME:** 20 MINUTES, PLUS TIME FOR MARINATING

*There is no shortage of ways to serve this spicy and succulent tempeh. It goes well with mashed potatoes and Jalapeño Corn Gravy (although, doesn't everything?) (page 216). Or try sautéed greens and baked sweet potatoes. If you wanna go all out, serve with Creole Stuffed Peppers (page 61) and Messy Rice (page 118).*

**tip**

➤ If you don't cook with wine, use vegetable broth here instead.

*Our preferred cooking method here is grilling, but we give you broiling and panfrying directions as well.*

1 (8-ounce) package tempeh

½ cup wine

    (whatever kind you've got on hand, just nothing sweet, Manischewitz lovers!)

¼ cup hot sauce

2 tablespoons olive oil

2 tablespoons soy sauce

3 tablespoons fresh lemon juice

    (juice of 1 lemon)

2 cloves garlic, crushed

1 teaspoon ground cumin

½ teaspoon dried oregano

⅛ teaspoon cayenne

    (we know, with hot sauce? Yes.)

BRING A medium-size pot of water to a boil.

Whisk all the marinade ingredients together in a bowl large enough to fit the tempeh slices.

Cut the tempeh in half, widthwise, then cut each of the resulting squares diagonally, to form four large triangles. When the water is boiling, lower the heat to a simmer, and cook the tempeh triangles for 10 minutes. This steams the tempeh and removes any bitterness, plus readies the tempeh to absorb the marinade.

Use tongs to immediately place the tempeh in the marinade bowl. Let marinate for 1 hour, flipping the tempeh every now and again to cover with the marinade.

### Grilling Instructions:

Preheat a greased cast-iron grill pan over medium-high heat. To grease it, brush lightly with olive oil or, if you have a spray bottle of olive oil, that works, too. (Get a spray bottle of olive oil already!)

Grill each side of the tempeh for 5 minutes. When the second side is almost done, spoon some of the marinade over the tempeh and let it cook for 30 more seconds.

### Panfrying Instructions:

Preheat a heavy-bottomed pan over medium heat. Add about a tablespoon of oil to the pan. Cook the tempeh for about 10 minutes, turning often and spooning a bit more marinade over the tempeh as you turn it.

### Broiling Instructions:

Preheat the oven to broil. Place the tempeh in an oven-safe pan (such as cast iron) or a rimmed baking pan. Spoon some of the marinade over the tempeh and broil for 5 minutes. Flip it and spoon some more marinade over it, and cook for another 5 minutes. When the second side is almost done, spoon some of the marinade over the tempeh and let cook for 30 more seconds.

## SMOKY GRILLED TEMPEH

SERVES 4 AS A SIDE, 2 AS A MAIN

TIME: 20 MINUTES, PLUS TIME FOR MARINATING

*This juicy tempeh is perfect alongside Sautéed Collards (page 106), which in turn make use of the tempeh marinade, so everyone is living in perfect harmony. It's equally delish with the Cheater Baked Beans (page 122), some greens, and a baked sweet potato. This tastes sort of like the Tempeh Bacon from* Vegan with a Vengeance, *so if you like that you will like this.*

Note: this recipe has the same basic directions as the Hot Sauce–Glazed Tempeh (page 129). Grilling is our preferred method but we give you broiling and panfrying directions as well.

1 (8-ounce) package tempeh

¾ cup vegetable broth

2 tablespoons soy sauce

**2 tablespoons apple cider vinegar**

**2 tablespoons liquid smoke**

**2 tablespoons olive oil**

**2 teaspoons pure maple syrup**

**2 cloves garlic, crushed**

BRING A medium-size pot of water to boil.

Whisk all marinade ingredients together in a bowl large enough to fit the tempeh slices.

Cut the tempeh in half, widthwise, then cut each of the resulting squares diagonally, to form four large triangles. When the water is boiling, lower the heat to a simmer, add the tempeh triangles, and cook for 10 minutes. This steams the tempeh and removes any bitterness, plus readies the tempeh to absorb the marinade.

Use tongs to immediately place the tempeh in the marinade bowl. Let marinate for 1 hour, flipping the tempeh every now and again to cover with the marinade.

### Grilling Instructions:

Preheat a greased cast-iron grill pan over medium-high heat. To grease it, brush lightly with olive oil, or use a spray bottle of olive oil.

Grill each side of the tempeh for 5 minutes. When the second side is almost done, spoon some of the marinade over the tempeh and let cook for 30 more seconds.

### Panfrying Instructions:

Preheat a heavy-bottomed pan over medium heat. Add about a tablespoon of oil to the pan. Cook the tempeh for about 10 minutes, turning often and spooning a bit more marinade over the tempeh as you turn it.

### Broiling Instructions:

Preheat the oven to broil. Place the tempeh in an oven-safe pan (such as cast iron ) or a rimmed baking pan. Spoon some of the marinade over the tempeh

and broil for 5 minutes. Flip it and spoon some more marinade over it, and cook for another 5 minutes. When the second side is almost done, spoon some of the marinade over the tempeh and let it cook for 30 more seconds.

## SIMPLE SEITAN

MAKES 1 POUND

Ⓕ

**TIME:** 1 HOUR 30 MINUTES

*This is the* Vegan with a Vengeance *seitan recipe simplified. After publishing that book we got a lot of questions, often asking if one could substitute this, leave out that—sometimes just asking how we got to be so beautiful. While we won't reveal our beauty secrets, we will present you with this bare-bones boiled seitan recipe with clearer directions, simpler ingredients, and just the right amount of seitan for most recipes in this book.*

**1 cup vital wheat gluten flour**

**3 tablespoons nutritional yeast**

**½ cup cold vegetable broth**

**¼ cup soy sauce**

**1 tablespoon olive oil**

**2 cloves garlic, pressed or grated on a microplane grater**

Broth:

**8 cups cold water plus 3 vegetable bouillon cubes, or 4 cups broth plus 4 cups water**

**¼ cup soy sauce**

MIX TOGETHER the gluten flour and yeast in a large bowl. In a smaller bowl, mix together the veggie broth, soy sauce, olive oil, and garlic. Pour the wet into the dry and stir with a wooden spoon until most of the moisture has been absorbed and the wet ingredients are partially clumped up with the dry ingredients. Use your hands to knead the mixture for about 3 minutes, until the dough is elastic. Divide with a knife into three equal pieces and then knead those pieces in your hand just to stretch them out a bit.

*Prepare the broth:*

Fill a stockpot with the water, bouillon cubes, and soy sauce, and add the wheat gluten pieces. Cover and bring to a boil but watch carefully; you don't want it to boil for very long or the outside of the seitan will be spongy. Try to catch it as soon as it boils and then lower the heat as low as it will go so that it's at a low simmer.

Partially cover the pot so that steam can escape and let simmer for an hour, turning the seitan occasionally. Turn off the heat and take the lid off; let sit for 15 minutes.

Remove from the broth and place in a strainer until it is cool enough to handle. It is now ready to be sliced up and used. If you have extra seitan, store in the cooking liquid in a tightly covered container.

## SEITAN CUTLETS

MAKES 6 CUTLETS

Ⓕ

**TIME:** 1 HOUR 30 MINUTES

*These baked cutlets are great for things like seitan Parmesan, or just as a meaty main dish with mustard sauce (page 204), red wine roux (page 204) or the sweet Vidalia onion sauce (page 216). They are firmer and chewier than boiled seitan; when sliced thinly across, they can be used in any of the seitan recipes in this book.*

*They're also wonderful left whole and grilled and then smothered in whatever sauce you choose. To grill, coat your grill pan with oil and place over high heat. Lightly press any extra water out of the seitan with your hands. Coat with a little olive oil and grill on each side for about 5*

*minutes, pressing down with tongs to get grill marks.*

*You can also dredge them in flour and fry them in a little oil on each side for about 4 minutes.*

**Broth:**
**6 cups vegetable broth**
**3 tablespoons soy sauce**

**Cutlets:**
**1¼ cups vital wheat gluten**
**½ cup cold vegetable broth**
**¼ cup soy sauce**
**1 tablespoon olive oil**
**2 cloves garlic, pressed or grated on a microplane grater**
**1 teaspoon grated lemon zest (optional)**

PREHEAT THE oven to 350°F.

*Prepare the broth:*

Bring to a boil in a pot and then turn off the heat and keep covered.

*Prepare the cutlets:*

Place the wheat gluten in a mixing bowl. Pour the cold vegetable broth (not the vegetable broth you boiled, but the broth in the gluten ingredients) into a measuring cup. Then pour in the soy sauce. Add the oil, garlic, and lemon zest, and mix. Pour the wet mixture into the flour and combine with a wooden spoon until most of the moisture has absorbed and it's partially clumped up with the flour. Use your hands to knead for about 3 minutes, until the dough is elastic. Divide into six equal pieces; the best way to do this is to roll it out into somewhat of a log shape and then slice it with a knife.

Take each piece and stretch and knead it into an oblong cutlet shape that is a little less than ½ inch thick. Use your body weight to press it and stretch it on a hard surface; there will be some resistance but just keep at it.

Pour the heated vegetable broth into a 9 × 13-inch glass baking pan or a ceramic casserole (If all you have is metal, that's okay). Place the cutlets in the broth, then bake for about 30 minutes uncovered, turn the cutlets over (use tongs for this and it's easy), and bake for an additional 20 minutes.

Remove from the oven and place the cutlets in a colander to drain. The cutlets are now ready to use in whatever seitan recipe you choose. If you have extra seitan, store it in the cooking liquid in a tightly covered container.

## CHICKPEA CUTLETS

MAKES 4 CUTLETS

TIME: 30 MINUTES

*We try not play favorites, but this is one of our babies and a recipe that we are sure will take over food blogs worldwide. A combination of chickpeas and vital wheat gluten formed into savory cutlets, it's perfect for when you want something "meaty" but don't want to go through the trouble of making seitan. We serve these cutlets in myriad ways, packed into sandwiches or smothered in mustard sauce, with a side of mashed potatoes and roasted asparagus. It's vegan food that you can eat with a steak knife and, best of all, it is fast and easy. You'll probably want to double the recipe if you're serving it to guests.*

1 cup cooked chickpeas
2 tablespoons olive oil
½ cup vital wheat gluten
½ cup plain bread crumbs
¼ cup vegetable broth or water
2 tablespoons soy sauce
2 cloves garlic, pressed or grated with a microplane
   grater
½ teaspoon lemon zest

½ teaspoon dried thyme
½ teaspoon Hungarian paprika
¼ teaspoon dried rubbed sage
Olive oil for panfrying

IN A mixing bowl, mash the chickpeas together with the oil until no whole chickpeas are left. Add the remaining ingredients and knead for about 3 minutes, until strings of gluten have formed.

Preheat a large heavy-bottomed nonstick or cast-iron skillet over medium heat. Meanwhile, divide the cutlet dough into four equal pieces. To form the cutlets, knead each piece in your hand for a few moments and then flatten and stretch each one into a roughly 6 × 4-inch rectangular cutlet shape. The easiest way to do this is to first form a rectangular shape in your hands and then place the cutlets on a clean surface to flatten and stretch them.

Add a moderately thin layer of olive oil to the bottom of the pan. Place the cutlets in the pan and cook on each side for 6 to 7 minutes. Add more oil, if needed, when you flip the cutlets. They're ready when lightly browned and firm to the touch.

Just in case you were wondering, you can also bake these too! Baking these patties gives them a toothsome chewy texture and firm bite. Preheat oven to 375°F, lightly oil baking sheet. Brush both sides of each patty with olive oil, place on baking sheet and bake for 20 minutes. Flip patties and bake another 8-10 minutes till firm and golden-brown.

# SOUPS

SOUP IS SO basic that all too often it's totally ignored in cookbooks. Everyone's always rushing willy-nilly to check out the chocolate cake situation or the latest developments in lasagne. Don't be a follower like them; stop for a moment and really think about the abundance that soup is and how it can change your life.

Soup can be smooth or chunky, creamy or clear, hearty or refreshing. The variations are really endless! Looking to drop a few pounds while eating fabulously? Make soup. Almost all of these recipes are low fat (and can be made even lower fat or fat free; see page 21) and absolutely loaded with tummy-filling fiber and nutrient-loaded veggies. Bean-based soups have the added benefit of plenty of protein. Eating a large bowl of soup for dinner is an easy way to avoid eating too many calories in the evening, when they're more likely to be stored as fat (as opposed to being burned off though activity).

More important, soup can be serious food, not just the stuff you sip before an entrée. Take a wander in midtown New York on any weekday around lunchtime—what you'll most likely see are people standing in line for soup. And we're talking about the suit-and-tie, pumps-and-purses, no-nonsense, office-working crowd. They don't mess around when it comes to that precious lunch hour, and neither should you. Be a smart New Yorker (or Green Bayer, San Diegan, Portlander . . .) and write "making (really awesome) soup" into your weekly planner.

# BLACK BEAN–VEGETABLE SOUP

SERVES 6 TO 8

Ⓒ Ⓖ Ⓕ ⬭

**TIME:** 1 HOUR 45 MINUTES (NOT INCLUDING SOAKING BEANS)

*Like that little black dress, a good black bean soup can really take you places and fit any occasion. To make sure that the beans' deep, purple-black color stays true, we first completely cook the beans solo and then add the accompanying sautéed veggies afterward for a long, final simmer. Serve as is or topped with a swirl of Lime Crema (from the Baja Tacos recipe, page 96) or Sour Cilantro Cream (page 209), a twist of lime juice, or some diced avocado.*

## Beans:

1 pound dried black beans, rinsed, soaked for 6 to 8
   hours or overnight
6 cups water
2 bay leaves
Pinch of baking soda

> ➤ We've added enough total liquid to create plenty of broth in this recipe; if you like your black bean soup more stewlike, add only two or three cups of veggie broth toward the end.

> ➤ For a creamy-textured black bean soup, remove a one or two cups of cooled soup and puree in a blender. Stir back into the soup and simmer for another 15 minutes. If you have leftover soup a few days down the road, try pureeing the whole thing and simmering until very hot. Season with a little more vinegar.

## Soup:

3 tablespoons olive oil
2 medium-size onions, diced finely
4 cloves garlic, minced
1 green bell pepper, seeded and diced finely
1 jalapeño, seeded and minced
1 stalk celery, diced finely
1 carrot, peeled and diced finely
1½ teaspoons ground cumin
2 teaspoons dried oregano
1 teaspoon dried thyme
1 tablespoon white wine vinegar or sherry vinegar
2 teaspoons salt, or to taste
Freshly ground black pepper
3–4 cups vegetable stock

## For garnishing each serving of soup:

lime wedges, chopped avocado, minced fresh cilantro

PREPARE THE beans: Drain the soaked beans, rinse again, and place the beans in a very large stockpot. Pour in the 6 cups of water and add the bay leaves and baking soda. Cover and bring to a boil, boil for about 3 minutes, and then lower the heat to medium-low. Allow to simmer for 1 to 1½ hours, until the beans are very tender and their skins are soft. Remove the bay leaves.

During the last 30 minutes of the beans' cooking, prepare the vegetables: Preheat a large heavy-bottomed skillet over medium heat. Sauté the garlic in the oil until the garlic begins to sizzle, stir for 30 seconds, and add the onions and bell pepper. Stir and cook for 12 to 15 minutes, until the onions and peppers are very soft, then add the jalapeño, celery, and carrot. Cook for another 10 minutes, until the carrot has begun to soften, then remove from the heat.

When the beans are completely tender, stir in the sautéed vegetables and any remaining oil, plus the cumin, oregano, thyme, and vegetable stock. Cover the pot, raise the heat to high, and bring to a boil. Lower the heat to medium-low, partially cover the pot, and simmer for 35 to 40 minutes, until the carrot and celery are tender.

Remove from the heat, allow to cool 10 minutes, add the vinegar, and season to taste with salt and pepper. Like most soups, this soup will be richer and more flavorful the next day.

Garnish each serving of soup with chopped cilantro and chopped avocado. Serve with lime wedges.

## ACORN SQUASH, PEAR, AND ADZUKI SOUP WITH SAUTÉED SHIITAKES

SERVES 6

Ⓖ

**TIME:** 1 HOUR

*This is a precious jewel of a soup studded with pretty, red adzuki beans along with just a hint of fragrant five-spice. We love the salty sesame shiitake mushrooms that adorn the soup and draw all the flavors together.*

**tip**

➢ Acorn squash is a pain in the tuchus to peel. The best way we've found is to cut the squash in half and seed it, then cut into chunks (¾ inch, in this case). Use a paring knife to slice off the skin.

➢ To remove the seeds from pears, peel and slice in half, then use a measuring teaspoon to scoop the seeds right out.

2 tablespoons peanut oil
1 large yellow onion, cut into ¼-inch slices
1 red bell pepper, cut into ¼-inch slices
2 teaspoons minced ginger
2 cloves garlic minced
½ teaspoon salt

½ teaspoon Chinese five-spice powder
2 acorn squashes, seeded, peeled, and cut into ¾-inch chunks
2 firm Bartlett pears, peeled, seeded, and sliced into thin (not paper-thin) slices roughly 1 inch long
4 cups vegetable stock
1 (15-ounce) can adzuki beans, drained and rinsed (about 1½ cups)
About 1 tablespoon fresh lime juice
Mushrooms:
4 ounces fresh shiitakes, sliced in half (about 1½ cups)
2 teaspoons peanut oil
½ teaspoon toasted sesame oil
1 tablespoon soy sauce

PREHEAT A large stockpot over medium heat. Sauté the onions and peppers in the oil for about 10 minutes, or until the onions just begin to brown.

Add the ginger and garlic, and sauté for 1 more minute. Stirring often, add the salt, five-spice, acorn squash, and pear, and cook for another minute before adding the vegetable stock. Cover and bring to a boil. Once the soup is boiling, lower the heat to medium-low and simmer briskly for about 20 more minutes, or until the squash is tender.

Puree half the soup, using either an immersion blender or by transferring half the soup to a food processor or blender, processing, and pouring it back into the rest of the soup (don't forget, if using a blender or food processor, to let the soup cool a bit so that the steam does not compress in the processor and hurt you).

Add the adzuki beans and lime. Cover and simmer over low heat just until the beans are heated through, 7 to 10 minutes.

*Meanwhile, prepare the mushrooms:*

Preheat a heavy-bottomed skillet over medium-high heat. Add the oils and sauté the mushrooms for about 7 minutes, until they are soft. Mix in the soy sauce and stir constantly until it is absorbed (about 1 minute).

Ladle the soup into bowls and top with the sautéed mushrooms.

## TOMATO-RICE SOUP WITH ROASTED GARLIC AND NAVY BEANS

SERVES 10 TO 12

Ⓢ Ⓖ Ⓕ ㊺ ⬯

**TIME:** 45 MINUTES

*Roasted garlic gives this pantry-staple tomato soup a little something special. Navy beans add protein and make it a complete meal. And since this recipe makes so much, it's a perfect contender for freezing and eating throughout the month. Or, you can keep it in the fridge to eat throughout the week and forget that you ever ate anything else.*

**tip**

➤ Use long-grain brown rice, not short-grain, because that kind doesn't like to cook in tomato broth.

➤ If you don't have any roasted garlic hanging around and don't intend on making any, then sauté 6 cloves of minced garlic along with the onion.

2 bulbs garlic

1 tablespoon olive oil

1 medium-size yellow onion, diced as small as possible

1 cup long-grain brown rice

2 bay leaves

2 teaspoons dried thyme

1 teaspoon dried marjoram

2 teaspoons salt

Several pinches of freshly ground black pepper

2 (28-ounce) cans crushed tomatoes

1 (15-ounce) can navy beans, drained and rinsed (about 1½ cups)

PREHEAT THE oven to 425°F. Following the directions on page 32, roast the garlic for about 45 minutes, until soft. You should be able to feel if it's soft by pressing with a knife or your finger. Don't burn yourself, though.

Preheat a soup pot over medium heat. Sauté the onions in the olive oil for 5 to 7 minutes, until translucent.

Add the rice, bay leaves, thyme, marjoram, salt, and pepper and cook, stirring, for about 2 minutes. Add the crushed tomatoes, then fill up the can with water twice and add the water (so that's 56 ounces of water).

Bring to a boil, then lower the heat to medium-low, cover, and simmer for about 45 minutes.

Remove the garlic from the oven. When it is cool enough to handle, squeeze the roasted garlic out of its skin and into a small bowl. Use a fork to mash the garlic to a relatively smooth consistency, then add to the soup once the rice is nearly tender.

When the rice is completely cooked, add the beans and heat through. Then it's ready to serve—just remove the bay leaves beforehand.

## ANCHO-LENTIL SOUP WITH GRILLED PINEAPPLE

SERVES 6

Ⓢ Ⓖ Ⓕ ㊺

**TIME:** 45 MINUTES

*Okay, even though this recipe involves you making your own chile powder, we promise this is a fast soup that is even a little fancy. Not to mention yummy, warm and comforting. The tart-sweet pineapple couples well with the deep, smoky chiles. Ancho chiles are fairly mild, so don't worry that this soup will be too spicy, unless you're a real big wimp. In fact, serve with hot sauce to prove your manhood.*

Chile powder:

> 1 tablespoon cumin seeds
>
> 1 tablespoon coriander seeds
>
> 2 dried ancho chile, seeds removed,
>   ripped into bite-size pieces

Soup:

> 2 tablespoons olive oil
>
> 1 large onion, cut into small dice
>
> 3 cloves garlic, minced
>
> 2 bay leaves
>
> 1 teaspoon salt
>
> 2 cups green lentils, washed
>
> 7–8 cups vegetable stock or water or a mix of both
>
> 3 tablespoons of lime juice, or to taste
>
> Nonstick cooking spray
>
> 6–8 pineapple rings
>
> Slices of lime
>
> Hot sauce

WE'RE GOING to make our own ancho chile powder! Preheat a small skillet over medium-low heat. Add the cumin seeds and ancho chile pieces and stir often, until fragrant and toasted, 3 to 5 minutes.

Transfer to a spice grinder (we use a clean coffee grinder) or small food processor and grind to a coarse powder. Some bigger pieces of chile are okay. Add the coriander seeds and pulse a few times to crush them—you don't want them completely ground to a powder, just broken up pretty well.

Preheat a big stockpot over medium heat. Sauté the onions in the olive oil until transparent, 5 to 7 minutes. Add the garlic and cook for another minute. Add the chile powder and mix into the onions. Add the bay leaves, salt, lentils, and 7 cups of water. Mix well. Raise the heat to high, cover, and bring to a boil. Once the soup is boiling, lower the heat to medium-low and let simmer for 30 minutes, stirring every now and again.

Meanwhile, heat your grill pan over high heat or preheat a broiler. Spray your grill pan with cooking spray and grill the pineapple slices for 4 minutes on each side, or until grill lines appear. If using a broiler, cook on one side for 3 minutes and on the other for

about 2 minutes, until the pineapple begins to brown and slightly caramelize.

Once the lentils are tender, add an extra cup of water/stock if you think the soup needs thinning. Add the lime juice and stir.

Remove the bay leaf. Use an immersion blender to puree about half the soup. If you don't have an immersion blender, use a potato masher to mash it up a bit, until the desired thickness is achieved. Taste and adjust the salt.

*To serve:*

Ladle into bowls and top with a pineapple ring, a slice of lime, and a few dots of hot sauce.

## BROCCOLI-POTATO SOUP WITH FRESH HERBS

SERVES 6 TO 8

**TIME:** 50 MINUTES

*This vibrant soup is a great start to a Mediterranean meal. Try it our way with fresh dill and mint, but keep in mind that it's also really versatile. So if the day should come when all you've got is some potatoes, onions, and garlic, you can use this recipe as a guideline and add the herbs and spices of your choice. But if you mess it up with some crazy substitution, please don't go giving us two-star reviews on Amazon.*

> 2 tablespoons olive oil
>
> 1 medium-size onion, cut into ¼ inch dice
>
> 3 cloves garlic, minced
>
> ½ teaspoon dried tarragon
>
> Several pinches of freshly ground black pepper
>
> 1 teaspoon salt
>
> 6 cups vegetable stock, or 4 cups veggie stock plus 2 cups water, whatever
>
> 2 pounds potatoes, peeled and cut into ½-inch chunks

4 cups chopped broccoli (including the stalks: chop them into thin slices, and the tops into small florets)

¼ cup chopped fresh dill

¼ cup chopped fresh mint

HEAT A soup pot over medium heat. Sauté the onion in the olive oil for 5 to 7 minutes, until softened. Add the garlic, tarragon, black pepper, and salt, and cook for 1 more minute. Pour in the vegetable stock and add the potatoes. Cover and bring to a boil. Once the soup is boiling, lower the heat and let simmer for 15 minutes. Add the broccoli and cook for 15 more minutes.

Use an immersion blender to blend about one-third of the soup; we like to keep it chunky with lots of whole potato chunks. If you don't have an immersion blender (get one!), transfer about one-third of the soup to a blender or food processor and puree, then add it back to the rest of the soup.

Add the fresh dill and mint, then let the soup sit for about 10 minutes to let the flavors meld. Serve!

## CHICKPEA-NOODLE SOUP

SERVES 6

**TIME:** 50 MINUTES

Chickpea Soup for the Vegan Soul. *This is some Oprah's Book Club stuff right here: a great soup for when you're feeling under the weather and need something tasty to slurp on while you watch TV and pity yourself. But don't let that dissuade you if you feel fine and just happen to want a nice, comforting bowl of soup.*

2 tablespoons olive oil

1 large yellow onion, sliced thinly

1 cup peeled, thinly sliced carrots (or chopped baby carrots)

2 cloves garlic, minced

2 cups sliced cremini mushrooms

½ teaspoon celery seeds

1 teaspoon dried thyme

½ teaspoon dried rosemary, crushed in your fingers

½ teaspoon ground black pepper

2 tablespoons mirin (optional)

⅓ cup brown rice miso

6 cups water or vegetable stock

2 cups cooked dried chickpeas, or 1 (15-ounce) can, drained and rinsed

6 ounces soba noodles

*tip*

➤ We use brown rice miso here, which has a nice winelike taste and isn't too salty, but you can use any kind of miso you like. If using a stronger miso, such as barley miso, first use ¼ cup and add more to taste from there.

➤ Some soba noodles come wrapped in 3-ounce serving sizes. If yours aren't wrapped, you can measure 'em this way: the circumference of one 3-ounce bundle is about the size of a quarter.

➤ Soba noodles expand a lot when they're soaking, so this isn't the best soup to keep in the fridge overnight. If you don't plan on eating it all in one day, use instead regular pasta noodles broken in half or thirds.

➤ Need a little green? Add some chopped greens toward the end of the cooking process. Spinach, kale, chard—whatever you've got. Let them wilt and then serve.

PREHEAT A soup pot over medium-high heat. Sauté the onions and carrots in the oil for about 10 minutes. Add the garlic, mushrooms, and herbs, and sauté for another 5 minutes. Deglaze the pot with the mirin (or just a splash of water). Add the 6 cups of water and the chickpeas. Cover and bring to a boil.

Once the broth is boiling, break the soba noodles into thirds and throw them in. Lower the heat to medium so that the soup is at a low boil. Cover and cook for 15 minutes, stirring occasionally.

Add the miso and stir until it's incorporated. Taste and adjust the salt, and add a little extra miso if you would like a stronger, saltier flavor.

## PORCINI–WILD RICE SOUP

SERVES 6

🅖 🅕 ⬚

TIME: A LITTLE OVER 1 HOUR, MOST OF IT INACTIVE

*Woodsy and earthy, this soup is rich with mushroom flavor. It is topped off with fresh chervil, which has a delicate, lemony taste that is not quite comparable to any herb, though if you can't find it, chopped fresh parsley works nicely. Go on a mission to find the chervil; if nothing else, it would make a great blog entry.*

*Garnished or not, this is an easy recipe for what tastes like a ten-dollar bowl of soup at a swanky Manhattan sidewalk café. Perfect for serving your yuppie friends.*

½ ounce dried porcini mushrooms

2 cups boiling water

2 tablespoons olive oil

1 large yellow onion, sliced thinly

4 cloves garlic, minced

2 tablespoons fresh thyme

1 teaspoon salt

Several pinches of freshly ground black pepper

8 ounces cremini mushrooms (about 3 cups), sliced thinly

1½ cups wild rice (try to find a wild rice blend with several kinds mixed together)

4 cups vegetable stock, plus extra if needed

1 carrot, peeled

Several sprigs of fresh chervil for garnish

PLACE THE porcinis in a bowl. Measure 2 cups of boiling water and pour over the porcinis. Cover with a plate and set aside.

Preheat a stockpot over medium-high heat. Add the olive oil and sauté the onions for about 3 minutes. Add the garlic, fresh thyme, salt, and pepper. Cook for about 10 minutes or until browned, stirring frequently.

Add the sliced creminis and sauté for about 3 minutes. In the meantime, remove the porcinis from their broth (with tongs or a fork). Slice them thinly and add to the stockpot along with the porcini broth. Let the mixture cook for a few more minutes.

Add the wild rice and the vegetable stock. Cover and bring to a boil. Once the soup is boiling, lower the heat to low and simmer for about 45 minutes.

When the rice is tender, grate in the carrot, turn off the heat, and let sit for 10 more minutes. If the soup is too thick, add another cup or so of water or broth. Ladle into bowls and garnish with sprigs of fresh chervil.

## DOUBLE PEA SOUP WITH ROASTED RED PEPPERS

SERVES 6 TO 8

🅢 🅖 🅕 ⬚

TIME: 1 HOUR 20 MINUTES

*Split pea soup is practically a pop-culture icon, in the world of soups, that is. Or at least we think so. Our split pea is a little amped-up, featuring extra herbs and spices, a new texture thanks to the addition of fresh green peas, and a little bit of smoky-sweetness from roasted red peppers. A big bowl makes a perfect light yet nourishing meal, especially when served alongside crusty bread and Hummus (page 67) for dipping.*

3 tablespoons olive oil

1 large onion, chopped finely

2 carrots, peeled and cut into small dice

2 stalks celery, chopped into ¼-inch pieces

2½ quarts water

## SPICY TEMPEH NORI ROLLS

(page 47)

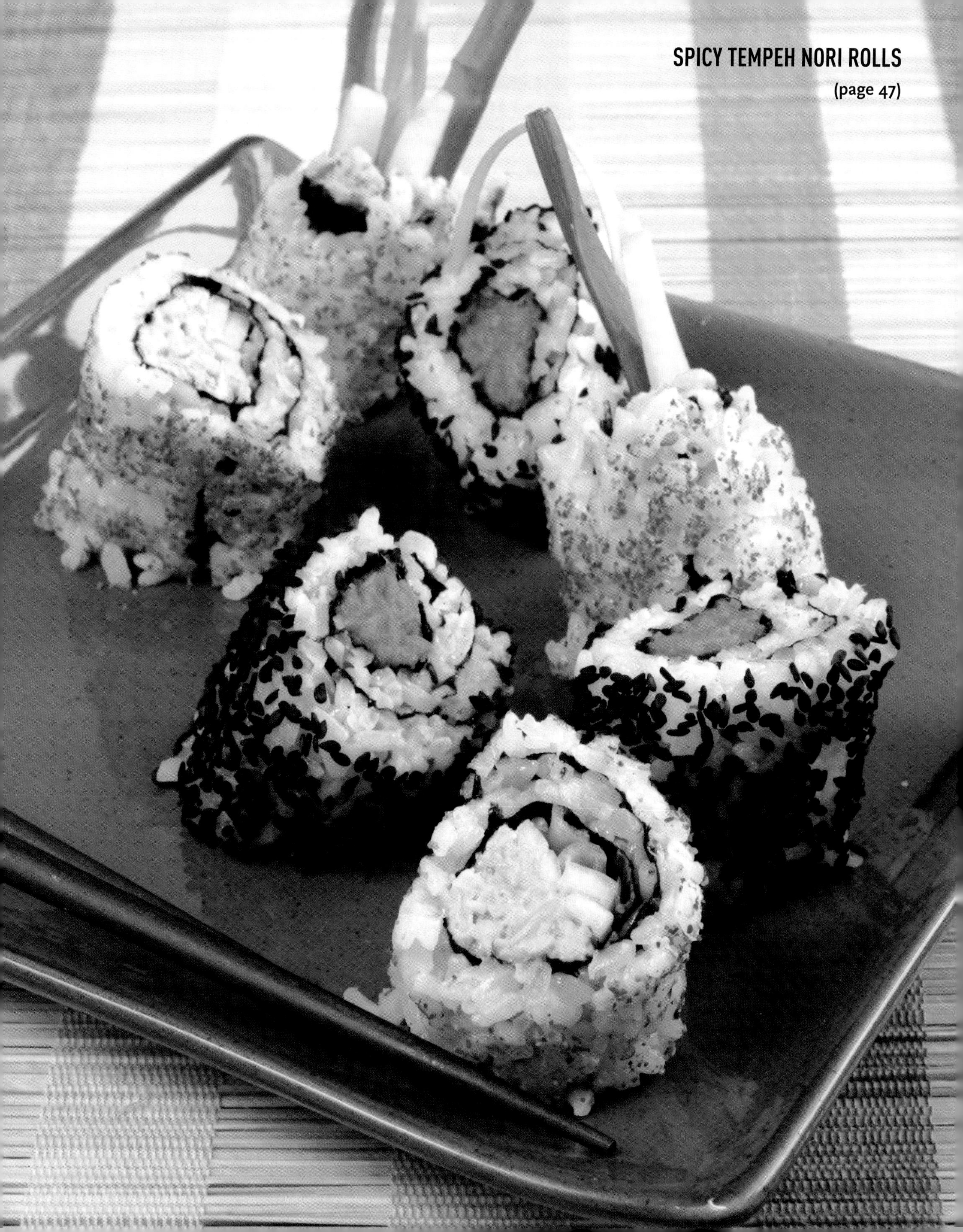

PORTOBELLO SALAD WITH SPICY
MUSTARD DRESSING (page 87)

**BAKED BBQ TOFU** (page 128)
**WITH APRICOT BBQ SAUCE**
(page 207)

**HOT SAUCE-GLAZED TEMPEH**

(page 129)

**POTATO AND KALE ENCHILADAS WITH ROASTED CHILE SAUCE** (page 162)

**GRILLED YUCA TORTILLAS** (page 49)

**KABOCHA-UDON WINTER STEW**
(page 180)

**BAKED POTATO & GREENS SOUP WITH POTATO-WEDGE CROUTONS** (page 146)

**LEMONY ROASTED POTATOES** (page 109)

**CHICKPEA CUTLETS** (page 133)

ROASTED FENNEL
AND HAZELNUT
SALAD WITH
SHALLOT DRESSING
(page 86)

SPICY TEMPEH AND BROCCOLI RABE
WITH ROTELLE (page 190)

**VANILLA-YOGURT POUND CAKE**

(page 254)

**GREEN TEA ICE CREAM SANDWICHES** (page 260, 261)

**CHOLENT** (page 182)

**EGGPLANT-POTATO MOUSSAKA WITH PINE NUT CREAM** (page 164)

**PINEAPPLE CASHEW QUINOA STIR-FRY** (page 175)

ACORN SQUASH, PEAR, AND ADZUKI SOUP
WITH SAUTÉED SHIITAKES (page 136)

**AUTUMN LATKES**
(page 53)

**CORN AND EDAMAME-
SESAME SALAD** (page 82)

BANANA-NUT WAFFLES (page 75)
AND CHOCOLATE CHIP BROWNIE WAFFLES (page 74)

**FUDGY WUDGY BLUEBERRY BROWNIES** (page 243)

**INDIVIDUAL HEART-SHAPED APPLE GALETTES** (page 249)

**ROASTED EGGPLANT AND SPINACH
MUFFULETTA SANDWICH** (page 100)

1 pound dried split green peas

1-inch cube fresh ginger, peeled

1 bay leaf

2 teaspoons dried thyme

1 teaspoon dried tarragon

½ teaspoon ground coriander

½ teaspoon ground cumin

1 (16-ounce) bag frozen green peas

2 roasted red reppers (page 33), cut into ½-inch
   pieces, diced

Freshly ground pepper

1½ teaspoons salt, or to taste

PREHEAT A large stockpot over medium heat. Sauté the onion 5 to 7 minutes, until softened. Add the carrots and celery, and sauté for another 5 minutes until the veggies are soft and slightly golden.

Add the water, split peas, ginger, bay leaf, thyme, tarragon, coriander, and cumin. Cover, raise the heat to high to bring to a rolling boil, then lower the heat to medium-low and allow the soup to simmer, covered, for 45 to 50 minutes until the split peas turn soft and mushy.

Stir in the frozen green peas and diced roasted pepper. Cover, and raise the heat to bring to a boil again, then lower the heat and simmer for another 20 minutes, or until green peas are tender.

Remove the ginger cube and bay leaf. Allow to sit for 15 minutes before serving.

## FRENCH LENTIL SOUP WITH TARRAGON AND THYME

SERVES 8

**TIME:** 1 HOUR

*This is the last lentil soup recipe you will ever need. Tarragon adds a wonderful peppery, licorice flavor that complements this soup like nobody's business. Just try to keep leftovers of this soup stored in the fridge—you will*

*find yourself going back for more all night. After three helpings, keep the lid on it to retain some sense of dignity.*

1 tablespoon olive oil

1 large yellow onion, diced

1 large carrot, peeled and cut into fine dice

5 plum tomatoes, seeded and diced

4 cloves garlic, minced

2 teaspoons dried tarragon

1 teaspoon dried thyme

1 teaspoon paprika (Hungarian if you've got it)

6 cups water or vegetable broth

2 cups French lentils

2 bay leaves

1½ teaspoons salt

**Several pinches of freshly ground black pepper**

PREHEAT A large soup pot over medium heat. Sauté the onion and carrots for about 10 minutes, until the onions have browned a bit. Add the garlic, tarragon, thyme, and paprika, and sauté for 2 more minutes. Add the tomatoes and a little splash of water if necessary, and stir to deglaze the pot. Cover and cook for 5 minutes.

Add the water, lentils, bay leaves, salt, and pepper, then cover and bring to a boil. Once the soup is boiling, lower the heat to a simmer and cook, covered, for about 45 minutes, or until the lentils are tender. If the soup looks too thin, uncover and simmer for a couple more minutes. If it looks too thick, add a little more water. Serve with good, crusty bread.

## GAZBORSCHT

MAKES A WHOLE HELL OF A LOT, ABOUT 10 SERVINGS

**TIME:** 20 MINUTES, PLUS TIME TO CHILL

*One hot summer's day, Isa wanted cold borscht and her man wanted gazpacho. What developed is a surprisingly delicious, earthy version of the Spanish soup or, if you pre-*

*fer, a piquant version of the Eastern European soup. In any case, it's very refreshing and makes a lot so you can keep it in the fridge for when you want to cool down during a hot summer week. A food processor is pretty necessary here, or else you will be shredding beets until your dying day.*

**tip**

➤ If you want to add a little heat, throw in a seeded jalapeño or two.

3 cups peeled, shredded beets

5 cups water

2 tablespoons tomato paste

1 teaspoon salt

1 seedless cucumber, chopped coarsely

3 average sized tomatoes, chopped coarsely

1 small white onion, chopped coarsely

1 nice-size slice of good white bread (peasant bread or French bread)

2 tablespoons olive oil

¼ cup fresh lemon juice (from about 2 lemons)

½ cup loosely packed cilantro

Freshly ground black pepper

1 avocado, pitted, peeled, and sliced when ready to serve, for garnish

PLACE THE shredded beets in a soup pot and add the water, tomato paste, and salt. Partially cover the pot, leaving a little room for steam to escape. Bring the water to a boil and then simmer for 5 minutes; the shredded beets should be tender but have a little crunch. Remove from the heat and let cool completely.

In a food processor fitted with a metal blade, place half the cucumber, half the tomatoes, and half the onion. Add 1 cup of the cooled beets and their liquid, and the bread, olive oil, and lemon juice. Process for about 15 seconds; the mixture should be chunky but you shouldn't be able to detect the bread.

Add the rest of the cucumber, tomato, and onion, plus the cilantro, to the processor. Pulse about ten times so that the soup is still chunky. Add this mixture to the rest of the cooled beets. Add freshly ground black pepper and salt to taste.

Pour into a container, cover, and chill for at least 30 minutes or until ready to serve. Garnish each bowl with thin slices of avocado.

## HOMEMADE VEGETABLE BROTH

**TIME:** 2 HOURS (MOSTLY INACTIVE)

*A rich vegetable broth for when you want to go the extra mile. This is a great way to use up the older veggies in your crisper, you can use different veggies such as celery, squash, potatoes or mushrooms, make sure there is enough water to cover everything. Keep the skins on the onions for added color and flavor. Try other herbs like thyme, rosemary, bayleaves and peppercorns for a stronger broth.*

1 tablespoon olive oil

1 large onion, skin included, roughly chopped

2 large carrots, peeled and roughly chopped

2 parsnips, peeled and roughly chopped

3 whole cloves garlic, crushed

2 leeks, cleaned well and roughly chopped

handful (a loosely packed cup) fresh parsley

9 cups water

1 teaspoon salt

IN a large stockpot, heat the oil. Saute onions for about 5 minutes on medium heat. Add all other ingredients and bring to a boil. Reduce heat and let simmer for an hour and a half, uncovered.

Let broth cool until it's an okay temperature to handle. Strain into a large bowl with cheese cloth or a very fine mesh strainer. Press the vegetables with a gentle but firm pressure to get all the liquid out. This will keep in the fridge in a tightly sealed container for up to 3 days, or freeze for up to 3 months.

## HOT AND SOUR SOUP WITH
## WOOD EARS AND NAPA CABBAGE

SERVES 6

**TIME:** 55 MINUTES

*This is a totally inauthentic hot and sour soup, perfect for when you want to break out the cute Asian bowls and spoons. Wood ear mushrooms give the soup that traditional Chinese look and texture and they soak up all the flavors of the broth quite nicely. They can be a pain to find, so if you need to sub dried shiitakes, go ahead. We were able to track some down at a local Asian market, but ask at any natural foods or gourmet market; there's a good chance they have some.*

½ **ounce dried wood ear mushrooms**

2 **cups boiling water**

8 **leaves napa cabbage**

4 **cups vegetable broth**

¼ **cup soy sauce**

¼ **cup rice vinegar**

3 **teaspoons Asian hot chile oil**

½ **teaspoon sesame oil**

1 **teaspoon ground white pepper**

1½ **cups thick-sliced white mushrooms**

1 **heaping tablespoon arrowroot or cornstarch**

1 **cup cold water**

1 **pound extra-firm tofu, pressed and cut into matchsticks (see tip)**

½ **cup shredded carrots**

1 **cup chopped scallions**

PLACE THE wood ear mushrooms in a bowl and pour boiling water over them so that they are submerged by a few inches. Cover with a plate and let sit for 20 minutes.

To prepare the napa leaves, lay them on top of each other so that they're spooning. Thinly slice across them widthwise. Set aside.

Pour the vegetable broth, soy sauce, rice vinegar, hot chile oil, sesame oil and white pepper into a soup pot. Cover and bring to a boil. Once the broth is boiling, add the cabbage and the fresh mushrooms. Cook until the cabbage is completely wilted, about 5 minutes.

The wood ears should be ready at this point, so remove them from the bowl, cut into bite-size pieces, and add them to the soup as well.

Mix the arrowroot with the water until dissolved. Add to the soup and stir until just slightly thickened, a minute or two. This soup isn't going to be very thick, just more cloudy than anything else. But the starch gives the soup a little body.

Add the shredded carrots and tofu, and cook just until heated though, about 5 more minutes. Ladle into bowls and garnish with scallions to serve.

### tip

➤ This recipe calls for Asian hot chile oil but if you don't have any and don't think you will ever use it, add 2 extra teaspoons of white pepper, but don't sub hot sauce, cheapskate! The chile oil is great, though, and you will probably love it in stir-fries, so try to get it!

➤ Raw napa cabbage looks like very pale green romaine lettuce. It isn't as tough as European cabbage, so you can use your leftovers on sandwiches instead of lettuce to add a pleasant crunch.

➤ The tofu slicing doesn't have to be perfect; basically, what you want are long, thin rectangles that are small but big enough that they won't fall apart. If you want to just make small cubes instead, that's fine, too. To make the matchsticks, cut the tofu into eight slices widthwise. Then slice those slices widthwise about ten times.

## MIDSUMMER CORN CHOWDER WITH BASIL, TOMATO, AND FENNEL

SERVES 6 TO 8

TIME: 1 HOUR 30 MINUTES

*This fresh, soothing corn chowder uses the best of the season's produce. You can expect the unexpected with the bold and tasty addition of fresh basil and fennel bulb. Make this on a lazy summer evening when you don't need to be anywhere anytime soon, and use that extra time to prepare the Fresh Corn Stock (next recipe), which gives this soup a rich, complex base. We like this corn chowder recipe because it doesn't rely on the addition of any soy dairy products (which usually is the case with vegan creamy soups) to achieve a smooth, velvety texture.*

### tip

➤ If there's no time for broth-making, Mr. or Ms. Jet-setter, and you absolutely insist on using just water, try simmering the soup with the corn cobs tossed in after adding the water, taking care to remove them before you add the tomatoes and basil.

*This soup just screams "I just came back from the farmers' market! Look at my bulging canvas sack!" Here's an opportunity to try out different varieties of local, fresh corn in the peak of summer, purple or Thai basil, Yukon gold or Russian banana potatoes, and any heirloom tomatoes.*

6 ears fresh corn, husks and silk removed
3 tablespoons olive oil
3 cloves garlic, minced finely
1 large onion, cut into fine dice
1 small bulb fennel (about ½ pound), diced
1 stalk celery, chopped finely
1 large carrot, diced
1 pound white, waxy potatoes (about 2 medium-size), peeled and diced
2 teaspoons dried thyme
2 quarts Fresh Corn Stock, vegetable broth, or water
1 pound tomatoes, seeded and chopped finely
⅓ cup fresh basil leaves, tightly rolled and chopped into thin strips
Salt and freshly ground pepper

ON A large cutting surface or in a large bowl, hold an ear of corn by the thicker end and run a sharp knife carefully down the length of the ear, close to the cob, to slice off the kernels of corn. Repeat with the remaining ears. Set aside the kernels, break each cob in half to use in the corn stock, or add to the soup when simmering.

Preheat a large soup pot over medium-high heat. Sauté the garlic in oil for 30 seconds, then add the onion. Stir and cover, sweating them for about 5 minutes. Add the carrot and celery, stir, cover, and cook for another 2 minutes. Add the fennel, stir, cover, and cook for another 2 to 3 minutes; then add the chopped potato, stir, cover, and cook for an additional 3 minutes. Finally, add the corn, stir, cover, and cook for 5 minutes.

Add the stock, stir, cover, and bring to a boil. Lower the heat to medium and allow the soup to simmer, covered (with lid tilted so a small amount of heat can escape), for 45 minutes. Turn off the heat, ladle 1½ cups of the soup into a separate large bowl, and allow to cool until only slightly warm.

Puree the bowl of soup with an immersion blender, then add back to the remaining soup in the pot. Place the pot over medium heat, add the chopped tomatoes and basil, and simmer for an additional 10 minutes, until the soup is hot.

## FRESH CORN STOCK

*This stock is very free form. Try tossing flavorful vegetable scraps (such as onion skins, carrot peelings, etc.) in with the rest of the ingredients.*

8 cups water

6 corn cobs, broken in half

2 carrots, chopped coarsely

2 stalks celery, with leaves

1 leek, washed well and chopped coarsely

1 onion with skin, cut into chunks

Handful of fresh parsley, torn coarsely

1 teaspoon whole black or red peppercorns

Optional:

carrot tops, additional celery leaves and stems,
additional onion skins, lacy fronds from the
fennel tops

IN a large stockpot, combine the water, corn cobs, carrot, celery, leek, onion, parsley and peppercorns. Add one or more of the optional vegetable trimmings. Cover and bring to a rolling boil. Remove cover, reduce heat to medium-high and allow to simmer for 1 to 1½ hours.

Allow the stock to cool until tepid. Strain the stock with either a large metal strainer or cheesecloth. It can be refrigerated in a covered container for up to a week.

## ROASTED YELLOW PEPPER AND CORN BISQUE

SERVES 6 TO 8

**TIME:** 1 HOUR 20 MINUTES, LOTS OF IT INACTIVE

*Yellow peppers, yellow corn, and yellow summer squash make for a bright and beautiful—you guessed it—yellow soup. Red chile peppers dot this soup and save it from a monochrome yellow, plus they add just a little spice. Partially pureeing everything makes this bisque really luscious and creamy, while nutmeg and lime tie the whole shebang together. Again, this is a great farmers' market soup, when everyone has yellow squash up the wazoo and you are sick another night of yellow squash sauté.*

*tip*

> To better manage your time, you can prep the roasted peppers up to a day ahead and leave them tightly sealed in the fridge overnight.

4 yellow bell peppers

3 cups fresh corn, cut from the cobs (you can use frozen, too, but fresh tastes better)

1 tablespoon vegetable oil

1 medium-size Vidalia or Walla Walla onion, diced

3 cloves garlic

2 hot red chiles, seeded and sliced thinly

1 yellow summer squash, cut in half lengthwise and sliced thinly (about 3 cups)

3–4 cups vegetable broth

1½ teaspoons salt

1 (14-ounce) can coconut milk (lite is fine)

1 tablespoon pure maple syrup

Juice of 1 lime, or to taste

1 whole nutmeg

PREHEAT THE oven to 375°F. Cut the stems off the peppers and pull out the seeds. Place on a rimmed baking sheet (cover with baking parchment to protect the sheet, or just ignore that if you don't care about your sheet) and bake for about 40 minutes, turning once. The peppers should be very soft and collapsed.

When the peppers are done, place them in a plastic bag for about 30 minutes. This will steam them and make the skin very easy to peel away. Remove from bag, peel away the skin, and roughly chop the peppers.

Preheat a soup pot over medium-high heat. Sauté the onion in the oil for 5 to 7 minutes, until softened and translucent. Add the garlic and chiles. Sauté for another minute or so. Add the corn and squash, and cook for 3 to 5 minutes, until moisture begins to release from the squash. Add the roasted peppers, vegetable broth, and salt. Cover and bring to a boil. Once the soup is boiling, lower the heat and simmer for about 20 minutes, covered.

Add the coconut milk and puree the soup, either by using an immersion blender or by slightly cooling and then transferring the soup to a food processor or blender in batches.

Let the soup heat through again and grate the nutmeg with a microplane grater directly into the soup. Add the maple syrup and lime, stir, and serve!

## BAKED POTATO AND GREENS SOUP WITH POTATO-WEDGE CROUTONS

SERVES 6

TIME: 30 MINUTES, NOT INCLUDING BAKING THE POTATOES

*Kids really love this soup, as far as we can tell, so if your kids says they don't, please explain that we said yes, they do. There's a giant french fry in it, for heaven's sake— that is, a potato wedge that's been dredged in cornmeal and lightly fried. As for the healthy part, we use kale here, but escarole or spinach would be good, too. Make the baked potatoes the night before so that you can have this soup ready in thirty minutes. Or microwave them instead; just don't tell us about it. Sincerely, the Anti-Microwave Squad.*

6–8 baking potatoes (3½ pounds), baked and cooled

2 tablespoons olive oil

1 large yellow onion, sliced into short strips

3 cloves garlic, minced

½ teaspoon fennel seeds, crushed

1 teaspoon dried thyme

½ teaspoon dried rubbed sage

1 teaspoon salt

Plenty of freshly ground black pepper

¼ cup dry white wine (or just more broth if you prefer)

4 cups vegetable broth

4 cups kale, torn into bite-size pieces (about 6 leaves, rough stems removed)

¼ cup plain soy milk

Potato wedges:

2 heaping tablespoons coarse cornmeal

¼ teaspoon dried thyme

½ teaspoon paprika

Generous pinch of salt

2 cloves garlic, minced

Olive oil in a spray bottle (or enough for light frying)

➤ This soup tastes great with either homemade or store-bought vegan bacon. *Vegan with a Vengeance* has a great tempeh bacon recipe that will work. But you don't need to own the book since the entire world has published the recipe on their blog; just Google it!

➤ Don't know how to bake potatoes? Sigh. Preheat the oven to 350°F, poke the potatoes with a fork a few times, and wrap them in aluminum foil. Place in the oven and bake for about an hour or until easily pierced with a fork.

ONCE YOUR potatoes are baked and cool enough to handle, preheat a soup pot and sauté the onions in the olive oil over medium-high heat until good and brown, about 12 minutes.

*While the onions cook, prep the potatoes:*

Slice the baked potatoes in half lengthwise. Reserve three of the halves to make the potato wedges. Slice the rest into ¾-inch chunks.

Once the onions are browned, add the garlic, fennel, thyme, sage, black pepper, and salt. Cook for 2 more minutes, then add the wine to deglaze the pan. Add the chunks of potatoes and the broth, cover, and lower the heat a bit to bring to a low boil. Mix in the kale. Cover and cook for 15 to 20 more minutes.

*Meanwhile, prepare the potato wedges:*

Slice the reserved potato halves in half lengthwise so you have six pieces. Preheat a heavy-bottomed skillet over medium-high heat. Combine all the ingredients for the wedges (except for the oil) on a plate. Wet the potato wedges with a little bit of water and dredge the two cut sides in the cornmeal mixture.

Lightly coat the skillet with oil. Cook the potatoes on each cut side for about 4 minutes, or until golden and crispy. Spray with oil as you alternate cooking sides.

The soup should be done by this point. Use a potato masher to mush up about half of the soup (for once, don't use an immersion blender; it will make the potatoes pasty and yucky), add the soy milk, and mix. If it's too thick, add a little water or vegetable stock.

Ladle into bowls and top with a potato wedge crouton.

## SPICY PEANUT AND EGGPLANT SOUP

SERVES 6 TO 8

TIME: 1 HOUR 20 MINUTES

*This is such a naughty (read: not low fat!) soup and so outrageously rich and savory, it's all too easy to ask for a second helping . . . or two. This thick concoction of meltingly tender eggplant, warming spices, and peanuts was a big hit with our testers. It's a meal in itself, but would also pair nicely with a bowl of steamed jasmine rice and a simple green salad. A sure thing against the wintertime blues—and true to soup form, tastes even better when heated up the next day.*

1 pound eggplant, peeled, chopped in ½-inch cubes

1 teaspoon salt, plus additional to season soup

5 large shallots, peeled and sliced very thinly

¼ cup peanut oil

1 medium-size yellow onion, diced

1 hot chile, seeded and minced

1-inch cube fresh ginger, peeled and minced

1½ teaspoons ground cumin

⅛–¼ teaspoon ground cayenne (optional)

2 teaspoons ground coriander

½ teaspoon ground turmeric

⅓ cup tomato paste

1 (16-ounce) can roasted diced tomatoes with juice

5 cups water or vegetable broth

½ cup creamy or chunky natural peanut butter

½ pound green beans, fresh or frozen, trimmed and cut into 2-inch pieces

2 tablespoons fresh lemon juice

Optional garnishes: ⅓ cup coarsely chopped cilantro, whole cilantro leaves, and chopped roasted peanuts

*tip*

➤ For more spicy heat in this soup, keep the seeds intact in the chile pepper and add to the stew.

TOSS THE eggplant cubes with the teaspoon of salt in a large bowl or colander. Allow to sit 30 minutes to soften, then gently rinse the eggplant with cold running water and drain.

While the eggplant is being brined, preheat a large stockpot over medium-high heat. Sauté the shallots in 2 tablespoons of the oil for about 20 minutes until very soft, browned, and slightly caramelized. Scoop the shallots out of the pot and set aside in a medium-size bowl.

Add 1 tablespoon of the oil to the pot and add the eggplant, stirring to coat with the oil. Stir and cook the eggplant for 12 to 15 minutes, until slightly tender. Transfer the eggplant to the same bowl as the shallots.

Add the remaining oil to the pot and allow it to heat, add the ginger and chile, and fry for 30 seconds. Add the ground cumin, coriander, turmeric, and fry for another 30 seconds, then add the onion. Stir and fry until the onion is just slightly soft and translucent, 5 to 6 minutes. Add the tomato paste and stir-fry the mixture for another minute.

Add the diced tomatoes, water, eggplant, string beans, and shallots to pot. Stir well and raise the heat to medium-high. Bring to a boil and boil for 5 minutes, then lower the heat and simmer.

In a separate bowl, stir the peanut butter to incorporate any separated oils. Add a ladleful of hot soup. Stir the peanut butter with the soup until creamy; the peanut butter should be completely emulsified. Scrape the peanut butter mixture into the rest of the simmering soup, stirring to mix.

Simmer the soup over medium-low heat, covered, for 35 to 45 minutes, or until the eggplant is very tender. Remove from the heat and stir in the cilantro and lemon juice. Salt to taste after the soup has cooled for at least half an hour. Top with the suggested garnishes, if desired.

## CREAMY TOMATO SOUP

SERVES 8

TIME: 45 MINUTES

*This soup packs a double one-two punch of tomato. Just when you're thinking it's made from regular old tomato—BAM—a sun-dried tomato gets you in the jaw and you are out for the count. You wake up on Avenue C and 4th Street wearing one shoe that is not vegan and you have no idea what happened.*

2 tablespoons olive oil

1 medium onion, chopped coarsely

3 cloves garlic, chopped

½ teaspoon dried rosemary (crushed between your fingers)

½ teaspoon dried thyme

½ teaspoon dried oregano

1 teaspoon salt

Lots of freshly ground black pepper

1 pound waxy potatoes (2–4 average-size potatoes; weigh them to be sure), peeled and cut into 1-inch chunks

1 cup sun-dried tomatoes (*not* the kind packed in oil, just honest-to-goodness sun-dried tomatoes)

6 cups water or vegetable broth

1 (28-ounce) can crushed tomatoes (the fire-roasted are especially worth it here)

Juice of ½ lemon, or to taste

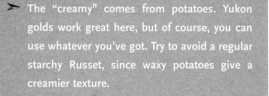

➤ The "creamy" comes from potatoes. Yukon golds work great here, but of course, you can use whatever you've got. Try to avoid a regular starchy Russet, since waxy potatoes give a creamier texture.

➤ This is a great soup to go along with panini or vegan grilled cheese.

PREHEAT A large soup pot over medium heat. Sauté the onions until translucent, 5 to 7 minutes. Add the garlic, herbs, salt, and pepper. Sauté for 1 more minute, until the garlic is fragrant.

Add the potatoes and sun-dried tomatoes. Pour in the water. Cover and bring to a boil. Once the soup is boiling, lower the heat to medium, cover, and let simmer for about 20 minutes, until the potatoes are tender and the sun-dried tomatoes are soft.

Add the crushed tomatoes and heat through. If you have an immersion blender, you're in luck! Puree the living hell out of it until it is very smooth. If you don't have one, just transfer the whole shebang to a food processor or blender, in cooled batches, then transfer back to the pot. Add the lemon juice and adjust the salt if you need to.

Serve!

*Variation:*

Tomato-Basil Soup: Add a half cup of shredded basil after pureeing.

## SMOKY RED PEPPERS 'N' BEANS GUMBO

SERVES 6 TO 8

**TIME:** 1 HOUR 30 MINUTES

*Thick but not too thick, a stick-to-your-ribs veggie gumbo has a hint of smokiness from juicy, roasted red peppers. And a little help from the magic of liquid smoke (and it's vegan, like a dream come true, so relax!). Traditionally, gumbos are served with a scoop of white rice in the middle, but this also pairs nicely with Skillet Corn Bread (page 223) or crusty French bread and a crisp green salad.*

⅓ cup nonhydrogenated vegan margarine

¼ cup all-purpose flour

2 medium-size onions, cut into small dice

2 green bell peppers, cut into small dice

1 stalk celery, sliced very thinly

4 cloves garlic, minced

1 (10-ounce) package frozen okra, slightly thawed and sliced thinly

1 (28-ounce) can diced tomatoes with juice, preferably fire-roasted tomatoes

3 roasted red peppers, jarred or homemade (page 33), chopped into fine dice

1 (16-ounce) can kidney beans, drained and rinsed

3 cups vegetable broth

1 cup ale-style beer

3 tablespoons tomato paste

2 teaspoons oregano

¼ teaspoon allspice

½ teaspoon liquid smoke flavoring

Pinch of freshly grated nutmeg

2 bay leaves

4–5 sprigs of thyme

Pinch of cayenne

1 teaspoon salt, or to taste

Several pinches of freshly ground black pepper

### tip

➤ Leftover Simple Seitan (page 131), diced small, makes an delicious addition. Add it to the vegetables when sautéing them in the roux.

➤ Frozen okra makes this recipe a breeze; it slices up easily with little mess. If you've never used it before, you'll be blown away by that perfect rectangle of frozen okra, or at least marginally amused. Of course, sliced fresh okra (½ to ¾ pound) may be used instead.

FIRST WE'RE going to make a roux: Preheat a large heavy-bottomed stockpot over medium-low heat. Place the margarine in the pot and stir until melted. Sprinkle in the flour and stir to dissolve it. Cook the flour mixture, stirring frequently, until it is a rich caramel color and smells toasty, anywhere from 10 to 14 minutes.

Add the chopped onions and peppers to the roux mixture, stirring to coat completely. Raise the heat to medium-high and cook until the vegetables are very soft, at least 12 minutes.

Add the celery, garlic, and okra, and cook for another 6 minutes. Add the tomatoes, roasted red peppers, kidney beans, and vegetable broth. Whisk together the beer and tomato paste and add that to the mixture, stirring to incorporate completely. Stir in the allspice, liquid smoke, and grated nutmeg, and lastly, tuck in the bay leaves and thyme sprigs.

Raise the heat and bring the mixture to a gentle boil, then lower the heat back to medium and partially cover. Allow the mixture to simmer 35 for 45 minutes, stirring occasionally, until the okra is very tender. Allow to cool at least 15 minutes before serving, then season with salt, pepper, and cayenne.

# CASSEROLES

PERHAPS AT FIRST the word casserole evokes images of a '70s mom. You know, she's the not-quite-picture-perfect version of '50s mom: hair a bit messed up, mascara running, her apron slightly askew over her no-iron poly-blend twin set. But there she is, our hero, with her plaid oven mitts, getting dinner on the table even though she just returned from work an hour ago. And all she had to do was open a couple of cans, pour 'em into a ceramic, and throw it in the oven—patriarchy has never been easier!

Well, there's no canned mushroom soup here in our modern, new-fangled kitchen and we smudge our mascara on purpose. When we talk about casseroles, really what we mean are one-dish meals that are baked. They aren't necessarily faster than other dinners, but the oven time does give you downtime to do your nails, organize a "Take Back the Night" demo, or call your mom and apologize for being such an ingrate. So don't let the longer cooking times for these recipes worry you.

These comfort meals—kugel, enchiladas, potpies of every description—come from all over the world. Some fall under the category of "side dish" and some are what laymen might call "main dishes," but if it goes into the oven in a baking dish, it's a casserole to us.

## SPINACH-NOODLE KUGEL

SERVES 8
**TIME:** ABOUT AN HOUR

*So you've never made kugel before? If the word* kugel *scares you, just call this Spinach-Noodle Casserole. If* matzo *scares you, then use bread crumbs. See? There's no reason to be scared. This goes great alongside the lentil salad. And of course, serving with potato pancakes and applesauce would be awesome. Just a note: the frozen spinach needs to be completely thawed, so remember to leave it in the fridge overnight or well in advance.*

> 3 cups uncooked rombi pasta (or mafalde or any short, cut ribbon noodles, or broken-up lasagna noodles)
> 3 (10-ounce) packages frozen chopped spinach, thawed
> 1¼ cups matzo meal (from about 4 matzos) or plain bread crumbs
> 1 small onion, finely chopped (about a cup)
> 12 ounces extra-firm silken tofu (the vacuum-packed kind)
> 1 cup vegetable broth
> 2 tablespoons olive oil
> ¼ cup lightly packed, chopped fresh dill
> 2 tablespoons lemon juice
> ¾ teaspoons salt (use ¼ teaspoon less if your matzo is salted)
> ½ teaspoon ground black pepper
> Nonstick cooking spray

BOIL A pot of water and cook the noodles according to the package directions. Preheat the oven to 350°F. Meanwhile, place thawed spinach in a colander and leave it in the sink to drain.

If making your own matzo meal, place the matzos in the food processor fitted with a metal blade and pulse until they are crumbs. Transfer to a medium-size mixing bowl.

Add the vegetable broth, oil, and tofu to the food processor and puree until smooth, scraping down the

sides to make sure you get everything. Add the tofu mixture to the mixing bowl.

Press the spinach in the colander to get out as much water as you can, then add it to the mixing bowl. By this time, your pasta should be done, so drain it and run it under cold water.

Add the pasta along with the remaining ingredients (except, of course, for the cooking spray—cans don't taste good) to the mixing bowl and mix very well. Use your hands if you have to.

Coat a 9 × 13-inch glass casserole dish with cooking spray. Press the kugel into the casserole dish. Bake for 30 minutes. Remove from the oven and let sit for 5 to 10 minutes before slicing.

## SOUTHWESTERN CORN PUDDING

SERVES 6

**TIME:** 1 HOUR 20 MINUTES

*This insanely flavorful, velvety side dish is the perfect accompaniment to any Southwestern meal—that is, whatever else you're making with cilantro and scallions and jalapeños and stuff in it. Or, serve with Green Pumpkin-Seed Mole (page 210) and Chile Cornmeal-Crusted Tofu (page 125).*

> 2 tablespoons corn oil
> 4 cups fresh corn (about 6 ears)
> 1 red bell pepper, seeded and chopped finely
> 2 jalapeños, chopped finely
> 1 cup coconut milk
> ¼ cup cornstarch
> ½ cup cornmeal
> 2 tablespoons pure maple syrup
> 1 cup finely chopped scallions
> ¼ cup finely chopped fresh cilantro
> 1 teaspoon salt
> ¼ teaspoon cayenne

PREHEAT THE oven to 350°F and lightly grease an 8-inch square baking or casserole dish. A cast-iron pan would work here, too (in fact, to cut down on dishes, you can sauté the corn in a cast-iron pan and later use it to bake the batter).

Sauté the corn, bell pepper, and jalapeños in a large skillet for 10 to 12 minutes, stirring occasionally; the corn should be very lightly browned. Meanwhile, stir together the cornstarch and coconut milk until the cornstarch has mostly dissolved.

When the corn and peppers are ready, transfer 2 cups of them to a blender or food processor. Add the coconut milk and cornstarch mixture, and pulse about twenty times, until the mixture is mostly pureed but not completely smooth.

Transfer to a large mixing bowl and mix with the remaining corn, cornmeal, maple syrup, scallions, cilantro, salt, and cayenne.

Pour the batter into a baking dish (or your cast-iron pan) and bake for 40 minutes. Let cool for about 10 minutes before slicing and serving.

## CARAMELIZED ONION-BUTTERNUT ROAST WITH CHESTNUTS

Serves 6 to 8

**TIME:** 1 hour 30 minutes

*Holidays a pain in the butt? Just imagine perfectly roasted chestnuts in a rich, savory medley of tender butternut squash, white beans, and caramelized onions in this stuffinglike casserole—little bit like the best parts of a holiday meal all rolled up into one. It's only natural to want to serve this with simply roasted Brussels sprouts (page 31) and Holiday Cranberry Sauce (213). Enjoy this special casserole in those early fall months when the holidays seem so far away and all you crave are the fixins' of Thanksgiving dinner.*

*P.S. We'll admit that peeling a pound of chestnuts could have you longing for a drive around the mall parking lot. So if you'd rather not channel all your jolly, festive anxiety into peeling these little bastards, you can also grab prepeeled or even jarred chestnuts for this recipe.*

**tip**

➤ This dish is best made with fresh chestnuts when they are in prime season, between October and January. After that, the freshness of most nuts in stores is often dubious; all too often we've purchased a pound and found out after peeling them that many a chestnut to be nasty, moldy, and shriveled. Instead, look for prepeeled, frozen, or jarred chestnuts available during the fall/winter months in many gourmet, natural, or specialty shops. Plus, they easily cut the prep time in half, giving you more time to procrastinate gift buying!

**Casserole:**

1 pound onions, peeled and sliced thinly

⅓ cup olive oil

1 pound chestnuts, fresh in the shell or frozen/jarred and prepeeled

2 pounds butternut squash (1 medium-size squash), peeled and cut into ½-inch cubes

1 (15-ounce) can white beans, such as cannellini or navy, drained and rinsed, or a (10-ounce) package of prepared baby lima beans

2 teaspoons dried thyme

1½ teaspoons ground coriander

½ teaspoon freshly grated nutmeg

1½ teaspoons salt, or to taste

Freshly cracked pepper

½ cup vegetable broth

**Crumb topping:**

½ cup dry white bread crumbs

2 tablespoons olive oil

½ teaspoon dried rubbed sage

Pinch of ground cayenne

½ teaspoon salt, or to taste

Freshly cracked pepper

PREHEAT THE oven to 375°F.

*Prepare the casserole:*

Place the onions and olive oil in a 9 × 13-inch baking dish, tossing to coat the onions with oil. Bake for about 30 minutes, stirring 3 or 4 times with a wooden spatula, until the onions are browned and sizzling. Remove from the oven and set aside.

While the onions are roasting, prepare the whole, unpeeled chestnuts according to the directions for the Chestnut-Lentil Pâté (page 63). If using prepeeled chestnuts, skip this step and thaw if frozen, drain if jarred. Coarsely chop the peeled chestnuts and add to the pan with roasted onions.

Add the diced butternut squash, white beans, thyme, coriander, nutmeg, salt, pepper, and broth to the baking pan, stirring so that the chestnuts, squash, and beans are well coated. Tightly cover the baking pan with aluminum foil and bake for 35 to 45 minutes, until the squash and chestnuts are tender.

*Prepare the crumbs:*

Toss together the bread crumbs, oil and sage in a bowl. Season to taste with salt, pepper, and cayenne. Remove the foil from the baking pan, top with the crumb mixture, and bake for another 15 minutes, until the top is lightly browned.

# ASPARAGUS QUICHE WITH TOMATOES AND TARRAGON

SERVES 6 TO 8

1 HOUR 30 MINUTES, PLUS COOLING TIME

*Real men are vegan, and they do eat vegan quiche. We really wanted to make a vegan quiche that didn't include tofu or nutritional yeast because every vegan cookbook in the world has one of those. So instead we created a blend of beans and walnuts, making this quiche tender and creamy with a crispy crumb top. It's a pleasure to sink your fork into during brunch, lunch, or dinner. Serve with a Caesar Salad (page 81) on the side.*

1 recipe Basic Single Pastry Crust (page 262)

4 tablespoons olive oil

1 pound asparagus, rough ends discarded

2 shallots, skins removed, chopped coarsely

3 cloves garlic

1 cup walnuts

1½ cups cooked navy beans, or 1 (15-ounce) can, drained and rinsed

¼ cup loosely packed fresh tarragon, plus 2 tablespoons finely chopped

2 tablespoons cornstarch

¾ teaspoon salt

¼ teaspoon ground nutmeg

Several pinches of freshly ground black pepper

⅓ cup plain whole wheat bread crumbs

4 slices beefsteak or Holland tomato, or any really big tomato

PREHEAT A large skillet over medium-high heat. Cut the tips off four pieces of the asparagus and set aside for garnish. Slice the rest into ½-inch lengths.

Sauté the asparagus (except for the reserved tips) in a tablespoon of the olive oil for about 7 minutes, stirring occasionally.

While the asparagus is cooking, place the walnuts, the ¼ cup of tarragon, and the nutmeg, salt, and pepper in a food processor. Pulse into crumbs, so that no whole walnuts are left.

Remove the asparagus from the pan and transfer to a shallow bowl to cool a bit. Sauté the shallots in another tablespoon of the olive oil for about 3 minutes. Add the garlic and sauté for 3 more minutes, being careful not to burn it. Transfer the shallots and garlic to the asparagus and let cool for a few more minutes.

When the vegetables have stopped steaming, add them to the food processor. Pulse a few times and scrape down the sides. Add the beans and puree until relatively smooth, although the walnuts will still be grainy. Add the cornstarch (sift first, if very clumpy) and pulse until thoroughly combined. Transfer the mixture to a bowl (use the bowl the veggies were cooling in, to cut down on dish duties), cover, and refrigerate for about 45 minutes.

Preheat the oven to 350°F.

Roll out the pastry dough to fit an 8-inch glass pie plate. Cover with aluminum foil and bake for 15 minutes.

Remove the baked crust from the oven. Spoon the asparagus filling into the crust and smooth out evenly. Sprinkle the top with half the bread crumbs and drizzle with 1 tablespoon olive oil. Then, place the tomato slices on top of the bread crumbs with an asparagus tip between each tomato. Sprinkle on the remaining bread crumbs, some freshly ground black pepper, a few pinches of salt, and the chopped tarragon. Drizzle again with the remaining tablespoon of olive oil.

Bake for 45 minutes. Let cool for about 20 minutes before serving. Serve warm or at room temperature.

## EGGPLANT ROLLATINI WITH SPINACH AND TOASTED PINE NUTS

MAKES 12 ROLLATINI, SERVES 4 TO 6
**TIME:** 1 HOUR 30 MINUTES

*In Brooklyn, people's worth is directly proportional to their ability to make an eggplant rollatini. If they can't perform, they are taken care of. While we're not going to kill you if you don't make this, we will be severely disappointed. This dish is so good it wins over nonvegans every time!*

*There are lots of little steps here but they are all pretty simple and this meal is worth it. It's not a weeknight dinner, more for company and special occasions when you want to be at the top of your vegan game. Since this can be a heavy meal if you are frying it, it's great to serve with steamed broccoli doused with the leftover marinara sauce. But if you wanna be real Brooklyn (and you do), make a double batch of sauce and serve with spaghetti. Two rollatini per person should get the job done.*

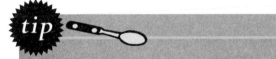

➤ Note that you aren't going to use all the eggplant. Since the skin can't be used here, you'll need to slice off two sides. Plus, there will likely be slices that are sacrificed because it is a little difficult to get them relatively uniformly thin. Save the scraps and use them in a soup or stew, or grill them and make a salad a day or two later.

➤ Which brings us to the best way to evenly slice eggplant: First, use a large chef's knife to cut off the top and bottom. Stand up the eggplant on the cutting board. Next, slice off one side (that slice won't be used, since it has a lot of skin). Then, still holding the eggplant upright, begin to slice off ⅛-inch-thick pieces, going as slowly as you need to.

3 large eggplants (a little over 3 pounds)

1 recipe (4 cups) Marinara Sauce or a variation of it
(we love the olive variation here) (page 205)

1 recipe Tofu Ricotta (page 206)

12 large spinach leaves, washed very well and
stemmed

### Dipping mixture (before breading):

1 cup cold water

¼ cup cornstarch

### Breading mixture:

2 cups bread crumbs

1 teaspoon dried thyme

½ teaspoon dried oregano

½ teaspoon dried basil

Optional: ¼ cup toasted pine nuts
(we know they are expensive)

1 recipe Almesan (page 207)

Chopped basil for garnish

CUT THE eggplant lengthwise into twelve slices about ⅛-inch thick. You don't need to actually measure them, and it's okay if they are a little thicker or thinner in some areas. See the tip for help with this.

Generously sprinkle salt on both sides of eggplant and rub it in. Set in a colander to drain for 30 minutes. Meanwhile, you can make your sauce, make your Almesan, toast your pine nuts, and prep your other ingredients.

### Make the dipping and breading mixtures:

Mix the cornstarch with the water in a bowl that is large enough to fit your eggplant slices. Mix together all the breading ingredients on a large dinner plate.

Rinse the eggplant with cold water and set aside. Whether you are baking or frying the eggplant, have a 9 × 13-inch baking pan at the ready and preheat the oven to 350°F.

### To Fry:

Preheat a large heavy-bottomed skillet over medium-high heat. Let it heat for at least 3 minutes. Pour in and heat about ⅛ inch of oil. Let it get hot but not smoky; if it smokes, lower the heat just a bit. To test the oil for the correct temperature, sprinkle in a small amount of bread crumbs. If bubbles form rapidly around the crumbs, the oil is ready.

Dredge an eggplant slice in the dipping mixture. Sometimes the starch settles at the bottom of the bowl, so mix it with a fork if need be. Gently press the eggplant into the breading mixture on both sides so that the crumbs are firmly in place.

Prep a second slice the same way, then place both slices in the pan and cook on each side for 1½ to 2 minutes. Use tongs to flip the slices. The eggplant should be tender and golden brown on both sides. When done, transfer to paper towels to drain the oil and proceed with remaining eggplant slices.

### To Bake:

Follow the same directions for breading as above. Grease two baking sheets with olive oil, place all the eggplant slices on the sheets, and spray the breaded slices with olive oil. If you don't have olive oil spray, cooking spray can be used but it doesn't come out as well. You can also drizzle oil over the slices, but they may come out uneven. Bake at 350°F for 20 to 25 minutes; no need to flip them. When ready, they should be tender and flexible. If you can't fit both sheets on one rack in your oven, then rotate them halfway through the baking process.

### To Assemble:

Let the slices cool enough that you can handle them, usually 10 minutes. Pour 1½ cups of sauce into a 9 × 13-inch casserole dish.

With the narrower end pointed toward you, place a leaf of spinach on the lower third of the eggplant slice.

Place 2 heaping tablespoons of ricotta on the spinach, sprinkle a few pine nuts on top of that (if using), and then roll up. It's should be easy! Place the rolled eggplant slices, seam side down, in the baking pan. When everything is rolled, pour another cup or so of sauce over the rollatini. Bake for about 20 minutes; really, you just want to heat the ricotta through.

*To serve:*

Sprinkle a little Almesan on top of each rollatini and garnish with chopped basil leaves.

## SWEET POTATO–PEAR TZIMMES WITH PECANS AND RAISINS

SERVES 6

**TIME:** 1 HOUR 15 MINUTES

*This can just as easily be called Roasted Sweet Potatoes and Pear, but* tzimmes *is what we Jews call it, isn't that adorable? The idea is actually to overroast everything so it gets a bit chewy on the outside while still creamy on the inside. This would be a good side to round out a dinner with the spinach kugel (page 151). But you can also just serve it with Tangerine Baked Tofu (page 126) and a green. Take this to your next Passover meal and please the whole* meshpuchah!

- **2 pounds sweet potatoes, peeled and cut into ¾-inch chunks**
- **3 firm Bartlett pears, seeded and cut into ¾-inch chunks**
- **1 tablespoon vegetable oil, plus spray on a little more if it needs it**
- **2 tablespoons mirin or any sweet cooking wine**
- **1 tablespoon pure maple syrup**
- **½ teaspoon ground cinnamon**
- **¼ teaspoon salt**
- **¾ cup pecan halves**
- **¾ cup golden raisins**

PREHEAT THE oven to 350°F.

Place the sweet potatoes and pears on a large, rimmed baking sheet. Sprinkle with the oil and mirin, and mix it all up to make sure everything is coated. Add the maple syrup, cinnamon, salt, and pecans, and toss to coat.

Cover with aluminum foil and bake for 30 minutes. Remove the foil and add the raisins. Using a thin, flexible spatula, carefully toss and mix, being careful not to break up the sweet potatoes. But tzimmes are a forgiving dish, so if some get mushed up that's perfectly acceptable.

Return to the oven uncovered and bake for 30 more minutes, tossing every now and again. Serve warm or at room temperature.

## MOLE SKILLET PIE WITH GREENS

SERVES 4 TO 6
**TIME:** 1 HOUR

*A cacophony of Tex-Mex good things that go "yum" in the belly. Chile-Chocolate Mole (page 210) smothers tender greens and plump beans, topped with a moist corn bread biscuit crust that's baked to a golden hue. You don't need a cast-iron skillet to enjoy this potpie; any deep casserole dish will do. Just as easily, use any leftover cooked vegetables and these will find a proper home in this luscious, saucy pie. Serve with a side of Mexican Millet (page 118) or simply sautéed corn kernels, if your little heart desires.*

**Filling:**
- **3 tablespoons grapeseed or peanut oil**
- **1 yellow onion, diced**
- **1 small carrot, diced**

½ pound greens, such as collard, kale, spinach or chard, chopped finely and steamed until tender

1 (15-ounce) can black, pinto, or white beans, rinsed and drained

1–1½ cups Chile-Chocolate Mole (page 210), plus additional for serving

### Corn bread crust:

1 cup soy or rice milk

1 teaspoon apple cider vinegar or lime juice

3 tablespoons canola or peanut oil

1 cup whole wheat pastry flour

½ cup cornmeal

1 tablespoon sugar

1¼ teaspoons baking powder

¼ teaspoon baking soda

¼ teaspoon salt

Sesame seeds (optional)

PREHEAT THE oven to 400°F.

### Prepare the filling:

Heat the grapeseed oil in a heavy cast-iron skillet over medium heat, then add the onion and sauté for 5 minutes. Add the carrot and continue to cook until the onion is tender and starts to turn golden, another 5 to 6 minutes.

Transfer to a large bowl and combine with the steamed greens, beans, and 1 cup of the mole sauce. Stir to coat everything with the sauce; if the mixture looks a little dry, add up to ½ cup more mole sauce. Place the mixture back in the skillet and smooth out the top. You should have a little over ½ inch of space between the veggies and the rim of the skillet; if it's filled to the top, remove a little, since the crust will require the extra room.

### Prepare the crust:

Combine the soy milk and vinegar in a measuring cup. Place the oil in a large bowl, beat in the soy milk

mixture, and sift in flour, cornmeal, sugar, baking powder, baking soda, and salt. Mix until just moistened (don't overmix).

Pour over the vegetables in your skillet and smooth to cover. Sprinkle on some sesame seeds, if desired, and bake for 30 to 35 minutes, until the crust is done and golden. Allow the pie to cool for 10 minutes (or until the filling stops bubbling), slice, and serve with extra mole sauce.

## JAMAICAN YUCA SHEPHERD'S PIE WITH SWEET POTATO, KIDNEY BEANS, AND PLANTAINS

SERVES 8

TIME: 1 HOUR

*New York is home to a huge Jamaican community and since there are lots of vegan Rastafarians, there's tons of vegan food, or Ital, to be had. Jamaican curries differ from Indian curries in that they are often a bit sweeter. Jamaican curry powder also has a different blend of spices, typically including star anise, aniseeds, and coriander. This curry is one of our favorites—sweet potatoes, kidney beans, corn, and plantains (we also snuck some lima beans in there in hopes that you'll cultivate some love for the little guys) in creamy coconut milk. You can serve this as a curry over rice, but we've turned it into a shepherd's pie with a layer of yuca on top.*

**tip**

➢ The easiest way to peel yuca is to remove the rough ends and cut the yuca widthwise into thirds. Place a piece vertically on the cutting board, secure with your nonwriting hand and use a paring knife to slice the skin off.

> Scotch bonnets are a really hot pepper so, instead of cutting them up, it's common in Jamaican cuisines to just score the sides in four places. To do this, use a paring knife to cut slivers up the sides. It releases all the peppery flavor without the searing hot heat, so it's spicy but not too spicy. Be careful not to crush the peppers when stirring; keep them intact and remove them when the curry is done cooking. If you can't find Scotch bonnets, you can use two serrano peppers instead.

**tip**

3–3½ pounds yuca, peeled and cut into 1½-inch chunks

1¾ teaspoons salt

3 tablespoons olive oil

1 yellow onion, diced

1 green bell pepper, seeded and diced

3 cloves garlic, chopped finely

1 tablespoon finely chopped fresh ginger

2 sweet potatoes, peeled and cut into ¾-inch chunks

2 Scotch bonnet peppers, scored down the sides (see tip)

2 bay leaves

2 sprigs fresh thyme

⅓ cup water

1 (15-ounce) can coconut milk

½ cup fresh corn (from 1 ear of corn)

1 cup cooked kidney beans, or 1 (15-ounce) can, drained and rinsed

¾ cup cooked lima beans, or 1 (8-ounce) can, drained and rinsed

2 ripe yellow plantains that have just begun to blacken, sliced in half lengthwise and cut into ½-inch pieces

1 tablespoon Jamaican curry powder

FIRST, PREPARE your yuca: Place the yuca in a medium-size stockpot and cover with water until it's submerged.

Cover and bring to a boil, add 1 teaspoon of the salt, and lower the heat to medium. Let the yuca boil for about 20 minutes, until tender enough to mash.

*Meanwhile, prepare the filling:*

Preheat a medium-size stockpot over medium-high heat. Place the 2 tablespoons of the oil, onions, green bell pepper, garlic, and ginger in the pot. Sauté for about 5 minutes. Add the sweet potatoes, Scotch bonnets, thyme, salt, and water. Cover and cook for about 15 minutes, stirring occasionally, until the sweet potatoes are easily pierced.

Set your oven to broil.

Add the remaining ingredients to the filling mixture in the stockpot and lower the heat. Cook for about 5 more minutes, until everything is heated through. Remove the thyme sprigs, bay leaves, and Scotch bonnets and discard.

By this point, the yuca is probably done. Drain the yuca and then immediately place it back in the pot you boiled it in. Add the remaining tablespoon of oil to the yuca and mash with a potato masher. It usually takes about 15 mashes to get it to the right consistency, creamy but chunky.

Pour the curried filling into a 9 × 13-inch baking dish. Use a large wooden spoon or spatula to scoop the yuca over it in several mounds. Press the yuca mounds down to spread over the curry. It's okay if some of the filling is peeking through in places.

Place in the oven and bake for about 10 minutes, then transfer to the broiler for about 2 minutes. Keep a close eye; the top should be gently browned.

Let sit for about 10 minutes before serving. Serve in rimmed plates or shallow bowls because it will be very saucy.

## ALMOST ALL-AMERICAN
## SEITAN POTPIE

SERVES 6 TO 8

**TIME:** 1 HOUR 20 MINUTES

*As American as chickpea flour and seitan, this potpie is just a little reminiscent of a certain frozen potpie that equaled big excitement at dinnertime when we were kids. Certainly more tasty and minus the freezer burn, so everybody's happy. Silky gravy envelops chewy chunks of seitan and down-home root veggies and peas. Top it all with a flaky whole wheat crust (or use all-purpose flour to keep it traditional) and you've got a complete, family-pleasing meal. If you need something green to round out it out, steamed broccoli or spinach salad will do the job.*

*The steps involved in this recipe may look epic but, once the crust is rolled out and chilling, the rest is just chopping and stirring. The filling, or even the entire pie, can be assembled a day or two ahead and popped in the oven a little less than an hour before dinner.*

**tip**

➤ This potpie is best made in a deep-dish casserole, or even better, make individual potpies in deep, ovenproof bowls or extra-large ramekins. Instructions for individual pies follow the main instructions.

➤ If you're feeling particularly industrious, double the crust recipe and prepare a bottom crust. It doesn't need to be chilled before fitting into the casserole dish; just roll out, fit, and trim, then cover the entire pie with plastic wrap and keep in the refrigerator while preparing the top crust and filling.

**Crust:**

  **2 cups all-purpose flour, or 1 cup each whole wheat and all-purpose**

  **¼ cup cornmeal**

  **2 teaspoons sugar**

  **1 teaspoon salt**

  **½ teaspoon baking powder**

  **½ cup cold nonhydrogenated vegan shortening**

  **½–¾ cup cold water**

  **2 teaspoons apple cider vinegar**

**Seitan filling:**

  **5 tablespoons grapeseed or peanut oil**

  **1 recipe Simple Seitan (page 131), chopped into ½-inch cubes (about 3 cups)**

  **1 teaspoon soy sauce**

  **¼ cup chickpea (garbanzo bean) flour**

  **1 large onion, cut into fine dice (about 2 cups)**

  **1 large carrot, peeled and cut into fine dice**

  **½ pound white potato or celery root, scraped and cut into fine dice**

  **1 stalk celery, cut into fine dice**

  **1 cup small, sweet green peas or corn kernels**

  **⅔ cup white wine or vegetable broth**

  **1 ½ cups vegetable broth**

  **1 teaspoon dried thyme**

  **1 teaspoon mustard powder**

  **½ teaspoon ground sage**

  **Salt and freshly ground pepper**

HAVE A 3-quart square or oval deep-dish (9½ × 11 × 2½-inch minimum) casserole ready.

*Prepare the crust first:*

Combine the flour, cornmeal, sugar, salt, and baking powder in a large mixing bowl. Add the shortening by the tablespoon, in small chunks, and cut it into the flour with a pastry cutter or two knives held together. Cut in the shortening until the mixture is crumbly.

Pour ¾ cup of cold water into a small bowl and toss in a few ice cubes. Measure out ½ cup of ice water and stir the vinegar into it. Add the vinegared water to the dough in three batches, gently mixing it in dough with a fork, until the dough holds together when pinched. If need be, add up to ¼ cup more water, a tablespoon at a time until all the dry ingredients are moistened and a firm dough is formed.

Gently press the dough into a ball. Sprinkle a clean work surface with flour, then roll the dough out to a shape of the casserole dish you'll be using but roughly 2 to 3 inches larger.

Place baking parchment or waxed paper on a cutting board and roll the dough from the rolling pin directly onto the paper. Cover the entire thing with plastic wrap or wrap in more waxed paper, and refrigerate while making the filling.

Preheat the oven to 375°F.

### Prepare the filling:

Heat a soup pot over medium heat and add 2 tablespoons of the oil. Add the chopped seitan, sprinkle with soy sauce, and sauté 8 to 10 minutes until the seitan is sizzling and lightly browned on the edges. Remove the seitan from the pot and set aside in a medium-size bowl.

Next, make a chickpea flour roux: Add remaining 3 tablespoons of oil to the pot and stir in the chickpea flour. Stir frequently and toast the flour for about 10 minutes, until fragrant and a deep mustard color. Stir in the chopped onion, cook for 4 minutes, and add the carrot, potato, and celery. Cook for 8 minutes, until the vegetables are softened. Stir frequently!

Pour in the white wine, stirring to dissolve the browned bits of roux from the bottom of the pot. Cook for 2 minutes to reduce a little bit, then stir in the frozen peas. Pour in about half of the vegetable broth and add the thyme, mustard powder, and sage. Bring the mixture to a simmer. Stir in the remaining broth and bring to a simmer again. Cook for another 6 to 8 minutes, until the broth has reduced slightly and a thin gravy has formed. Remove from the heat and season with salt and freshly ground pepper.

Remove the piecrust dough from the fridge. Ladle the filling into the casserole dish. Top with the crust, pressing the edges down lightly and leaving about 1½

inches of dough hanging over the sides of the dish (trim any excess dough beyond the 1½ inches with kitchen scissors or a sharp knife). Form a raised edge by turning or rolling up the dough at the edges of the casserole dish. Use a fork to crimp these edges, and poke a few holes with that fork onto the top of the crust, to allow steam to escape.

Place in the preheated oven; this pie tends to bubble and gravy could spill, so it's a good idea to place a large, rimmed baking sheet (or big swaths of aluminum foil) on the rack beneath it. Bake for 40 to 45 minutes, until the filling is bubbling and the crust is lightly browned and flaky. If you like, brush the top with a little soy milk once or twice during baking, for a light sheen on the crust.

Allow the pie to cool at least 10 minutes before serving; the filling will be boiling hot straight out of the oven.

### For Individual Pies:

Use deep, ovenproof bowls or deep mini-pie tins. For the crust, cut the dough into the appropriate number of sections, one per bowl. Form the sections into balls and roll out to the shape of the bowls/tins, plus an inch or two. Proceed as directed for the crust, stacking the individual crusts between sheets of waxed paper before chilling.

Prepare the filling as directed, dividing among the bowls. Top with the crust, seal, and crimp as for a large pie, and bake for 30 to 35 minutes at 375°F.

## CAULIFLOWER AND MUSHROOM POTPIE WITH BLACK OLIVE CRUST

SERVES 4 TO 6

**TIME:** A LITTLE OVER AN HOUR

*You'll almost look forward to the next freezing cold night as a chance to have this old-fashioned kind of pot-pie in the oven, filling the kitchen with a homey, Hallmark-card worthy aroma. Fresh cauliflower teams up with succulent mushroom in a velvety leek and herb gravy. And what's not to love about a satisfying biscuit-style top crust flecked with savory black olives? This hearty pie is best served with Sautéed Collards (page 106) or a simple green salad.*

**Sauce:**

- 3 tablespoons vegan margarine
- 4 tablespoons all-purpose flour
- 2 cups unsweetened plain soy or oat milk
- 1 bay leaf
- 2 teaspoons dried tarragon
- ½ teaspoon dried thyme
- ½ teaspoon dried marjoram
- ¼ teaspoon mustard powder
- 1 teaspoon salt
- Ground pepper

**Vegetables:**

- 1 pound cauliflower, trimmed, washed, and cut into bite-size pieces
- 2 tablespoons grapeseed or olive oil
- 1 leek, sliced thinly
- 1 small carrot, cut into small dice
- ½ pound cremini mushrooms, washed, trimmed, and sliced into large chunks
- 1 teaspoon sherry or white wine vinegar

**Black olive biscuit crust:**

- 1¼ cups all-purpose flour or a combination of whole wheat pastry and all-purpose

- 1 teaspoon baking powder
- 1 teaspoon salt
- Pinch of dried thyme leaves
- 3 tablespoons vegan margarine, chilled
- 4–5 tablespoons cold water
- ⅓ cup pitted black olives (kalamata recommended), chopped coarsely

PREHEAT THE oven to 375°F. Use a large, oven-to-table Dutch oven. If you don't have one, used a large, heavy-bottomed pot to prepare the filling and a large, deep casserole dish to bake the finish potpie.

*Prepare the sauce:*

In a heavy-bottomed saucepan (not the Dutch oven) over medium heat, melt the margarine and sprinkle in the flour. Stir to form a thick paste. Cook the mixture until fragrant, bubbling, and lightly browned, 4 to 5 minutes.

Temporarily turn off the heat. Slowly pour in the soy milk, using a wire whisk to stir until smooth. Whisk in the dried herbs, mustard powder, salt, and add bay leaf. Turn on the heat to medium and cook, stirring constantly with whisk, for 8 to 10 minutes, until a thick sauce forms. Turn off the heat, remove the bay leaf, and adjust the salt and pepper to taste.

Heat the oil in the Dutch oven over medium heat. Add the leeks and carrots, and sauté for 6 to 8 minutes, until softened. Add the mushrooms and vinegar, stir, and cook another 6 to 8 minutes until most of the excess liquid from the mushrooms has evaporated. Add the cauliflower, stir briefly, cover partially, and steam for about 8 minutes, until the cauliflower has just begun to soften. Remove the lid, turn off the heat, and set aside.

*While the cauliflower is cooking, prepare the biscuit crust:*

Sift together the flour, baking powder, salt, and thyme in a small bowl. With a pastry cutter or two knives held together, cut in the cold margarine until crumbs form, then drizzle in 3 tablespoons of cold water and mix. Drizzle in additional tablespoons of cold water, one at a time, until a soft dough forms (but be careful not to overwork it). Fold in the olives.

Pat out the dough on a lightly floured surface or give it a few rolls with a rolling pin, to form a circle or appropriate shape slightly smaller than the Dutch oven. Using a sharp knife, cut the dough into diamonds (you'll be placing small squares of dough over the casserole, rather than one big disk of dough).

### To assemble:

Give the sauce a good whisking (no worries if a skin has formed over it), pour into the cauliflower mixture, and stir completely to blend the veggie juices and sauce. Arrange the diamonds of dough over the mixture and brush with soy milk. Bake for 35 to 40 minutes, until the cauliflower is tender and the biscuits are cooked.

Allow to cool at least 10 minutes before serving, as the filling will be boiling hot straight out of the oven.

## POTATO AND KALE ENCHILADAS WITH ROASTED CHILE SAUCE

SERVES 4 TO 6

Ⓢ Ⓖ

TIME: 1 HOUR

*Just like tamales, enchiladas are a gift from Mexican cooking that requires just a little extra work than most casseroles do. Enchiladas taste even better the next day and even your kitchen-fearing domestic partner or kids could reheat without having to call 911.*

*In this alternative to traditional fillings, mashed potatoes and tender braised kale are spiked with lime, chile, and toasted pepitas, all wrapped in corn tortillas and a flavorful chile sauce. Accompany individual servings with a dollop of Sour Cilantro Cream (page 209) and a side of Mexican Millet (page 118).*

*tip*

➤ There's a dozen different ways to assemble enchiladas, but we prefer intersecting two lightly toasted, sauce-soaked tortillas like a spicy red Venn diagram to form one big tortilla so that we can get as much filling as possible into each enchilada.

➤ If you can't find any fresh green chiles, a 4-ounce can of green roasted chiles will do in a pinch.

### Enchilada Chile Sauce:

**2 tablespoons grapeseed or olive oil**

**1 onion, cut into small dice**

**3 large green chiles (such as Anaheim or even Italian-style long green peppers), roasted, seeded, peeled (see page 33), and chopped coarsely**

**2–3 teaspoons chile powder, preferably ancho**

**1½ teaspoons ground cumin**

**1 teaspoon marjoram or Mexican oregano (epazote)**

**1 (28-ounce) can diced tomatoes with juice (roasted preferred)**

**1 teaspoons sugar**

**1½–2 teaspoons salt**

### Potato and Kale Filling

**1 pound waxy potatoes (Yukon gold or red)**

**½ pound kale, washed, trimmed, and chopped finely**

**3 tablespoons grapeseed or olive oil**

**4 cloves garlic, minced**

**½ teaspoon ground cumin**

**¼ cup vegetable broth or water**

**3 tablespoons lime juice**

**¼ cup toasted pepitas (pumpkin seeds, page 210), chopped coarsely, plus additional for garnish**

**1½ teaspoons salt, or to taste**

**12–14 corn tortillas**

PREHEAT THE oven to 375°F and have ready a shallow casserole dish, at least 11½ × 7½ inches.

*Prepare the enchilada sauce first:*

In a large, heavy-bottomed saucepan over medium heat, sauté the onions in oil for 4 to 7 minutes, until softened. Add the remaining sauce ingredients, bring to a simmer, and remove from the heat. When the mixture has cooled enough, taste and adjust the salt if necessary. Puree with an immersion or regular blender until the mixture is smooth and even.

*Prepare the filling:*

Peel and diced the potatoes, then boil them until tender, about 20 minutes. Drain and set aside. Cook the grapeseed oil and minced garlic in a saucepot over medium-low heat, stirring occasionally until the garlic is sizzling and slightly browned (be careful not to let it burn). Add the kale, sprinkle with a little salt, and raise the heat to medium, stirring constantly to cover the kale with the oil and garlic. Partially cover the pot to steam the kale until it has wilted, 4 to 6 minutes.

Remove the lid and mix in the potatoes, vegetable stock, lime juice, pumpkin seeds, and salt. Use the back of a wooden spoon to mash some of the potatoes. Cook another 3 to 4 minutes, until the stock is absorbed. Add more salt or lime juice to taste.

*Create an enchilada assembly line:*

Have ready a pie plate filled with about ¾ cup of enchilada sauce, a casserole dish, a stack of corn tortillas, a lightly greased, heated griddle or cast-iron pan (for softening the tortillas), and the potato and kale filling.

Ladle a little bit of the enchilada sauce onto the bottom of the casserole dish and spread it around. Take a corn tortilla, place it on the heated griddle for 30 seconds, then flip it over and heat until the tortilla has become soft and pliable. Drop the softened tortilla into the pie plate filled with sauce; allow it to get completely covered in sauce, flip it over, and coat the other side.

Now, place the tortilla either in the casserole dish (the easiest way) or on an additional plate. Layer it with another heated, sauce-covered tortilla or just use one per enchilada; either way, run the potato filling down the middle and roll it up. Continue with rest of tortillas, tightly packing enchiladas next to each other.

Pour about a cup of sauce over the top (reserving some for later), cover tightly with aluminum foil, and bake for 25 minutes. Remove the foil and bake for another 10 to 15 minutes, until edges of the tortillas poking out of sauce look just a little browned. Allow to cool slightly before serving. Top individual servings with any remaining enchilada sauce, warmed slightly.

## EGGPLANT-POTATO MOUSSAKA
## WITH PINE NUT CREAM

SERVES 6 TO 8

**TIME:** 1 HOUR 20 MINUTES

*Our version of this traditional Greek casserole tastes
like it was made in a restaurant. A magical restaurant
that only makes vegan moussaka all day long and
delivers it instantly to anyone who reads this recipe
aloud three times and clicks her heels. Okay, that part
is a lie, but we promise, if you follow the instructions,
this outrageous casserole will be yours. Just imagine
delicate layers of roasted eggplant, potatoes, and zucchini topped with a sublime cinnamon-spiked tomato
sauce and a creamy pine nut custard. Our testers and
friends can't stop raving about the pine nut cream
and often just make that to incorporate into other
baked dishes.*

*This reheats nicely and tastes even better the next day.
Serve with slices of crusty peasant bread, and a simple
tomato and cucumber salad dressed with Mediterranean
Olive Oil and Lemon Vinaigrette (page 94).*

> ⭐ *tip* 🥄
>
> The zucchini will likely be very watery after roast-
> ing, so when it's cool enough to touch, gently
> but firmly squeeze the slices, by the handful, to
> remove any excess water. This will prevent an
> overly wet casserole and will help concentrate
> the flavors. See our tips for roasting summer
> squash (page 35), for further suggestions.

**Vegetable layer:**

- 1 pound eggplant
- 1 pound zucchini
- 1½ pounds Russet or baking potatoes (large, long
  potatoes work perfectly in this recipe)
- ¼ cup olive oil

**Sauce:**

- ¼ cup olive oil
- 4 large shallots, sliced thinly
- 3 cloves garlic, minced
- ⅓ cup vegetable broth or red wine
- 2 (15-ounce) cans crushed tomatoes, with juice
- 2 teaspoons dried oregano
- ¼ teaspoon ground cinnamon
- 1 bay leaf
- Salt

**Pine Nut Cream:**

- 1 pound soft silken tofu
- ½ cup pine nuts, plus additional for garnish
  (optional)
- 3 tablespoons lemon juice
- 1 teaspoon arrowroot powder
- 1 clove garlic
- Pinch of freshly grated nutmeg
- 1¼ teaspoons salt, or to taste
- white pepper

½ cup dry, fine white bread crumbs

PREHEAT THE oven to 400°F. Lightly oil three baking
sheets or shallow pans.

*Prepare the vegetables:*

Wash the eggplant and zucchini, and trim the
stems. Scrub and peel the potatoes. Slice the eggplant,
zucchini, and potatoes lengthwise into approximately
¼-inch-thick slices. Rub the eggplant slices with a little
salt and set aside in a colander in the sink or in a big
bowl for about 15 minutes to drain. Briefly rinse with
cold water and pat dry with a paper towel.

Place each vegetable on a separate baking sheet.
Distribute the ¼ cup of oil among the three sheets
and sprinkle vegetables with salt (except the eggplant,
if salted already). Toss to coat the vegetables on each
sheet, making sure each piece is completely coated
with oil. Drizzle a little extra oil on the eggplant, as it

has a slight tendency to stick (or if you're really paranoid, place the eggplant slices on oiled baking parchment). Spread out the vegetables on each sheet; some overlapping is okay. Roast the pans of zucchini and eggplant for 15 minutes, or until tender. Roast the potatoes for about 20 to 22 minutes, until the edges are lightly browned. Allow the vegetables to cool.

*While the vegetables are cooking,*
*prepare the tomato sauce:*

Combine the remaining ¼ cup olive oil and minced garlic in a large heavy-bottomed saucepan. Heat over medium heat and let the garlic sizzle for about 30 seconds, then add the shallots and cook until soft and translucent, 3 to 4 minutes. Add the wine and simmer until slightly reduced, another 3 minutes. Add the crushed tomatoes, oregano, ground cinnamon, and bay leaf. Partially cover and simmer over medium-low heat for 12 to 14 minutes, stirring occasionally. The sauce should reduce slightly. Turn off the heat, remove the bay leaf, and adjust the salt.

*Make the pine nut cream:*

In a food processor, blend the pine nuts and lemon juice, scraping the sides of the bowl with a rubber spatula, until a creamy paste forms. Add the tofu, garlic, arrowroot, nutmeg, salt, and white pepper. Blend until creamy and smooth.

Lightly oil a 9 × 13-inch pan and preheat the oven again to 400°F, if necessary. Spread ¼ cup of sauce on the pan, then add successive layers in order of eggplant, potatoes, sauce, and half the bread crumbs. Spread all the zucchini on top of this. Top with a final layer each of eggplant, potatoes, sauce, and bread crumbs. Use a rubber spatula to evenly spread the pine nut cream over the entire top layer. Scatter a few pine nuts on top, if desired.

Bake for 35 to 40 minutes, until the top is lightly browned and a few cracks have formed in the topping. Allow to cool 10 minutes before slicing and serving.

## KASHA PHYLLO PIE

SERVES 6 TO 8

**TIME:** ABOUT AN HOUR

*This filling wintertime pie is a little like a great big mushroom and kasha knish. It's wrapped up in layers of flaky, melt-in-your-mouth phyllo dough with a sneaky layer of crunchy sauerkraut tucked in its center. The filling can be made days in advance and the pie assembled and baked later (but don't assemble the pie until you're ready to serve it, to keep the dough from getting soggy). Serve with a dollop of your favorite spicy brown mustard or Horseradish-Dill Sour Cream (page 208), or doused in Mustard Sauce (page 204).*

Filling:

3 tablespoons olive oil

1 medium-size onion, cut into small dice

1 stalk celery, cut into small dice

½ pound cremini mushrooms, sliced thinly

1 small carrot, grated

1 teaspoon caraway seeds

1 teaspoon ground coriander

1¼ cups whole roasted buckwheat groats (roasted kasha)

2¼ cups vegetable stock, preferable mushroom-flavored, heated to almost boiling

½ teaspoon salt

Freshly cracked black pepper

1 cup sauerkraut, well drained of excess liquid

Phyllo:

1 16-ounce package of frozen phyllo dough, thawed according to package directions

⅓ cup or more of olive oil for brushing

PREPARE THE filling: Heat the olive oil in a 3-quart saucepan over medium heat and add the onion and celery. Stir-fry the vegetables until slightly soft, 4 to 5 minutes, then add the mushrooms and cook until most of mushroom liquid is evaporated, another 6 to 8 minutes. Add the grated carrot, stir-fry for 2 more minutes, then add the caraway seeds, coriander, salt, pepper, and buckwheat groats. Stir to coat the groats with oil and

pour in the hot vegetable stock. Bring the mixture to a boil, lower the heat to a low simmer, and cover.

Cook for 12 to 14 minutes until the liquid is absorbed and the buckwheat is tender. Remove from the heat, fluff with a fork, and partially cover. Allow the mixture to sit for 10 to 15 minutes so that kasha is cool to the touch before you proceed with assembling the pie.

Preheat the oven to 375°F. Lightly oil a medium-size casserole dish. Set up your work area to work with phyllo dough. We like to spread out a clean, damp tea towel on a cutting board, and to keep nearby the stack of phyllo covered in a plastic wrap and draped with another damp towel. Consult the package directions if you're looking for additional support.

Lay a sheet of phyllo dough on your work area. Quickly brush it with olive oil and layer with another sheet. Repeat four or five more times, then fold the entire thing in half and press into the bottom of the casserole dish to form a bottom crust. Push up the edges of the dough along the sides to form the sides of the pie.

Press one-half of the kasha mixture onto the dough. Spread the drained sauerkraut over kasha and sprinkle with a little freshly cracked pepper. Top with the remaining kasha and press the mixture to edges of the pie to even out. Repeat the process of layering and folding the phyllo dough (as for the bottom crust) to form the top crust of the pie, then press this top crust onto the kasha filling and fold any hanging edges into the sides of the pie.

Brush the top with a little more olive oil and bake for 30 to 35 minutes until the phyllo is puffed and golden. Cool for 10 minutes before serving and cut the pieces with a very sharp, thin, serrated knife.

## tip

➤ Kasha, or buckwheat, is a hearty, protein-packed grain (actually an herb, botanically speaking!) that's kept people alive in many parts of Asia and Eastern Europe for thousands of years. It can do the same for you; however, it does have a distinctive, "earthy" taste that might take some getting used to, for those uninitiated in the ways of buckwheat. This pie is a must for kasha fans, though! Look for whole, roasted buckwheat groats in the rice and pasta or kosher foods section of well-stocked grocery stores.

➤ Use the best possible sauerkraut you can get, so stay away from the canned stuff. Look for fresh, water-packed varieties found in the refrigerated section of the grocery store.

➤ Working with temperamental phyllo, a thin pastry dough, can sometimes make you curse the Greek gods, but with a little practice and some careful arrangement of your work "materials," you'll fly though it. For this dish, have the phyllo arranged right next to the casserole dish and keep the dough covered with either plastic wrap or a lightly damp, clean dish towel, so that it doesn't dry out. (Make sure to keep phyllo covered when not using, even between adding layers.) Keep a bowl with the olive oil and a brush near the phyllo as well. You will get olive oil all over the place, but soldier though it like a Spartan warrior.

# TEMPEH SHEPHERDESS PIE

SERVES 8

**TIME:** 1 HOUR 20 MINUTES

*As we were developing this recipe we found ourselves pondering some deep questions. Sheep herding is not vegan by definition, so why does every vegan cookbook have a vegan shepherd's pie? And do vegan shepherdesses dream of electric sheep? Our answer to these riddles is the winning combo of tempeh, peas, and corn, in a zesty mushroom gravy instead of a tomato-based one, because we prefer to dream that way.*

## tip

➤ For a fun and colorful variation, use mashed sweet potatoes, instead of regular mashed potatoes, as the topping.

**Tempeh layer:**

2 (8-ounce) packages tempeh

⅓ cup tamari or soy sauce

2 cups water

2 tablespoons plus 1 teaspoon olive oil

1 large onion, cut into ½ inch dice

3 cloves garlic, minced

8 ounces cremini mushrooms, sliced (about 3 cups)

1 teaspoon dried thyme

1 teaspoon ground coriander

Lots of freshly ground black pepper

1 cup frozen peas

1 cup fresh or frozen corn

2 cups vegetable broth

¼ cup all-purpose flour

¼ cup finely chopped fresh parsley, plus a little extra for garnish

**Potato layer:**

3 pounds Yukon gold potatoes, peeled and cut into 1-inch chunks

⅓ cup plain soy milk (preferably unsweetened), warmed or at room temperature

¼ cup grapeseed oil

¾ teaspoon salt, or to taste

Plenty of freshly ground black pepper

IN A large skillet, crumble the tempeh into small, bite-size pieces. Add the water, tamari, and 1 teaspoon of oil. Cover and let boil for about 10 minutes. Start boiling the potatoes in the meantime (directions below).

Remove the lid from tempeh and continue to boil until most of the water has evaporated, about 5 more minutes. Drain the tempeh in a colander and return the pan to the stove top over medium-high heat (you don't need to wash it).

Sauté the onions in the remaining olive oil for 5 minutes. Add the garlic and sauté for 1 more minute. Stir in the tempeh, along with the sliced mushrooms and the spices. Cook for about 10 more minutes over medium heat until the mushrooms are juicy and the tempeh is slightly browned. While this cooks, your potatoes should be ready for mashing and you can go ahead and preheat the oven to 375°F.

Add the corn and peas, and cook until heated through. You may need to add a little extra oil here; if you have a spray bottle of it, you should use it.

Mix together the vegetable broth and the flour until pretty much dissolved (a few lumps is okay). Add to the tempeh, along with the parsley, and stir. Let thicken for about 3 minutes, stirring occasionally. It will thicken more as it bakes.

## Prepare the potatoes:

Place the potatoes in a soup pot and cover with water (the water should be about 1 inch above the potatoes). Cover and bring to a boil. Let boil for 20 minutes, or until they easily cut with a fork. Drain and return to the pot. Use a potato masher to mash them up a bit, then add the soy milk, oil salt, and pepper. Mash very well, until creamy. Cover to keep warm until ready to use.

*Assemble the pie:*

Place the tempeh filling in a 9 × 13-inch casserole dish. Spoon the potatoes over the filling (although, truth be told, we use our hands for this because it's just easier).

Place in the preheated oven and bake for 20 minutes; the potatoes should be slightly browned on top. If they are not, place under a broiler for 2 to 3 minutes. Remove from the oven, garnish with chopped parsley, use a spatula to cut into eight squares, and serve.

# ONE-POT MEALS AND STOVE-TOP SPECIALTIES

THIS CHAPTER IS very much a two-part biopic—"a tale of two recipes," one might say—but even better because you won't be tested on any of the material. It centers on the secret lives of food that's cooked on top of the stove. Some meals use but one pot, some use a few more. Both make the tummy feel full of joy and, well, fullness.

Part I. We like the sound of "One-Pot Meals." It makes us feel like we're hanging out in a *Little House on the Prairie* remake, chopping wood, building barns, sewing quilts, and at the end of the day getting ready for a big dinner scooped out of a big, cast-iron pot.

"And what do those city girls know about cast-iron pots?" you ask? Enough that somehow stews and casseroles just taste better cooked in them. Good one-pots also include enameled cookware and stoneware, which are pricey but worth trading a few blankets for. We'll often recommend starting a recipe on top of the stove, then moving it to the oven to finish cooking. We're not being fickle, it's just the best way to give dumpling biscuits the perfect toasted top or to ensure that a steaming vat of jambalaya rice cooks up tender instead of burned. But if you haven't traveled down to the general store yet for a stove-to-table pot, fear not. You can just as easily transfer the recipe from a pot on the stove and into an oven-safe dish to complete the cooking process.

Part II. Let us turn to our attention for a moment to "Stove-Top Specialties," shall we? This is just a catch-all name for meals that require you to use those pots (and pans) you thought might never see some action (we're looking at you, Mister or Miss Ramen-Noodle). If you're scared you'll have to pull out all the stops like some kind of TV chef, be assured we'll keep your budding career in check—these recipes simply require just an extra sauté pan or small saucepan. As you'll see, stove-top meals include flavorful and thrilling sautés of vegetables, seitan, and tofu. Normal people (read: not the authors of the *Veganomicon*) would probably call these dishes "entrées."

## SEITANIC RED AND WHITE BEAN JAMBALAYA

SERVES 6

**TIME:** 1 HOUR 25 TO 35 MINUTES, DEPENDING ON THE RICE

*Warning: Just a taste of this luscious, tomato-laced con-coction of rice, vegetables, and seitan, and you just might feel like shouting at the devil. But please, don't do it with huge, teased metal-band hair or while wearing skin-tight black pleather pants, lest you scare the kids. Perfectly sin-ful for hardcore meat-eaters and vegans alike, seitanic jambalaya is a favorite at parties, potlucks, or wherever a* hungry, Cajun-spice lovin' crowd may be. Serve with French bread rolls, Sautéed Collards (page 106), and your favorite Louisiana-style hot sauce.

*tip*

➤ If using fresh thyme, just poke the sprigs into the rice before baking. The leaves will fall off the stems while it's cooking. Just remove the stems before serving.

➤ Have a favorite Cajun-style seasoning mix? Use three or more teaspoons in place of the dried herbs and spices, but still add the fresh thyme.

IF you haven't used the technique of deglazing (page 19) yet, here is the place to give it a shot. If bits of seitan stick to the bottom of the pot and start to burn while you're sautéing, deglaze the pot with a few tablespoons of cooking sherry. Then remove the seitan from the pot and continue as directed. The browned bits add lots of flavor, while the deglazing prevents them from sticking around and burning when cooking the vegetables.

6 tablespoons olive oil

1 recipe Simple Seitan (page 131), or 16 ounces store-bought seitan, diced or pulled apart into bite-size pieces

1 green bell pepper, seeded and cut into ½-inch dice

1 large yellow onion, cut into ½-inch dice

2 stalks celery, cut into small dice

4 cloves garlic, minced

3 heaping tablespoons tomato paste

½ cup cooking sherry or vegetable broth

2 cups long-grain rice, brown or white

1 (28-ounce) can diced tomatoes

1 (15-ounce) can white kidney (cannellini) beans

1 (15-ounce) can red kidney beans

1 bay leaf

4–6 sprigs fresh thyme (optional but really great here)

1 teaspoon dried thyme

1 teaspoon dried marjoram

1 teaspoon dried paprika

½ teaspoon celery seed

½ teaspoon onion powder

¼ teaspoon cayenne, or to taste

4 cups vegetable broth

1 teaspoon salt

Several pinches of freshly ground black pepper

Chopped, fresh flat-leaf parsley for garnish

PREHEAT THE oven to 375°F.

Preheat a large (the biggest you have) oven-to-table Dutch oven or heavy-bottomed pot over medium-heat. Sauté the seitan in 2 tablespoons of olive oil for 4 to 6 minutes, until lightly browned. Remove from the pot and set aside. Add the remaining olive oil to the pot, then stir in the onion, celery, green pepper, and garlic. Sauté for 12 to 14 minutes, until the vegetables are very soft and a tad mushy. Stir in the tomato paste and cook, stirring frequently, for another 4 minutes.

Stir in the cooking sherry to deglaze the vegetables, cook for 30 seconds, then add the rice. Stir the rice for about 4 minutes, then stir in the diced tomatoes, seitan, beans, bay leaf, all of the herbs, and the salt and pepper. Bring to a simmer, pour in the vegetable broth, and return to a simmer. Taste the broth and adjust the salt and pepper to taste.

If using a Dutch oven, cover and place in oven for 30 to 35 minutes, until the rice is tender. If using a pot, transfer to a deep casserole dish, cover tightly with aluminum foil, and bake for 30 to 35 minutes. If using brown rice, increase the baking time to 40 to 45 minutes.

Remove from the oven, stir the jambalaya, then cover and allow to sit for about 10 minutes before serving. Garnish with chopped parsley if desired.

## MANZANA CHILI VERDE

SERVES 4 TO 6

TIME: 1 HOUR

*This mild green chili has a secret weapon! Okay, it isn't so secret if you speak Spanish—it's apples. They give this chili mellow notes of sweet and tart. Tomatillos, poblano peppers, jalapeños, and cilantro give this chili its flavorful verde-ness; little white beans and cubes of tender white potatoes give it heartiness. Perfect with Jalapeño Onion Corn Bread (page 223). The next time your family or loved ones complain that all you vegans ever make is chili, serve this one and graciously accept their apology.*

1 pound baby Yukon golds or other thick-skinned potato, cut into ½-inch pieces

2 tablespoons vegetable oil

1 large yellow onion, cut into small dice

3 jalapeños, seeded and sliced thinly

2 poblano peppers, seeded and chopped into 1-inch pieces

4 cloves garlic, minced

3 teaspoons ground cumin

1 teaspoon dried oregano (preferably Mexican oregano)

1 teaspoon salt

⅓ cup dry white wine

1 pound tomatillos (about 10 small to medium ones), papery skin removed, washed, chopped into ½- to ¾-inch pieces

2 Granny Smith apples, cored, quartered, and sliced thinly

2 cups vegetable broth

1 cup loosely packed fresh cilantro

¼ cup chopped scallions, plus extra for garnish

1 (15-ounce) can small white beans, such as navy or cannellini, drained and rinsed (1½ cups)

Juice of 1 lime

Avocado slices for garnish

> If you can't find poblanos, plain old green bell
> peppers taste good, too. Also, as always, if you
> like things on the spicier side, keep the seeds
> from a jalapeño or two

PLACE THE chopped potatoes in a small saucepan, cover with water, and bring to a boil. Let boil, covered, for a little less than 20 minutes, until the potatoes are easily pierced with a fork. Drain and set aside. Of course, you should be preparing everything else while it is boiling.

Preheat a soup pot over medium-high heat. Sauté the onion, jalapeños, and poblanos in oil for about 10 minutes, until everything is softened and the onions are slightly browned.

Add the garlic, cumin, oregano, and salt. Sauté for 1 more minute, until the garlic is fragrant. Add the white wine and tomatillos, raise the heat a bit to let the wine reduce and tomatillos release their juices, about 5 minutes.

Add the apples, vegetable broth, scallions, and ½ cup of cilantro. Lower the heat to a simmer (medium-low), cover, and cook for 20 minutes.

Use an immersion blender to partially puree everything. If you don't have one, then let the mixture cool slightly and transfer to a blender or food processor; pulse until just slightly chunky. Don't forget that if you are using a blender, you need to be careful not to have a steam explosion, so pulse quickly and then lift the lid to let steam escape, then pulse again and repeat. Or just go get yourself an immersion blender, it will save your life! If using a blender or food processor, transfer the mixture back to pot.

Taste for sweetness/tartness. Tomatillos are sometimes bitter; if that is the case, add a teaspoon or two of sugar and that should level things out. Add the cooked potatoes and the beans, and simmer for a few more minutes, until everything is heated through.

Add the remaining cilantro and the lime juice. Ladle into bowls, garnish with avocado and scallions, and serve.

## LEEK AND BEAN CASSOULET WITH BISCUITS

SERVES 6

**TIME:** 1 HOUR 20 MINUTES

*This is home-cooked comfort food to the max. Leeks, potatoes, carrots, peas, and white beans in a savory stew, with biscuits that are baked right on top of it. Isa often wishes that someone would have this ready and waiting for her at the end of a rainy day, but she doesn't leave her apartment so that isn't going to happen. You however are probably not such a recluse, so request that your loved ones have this ready and waiting for you, or do the same for them.*

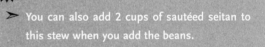

> You can also add 2 cups of sautéed seitan to
> this stew when you add the beans.

> If you don't have an oven-safe skillet, transfer
> this to the same size casserole dish.

**Stew:**

**2 Yukon gold potatoes, cut into ½-inch dice**

**3 cups vegetable broth**

**3 tablespoons cornstarch**

**2 tablespoons olive oil**

**2 leeks, washed well and sliced thinly (about 2 cups)**

**1 small onion, cut into medium-size dice**

**1½ cups carrots, peeled and cut into ½-inch dice**

**2 cloves garlic, minced**

1 heaping tablespoon chopped fresh thyme, plus
    extra for garnish
Several pinches of freshly ground black pepper
½ teaspoon salt (more or less depending on how
    salty your broth is, so taste first)
¾ cup frozen peas
1 (15-ounce) can navy beans, drained and rinsed
    (about ½ cups)

### Biscuits:

¾ cup plain soy milk
1 teaspoon apple cider vinegar
1½ cups all-purpose flour
2 teaspoons baking powder
¼ teaspoon salt
¼ cup nonhydrogenated vegan shortening

PREHEAT THE oven to 425°F.

Place the potatoes in a small pot and cover with water. Cover and bring to a boil. Once boiling, let cook for about 10 minutes, until the potatoes are just tender enough to be pierced with a fork. Drain immediately so that they do not overcook. While they are boiling, you can prep the rest of the veggies and start preparing the biscuits—the potatoes should definitely be done by the time you are.

Now, prepare everything for the biscuits. You're not going to make them yet, but it's good to have everything ready when it comes time to top the stew. Add the vinegar to the soy milk in a measuring cup and set aside to curdle. Mix the flour, baking powder, and salt in a medium-size mixing bowl.

### Now leave that alone and start the stew:

Mix the cornstarch into the vegetable stock until dissolved.

Preheat an oven-safe skillet, preferably cast iron, over medium heat. Sauté in the oil the leeks, onions, and carrots until very soft and just beginning to brown, about 10 minutes. Keep the heat moderate so that they don't burn.

Add the garlic, thyme, freshly ground black pepper, and salt, and cook for 1 more minute. Add the cooked potatoes and frozen peas, then pour in the vegetable stock mixture. Raise the heat just a bit; it will take a few minutes but the liquid will start simmering. Once it does, lower the heat again. Let it simmer for about 7 minutes, stirring occasionally, but no longer than that. If you need more time for the biscuits, then turn off the heat under the stew.

### Back to the biscuits:

Add the shortening to the flour in small slivers and work it into the dough with a fork or with your fingers until large crumbs form. You don't want to cream it in; there should be clumps. Drizzle in the soy milk and mix with a fork until everything is moistened (some dry parts are okay).

Wash and dry your hands, then lightly flour them and get them dirty again. Gently knead the dough about ten times right in the bowl, just so that it is holding together and not very sticky. If it seems sticky, as in sticking to your fingers, then gently work in a little more flour. Set that aside and check on your stew.

The stew should be simmering and slightly thickened. Mix in the beans. Now, let's add the biscuits. Pull off of chunks of dough that are about slightly larger than golf balls. Gently roll them into balls and flatten a bit; they do not have to be perfectly round. Add them to the top of the stew, placed an inch or so apart.

Transfer the whole megillah to the preheated oven. If you are worried about spillover, place it on a rimmed baking sheet, but we've never had that problem. Bake for about 15 minutes. The biscuits should be just slightly browned and firm to the touch.

Remove from the oven and use a large serving spoon to place some of the stew and a biscuit in each shallow, individual bowl. Sprinkle with a little chopped, fresh thyme.

Serve at last! Especially yummy when you break up your biscuit and mix it in a bit with your stew.

## SEITAN PICCATA WITH OLIVES AND GREEN BEANS

SERVES 4

**TIME:** 40 MINUTES

*Okay, enough messing around with everything else we call "recipes," piccata is where it's at. If you've ever wanted to impress someone with something other than your ability to touch your tongue to your nose, then serve them piccata. Never had it before? It's capers and white wine and garlic and shallots and lemon and breaded seitan, and it's easy to make. Are you sold? We serve it with olives and crunchy string beans over a big pile of mashed potatoes, and we serve it often.*

1 pound seitan

About ⅓ cup all-purpose flour

Olive oil (enough to coat the bottom of the pan)

1 scant cup thinly sliced shallots (3 to 5, depending on the size)

4 cloves garlic, chopped

⅓ cup dry white wine

2 cups vegetable broth

¼ teaspoon salt

Several pinches of freshly ground black pepper

Small pinch of dried thyme

¼ cup capers with a little brine

½ cup pitted kalamata or black olives, cut in half

Juice of 1 lemon (2–3 tablespoons)

3 tablespoons finely chopped fresh parsley

½ pound green beans, ends trimmed

PREHEAT A large heavy-bottomed skillet over medium-high heat.

Cut the seitan into long, thin pieces, slicing off any rounded ends so that they will lay flat. Ideally, the slices should be a little over ¼ inch thick, 3 inches long, and 2 inches across, but who is counting?

Coat the bottom of the skillet with oil and let it get hot. Dredge half the seitan slices in flour to coat. Add to the pan and cook until lightly browned, about 2 minutes on each side. Proceed to coat the other slices and repeat. Place the cooked seitan slices on a tray or plate covered with aluminum foil, to keep warm. Do not rinse out the skillet or turn the heat off, as you're going to make the sauce in it.

Bring a pot of water to a boil for the green beans, but don't boil them just yet. You just want to have the water at the ready.

If there is enough oil left in the seitan pan to sauté the shallots and garlic, then do so; if not, add a little oil and sauté them for about 5 minutes, stirring often so as not to burn.

Add the white wine to the sauce and raise the heat to bring to a rolling boil. Add the vegetable broth, salt, black pepper, and thyme. Again, bring to a rolling boil and let the sauce reduce by half; this should take about 7 to 10 minutes.

Add the capers and olives to heat through, about 3 minutes. At this point, add the beans to the boiling water and let them cook for 2 minutes, then strain.

Add the parsley and lemon to the sauce and turn off the heat.

*To serve:*

Make a pile of mashed potatoes. Place the seitan over the mashed potatoes and insert the green beans around the seitan, vertically. Use a ladle to douse everything in plenty of sauce. Serve immediately.

## BBQ BLACK-EYED PEA–COLLARD ROLLS

MAKES 12 ROLLS, SERVES 3 TO 4

**TIME:** 40 MINUTES

*Black-eyed peas love BBQ sauce and everyone loves rolling things. The combination makes this meal extra special. One bunch of collards should give you enough to prepare this recipe. It's yummy with mashed potatoes and Jalapeño-Corn Gravy (page 216) or any gravy, really. Prepare the BBQ sauce first and boil water for the collard leaves, then when the BBQ sauce is almost finished, begin cooking the mushrooms and beans. For a really quick and easy meal, prepare the sauce a day in advance.*

- 12 large collard leaves
- 1 tablespoon vegetable oil
- 8 ounces cremini mushrooms, sliced thickly
- 4 cups chopped collards
- 1 (15-ounce) can black-eyed peas, drained and rinsed (1½ cups)
- 3 cups Backyard BBQ Sauce (page 207)

> ### tip
>
> ➤ To prepare the collard leaves for this recipe, pick the biggest, prettiest collard leaves of the bunch. Slice off the rough stems and a few inches of the stem that grows into the leaf because, if it's too stiff, it might make rolling difficult. To do that, run the tip of your knife alongside either side of the stem and then slice it.

BRING A large pot of water to a boil.

When the water is boiling, submerge the collard leaves and cover for 6 minutes. When done, use tongs to transfer them to a strainer and let cool. Handle them gently so that they don't rip.

Preheat a large skillet over medium heat. Sauté the mushrooms in the oil for about 5 minutes, until softened. Add the chopped collards. Cook for 7 to 10 minutes, or until most of the moisture has cooked off. Add the black-eyed peas and cook through. Pour on 2 cups of the BBQ sauce and cook for about 5 more minutes. If it looks watery, turn the heat up a bit and cook a few more minutes.

Let cool just a bit so that you can make the rolls without burning yourself.

Place a collard on a flat work surface with the side that has not been sliced facing you. Place about 2 tablespoons of the black-eyed peas and company in the lower third of the collard. Fold the bottom up over the mixture, then fold in the sides. Roll the collard up, gently but firmly. If the filling is spilling out, remove some of the black-eyed peas and try again.

Continue rolling the remaining collards. When ready to serve, spoon extra BBQ sauce over the rolls.

## PINEAPPLE-CASHEW-QUINOA STIR-FRY

SERVES 4

**TIME:** ABOUT 30 MINUTES, NOT INCLUDING COOLING THE COOKED QUINOA

*Love pineapple and wish you could eat it in something other than dessert? Well then, welcome to your pineapple heaven; it's all here in the South Asian–inspired dish. Quinoa, the high-protein South American grain, is delicately flavored by being cooked in a little pineapple juice, then it's the base for this colorful and speedy stir-fry featuring crisp veggies, fresh ginger and crunchy cashews. Make the quinoa a day or two in advance, store it in the fridge, and you'll be able to put this stir-fry in a snap for an easy weeknight dinner. It's a meal in itself, or serve alongside any marinated and grilled tempeh (page 97) or tofu (page 126).*

➤ Hit a deli or grocery store's salad bar (or produce section) for precut, ready-to-use fresh
pineapple.

➤ Use up leftover quinoa in this recipe (but try it
just once by cooking quinoa in pineapple
juice). For a truly gorgeous dish, use a blend of
the white quinoa and the heirloom variety Red
Inca, which cooks up a deep russet color. Use
about half and half each kind of quinoa and
cook them together.

## Quinoa:

1 cup quinoa, well rinsed and drained

1 cup pineapple juice

1 cup cold water

¼ teaspoon soy sauce

## Stir-fry:

4 ounces cashews, raw and unsalted

3 tablespoons peanut oil

2 scallions, sliced thinly

2 cloves garlic, minced

1 hot red chile, sliced into very thin rounds

½-inch piece ginger, peeled and minced

1 red bell pepper, seeded and diced

1 cup frozen green peas or cooked edamame

½ cup fresh basil leaves, rolled and sliced into thin
shreds (just like slicing collard greens)

2 tablespoons finely chopped fresh mint

10 ounces fresh pineapple, cut into bite-size chunks
(about 2 cups)

3 tablespoons soy sauce

3 tablespoons vegetable stock

1 tablespoon mirin

Lime wedges for garnish

PREPARE THE quinoa first: Combine the quinoa, juice,
water, and soy sauce in a medium-size pot. Cover,
place over high heat, and bring to a boil. Stir a few
times, lower the heat to medium-low, cover, and cook
for 12 to 14, minutes until all the liquid has been
absorbed and the quinoa appears plumped and
slightly translucent. Uncover, fluff, and let cool.

For best results, place the quinoa in an airtight container and refrigerate overnight. If you're in a hurry,
chill the covered quinoa for at least an hour. When
ready to use, break up any chunks of the cold quinoa
with a fork.

### Prepare the stir-fry:

Use the largest nonstick skillet you have (at least 11
inches in diameter) or a wok. Have all of your ingredients chopped and easily within reach. Place the
cashews in the dry pan and heat over low heat, stirring
them, until lightly toasted, 4 to 5 minutes.

Remove the cashews from the pan, raise the heat
to medium, and add the peanut oil, scallions, and garlic. When the garlic starts to sizzle, add the sliced
chile pepper and ginger. Stir-fry for about 2 minutes,
then add the bell pepper and peas. Stir-fry for another
3 to 4 minutes, until the bell pepper is softened and
the peas are bright green. Add the basil and mint, and
stir for another minute before adding the pineapple
and quinoa.

In a measuring cup, combine the soy sauce, vegetable stock, and mirin. Pour over the quinoa mixture.
Stir to incorporate completely and coat the quinoa.
Continue to stir-fry 10 for 14 minutes, until the quinoa
is very hot (it helps to use two spoons/spatulas to
scoop the quinoa around).

Serve with lime wedges and additional soy sauce,
to season individual servings to taste.

## LENTILS AND RICE WITH CARAMELIZED ONIONS AND SPICED PITA CRISPS

SERVES 4 TO 6

 if served without pita

**TIME:** 1 HOUR 20 MINUTES

*This is referred to as Mujadarah or Enjedra and a dozen other names in the Middle East. Terry says she could live for months on the simple and scrumptious meal of rice, lentils, and onions, and be assured she has damn well tried. Try it and be amazed how few ingredients can make something so yum. It's a different version of comfort food; here spiced red lentils transform into creamy, golden mash that just melts right into the fragrant rice and rich caramelized onions. Serve alongside braised chard or kale.*

### tip

➤ Substitute brown, green, or black lentils for the red lentils. Unlike red lentils, these varieties hold their shape so this dish will have more of a pilaflike consistency, but is still delicious.

3 large yellow onions, peeled and sliced into thin rings (about 2 pounds)

¾ cup olive oil

1 cup long-grain basmati rice (brown or white), rinsed

1 cup red lentils, rinsed

1 cinnamon stick

½ teaspoon ground allspice

1½ teaspoon ground cumin

*generous pinch of ground cloves*

PREHEAT THE oven to 400°F.

In a large, deep baking pan, toss the onion rings with the olive oil to coat. Be sure to separate the rings and spread them out in the pan. Roast in the oven for 25 to 30 minutes, stirring often. The idea is the get most of the onion rings deep brown, crisp, and even burned on the edges. The deeper they roast, the sweeter they'll taste. When done, remove from the oven and set aside.

Bring 4 cups of water to a boil in a large, heavy-bottomed pot. Add the rice, cinnamon stick, ground cloves, and *ground* allspice. Bring back to a boil, then lower the heat, cover, and simmer for 15 minutes.

Uncover and add the lentils, cumin, and ~~allspice~~; stir gently only a few times (too much stirring can break the rice grains); cover, bring to boil again, lower the heat to low, and cook for an additional 45 minutes, until the liquid is completely absorbed. Remove from the heat and set aside the covered pot for 10 minutes.

Use a fork to gently fluff the lentils and rice. Remove the cinnamon stick. Gently fold the caramelized onions into the lentils and rice, making sure to drizzle on any remaining olive oil from the roasting pan. Stir thoroughly. Serve warm or at room temperature.

## SPICED PITA CRISPS

SERVES 4

**TIME:** 15 MINUTES

*Crunchy, easy to make, and great with any dip or spread, too. A nice way to use up pita that's just a little past its prime.*

4 white or whole wheat pitas

Olive oil for brushing

1 teaspoon or more per pita of the following spices; pick just one and stick with it, or be like a crazy person and experiment with these mixtures:

Garam Masala

Garlic powder, cumin, cayenne, and salt or

Lemon pepper, garlic powder, and salt

PREHEAT THE oven to 350°F.

Slice open a pita along the edges, and carefully

open and separate each half. Brush with olive oil, then sprinkle with your seasoning(s) of choice. Spread the pitas on cookie sheets (a little overlapping is okay) and bake for 8 to 10 minutes, until golden brown and crisp. Watch and be careful not to burn.

Cool on the cookie sheets and store in plastic bags.

## SPAGHETTI SQUASH MEXICANA WITH TROPICAL AVOCADO SALSA FRESCA

SERVES 4 TO 6

🟢 🟢 🟢

**TIME:** 1 HOUR 15 MINUTES

*If you throw the word* Mexicana *on something it automatically connotes that there's black beans and corn in it, right? Okay, good. This is baked spaghetti squash tossed with mildly spicy black beans and corn, topped off with a fruity salsa fresca. We used pineapple, but you can use mango or papaya, if you prefer. Spaghetti squash gets its name because, when cooked, the flesh divides into pretty strings that resemble, you guessed it, spaghetti. It's a good idea to make the roasted squash a day in advance; that way you can have this dish on the table in under half an hour.*

### tip

> Our testers had good results microwaving the spaghetti squash instead of baking it. Since we don't have microwaves (as we keep repeating), we weren't able to test that, but do an Internet search for how to microwave a spaghetti squash and have at it. Is it wrong for a cookbook to tell you to Google something? Probably, but no more wrong than having a microwave.

**1 spaghetti squash (use one in the 3-pound range)**

Tropical salsa fresca:

**1 cup chopped tomato (½-inch chunks)**

**1 cup chopped pineapple, mango, or papaya (½-inch chunks)**

**1 avocado, peeled, pitted, and cut into ½-inch chunks**

**¼ cup lightly packed chopped fresh cilantro**

**Juice of 1 lime**

Bean mixture:

**1 tablespoon vegetable oil**

**1 medium-size yellow onion, cut into small dice**

**2 jalapeños, seeded and chopped small**

**3 cloves garlic, minced**

**2 teaspoons coriander seeds, crushed**

**1½ teaspoons chile powder**

**½ teaspoon ground cumin**

**¼ teaspoon ground cinnamon**

**½ teaspoon salt**

**½ cup red cooking wine**

**1 cup fresh or frozen corn (if frozen, partially thawed)**

**1 (15-ounce) can black beans, drained and rinsed (1½ cups)**

**2 teaspoons hot sauce, or to taste**

FIRST, BAKE the squash: Preheat the oven to 375°F. Cut the squash in half across its waist (widthwise). Scoop out the seeds. Prick the squash halves with a fork five or six times. Fill a baking dish with about an inch of water and place the squash cut side down in the dish. Bake for about 45 minutes, or until the skin is easily pierced with a fork.

*Meanwhile, prepare the salsa:*

In a small mixing bowl, toss all those ingredients together. Cover and refrigerate until ready to use.

*Then prepare the bean mixture:*

Preheat a large, heavy-bottomed skillet over medium-high heat and sauté the onions and jalapeño in the oil for about 5 minutes. Add the garlic and coriander seeds, and sauté 2 more minutes. Add the remaining spices, salt, and the wine, raise the heat, and boil for about 2 minutes, stirring often.

Lower the heat and add the corn, black beans, and hot sauce. Cook for 5 to 7 more minutes, until the corn is heated through and the wine has reduced.

If the squash is not done by this point, cover the bean mixture. If they cool by the time the squash is ready, then gently reheat. The bean mixture should be hot when served.

When your squash is ready, remove from the oven and let cool for about 10 minutes until you can handle it without burning yourself. Cut the squash halves in half lengthwise. Shred and scoop out the flesh with a spoon, add to the bean mixture, and toss with tongs to separate the strings and mix.

Divide among individual plates and top with salsa fresca. Serve immediately.

## TOMATO AND ROASTED EGGPLANT STEW WITH CHICKPEAS

SERVES 6

**TIME:** ONE HOUR 10 MINUTES

*One bite of this stew will have you transported to a sunny hillside in Greece, or maybe Terry's renovated apartment in Astoria, Queens (that's what she gets for marrying a Spartan). Either way, roasted eggplant, garlic, and peppers make for a deeply satisfying Mediterranean dish. Serve with Soft Poppy-Seed Polenta (page 115) by scooping the polenta into the center of a wide bowl and ladling the stew around it. Garnish with fresh parsley if you roll like that and serve with hot sauce if you like things spicy.*

*This recipe looks really long but it's mostly our detailed notes on how to time everything right. Most of the cooking time isn't active; it's the veggies roasting and the soup simmering. Granted, there's a lot of steps and chopping of veggies, but worth it for the eggplant lover in your life.*

¼ **cup olive oil**

2 **large eggplants (3 pounds)**

1 **bulb garlic**

2 **red bell peppers, stems and seeds removed**

1 **white onion, sliced into thin half-moons**

3 **cloves garlic, minced**

½ **cup white wine**

2 **teaspoons dried tarragon**

1 **teaspoon dried thyme**

1 **teaspoon ground coriander**

½ **teaspoon paprika**

1 **teaspoon salt**

**Several pinches of freshly ground black pepper**

2 **bay leaves**

1 **(28-ounce) can whole peeled tomatoes**

1 **(15-ounce) can chickpeas, drained and rinsed, or 1** ½ **cups cooked chickpeas**

> *tip*

> ➤ You are going to need two large, rimmed baking sheets to get the job done and baking parchment to make sure that you don't ruin the baking sheets—unless they're already ruined and you don't care.

> ➤ If you don't have a pastry brush for applying the oil, a spray bottle of olive oil with work, too. Otherwise just drizzle it on

ARRANGE TWO oven racks so that one is in the upper third and the other is in the lower third. You're probably not going to be able to fit both of your pans on one rack. If you are, we hate that you've got a bigger oven than we do!

Preheat the oven to 450°F.

Quarter the eggplant lengthwise and slice across into ¾-inch slices.

Line two rimmed baking sheets with baking parchment and brush the parchment with the olive oil. Lay the eggplant slices on the baking sheets and brush or spray the tops with olive oil. Leave a little room on one pan for the peppers. Brush the outsides of the peppers with olive oil and place them, cut side down, on the pan.

Remove the papery skins from the garlic bulb (as much skin as will come off easily). Place the garlic on one of the pans as well.

Place the pans in the oven and roast for 25 minutes.

Remove the pans from the oven. Place the red pepper in a paper or plastic bag and close up the bag (so that the pepper skins steam off). Flip the eggplant pieces and brush a little oil on any pieces that look dry (they should be fairly browned, albeit unevenly).

Return the eggplant to the oven for an additional 15 minutes and remove the garlic, setting it aside to cool. The garlic should have been in for 40 minutes, but if you did the eggplant flipping with lightning speed, give the garlic a few more minutes to bake.

On the stovetop, preheat a soup pot over medium-high heat. Sauté the onions in 1 tablespoon of olive oil for 10 to 12 minutes, until lightly browned. The eggplant should be ready while the onion is browning, so remove the eggplant from the oven and set aside (if you are running out of counter space, use tongs to transfer the eggplant to a bowl).

Add the garlic to the onions and sauté for 2 more minutes. Add the white wine and herbs and cook for about 5 minutes. Add tomatoes, tearing up each tomato with your hands before adding to the pot, and add the remaining tomato juice from the can.

Add the eggplant to the pot and mix well. Don't be afraid of crushing the eggplant; in fact it's good if it gets a little crushed.

Remove the peppers from the bag and peel away the skin. If for some reason the skin won't peel, don't sweat it. Chop the peppers into bite-size pieces and add to the soup pot along with the chickpeas. Lower the heat and simmer for 20 minutes, stirring occasionally.

To prepare the garlic, wet your hands (to avoid sticking) and squeeze each roasted garlic clove into the soup pot. Mix well, turn off the heat, and let the stew sit for as long as you can stand to let the flavors to develop.

Serve!

## KABOCHA-UDON WINTER STEW

Serves 4

Ⓕ

**TIME:** about 35 minutes

*Feel healthy (or just fake it, deliciously) by eating this mellow broth loaded with sweet kabocha squash and vegetables. It's a welcome break from the usual heavy winter fare, but still it's light enough to be just as welcome in warmer weather. The clear broth is Japanese-style dashi broth flavored with dried shiitake mushrooms, sake, and sea vegetables. The chewy udon noodles make this a complete meal, but also try serving with packaged Japanese-style pickles alongside.*

*If you haven't guessed already, you'll need a few Japanese specialty items for this stew. We recommend making this if you've ever stepped into a huge, well-stocked Asian market, got really excited, brought home a big bag of groceries, then asked yourself "What the hell am I going to make with all this stuff?" Now you can go shopping with purpose!*

**Shiitake dashi broth:**

- **2 quarts cold water**
- **2 (4-inch) pieces kombu (kelp)**
- **⅓ cup shoyu (Japanese soy sauce)**
- **2 teaspoons sugar**
- **½ ounce dried shiitake mushrooms (4–5 dried)**
- **2 (¼-inch-thick) slices fresh ginger, lightly crushed with the side of a knife**

**Stew:**

- **½ pound fresh udon noodles**
- **1 large leek, washed well and sliced into ½-inch lengths**
- **1 large carrot, peeled and sliced into ½-thick pieces**
- **1½–2 pounds kabocha (about 1 small squash), unpeeled but seeded and sliced into 2 × 1-inch pieces**

6–8 ounces fried tofu pouches (aburage), or firm
silken tofu, sliced into strips or cubes

⅓ cup sake

2 tablespoons mirin

2 scallions, sliced very thin

Optional garnishes: Japanese hot pepper powder and
additional shoyu

PREPARE THE broth: Pour 2 quarts of water into a large soup pot and add the kombu, shoyu, sugar, dried shiitakes, and ginger. Bring the water to a boil, then lower the heat so that it gently simmers. Cook for 15 minutes.

Taste the broth and add a little more shoyu if it's not quite salty enough (but don't overdo it—it's easy to pour too much!). Remove the kombu, ginger, and mushrooms. Allow the mushrooms to cool enough to handle, slice very thinly, and return to pot. Cover the pot and keep the broth warm over a low flame.

In a separate pot, bring 3 quarts of water to a boil. Add the udon noodles and cook for 4 to 5 minutes, until tender. Use chopsticks to pull apart the noodles while they are cooking. Transfer to a colander in the sink, rinse well with cold water, and allow the noodles to continue to drain. If at any point the noodles get too gummy and sticky, rinse with warm water to separate.

Meanwhile, add the leek, carrot, kabocha, and tofu to the broth. Simmer over medium-low heat for 20 to 25 minutes, until the squash is tender and can be pierced easily with a fork. Stir in the sake and mirin.

Place portions of the rinsed udon noodles into large, deep, individual serving bowls. Use a slotted spoon to add vegetable chunks to the bowls, then a ladle to spoon on the stock. Sprinkle with chopped scallions. Eat with a large spoon and chopsticks.

*tip*

➤ Kabocha squash is an Asian pumpkin with deep orange, nutty-flavored flesh that's sweeter and slightly drier that regular pumpkin. A bonus for lazy cooks: the deep green, thin skin of kabocha squash cooks up tender and edible, so no need to peel. We have no problem finding it in supermarkets but, if you can't find it, use peeled sugar pumpkin, acorn, delicate, or butternut. You'll probably need to extend the cooking time for these squash, cooking an additional 10 to 15 minutes until the squash is tender.

➤ Kombu, dried giant kelp, is a standard ingredient in Japanese soups and condiments. When cooked in a stock or broth, it will unfold into a really big sheet. Don't freak out, just let the stock cook as directed and then remove and discard the kelp when it's done.

➤ Dried udon works just fine here, too. Cook the noodles according to the package directions and rinse in cold water, then keep them handy in a colander. Rinse in warm water when ready to add to stir-fry.

## BRAISED SEITAN WITH BRUSSELS, KALE, AND SUN-DRIED TOMATOES

SERVES 4

TIME: 30 MINUTES

*This makes an easy weeknight meal served over mashed potatoes, pasta, or rice. Make it a little more fancy with either Soft Poppy-Seed Polenta (page 115) or Broccoli Polenta (page 114). A warm and flavorful Fork You to winter.*

2 tablespoons olive oil, plus a little extra if needed

6 average-size shallots, sliced thinly

2 cups seitan, sliced on the diagonal into bite-size pieces

½ pound Brussels sprouts, quartered (about 2 cups once sliced)

4 cloves garlic, minced

½ teaspoon dried thyme

½ teaspoon dried basil

¼ teaspoon dried tarragon

½ teaspoon salt

Several pinches of freshly ground black pepper

½ cup sun-dried tomatoes, chopped into bite-size pieces

2 cups vegetable broth

¼ cup red wine (any wine will do, really)

4 cups chopped kale

PREHEAT A large, heavy-bottomed pan over medium-high heat. Sauté the shallots and seitan in 2 tablespoons of the olive oil for about 7 minutes, until they have both browned. Add the Brussels sprouts and sauté for 3 more minutes, adding a little extra olive oil if need be. Add the garlic, herbs, salt, and pepper, and sauté for another minute. Mix in the sun-dried tomatoes.

Add the vegetable broth and wine. Once the liquid is boiling, which should be pretty quick if the heat is right, add the chopped kale. Stir the kale until it is wilted.

Cover the pan, leaving a little room for steam to escape, and lower the heat. Simmer for 5 to 7 more minutes. Taste and adjust the salt, and serve immediately.

## CHOLENT

SERVES 6

TIME: 45 MINUTES

*Cholent is a Jewish beef stew that's typically served on the Sabbath. Here, we use textured vegetable protein (TVP), kidney beans, and lentils to create a thick, full bodied pot of stick-to-your-ribs yumminess. Caraway seeds give it the Eastern European flavor that sets it apart from your run-of-the-mill stew, so now would be a great time to add them to your spice rack arsenal. We like to just crush crackers over the top and serve, but rice would be good, too. Or serve with bread for scooping. Warning: You might start inexplicably calling people* meshugenahs *and* putzes *after you've eaten this.*

*This is one of those stews that really benefits from a night in the fridge, but don't let that deter you from eating it right away (or any day of the week).*

2 tablespoons olive oil

1 large onion, cut into medium-size dice

3 cloves garlic, minced

½ teaspoon tarragon

1 teaspoon caraway seeds

1 teaspoon salt

Several pinches of freshly ground black pepper

½ cup red cooking wine, water, or vegetable broth

2 bay leaves

½ cup French lentils, rinsed

1 cup peeled, sliced carrots (about ½ inch thick)

4 medium-size potatoes (about 1¼ pounds), peeled and cut into ¾-inch chunks)

1 (15-ounce can) tomato sauce

3 cups water

1 cup TVP chunks (*not* granules or crumbles)

1 cup frozen or canned and drained lima beans (green peas are fine if you hate lima beans, hater)

1 (15-ounce) can kidney beans, drained and rinsed (1 ½ cups)

PREHEAT A large soup pot over medium heat. Sauté the onions in the oil until translucent, 5 to 7 minutes. Add the garlic, tarragon, caraway seeds, salt, and pepper. Sauté until the garlic is fragrant, about a minute more.

Deglaze the pot with the red wine. Add the bay leaves, lentil, carrots, potatoes, tomato sauce, water, and TVP chunks. Mix together. Cover and simmer for about 30 minutes, until the potatoes and carrot are tender.

Add the lima and kidney beans and cook until heated through. Serve like crazy. *Ess gezunterhait.*

## PLANTAIN AND PINTO STEW WITH PARSNIP CHIPS

SERVES 4

TIME: 45 MINUTES

*In NYC, plantains abound in the supermarkets and we're always looking for new ways to use them. This is a spicy and flavorful yet delicate stew. Use fresh tomatoes instead of canned so that you don't get a concentrated flavor that overpowers the plantains. Choose plantains that are ripe yellow and flecked with black yet not completely blackened. The parsnip chips are optional but yummy!*

1 recipe parsnip chips (recipe follows)

1 tablespoon vegetable oil

1 large white onion, chopped finely

1 yellow pepper, chopped finely

3 jalapeños, seeded and chopped finely

3 cloves garlic, minced

8 plum tomatoes, diced

¼ cup cooking sherry (any cooking wine will do, or sub vegetable broth)

1 teaspoon salt

2 teaspoons ground cumin

1 (15-ounce) can pinto beans, drained and rinsed

2 ripe plantains, peeled, sliced in half lengthwise, and sliced into ½-inch pieces

1 cup chopped fresh cilantro

IN A soup pot over medium heat, sauté the onions, peppers, jalapeños, and garlic in the oil for 5 to 7 minutes, until the vegetables are softened. Add the tomatoes, sherry, salt, and cumin. Cover and bring to a simmer; let simmer for 15 minutes, stirring occasionally, until the tomatoes are cooked and broken down.

Add the pinto beans and plantains. Cover and simmer for another 20 to 25 minutes. The plantains should be soft and sweet. Add the cilantro and mix in so that it wilts.

Ladle into bowls and stick a few plantain chips into each bowl, like spears.

## PARSNIP CHIPS

*If you like sweet potato fries, you will like these. There are only two ingredients here, but sprinkling them with ground cumin is yummy, too. For parsnip fries, just cut them into ¼-inch-thick slices instead of ⅛-inch and bake for an additional 5 to 10 minutes.*

1 pound parsnips (2 medium-size)

2 teaspoons or so peanut oil

PREHEAT THE oven to 400°F.

Peel the parsnips and slice them lengthwise. Place them cut side down and slice into ⅛-inch-thick strips, or as close to that as you can get them.

Line them in a single layer on a baking sheet and drizzle with oil. Toss them around and try to get the oil over all of them, add a little more oil if necessary.

Bake for 15 minutes, then flip them (use tongs for this). Bake for an additional 10 to 15 minutes. The parsnips should be flecked with black and dark brown. If some are thinner than others, they will cook faster, obviously; remove the skinny ones from the baking sheet as they finish baking.

Sprinkle with salt and serve.

## PUMPKIN SAAG

SERVES 4 TO 6

TIME: 1½ HOURS

*Saag is Hindi for a curry that's made of greens—in this case, we use spinach. Baked pumpkin works as a flavorful backdrop to make this a healthier-than-usual saag (it's typically loaded with lots of ghee and cream or coconut cream). Masala complements the pumpkin nicely because of its autumnal blend of cinnamon, cloves, and cardamom. What we're going for here is mushy in a good way, with just a little bit of chunky pumpkin bites thrown in. Serve with basmati rice and some sort of chutney (page 212) and flat bread (page 222).*

**tip**

> Roast the pumpkin a day in advance so that you can throw this together the next day. Just wrap the baked pumpkin in plastic wrap, refrigerate, and you'll be good to go.

**3 pounds sugar pumpkin**
**3 tablespoons peanut oil**
**1 large white onion, diced finely**
**4 cloves garlic, minced**
**1½ teaspoons garam masala**
**¼ teaspoon ground cinnamon**
**½ teaspoon salt**
**⅛ teaspoon cayenne**
**1 cup water**
**1-inch cube fresh ginger, peeled**
**10 ounces fresh spinach (this is about 2 bunches), washed well and chopped coarsely**
**Juice of ½ lime**

PREHEAT THE oven to 350° F.

*First, bake the pumpkin:*

Carve out the top of the pumpkin to remove the stem. Use your strongest knife to cut the pumpkin in half along the vertical. Remove the seeds (reserve them to toast sometime) and scrape out the stringy stuff with a spoon. Place the pumpkin halves, cut side down, on a lightly greased baking sheet. Bake for about 45 minutes, until a fork can easily pierce the flesh.

Let the pumpkin cool completely. Peel away the skin and then chop the pumpkin up into 1-inch chunks.

Preheat a soup pot over medium-high heat. Sauté the onions in the peanut oil for about 5 minutes. Add the garlic and sauté for 2 to 3 minutes more, or until everything is honey brown.

Add the pumpkin and cook until heated through, about 3 minutes. Add the spices and salt, and grate the ginger directly into the pot (use a microplane grater, if possible). Add the water and cook for about 5 minutes, mixing often. Use your mixing spatula to mush the pumpkin up a bit, but leave some pieces chunky.

Add the spinach in batches (three or four should do it), mixing well after each addition.

Cook for about 10 more minutes, stirring often. Add the lime; taste and adjust the salt.

This is best if it's had time to sit for a while, but if you want to eat it immediately, we understand.

## VEGETABLES OR SEITAN SIMMERED IN MOLE SAUCE

*Who doesn't want chocolate for dinner? Presenting two variations on the same concept; tender vegetables or chewy seitan is slowly simmered in homemade chocolate mole sauce. Change the vegetables to suit the season, if you please. Serve with a starchy side such as Mexican Millet (page 118), plain steamed brown rice, cooked quinoa, or soft, warmed corn tortillas to sop up lots of the luscious sauce.*

## SWEET SQUASH IN MOLE SAUCE

SERVES 4 TO 6

**TIME:** 50 MINUTES, NOT INCLUDING PREPARING MOLE SAUCE

*This is a delectable stew of sublime mole sauce and a fresh tasting blend of summer squash and tropical calabaza pumpkin. Calabaza can be found in most any grocery that carries Latino groceries; it's usually conveniently precut into manageable-size chunks and can be easily peeled with a vegetable peeler. We love it so because it's the pumpkin that's commonly available year round (note our pumpkin fetish). Sugar pumpkin or butternut squash in season can be substituted instead.*

1 pound zucchini, yellow summer, or pattypan
    squash
2 tablespoons peanut oil
1 large onion, diced
1 pound calabaza or butternut squash, peeled,
    seeded, and diced in 1-inch cubes
2 cups Chile-Chocolate Mole (page 210)

> ***tip***
>
> ➤ Don't skip the salting-the-zucchini step; it really helps the zucchini slices keep their shape and fully develop their flavor. Salting does this by removing the excess water that usually makes sautéed summer squash fall apart. Cutting the squash into ½-inch-thick cuts will also help retain its shape.

TRIM AND slice the zucchini into ½-inch-thick rounds and place in a large colander. Sprinkle a few large pinches of kosher salt onto the zucchini and rub to coat each piece. Allow the colander to remain in the kitchen sink or over a bowl for at least 30 minutes to allow the excess moisture to drain from the squash. If you haven't prepared the mole sauce already, this is a good time to do so. Rinse and allow the zucchini to drain before using.

Heat the peanut oil in a large, heavy pot over medium heat. Add the onion and sauté until slightly softened and translucent, 5 to 7 minutes. Add the diced calabaza squash and 2 tablespoons of water, and partially cover. Steam for 8 to 10 minutes, until the squash is partially tender but not completely cooked.

Remove the cover, add the drained zucchini and sauté for 5 minutes. Add the mole sauce, lower the heat slightly, and stir to completely combine the squash juices with the sauce. Simmer for 10 to 12 minutes until both kinds of squash are tender.

## SEITAN IN MOLE SAUCE

SERVES 4 TO 6

**TIME:** 50 MINUTES, NOT INCLUDING PREPARING MOLE SAUCE

*Seared, succulent chunks of seitan and spicy-sweet mole sauce makes one heck of a hearty and warming winter dinner. Serve with a lightly steamed green, such as chard or collards, to offset some of the richness of the mole and seitan.*

2 tablespoons peanut oil
1 recipe Simple Seitan (page 131), cut into 1-inch
   chunks
2 large carrots, scraped and sliced ½-inch thick
1 large onion, diced
½ cup vegetable broth
2 cups Chile-Chocolate Mole (page 210)

PREHEAT A large pot over medium heat. Add 1 tablespoon of the oil and sauté the seitan for 4 to 5 minutes, until it is lightly browned.

Remove the seitan from the pot, set aside, and heat the remaining oil in pot. Add the onion, sauté for 6 to 8 minutes, until soft, add the carrots plus the vegetable broth, and cover. Steam the carrots for 8 minutes, until partially tender, remove the cover, and stir in the seitan and mole sauce. Mix completely and allow everything to simmer over medium-low heat for 10 to 12 minutes, until the carrots are tender.

## RED LENTIL–CAULIFLOWER CURRY

SERVES 4 TO 6

**TIME:** 1 HOUR

*There's always room for one more lentil recipe in the mighty tome that is the Veganomicon! And why not . . . lentils are such a tasty, filling, and fast-cooking legume, it would be stupid not to eat them more often. So here we have a healthy and comforting curry of red lentils, cauliflower, and a sneaky surprise, parsnip. Depending on what kind of curry powder you use, it can be mild or fiery. Serve with basmati rice, steamed chard or spinach, and Poppy Seed–Cornmeal Roti (page 221).*

3 tablespoons grapeseed or peanut oil
1 large onion, chopped
1 large chile pepper (jalapeño or serrano), minced
2 large shallots
1 (½-inch) piece fresh ginger, peeled and grated
1 large parsnip, peeled and chopped
2 teaspoons curry powder
½ teaspoon turmeric
½ teaspoon ground cinnamon
½ teaspoon ground cumin
½ teaspoon ground coriander
1½ cups red lentils, sorted and rinsed
4 cups vegetable broth or water
1½ –2 pounds cauliflower (about one medium-size
   head), trimmed and sliced into small florets
2 tablespoons chopped fresh cilantro
2 tablespoons lime juice
1½ teaspoons salt

HAVE ALL of the ingredients chopped and readily at hand. In a large stockpot, heat the oil over medium heat. Sauté the onion and shallots until tender and translucent, 5 to 7 minutes. Add the grated ginger and chile, and sauté for 1 minute. Add the spices and briskly stir-fry for 30 seconds, then add the parsnip and stir-fry for another minute.

Slowly pour in the vegetable broth, then stir in the lentils. Cover the pot, raise the heat to high, boil for 1 minute. Give the mixture a stir, then cover the pot and lower the heat to medium-low. Allow the lentils to simmer for 10 to 12 minutes. They should turn light yellow and look mushy.

Add the cauliflower florets, stirring to coat with the lentils. Partially cover and simmer for 20 to 25 minutes, until the cauliflower is tender but not completely falling apart. Remove from the heat and stir in chopped cilantro, lime juice, and salt.

Allow the curry to sit, covered, for about 15 minutes before serving to allow the flavors to meld and the mixture to cool slightly.

## SAUTÉED SEITAN WITH MUSHROOMS AND SPINACH

SERVES 4

**TIME:** 35 MINUTES

*One of our testers remarked that this is how Julia Child would have cooked if she had been vegan. Simple, fast preparation makes this a great choice for a weeknight date or for any time when you want something a little fancy but don't have much time. Serve over quinoa or mashed potatoes or rice or . . . you get the picture.*

    1 tablespoon olive oil
    2 cups seitan, sliced on the diagonal into bite-size pieces
    1 small onion, sliced into thick half-moons
    2 cups sliced white or cremini mushrooms
    3 cloves garlic, minced
    1 teaspoons dried thyme
    ½ teaspoon dried basil

    1 teaspoon salt
    Several pinches of freshly ground black pepper
    ¼ cup white wine
    ¼ cup vegetable broth or water
    6 cups spinach, washed well
    Lemon slices (optional)

PREHEAT A large, lidded skillet over medium-high heat. Sauté the seitan for about 2 minutes. Add the onions and sauté for another 5 minutes, until softened, covering the pan but lifting it to stir occasionally, to make the onions and seitan cook faster.

Add the mushrooms, garlic, thyme, basil, salt, and pepper, and sauté for another 8 minutes, again, covering but occasionally stirring. Once the mushrooms are cooked and soft, add the wine and broth. Add the spinach in batches and use tongs to incorporate them with everything else. Cook for about 5 more minutes.

Serve immediately, with slices of lemon, if desired.

# PASTA, NOODLES, AND RISOTTO

SOMETIMES PASTA JUST seems too good to be true. What did we ever do to deserve to be on the same planet with a food so easy to make, so (usually) inexpensive, and always fun to eat? The world needs more pastalike miracles.

Not only that, but pasta and noodles are a vegan godsend when it comes to making a quick, substantial weeknight dinner. A bag of whole wheat spirals is transformed by the addition of vegetables, a little olive oil, and garlic. We're especially in love with how a can of crushed tomatoes and a little time on the stove can make a homemade sauce that rivals anything you'll pour out of a jar. And although pasta is sometimes thought of as void of nutrition, we've been digging the fiber-ific whole wheat, brown rice, and quinoa varieties, as well as gluten-free brown rice pasta.

Even if you're an old hand at whipping up spaghetti, you'll find something to love in this collection of old-time favorites and exciting new combinations. You want lasagne? We got your lasagne layered with creamy basil–tofu ricotta and homemade sauce right here! Too lazy to make eggplant parm? We have roasted eggplant, garlicky bread crumbs and fettuccine to sooth your soul. Go east with a lively, rich Japanese-style curry stir-fry of udon with seitan. Or head to the coast and savor California-inspired spinach linguine, spiked with fresh lime juice and wrapped around delicately sautéed chunks of avocado.

Last but never the least, a duo of risottos will get you exited about standing over a hot stove in ways you never dreamed possible. Take your pick from lively lemon and fresh peas or tender asparagus scented with exotic lemongrass. Impress your guests or just even yourself with how a bag of rice and a little elbow grease can become the creamiest, comforting food in existence.

## SPAGHETTI AND BEANBALLS

SERVES 4

**TIME:** 40 MINUTES

*We usually don't eat spaghetti, opting instead for more interestingly shaped pastas, but we absolutely have to have spaghetti with meatball-type comfort meals or the world just feels off kilter. These "meatballs" can be baked or panfried, depending on your mood. Begin your sauce right before preparing the beanballs because you will need some of it for this recipe.*

**tip**

> Vital wheat gluten makes the beanballs chewier but, if you don't have any, go ahead and use whole wheat or all-purpose flour.

**Spaghetti:**

- 1 recipe (4 cups) Marinara Sauce, any variation (page 205)
- ½ pound whole wheat or regular spaghetti

**Beanballs:**

- 1 (20-ounce) can kidney beans, rinsed and drained (about 3 cups)

- 2 tablespoons soy sauce
- 2 tablespoons steak sauce or tomato paste
- 2 tablespoons olive oil, plus additional for frying or baking
- 2 cloves garlic, grated or minced finely
- ¼ teaspoon grated lemon zest
- ½ cup plain bread crumbs
- ¼ cup vital wheat gluten
- ½ teaspoon dried oregano
- ¼ teaspoon dried thyme

IF BAKING, preheat the oven to 375°F.

Put a large pot of salted water on the stove to boil, for the spaghetti.

*Prepare the beanball mixture:*

Mash the kidney beans in a mixing bowl until no whole beans are left. (We start with a potato masher and then use a fork to get any rebel beans that refuse to mash.) You don't want them to be completely smooth, you should still be able to recognize that they are kidney beans. Add the soy sauce, steak sauce, 2 tablespoons of the olive oil, the garlic, lemon zest, bread crumbs, wheat gluten, and herbs, and use a fork to mix everything together. Use your hands to knead the mixture for about a minute, until everything is really well combined and firm.

Roll the bean mixture into walnut-size balls (you should have twelve to fifteen of them). But don't make them too big; smaller makes for the best texture.

A few minutes after you've began cooking the bean-balls (directions follow), add the pasta to the water and cook according to the package directions, usually about 10 minutes.

### To assemble:

Drain your spaghetti and put it back in the pot. Pour your remaining marinara sauce over the pasta and mix. Use a pasta spoon to transfer the spaghetti to plates, then top with three or four beanballs and their sauce.

### To Bake the Beanballs:

Grease a rimmed baking sheet with olive oil. Place the balls on the sheet and then drizzle them with a little more oil, to coat. Bake for about 15 minutes, until lightly browned on the bottom, then flip them and bake for another 10 minutes. Remove them from the oven and pour about ⅓ cup of your marinara sauce onto them, flipping them around to coat. Bake for an additional 5 minutes.

### To Panfry the Beanballs:

Preheat a large skillet over medium heat. Pour about ¼ inch of olive oil into the pan, then add your meatballs (you might have to do this in two batches or two pans, if your pan isn't big enough). Cook for about 15 minutes, tossing them often, until browned on all sides. Add ⅓ cup of marinara sauce to the meatballs, and toss to coat. Cook for an additional 15 minutes.

# SPICY TEMPEH AND BROCCOLI RABE WITH ROTELLE

SERVES 4

45

**TIME:** 40 MINUTES

*The bittersweet flavor of broccoli rabe (also known as broccolini, broccoli rape, rapini, or rabini) matched with whole wheat pasta and peppery braised tempeh create a complex tasting meal reminiscent of the classic Italian dish featuring sausage. Our recipes testers loved how it was a perfect balance of pasta, protein, and greens; we love its spicy texture and savory bite. Spiral-shaped pasta nicely captures the tiny bits of tempeh, red pepper, and olive oil, but substitute any shape you like.*

½ **pound whole wheat rotelle or other spiral-shaped pasta**

Spicy fennel tempeh:
1 (15-ounce) **package tempeh, cubed**
½ **cup plus 2 tablespoons vegetable broth**
2 **tablespoons soy sauce**
2 **tablespoons tomato paste**
1 **clove garlic, pressed**
1 **tablespoon fennel seeds**
1½ **teaspoons red pepper flakes, or to taste**
1½ **teaspoons dried oregano**
½ **teaspoon red wine vinegar**

Broccoli rabe:
¼ **cup olive oil**
5 **cloves garlic, sliced thinly**
1 **bunch broccoli rabe (½–¾ pound), tough stems trimmed, chopped coarsely**
2–3 **tablespoons white wine, water, or vegetable broth**
2 **teaspoons red wine vinegar or balsamic vinegar**
**Salt and freshly ground pepper**

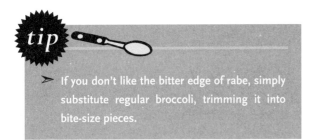

➤ If you don't like the bitter edge of rabe, simply substitute regular broccoli, trimming it into bite-size pieces.

BRING A large pot of salted water to boil, add the pasta and cook according to the package directions, usually about 10 minutes. Drain the pasta, toss with a teaspoon or two of olive oil and keep covered either in a large covered serving bowl or the cooking pot. While your pasta is boiling, prepare the other ingredients.

### Prepare the tempeh:

Place the tempeh in a large, nonstick skillet. In a measuring cup, whisk together the vegetable broth, tomato paste, soy sauce, garlic, fennel seeds, red pepper flakes, and oregano. Pour over the tempeh, stir to coat, and cook over medium heat until the liquid starts to simmer. Cover the pan and steam the tempeh for 8 minutes, or until most of the liquid is absorbed and the tempeh is tender. Stir a few times while tempeh is steaming.

Transfer the tempeh to a bowl and crumble about half of the cubes with the back of a spoon.

Wipe down the skillet to remove any leftover tempeh sauce, return the skillet to medium heat the and add 2 tablespoons olive oil. To test the heat, drop a bit of tempeh into the oil—when it sizzles, the oil is hot enough. Add the tempeh and stir-fry for 4 to 5 minutes, until it begins to brown. Remove from the heat, add to the pasta, and keep covered.

### Prepare the broccoli rabe:

Pour the remaining olive oil into the pan and add the sliced garlic. When the garlic begins to sizzle, stir and cook it for about a minute. Add the broccoli rabe,

stir to coat it with the oil, sprinkle with a little salt, and cover the pan. Cook for about 2 minutes. Sprinkle with 2 tablespoons of the white wine and steam for 8 to 10 minutes, until the broccoli rabe is bright green and its stems are tender (you might need to do this in two batches; just add the second batch of broccoli as soon as it the first batch has wilted enough to create room in your pan).

Remove the cover and continue to sauté for an additional minute or two, until any excess liquid is evaporated. Pour the cooked broccoli rabe onto the tempeh and pasta, sprinkle with red wine vinegar, season with salt and freshly cracked pepper, and toss everything to mix.

Use a pasta spoon to divvy up onto plates, or place everything in a big pasta bowl and serve family style.

## SPINACH LINGUINE WITH BASIL-CILANTRO PESTO AND ARTICHOKES

SERVES 4

🌀 ④⑤ 🍽

**TIME:** 35 MINUTES

*You will be craving this from now on, mark our words. Spinach linguine is sautéed with fragrant pesto, while red onions add just a hint of sweetness, color, and texture. Don't replace the red onions with regular ones unless you really have to. Artichokes round everything out and give a great bite. This also makes a great fast and fancy meal if your in-laws or the IRS decides to drop by for a surprise visit.*

➤ Make your pesto while the water for the linguine is boiling, so that you can time this right.

½ pound spinach linguine

2 tablespoons olive oil

1 medium-size red onion, sliced into thin half-moons

4 cloves garlic, thinly sliced

2 tablespoons white cooking wine, vegetable broth, or water, whatever

½ teaspoon salt

Several pinches of freshly ground black pepper

1 recipe Basil-Cilantro Pesto (page 214)

1 (15-ounce) can artichoke hearts, drained and sliced in half (don't use the jarred kind in oil, it's expensive and too oily for this; get the kind that comes in brine)

BRING A large pot of salted water to a boil and cook the linguine according to the package directions, usually about 10 minutes. Once you've added the pasta to the water, proceed with the recipe.

Preheat a large skillet over medium-high heat and sauté the onion in the olive oil until softened, 5 to 7 minutes. Add the garlic and sauté for a minute more. Add the white wine, salt, and pepper, and cook for another minute or two. Lower the heat to low. At this point, the linguine should be done.

When the linguine is ready, don't drain it. Use a pasta spoon to transfer it to the pan in batches. This is a good method because you can use the pasta water to thin out the pesto and make sure that everything gets evenly coated. When you add one batch, add a bit of the pesto, too, and using the pasta spoon, sauté to coat. Proceed with the rest of the pasta and pesto until you've added all of it. If it seems dry, add extra splashes of pasta water.

Add the artichoke hearts and toss to coat. Cook gently over low heat just until the artichokes are heated through, about 3 minutes. Serve immediately!

## PASTA DELLA CALIFORNIA

SERVES 4

TIME: 35 MINUTES

*If we said in the title that this was pasta with avocados, no one would take us seriously, so instead we call it Pasta Della California. Anything with avocado in it can be called "California," right? Anyway, this is so damn good. The pasta is sautéed in lots of garlic and lime along with broccoli and peppery arugula. Then the avocados are gently tossed in just until they are warm. So if the idea of "cooked" avocados scares you, don't worry. This is especially astounding with the Smoky Grilled Tempeh (page 130).*

**tip**

➤ Choose avocados that are ripe but still firm. An avocado that is too mushy and has brown spots will not work here. If it's warm in your house, once the avocado is ripe you should refrigerate it for several hours—this way, it will hold its shape when peeled and sliced. For this recipe, slice the avocado in half and remove the seed. Peel off the skin, then slice each half lengthwise down the middle. Next, slice across into chunks.

½ pound linguine

3 cups sliced broccoli (tops cut into small florets, stalks sliced thinly)

2 tablespoons olive oil

8 cloves garlic, minced (yes 8, that's not a typo!)

¼ teaspoon grated lime zest

½ teaspoon red pepper flakes

¼ cup white wine

1 cup vegetable broth

2 tablespoons lime juice (juice of 1 lime, depending on the juiciness of your lime)

½ teaspoon salt

**Several pinches of freshly ground black pepper**

**4 cups loosely packed arugula leaves**

**2 avocados, peeled, pitted, and sliced into 1-inch chunks (see tip)**

BRING A large pot of water to boil and prep all your ingredients while the water boils, because this dish comes together in no time. Once the water is boiling, add the pasta and cook according to the package directions, usually about 10 minutes. In the last minute of cooking you will be adding the broccoli, so keep that in mind.

Meanwhile, preheat a large nonstick skillet over medium heat. Add the olive oil, garlic, lime zest, and red pepper flakes, and gently heat, stirring often, for about 2 minutes, being careful not to burn the garlic. Pour in the wine and raise the heat to bring to a boil, to reduce the wine, about 2 minutes. Add the vegetable broth, lime juice, salt, and pepper, and bring again to a boil. Once the sauce is boiling, lower the heat to a simmer. Add the arugula.

By this point the pasta should be almost done, so add the broccoli to the boiling pasta and cook for 1 more minute. Drain all into a colander.

When the arugula is wilted, add the broccoli and pasta to the pan and use a pasta spoon to toss it around, making sure to get everything coated in garlic. Cook for about 3 more minutes. Add the avocado and turn off the heat. Gently toss the pasta for another minute to incorporate the avocado without smushing it, just until it is warmed through.

Serve with generous grinds of black pepper. There is usually a lot of garlic left in the pan, so be sure to spoon that over your bowls of pasta.

## PENNE VODKA

SERVES 4

**TIME:** 35 MINUTES

*No Brooklyn Italian restaurant is complete without this classic creamy tomato dish. We blend almonds into the sauce to get that expected creaminess and a little fresh basil to bring it home.*

**2 teaspoons olive oil**

**4 cloves minced garlic**

**¼ teaspoon crushed red pepper**

**28 ounce can crushed tomatoes**

**¼ cup vodka**

**¼ teaspoon dried thyme**

**¼ teaspoon dried oregano**

**½ teaspoon salt**

**A few dashes fresh black pepper**

**½ cup sliced or slivered almonds**

**¼ cup finely chopped fresh basil, plus a little extra for garnish.**

**½ pound penne**

BRING a pot of water to boil for the pasta. Preheat a saucepan over medium/low heat. Add the oil, garlic and crushed red pepper to the saucepan and sauté for about a minute, until fragrant, being careful not to burn. Add the crushed tomatoes, vodka, thyme, oregano, salt and black pepper. Cover, and turn the heat up a bit to bring to a simmer for about 20 minutes, stirring occasionally. Meanwhile, add pasta to the water and cook according to package directions.

Once the sauce has simmered for 20 minutes, add the almonds. Use an immersion blender to blend the almonds into the sauce until creamy and only slightly grainy (see page 211). The pasta should be done by now, so drain and set aside. Add the basil to the sauce, and mix the sauce and pasta together in the pot. Serve, garnished with a little extra chopped basil.

## PASTA E FAGIOLI

SERVES 4

**TIME:** 35 MINUTES

*Sometimes pronounced pasta fazool by real New Yorkers, fagioli is beans to you, bub. This is a simple but filling dish that is made from fresh plum tomatoes that are cooked down with garlic and herbs. The light fresh taste and texture goes well with the heartiness of the beans. We suggest white beans—cannellini, navy or great northern—but use kidney or garbanzos if that floats your legume boat.*

### For the sauce:

2 tablespoons olive oil

6 cloves garlic, minced

2 pounds plum tomatoes, diced medium

¼ cup dry white wine (or vegetable broth)

½ teaspoon dried thyme

½ teaspoon dried oregano

a few dashes fresh black pepper

1 teaspoon salt

16 oz can white beans, washed and drained

½ pound small tube pasta, like penette or tubetti, or even small shells

BRING a pot of water to boil for the pasta and preheat another large pan over medium heat. Add the oil and garlic to the large pan and sauté for about 1 minute, until garlic is fragrant. Add the tomatoes, wine, thyme, oregano, black pepper and salt. Bring to a boil, then lower to medium heat until the tomatoes are broken down and sauce is reduced and thickened, about 20 minutes. Meanwhile, add pasta to the water and cook according to package directions. Once the sauce is thickened, simmer on low heat to keep warm. Drain pasta and set aside. When sauce is finished, add the beans and pasta and use a pasta spoon to mix. Serve when pasta and beans are heated through, about 3 minutes.

## PUMPKIN BAKED ZITI WITH CARAMELIZED ONIONS AND SAGE CRUMB TOPPING

SERVES 6 TO 8

**TIME:** ABOUT AN HOUR

*This is a rich and creamy baked pasta casserole that blends the best flavors that fall has to offer. The pumpkin is subtle but sweet caramelized onion and a hint of nutmeg complement it nicely. Serve alongside some lightly braised chard or a simple arugula salad. Don't forget to tell your dinner companions that ziti means "bridegrooms" in Italian, then sit back smugly in your seat, satisfied with your foodie knowledge. They probably won't even hear you because they'll be too busy digging in.*

**tip**

➤ If you've never made homemade bread crumbs before, try it today, as store-bought crumbs won't have the same crunchy texture. It really makes a difference in this recipe—the top layer of crumbs contrasts wonderfully with the chewy, rich bottom layer of pasta. Simple tear up your old bread and process in a food processor until you get coarse crumbs.

¾ pound uncooked ziti or penne pasta

2 onions, sliced very thinly

3 tablespoons olive oil

1 recipe Cashew Ricotta (page 206)

1 tablespoon brown sugar

¼ teaspoon ground nutmeg

White pepper and cayenne

2 cups pureed pumpkin, or 1 (15-ounce) can pumpkin puree (don't use pumpkin pie mix)

¼ cup vegetable broth

**Sage bread crumbs:**

2½ cups bread crumbs, preferably fresh and homemade (made from about half a baguette or four
dinner rolls)

⅓ cup walnut pieces, chopped in a food processor
until resembling coarse crumbs

¼ cup nonhydrogenated vegan margarine

2 teaspoons dried, rubbed sage

1 teaspoon dried oregano leaves

½ teaspoon ground paprika

Salt and freshly ground black pepper

PREHEAT THE oven to 375°. Lightly grease a 9 × 11-inch lasagne-type baking pan with olive oil, or use two smaller pans.

Prepare the ziti according to the package directions, about 10 minutes. Drain, rinse with cold water, and drain again. Set aside.

*While the pasta is cooking make the caramelized onion:*

Preheat a large heavy-bottomed pan, preferably cast iron, over medium heat. Sauté the onions in oil until some onion bits are very brown and caramelized, 12 to 15 minutes. Set aside.

Place the Cashew Ricotta in a large bowl and fold in the pumpkin puree, brown sugar, nutmeg, white pepper, cayenne, and vegetable broth, and mix. Add the cooked ziti and caramelized onions, stirring to coat the pasta. Pour the mixture into the prepared baking pan and press lightly with a rubber spatula to level it.

*Make the sage bread crumbs:*

Melt the margarine in large, heavy-bottomed skillet over medium heat. Stir in the bread crumbs, walnuts, dried herbs, and paprika, and season with salt and pepper. Stir constantly until the mixture is lightly coated, 3 to 4 minutes. Remove from the heat and sprinkle evenly over the ziti.

Bake for 28 to 30 minutes, until the top of the ziti is golden brown. Cool for 10 minutes before slicing and serving.

## MAC DADDY

SERVES 8 TO 10
**TIME:** 1 HOUR 10 MINUTES

*Here he is, the ultimate in comfort food: our version of Mac and Cheese. We use mashed tofu to give this dish body and douse it in Cheezy Sauce (page 214) for creaminess. Serve with a very simple salad of baby greens with grapeseed oil and red wine vinegar. This is the perfect thing to use up all your vegetable odds and ends, so see our variations. Any vegan potluck would be incomplete without Mac Daddy, but since omnivores tend to be sketchy about nutritional yeast, save this for appreciative vegans and vegetarians.*

Double recipe Cheezy Sauce (page 214)

¾ pound elbow macaroni

1 pound extra-firm tofu

1 teaspoon salt

1 tablespoon olive oil

2 tablespoons fresh lemon juice

**tip**

➢ This dish freezes well. Store leftovers in a covered plastic container and freeze. When ready to eat, preheat the oven to 350°F, transfer the leftovers to a baking pan, cover with aluminum foil, and bake for about 30 minutes.

BRING A large pot of salted water to a boil. Add the macaroni and cook according to the package directions, about 10 minutes. Meanwhile, prepare your Cheezy Sauce.

Preheat the oven to 325°F. When the pasta is ready, drain and set aside. When sauce is ready, begin assembling.

*To assemble:*

Crumble the tofu into an 11 × 13-inch glass or ceramic baking dish. Mash the tofu with your hands until it resembles ricotta cheese. Add the salt, olive oil, and lemon juice, then stir.

Add ½ cup Cheezy Sauce to the tofu and stir. Use a dry measuring cup with a handle so that you can just dip it in to the sauce and pour—you don't need to be very precise. Add the macaroni to the tofu, along with 3 more cups of sauce, and stir well.

Smooth the top of the pasta mixture and press it down with a spatula to level it. Then pour the remaining sauce over the pasta and smooth again.

Bake for 30 minutes; the top of the macaroni should be slightly browned. It's a good idea to wait about 20 minutes before serving, so that it can cool down and firm up a bit, but if you can't wait, more power to you.

### Variations:

**Mac and Peas:** Add 2 cups of frozen peas when you add the macaroni to the casserole.

**Broc Mac Daddy:** Add 3 cups of small broccoli florets when you add the macaroni.

**Autumn Mac Daddy:** Add 3 cups of roasted or boiled butternut squash when you add the macaroni. Omit the thyme from the nutritional yeasty sauce and add 1 teaspoon of ground nutmeg.

**Spicy Mac Daddy:** Add ¾ teaspoon of red pepper flakes to the nutritional yeasty sauce when you add the black pepper.

**Mac and Greens:** Add 4 cups of finely chopped kale, spinach, or chard when you add the macaroni.

**Mac and Chicks:** Instead of tofu, use 2 cups of mashed chickpeas.

## LASAGNE MARINARA WITH SPINACH

SERVES 6 TO 8

(Tofu Ricotta variation)

**TIME:** 1 HOUR 10 MINUTES

*Lasagne is a great way to showcase how delicious vegan cooking can be. Our version brings together a variety of recipes in this book to create everyone's favorite baked pasta dish. It's endlessly versatile, depending on what flavor you feel like making the Marinara Sauce (page 205), what fresh vegetables are found at the market that day, which Tofu Ricotta (page 206) is used, and whether the luscious Pine Nut Cream (page 164) is featured on top. Lasagne can be served alone or with a hearty sprinkling of Almesan (page 207), breadsticks, and a crisp green salad.*

*If you have a favorite way of assembling lasagne, then go right ahead and use that instead of our method. We've included directions for the traditional boiled noodle and the "controversial" no-cook pasta method. Both methods work great here.*

**Double recipe Marinara Sauce (page 205), plain or any variation (roasted garlic is particularly good here)**
**Double recipe Tofu Ricotta or Cashew Ricotta (page 206)**
**1-pound package lasagna noodles, cooked according to package directions or left uncooked**
**2 pounds spinach or a mix of spinach and other greens (chard, dandelion, etc.)**
**2 tablespoons olive oil**
**Salt and pepper**
**1 recipe Almesan (page 207)**
**1 recipe Pine Nut Cream (optional)**

PREHEAT THE oven to 375°F degrees. Have ready a 9 × 13-inch deep lasagne pan and a double layer of aluminum foil that can tightly cover the pan. Also have ready the prepared Marinara Sauce and Tofu Ricotta.

Wash the spinach well, drain, and place in a steamer basket in a large pot. Cover and steam for 8 to 10 minutes, until the spinach is wilted and a deep green. Uncover and remove from the heat, allowing the spinach to cool to the touch. Squeeze handfuls of the spinach to remove the excess water and chop coarsely. Toss with the olive oil and season with salt and pepper.

Ladle about ½ cup of sauce into the bottom of the lasagne pan and layer with 5 to 6 noodles, either pre-cooked or raw. Add about half of the tofu ricotta, a layer of spinach, and about one-third of the sauce. Add another layer of noodles (4 to 5), the rest of the ricotta, the remainder of the spinach, and another third of the sauce. Top with the remaining noodles, then top the noodles with remaining sauce. Or, if you wish, you can combine the spinach with the ricotta before layering.

If using uncooked noodles, gently pour 1 cup of warm water over the top of the assembled casserole,

being careful to pour into the gaps between noodles and the edges of the pan as well. Skip this step if using cooked noodles.

If you wish, you may generously sprinkle Almesan on top of the lasagne before baking.

Tightly crimp two overlapping layers of foil over the top of the pan. Bake for 30 to 35 minutes, until the pasta is tender, then remove the foil and bake for another 20 minutes, until edges of noodles are slightly browned and sauce is bubbling. Allow to cool 10 minutes before slicing. Best if served with additional marinara sauce.

### Variation:

**Mushroom-Spinach Lasagne:** In addition to the spinach layers, add 1 pound of white button or cremini mushrooms, sliced thinly and sautéed in 2 tablespoons of olive oil. Cook until all of the water has evaporated and the mushrooms are browned and tender.

**White and Red Lasagne:** After removing the foil for the final baking step, top the lasagne with Pine Nut Cream. Bake for an additional 20 to 24 minutes, until the topping is lightly browned and cracked.

## tip

➤ The recipe calls for a double batch of Marinara Sauce, which makes an evenly moist but not overly saucy casserole. For deliciously saucy lasagne, triple the sauce and reserve one-third for ladling over individual servings.

➤ You can prepare the noodles either by the traditional "boiling first" method or by layering the uncooked noodles into the casserole and pouring a scant 1 cup of water over the entire assembled casserole before baking. The pre-cooking method is more work but results in a "neater" layered lasagne. The uncooked method is very easy and less messy but the noodles tend to curl up a bit during the baking, which doesn't matter much if additional sauce will be poured on top of individual servings.

## ASPARAGUS AND LEMONGRASS RISOTTO

SERVES 4 TO 6

Ⓖ

**TIME:** 1 HOUR 20 MINUTES

*Find your purpose in life with this unusual risotto. You begin by pondering your existence while stirring aromatic vegetables in Arborio rice. Then you gradually add a steaming broth scented with lemongrass and ginger. After stirring for a few years, you'll someday have this luscious, creamy asparagus risotto with a decidedly Thai twist. It's delightful served garnished with chopped roasted peanuts and a twist of lime, or serve alongside grilled Tangerine Baked Tofu (page 126) for a complete meal. Existential crisis over.*

### Lemongrass broth:

3 cloves garlic, whole and unpeeled

1-inch piece fresh ginger, sliced into ¼-inch slices

1 small stalk lemongrass, or 1 tablespoon dried, chopped lemongrass

**tip**

➤ Fresh lemongrass is available in well-stocked gourmet-type grocery stores or at Asian markets. If you can't find it, look for dried, chopped lemongrass in the spice aisle. When using dried lemongrass here, you'll need to make a mini-bouquet garni by tucking the dried lemongrass into a small, porous pouch along with the ginger and garlic, and knotting tightly on top. Long, empty tea bags sold for use with loose-leaf tea are ideal for this. You can also use cheesecloth and tie it into a little bundle, but double- or triple-layer it to make sure none of the lemongrass bits leak into the stock (just give the bundle a good squeeze before discarding).

3 cups vegetable broth

3 cups water

3 tablespoons soy sauce

### Risotto:

⅓ cup cooking sherry

1 pound asparagus

5 tablespoons peanut oil

1 cup basil leaves (Thai preferred), rolled and sliced into very thin strips

2 tablespoons chopped fresh mint

6 large shallots, sliced thinly

4 cloves garlic, minced

1 serrano red chile, sliced very thinly, or ½–1 teaspoon dried red pepper flakes

1½ cups Arborio rice

1 teaspoon sugar

2 tablespoons lime juice

Chopped roasted peanuts and lime wedges, for garnish

IF USING fresh lemongrass, peel away and discard any brown stems from the stalk. Slice the stalk in half lengthwise, cut those sections into 3 to 4-inch lengths, and then slice into thin matchstick pieces.

Lightly bruise the ginger slices by gently pounding them with the side of your knife. Crush the garlic cloves with the side of your knife as well, but keep whole; just lay the flat part of the blade over the clove of garlic and give it a good whack. Prepare your bouquet garni as described in the tip.

Place all the broth ingredients in a large stockpot and bring to a boil, then lower the heat to medium-low. Simmer for 10 minutes, then strain the broth, discarding the vegetables and herbs. Pour the broth back into the pot, cover, and place over low heat (as low as possible) to keep warm.

While you're cooking the broth, warm the cooking sherry in a separate, small saucepan over medium heat.

Slice the asparagus into ½-inch pieces, removing any tough parts from the bottom of the stem. Separate tips from the stems and place each in separate small bowls.

In a medium-size heavy-bottomed pot, sauté the asparagus tips in 1 tablespoon of the oil over medium heat until the tips are bright green and crisp-tender, 3 to 4 minutes. Return them to their small bowl. Add 1 more tablespoon of oil to the pot and sauté the sliced asparagus pieces until crisp-tender, 5 to 6 minutes. Add the basil and mint, sauté for 30 seconds, remove from the heat, and set the sliced asparagus mixture aside in a small bowl separate from the tips.

Add the remaining oil to the pot. Sauté the shallots and garlic, stirring occasionally, until shallots are very soft and just starting to brown, 6 to 8 minutes. Stir in the chile pepper and rice, and sauté for about 8 minutes, until the rice smells slightly toasted. Add the cooking sherry and stir constantly until the liquid is absorbed.

Now meditation time begins. Ladle about ½ cup of the broth at a time into the rice, stirring constantly until each addition is absorbed. Stir and cook until the rice is creamy but still somewhat firm in center. When broth is almost gone, stir the sugar and lime juice into the last of the broth before adding to the risotto. You may add more water or additional regular vegetable broth in ¼-cup increments if the broth runs out and the rice isn't cooked enough yet. This will take about 35 minutes.

Stir the asparagus stems (not tips) into the risotto and cook for another 5 to 10 minutes, until the asparagus has reached desired tenderness.

Garnish individual servings with the sautéed asparagus tips, chopped roasted peanuts, and lime wedges.

## GREEN PEA AND LEMON RISOTTO WITH ROASTED RED PEPPERS

SERVES 4

*This bright-tasting risotto features summer's vivid bounty. Use vegetable broth that isn't too strongly flavored, so*

*that the lemon, peas, and parsley really shine through. If your broth has a very strong taste, use only four cups of broth plus two cups of water.*

2 red bell peppers
6 cups vegetable broth
1 tablespoon olive oil
1 cup finely chopped shallots
4 cloves garlic, minced
½ teaspoon dried thyme
½ teaspoon dried rosemary
Several pinches of freshly ground black pepper
½ cup dry white wine
½ teaspoon salt
1½ cups Arborio rice
1½ cups fresh or frozen peas
2 teaspoons grated lemon zest
2 tablespoons fresh lemon juice
½ cup loosely packed chopped fresh parsley, (plus extra for garnish)

### Prepare the peppers:

Preheat the oven to 350°F. Slice the stems off the peppers and pull out the seeds. Quarter the peppers lengthwise. Line a rimmed baking sheet with baking parchment and place the peppers, cut side down, on the sheet. Lightly spray the peppers with olive oil and roast for 35 to 40 minutes, until the peppers have "collapsed" and are moist, juicy, and slightly blackened in some places.

### Prepare the risotto:

Warm the vegetable broth in a saucepan. Keep it warm on the lowest setting possible as you prepare the risotto.

Preheat a heavy-bottomed soup pot over medium heat. Sauté the shallots in the oil for about 5 minutes. Add the garlic, thyme, rosemary, and black pepper, and sauté for 2 more minutes.

Add the white wine and salt, and raise the heat so

that the wine boils and reduces for about 2 minutes. Lower the heat back to medium.

Add the rice and stir for about 3 minutes. The rice should soak up the liquid from the pot and have turned light brown. Add the broth by the cupful, stirring the risotto after each addition, until the broth is mostly absorbed (6 to 8 minutes). If the broth isn't absorbing, raise the heat a bit. It absorbs faster as the rice gets more and more tender.

With your last addition of broth, add the peas and stir. When the peas are warm and tender and most of the broth is absorbed, add the lemon zest, juice, and chopped parsley.

Cook, stirring, until all the broth is completely absorbed and the parsley has wilted. Spoon the risotto into a wide bowl or plate and overlap the red peppers on one side of the dish. Garnish with fresh parsley and serve.

## CURRIED UDON NOODLE STIR-FRY

SERVES 4

45

TIME: 35 MINUTES

*This saucy noodle dish is inspired by the slightly sweet, mellow curries that are hugely popular in Japan for lunch and dinner, or so we hear. A simple roux-based curry sauce is prepared first, then stirred into udon, bits of sautéed seitan, and crisp veggies. Experiment—change the vegetables, use tofu in place of seitan, try different brands of curry powder—the variations are endless.*

**½ pound fresh udon noodles or dried udon noodles**

Curry roux sauce:

**2 tablespoons peanut oil**
**2 tablespoons all-purpose flour**
**1½ teaspoons curry powder**
**½ teaspoon garam masala**

**½ cup vegetable broth**
**2 teaspoons sugar**

Udon stir-fry:

**2 tablespoons peanut oil**
**1 large yellow onion, sliced into thin strips**
**1 teaspoon grated fresh ginger**
**1 red bell pepper, seeded and sliced into thin strips**
**1 hot red chile pepper, sliced very thinly (optional)**
**2 Seitan Cutlets (page 132), panfried and sliced into thin strips**
**½ pound broccoli florets, sliced into bite-size chunks**
**¼ cup vegetable broth**
**2–3 tablespoons soy sauce, preferably shoyu (Japanese soy sauce)**

**tip**

➤ Use any curry powder you like, depending on your tolerance for heat. Even generic, grocery-store Indian or Jamaican curry powder works very nicely in this recipe.

➤ You can use either dried or fresh udon noodles for any recipe calling for them. Dried noodles are sold packaged like spaghetti and can be prepared the same way. Cook the noodles according to the package directions till just tender and rinse in cold water. Keep them handy in a colander until ready to use. Give them a brief rinsing in cold water before adding to a soup or stir-fry.

Fresh udon noodles are sold twisted in cute bundles. They require only a brief cooking time in boiling water (follow package directions), usually about 3 to 4 minutes. Use a pair of chopsticks to separate the bundles while they are cooking. Drain, rinse with cold water and store in that colander. Rinse in warm water to unstuck any noodles just before using.

PREPARE THE udon first: Cook the udon according to the package directions, about 5 minutes. Drain and rinse well with cold water.

*In the meantime, prepare the curry roux sauce:*

Combine the flour and 2 tablespoons peanut oil in a small saucepan. Cook over medium-low heat, stirring constantly with a wooden spoon, until the mixture browns to the color of rich caramel and smells toasty, about 10 minutes or less. Stir in curry powder and garam masala, and cook for another minute while stirring constantly. Switch to using a wire whisk, then pour in the vegetable broth in a steady stream. Whisk in the sugar and cook the roux, stirring constantly, until a thick sauce forms, about 2 minutes. Remove from the heat and set aside.

*To prepare the stir-fry:*

Heat the 2 tablespoons of peanut oil in a large (at least 11-inch) nonstick skillet or a wok and cook the sliced onion for 5 to 6 minutes, stirring occasionally, until the onion is softened and translucent. Add the ginger, red bell pepper, hot chile, and seitan, and stir-fry for another 5 minutes, until the pepper starts to soften. Add the broccoli and stir-fry for 4 to 5 minutes, until it turns bright green.

Return to the udon noodles—if they're sticking together, rinse briefly in warm water and drain. Add the udon to the stir-fried vegetables, sprinkle with soy sauce, and stir-fry for 2 to 3 minutes. It may help to use two large spatulas or extra-large chopsticks (the ones that come with some wok kits) while doing this.

Whisk ¼ cup of the vegetable broth into the curry roux sauce in the saucepan. Pour the sauce over the udon stir-fry and stir to coat everything completely with the sauce. Stir and cook for 2 to 3 minutes, until the sauce is simmering and the noodles are warm. Remove from the heat and serve.

# UDON WITH SHIITAKE MUSHROOMS AND KALE IN MISO BROTH

SERVES 4

**TIME:** 35 MINUTES

*Super-simple ingredients result in super-flavorful returns. That sounds a little like a fortune cookie. This is a great weeknight meal that's healthy and hearty. Make it even heartier by adding sautéed seitan to each serving.*

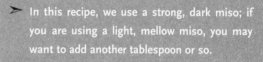

**tip**

➤ In this recipe, we use a strong, dark miso; if you are using a light, mellow miso, you may want to add another tablespoon or so.

➤ See previous page (Curry Udon Stir-Fry recipe) for tips on using dried or fresh udon noodles.

½ **pound fresh udon noodles or dried udon noodles**
2 **tablespoons vegetable oil**
1 **medium-size red onion, sliced into thin half-moons**
4 **ounces shiitake mushrooms, stems trimmed, sliced**
3 **cloves garlic, minced**
2 **teaspoons ginger, minced**
2 **tablespoons mirin (optional)**
2 **cups water**
3 **tablespoons miso (see tip)**
4 **cups chopped kale**
2 **teaspoons soy sauce, or to taste**

BRING A pot of water to a boil. Cook the udon according to the package directions, about 10 minutes. When done, drain and rinse with cool water until ready to use.

Meanwhile, preheat a large skillet over medium heat. Sauté the onion and mushrooms in the oil for 5 to 7 minutes, until the mushrooms are tender and the onions are softened but still have some crunch. Add the garlic and ginger, and sauté for another minute.

Add the mirin, water, and miso, and bring to a gentle boil. Lower the heat to a simmer and add the kale. Toss the mixture around with tongs until the kale has wilted. Add the noodles and use a pasta spoon to stir them into the broth for about 2 minutes.

Divide the udon and vegetables among bowls and spoon some broth over each serving.

# SAUCES AND FILLINGS

HERE YOU'LL FIND toppings and fillings we use throughout the book, but more important, you'll find sauces. We are going to go out on a limb and say that the sauce can make or break your cooking. Watch as you transform mere mortal vegetables into the foods of gods and goddesses! Marvel as your pasta goes from "Pasta again?" to "Pasta again!"

Consider this chapter a master class in sauce making. In fact, go ahead and call yourself a *saucier* just because you've glanced at it. Every culture in the world has its trademark sauce, making this section truly transcontinental. Not only is the perfect marinara now within your reach but you'll learn to make a roux, the toasted fat- and flour-based sauce that is the mama of French cooking; our spin on pesto, the classic Italian paste of herbs, nuts, and garlic; two kinds of mole, the classic Mexican blend of chiles and chocolate as well as a green one that uses pumpkin seeds; and barbecue sauce that is sure to get the kids lickin' their fingers.

Most of these sauces take less than twenty minutes to prepare and require minimum equipment for prepping, so stop pushing your food around on your plate barren, lonely, unsauced, and unloved. It's time to get saucy!

## MUSTARD SAUCE

MAKES ABOUT 1½ CUPS SAUCE

TIME: 20 MINUTES

*For mustard lovers only! Add a little elegance to your meal with this thick, tangy and savory sauce that's great over Chickpea Cutlets (page 133), baked or broiled tofu, and roasted vegetables—especially asparagus.*

2 tablespoons cornstarch

¾ cup vegetable broth

3 cloves garlic, minced

½ teaspoon dried thyme

1 tablespoon olive oil

½ cup sherry cooking wine

1 tablespoon soy sauce

¼ cup whole-grain Dijon mustard

1 tablespoon lemon juice

2 tablespoons capers (with brine)

MIX THE cornstarch with the vegetable broth in a measuring cup and set aside.

In a small saucepan over medium heat, sauté the garlic and thyme in the olive oil for about a minute.

Add the white wine and soy sauce, and raise the heat to high. Once the mixture is boiling, lower the heat to medium and simmer, to reduce for about 4 minutes. Add the vegetable broth mixture, mustard, lemon juice, and capers. Stir often, using a whisk. Once the sauce is bubbling, lower the heat to low and simmer for about 3 minutes. The sauce should be on the thick side.

Let cool a bit before serving; this sauce tastes great just above room temperature.

## RED WINE ROUX

MAKES 2 CUPS SAUCE

TIME: 15 MINUTES

*This luscious, French-inspired sauce packs a rich bouquet of flavors. Serve on anything seitan, tempeh, roasted cauliflower, or mashed potatoes. Our favorite way by far is to served on Chickpea Cutlet (page 133) and a side of French-Bakes (page 33) for a real un-meat and potatoes meal with just a touch of class.*

**tip**

➤ This sauce will thicken considerably as it cools and may form a skin on top. Don't worry, just give it a good whisk and reheat over a low flame.

➤ For best results, try to mince the vegetables as small as possible. Also, very dry wines taste best in this sauce.

1¼ cups boiling water

1 vegetable bouillon cube

2 tablespoons nonhydrogenated vegan margarine

3 tablespoons all-purpose flour

3 large shallots, minced finely

¼ cup finely minced celery

1 clove garlic, minced

¾ cup dry red wine

1 bay leaf

1 teaspoon dried marjoram

½ teaspoon dried thyme

½ teaspoon dried rosemary, crumbed between your fingers

2 tablespoons minced fresh chives

IN A small saucepan, dissolve the bouillon cube in boiling water. Keep the broth warm on the lowest flame possible.

Melt the margarine in a separate small, heavy-bottomed saucepan and stir in the flour with a wooden spoon. Cook over medium-low heat, stirring constantly, until the mixture is deep golden brown and smells toasty, 6 to 8 minutes. Stir in the minced shallots and garlic, coating with the sauce, and continue to cook, stirring, for another 5 minutes; it will resemble a coarse paste. Stir in the celery and cook for another 3 to 4 minutes, until the celery has softened a little.

Pour in the hot veggie bouillon and stir with a wire whisk to create a thick sauce. Add the bay leaf, marjoram, thyme, and rosemary. While stirring constantly, bring to a boil, then lower the heat and simmer for 2 minutes.

Gradually pour in the wine, continuing to stir with the whisk, and bring to a boil again. Lower the heat once more and simmer for 4 to 6 minutes, until slightly reduced and thickened (sauce is not as thick as a gravy but will cling to the back of a metal spoon).

Remove from the heat, stir in the chopped chives, and either ladle directly over food or serve alongside in a gravy boat.

### To reheat the sauce:

This sauce will become very thick if refrigerated, but it reheats easily. Place the sauce in a small saucepan, heat over medium-low heat while stirring occasionally, and whisk in a little vegetable broth until the desired consistency is reached.

## MARINARA SAUCE AND VARIATIONS

MAKES ABOUT 5 CUPS
(ENOUGH FOR 4 SERVINGS OF PASTA)

**TIME:** 20 MINUTES

*The secret to a great marinara sauce is K.I.S.S.—keep it simple, stupid! Oh yes, and a hell of a lotta garlic. Store-bought sauce tends to be too sweet and tastes, well, store-bought. We use this in all of our tomato-based Italian dishes from pasta to eggplant rollatini, and it doesn't take much time, so go ahead and pour some love onto your spaghetti. Go crazy with the variations that follow.*

**2 teaspoons olive oil**
**4 cloves garlic, minced**
**1 (28-ounce) can crushed tomatoes**
**¼ teaspoon dried thyme**
**¼ teaspoon dried oregano**
**½ teaspoon salt**
**Several pinches of freshly ground black pepper**

PREHEAT A saucepan over medium-low heat. Add the oil and garlic, and sauté for about a minute, until fragrant, being careful not to let it burn. Add the remaining ingredients, cover, and raise the heat a bit to bring to a simmer. Simmer for about 15 minutes, stirring occasionally.

### Variations:

Roasted Red Pepper Marinara Sauce: Add a chopped roasted red pepper along with the tomatoes. Blend the sauce when done cooking, if you like.

Mushroom Marinara Sauce: Increase the oil to 1 tablespoon, and sauté 1 cup of thinly sliced mushrooms before adding the garlic.

Roasted Garlic Marinara Sauce: Decrease the minced garlic to 2 teaspoons. Add a whole bulb of peeled roasted garlic to the sauce halfway through the cooking process. Blend the sauce when done cooking.

**Olive Marinara Sauce:** Add ½ cup of chopped black olives to the sauce about halfway through the cooking process.

**Caramelized Onion Marinara Sauce:** Increase the oil to 1 tablespoon. Sweat 1 cup of finely chopped white or yellow onion for about 15 minutes. (To sweat, keep the heat low and cover, stirring every few minutes, the onions should not brown.) Uncover and cook for 15 more minutes at higher heat, until browned and caramelized. Proceed with the rest of the recipe.

**We also like to mix and match some of these variations:** Caramelized Onion and Roasted Red Pepper, Mushroom and Olive, you get the idea.

## TOFU RICOTTA

MAKES 3½ CUPS

Ⓖ ㊺

TIME: 10 MINUTES

*Straight outta* Vegan with a Vengeance, *we've included the recipe in this book, too, because, well, tofu ricotta doesn't get better than this! We use it in Eggplant Rollatini (page 154) but feel free to use it anywhere that ricotta might be found; stuffed shells, as a pizza topping, you name it.*

1 pound extra-firm tofu
2 teaspoons lemon juice
1 clove garlic, minced
¼ teaspoon salt
Pinch of freshly ground black pepper

Handful of fresh basil leaves, chopped finely (10 leaves or so) (optional)
2 teaspoons olive oil
¼ cup nutritional yeast flakes

IN A large bowl, mush the tofu up with your hands, until it's crumbly.

Add the lemon juice, garlic, salt, pepper, and basil. Mush with hands again; this time you want it to get very mushy, so squeeze through your fingers and mush until it reaches the consistency of ricotta cheese, 2 to 5 minutes.

Add the olive oil, stir with a fork. Add the nutritional yeast and mix all ingredients well. Use a fork now, because the oil will make it sticky. Cover and refrigerate until ready to use.

## CASHEW RICOTTA

MAKES 2 CUPS

Ⓖ ㊺

TIME: 15 MINUTES

*Thick, creamy and extra-dreamy, this dairyless ricotta is what you want when that lasagne or stuffed shells requires something just a little bit more. Perfect when paired with sweet winter squash, such as Pumpkin Baked Ziti with Caramelized Onions (page 194). Also makes a smooth sandwich spread paired with crusty herbed peasant bread.*

½ cup raw cashew pieces (approximately 4 ounces)
¼ cup fresh lemon juice
2 tablespoons olive oil
2 cloves fresh or roasted garlic (page 32)
1 pound firm tofu, drained and crumbled
1½ teaspoons dried basil
1½ teaspoons salt

IN A food processor, blend together the cashews, lemon juice, olive oil, and garlic until a thick creamy paste forms. Add the crumbled tofu to the food processor, working in two or more batches if necessarily, until the mixture is thick and well blended. Blend in the basil and salt.

## ALMESAN

MAKES ⅓ CUP

TIME: 5 MINUTES OR LESS

*This is our vegan version of Parmesan, made with almonds, sesame seeds, and a little lemon zest. It's great for when your pasta needs a sprinkle of a little somethin' somethin'. If you have a mini processor, there is no better time to use it.*

¼ cup slivered or sliced almonds
1 tablespoon toasted sesame seeds
⅛ teaspoon salt
¼ teaspoon lemon zest

COMBINE ALL ingredients in a blender or food processor. Pulse until everything turns to tiny crumbs. That's it!

## BACKYARD BBQ SAUCE

MAKES ABOUT 4 CUPS

TIME: 40 MINUTES

*The basic components of a BBQ sauce are something sweet, something sour, and something tomato-y. This sauce is super versatile—you can replace the molasses with maple syrup or just plain sugar, you can replace the crushed tomatoes with tomato sauce or diced tomatoes (but you should puree it at the end if you use crushed tomatoes). Red pepper flakes add a little heat, but you*

*can use a bit of cayenne or hot sauce instead. The longer you cook this sauce, the thicker and more delicious it gets, but if all's you got is half an hour, it's still yummy!*

1 tablespoon vegetable oil
1 medium-size yellow onion, chopped as finely as
    you can
4 cloves garlic, minced
¼ teaspoon salt
1 teaspoon red pepper flakes
1 (28-ounce) can crushed tomatoes
⅓ cup molasses
⅓ cup white vinegar
2 tablespoons sugar
1 tablespoon prepared yellow mustard
    (Dijon is fine, too)
2 teaspoons liquid smoke

PREHEAT A saucepan over medium heat. Place the onions in the pan and sauté in oil until browned (about 7 minutes). Add the garlic and sauté for another minute. Add all the other ingredients except the mustard and liquid smoke, and cook for at least 30 minutes and up to 1 hour, uncovered, stirring occasionally. Lower the heat if the sauce begins to splatter everywhere. Add the mustard and liquid smoke, and taste for sweetness/sourness. Adjust the flavors if you think it's necessary, and cook for 5 more minutes. If you like a smooth BBQ sauce then puree it, but that's not entirely necessary.

## APRICOT BBQ SAUCE

MAKES ABOUT 4 CUPS

TIME: 40 MINUTES

*This is a fruity, kid friendly BBQ sauce that isn't too sweet. It's wonderful on any of the holy trinity (tofu, tempeh, or seitan). See the recipe for Baked BBQ Tofu (page 128). It's also wonderful on steamed veggies, especially broccoli. As with all recipes where you cook with fruit, the sweetness will need to be adjusted depending on how sweet your fruit is.*

1 tablespoon peanut oil

1 small yellow onion, diced

2 cloves garlic, chopped

1½ pounds apricots (6–8, depending on their size), pitted and sliced about ½ inch thick

½ cup vegetable broth or water

¼ teaspoon ground ginger

¼ teaspoon ground coriander

Several pinches of freshly ground black pepper

¼ cup molasses

2 tablespoons pure maple syrup

2 tablespoons tomato paste

3 tablespoons soy sauce

1 teaspoon liquid smoke

IN A small saucepan over medium-high heat, sauté the onions in oil for 7 to 10 minutes, until browned. Add the garlic, sauté for 2 more minutes. Add the vegetable broth to deglaze the pan. Add the apricots, black pepper, ginger, and coriander. Cover and bring to a boil. Once the sauce is boiling, lower the heat to medium-low and let cook for about 10 minutes, until the apricots are mushy.

Uncover and add the remaining ingredients. Cook for about 10 more minutes, stirring often and mashing the apricot as you stir. Taste the sauce and adjust the sweetness, if necessary.

Remove from the heat and let cool until it's not steaming, stirring occasionally to speed up the cooling. Transfer to a blender or food processor and puree until completely smooth. Keep refrigerated in an airtight container until ready to use.

## HORSERADISH-DILL SOUR CREAM

MAKES ABOUT 3 CUPS

**TIME:** 15 MINUTES, PLUS TIME TO CHILL

*This is our cream of choice for latkes both of the potato persuasion and the beet kind (see Autumn Latkes, page 53). It also makes a wonderful dressing, especially for cucumbers. We used fresh horseradish but if you can only find the jarred kind, go ahead and use it. Since it's stronger than fresh, add a tablespoon at first and taste from there.*

1 pound soft tofu

2 tablespoons fresh, grated horseradish

1 tablespoon apple cider vinegar

1 tablespoon agave or real maple syrup

¾ teaspoons salt

3 cloves garlic, crushed

¼ cup grapeseed oil

1 cup loosely packed fresh dill

REMOVE THE tofu from the package and shake off any excess water. Place in a blender or food processor (a food processor works better) along with the horseradish, apple cider vinegar, agave, and salt. Blend until smooth.

Preheat a small saucepan over medium-low heat. Place the crushed garlic and grapeseed oil in the pan. Cook gently, stirring occasionally, for about 2 minutes. The garlic should *blondir* (that means "lightly brown") but not burn. Remove the garlic from the oil and discard. Add the oil to the tofu mixture and blend again until smooth. Add the dill and horseradish, and blend until smooth—the cream will be light green with some flecks of dill. Scrape down the sides to make sure you get everything.

Taste and adjust the salt and vinegar, if necessary. Transfer to a bowl and seal tightly with plastic wrap and refrigerate for at least 30 minutes.

## SOUR CILANTRO CREAM

MAKES ABOUT 3 CUPS

**TIME:** 15 MINUTES, PLUS TIME TO CHILL

*Here's a nice replacement for sour cream on anything where cilantro would fit in: burritos, tacos, black bean soup, you name it. It's also a yummy salad dressing and great on black bean burger (page 98).*

- 1 pound silken tofu (*not* the vacuum-packed kind)
- 2 tablespoons fresh lime juice (from 1 lime)
- 1 tablespoon agave syrup
- ¾ teaspoons salt
- 3 cloves garlic, crushed
- ¼ cup grapeseed oil
- 2 cups loosely packed fresh cilantro (stems and leaves)

REMOVE THE tofu from the package and shake off any excess water. Place in a blender or food processor (a food processor works better) along with the lime juice, agave, and salt. Blend until smooth.

Preheat a small saucepan over medium-low heat. Place the crushed garlic and grapeseed oil in the pan. Cook gently, stirring occasionally, for about 3 minutes. The garlic should *blondir* (that means "to lightly brown") but not burn. Add to the tofu mixture and blend again until smooth. Add the cilantro and, guess what? Yep, blend until smooth and light green with some flecks of dark green. Scrape down the sides to make sure you get everything.

Taste and adjust the salt and lime, if necessary. Transfer to a bowl, seal tightly with plastic wrap and refrigerate for at least 30 minutes. It will get a little bit firmer but will still have a pourable consistency.

## SALSA VERDE

MAKES ABOUT 2 CUPS

**TIME:** 40 MINUTES

*What Mexican meal is complete without a little salsa verde? Maybe a Mexican meal using some other Mexican sauce, but that's neither here nor there. Salsa verde (green sauce to you, bub) is made with those mysterious tomatolike wonders, tomatillos. Serve chilled with chips and guacamole, or hot over enchiladas and burritos. This is a mild version, so add more jalapeños if you like it hot. Wear gloves to avoid touching the seeds, or your hands will burn all day. (If you're like us and don't have gloves, just be careful!)*

- 10 tomatillos (husks removed), cleaned and diced
- 1 teaspoon olive oil
- 3 cloves garlic, minced
- 1 jalapeño, seeded and minced
- ¼ teaspoon sea salt
- 1½ cups vegetable broth
- Juice of 1 lime
- 1 cup loosely packed fresh cilantro

IN A small saucepan over low heat, sauté the garlic and jalapeño in oil until fragrant, about 3 minutes.

Add the tomatillos and salt, sauté until the tomatillos begin to soften and release moisture, about 5 minutes. Add the vegetable broth, bring to a slow boil, and cook for about 20 minutes, stirring occasionally.

Remove from the heat, let cool until it is not steaming, then add the cilantro and lime juice. Pour into a blender and blend until relatively smooth, about 30 seconds.

## GREEN PUMPKIN-SEED MOLE

MAKES A LITTLE OVER 2 CUPS

🌀 Ⓖ ㊺ ⌷

**TIME:** 20 MINUTES

*A thick diplike sauce made from pumpkin seeds, herbs, tomatillos and peppers, this mole will turn any Mexican type of meal into a revolutionary uprising. Canned tomatillos makes this thick sauce a snap to prepare; the only cooking required is the toasting of the pumpkin seeds (also called* pepitas). *It's wonderful with rice and beans, and especially delish with Corn Pudding (page 15).*

1 cup hulled raw pumpkin seeds

4 whole black peppercorns

1 cup lightly packed fresh cilantro

1 cup lightly packed fresh parsley

1 (7- to 8-ounce) can tomatillos

1 serrano chile, stemmed, seeded, coarsely chopped

2 scallions, white part discarded, chopped coarsely

2 lettuce leaves (such as romaine or green leaf), torn into pieces

2 cloves garlic, chopped coarsely

¼ cup olive oil

**tip**

> Tomatillos are readily available in the "ethnic" section of most supermarkets. If you can't find them, you can use salsa verde; just check that the ingredients list contains nothing more than tomatillos, garlic, and cilantro.

HEAT A large skillet over medium-low heat. Toast the pumpkin seeds, turning occasionally, for 3 to 4 minutes. Transfer the seeds to a food processor or blender (a food processor works better). Add the peppercorns and pulse into a coarse powder.

Add everything else save the olive oil and grind into a thick paste. Add the olive oil and blend for about 30 seconds. Scrape down the sides of the processor to incorporate all the ingredients. Add salt to taste (it may not even be necessary).

## CHILE-CHOCOLATE MOLE

MAKES 3 CUPS

🌀 Ⓖ ㊺

**TIME:** 30 MINUTES

*Not authentic by any means, this spin-off of traditional mole poblano takes a few modern shortcuts to whip up a thick, rich sauce with a complex blend of hot, sweet, bitter, and nutty flavors. Highly versatile, this mole can be used for any number of Mexican specialties, such as enchiladas, tamales, tostadas, and so on. The simplest way to enjoy it as a hearty entrée is to simmer vegetables and other foods on the stove-top, as in* Vegetables or Seitan in Mole Sauce *(page 185).*

Spice mixture:

⅓ cup sliced almonds

⅓ cup crushed tortilla chips

2 tablespoons sesame seeds

1 teaspoon aniseeds

3–4 teaspoons chile powder, preferably a mix of ground ancho and chipotle

1¼ teaspoons ground cinnamon

1 teaspoon dried marjoram

½ teaspoon ground cumin

¼ teaspoon ground allspice

Mole base:

3 tablespoons peanut oil

4 garlic cloves, chopped

1 small onion, diced

2 cups hot vegetable broth, kept warm on the stove top

2 tablespoons creamy, all-natural peanut butter

1 (15-ounce) can diced tomatoes

3 ounces chopped semisweet vegan baking chocolate (60 percent cacao is best)

PREPARE spice mixture: Place the almonds, tortilla chip crumbs, sesame seeds, and aniseeds in a heavy-bottomed pot. Stir constantly to toast over medium heat for about 2 minutes, being careful not to let it burn. Remove from the heat and allow to cool slightly. Place the toasted ingredients in a food processor, add the chile powder, cinnamon, marjoram, allspice, and cumin, and pulse until the mixture is as finely ground as possible.

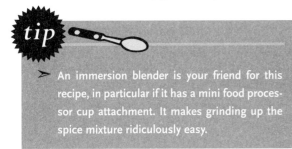

> An immersion blender is your friend for this recipe, in particular if it has a mini food processor cup attachment. It makes grinding up the spice mixture ridiculously easy.

*Prepare the mole base:*

In the same pot over medium heat, sauté the garlic in oil. When the garlic starts to sizzle, add the onion and cook, stirring occasionally, for 5 minutes. Meanwhile, combine the peanut butter and a few tablespoons of hot vegetable broth in a bowl, stirring until the peanut butter is emulsified and easy to pour.

Pour remaining vegetable broth, peanut butter mixture, spice mixture and diced tomatoes into the pot and stir to combine. Bring to a boil, lower the heat slightly to medium-low, and simmer for 8 to 10 minutes until sauce has slightly reduced.

Remove from the heat, puree until smooth, and return to stove over medium-low heat. Add the chopped chocolate, stirring constantly until melted and completely incorporated, at least 3 minutes.

Note: when using mole in cooked dishes, it's recommended to thin it a little with vegetable broth. If using as a dip or condiment there's no need .

*Some ideas for using this mole:*

Prepare Potato and Kale Enchiladas (page 162), substituting the mole for the enchilada sauce. Thin the mole with ½ cup of vegetable broth before using.

Drizzle onto tostadas, nachos, and tacos. Tuck into black bean burritos.

Serve the mole (warmed, thinned slightly with vegetable broth) over fresh steamed winter squash, green beans, or asparagus.

Mole makes an interesting dip alongside salsas and guacamole with tortilla chips (don't thin the mole with broth).

## MUSHROOM GRAVY

MAKES ABOUT 4 CUPS

**TIME:** 30 MINUTES

*We don't need to tell you what to do with it, do we? Smother it on absolutely everything!*

**2 cups vegetable broth**
**¼ cup flour (use ⅓ cup for a thicker gravy)**

**2 Tablespoons olive oil**
**1 medium onion, thinly sliced**
**10 ounces cremini mushrooms, thinly sliced (about 4 cups)**
**3 cloves garlic, minced**
**1 teaspoon thyme**
**½ teaspoon sage**
**¼ teaspoon salt**
**Several dashes fresh black pepper**
**¼ cup white cooking wine (or any non-sweet wine will do)**

MIX the flour into the vegetable broth until dissolved and set aside.

Preheat a large non stick pan over medium heat. Sauté the onion in the oil for about 5 minutes, until translucent. Add the mushrooms and sauté for 5 more minutes, until mushrooms are tender.

Add the garlic, thyme, sage, salt and pepper. Sauté for another minute. Add the wine and turn the heat up to bring to a simmer. Let simmer for about a minute, then lower the heat and add the flour vegetable broth mixture. Stir constantly until thickened, about 5 minutes. If not serving immediately then gently reheat when you are ready to serve.

## 5-MINUTE MANGO CHUTNEY

MAKES ABOUT 2 CUPS

🌀 🄖 🄕 🄸 🄐

TIME: 15 MINUTES, PLUS CHILL TIME

*This is totally inauthentic but so what, it's really yummy! And after you've prepped everything, you only need to cook it for five minutes. Serve with any Indian meal, on a curry, or on Samosa Stuffed Baked Potatoes (page 60). I like the sourness of the asafetida, but you can use any Indian-y sort of spice instead—such as curry powder or garam masala.*

### tip

> Asafetida is a pungent spice (a resin from sap, if you want to be technical about it) that hasn't quite caught on in the American kitchen just yet. You can find it in a fancy-shmancy gourmet store or in Indian markets. Definitely seek it out; one great bonus is that the tin it comes in is usually very cool looking and colorfully decorated.

2 teaspoons peanut oil
2 cloves garlic, minced
2 teaspoons grated fresh ginger
1 jalapeño, seeded and chopped
1 large mango, peeled and cut into bite-size pieces
    (you should get a little under 2 cups of fruit)
2 tablespoons sugar

2 tablespoons water
2 tablespoons red wine vinegar
½ teaspoon asafetida

PREHEAT A small saucepan over medium-low heat. Put the oil, garlic, ginger, and jalapeño in the pan. Sauté for about 1 minute. Add the mango, sugar, and water. Turn heat up to medium, cover and cook for 3 minutes, until it's boiling. Add the red wine vinegar and asafetida, and cook for another minute, uncovered.

Chill until ready to use. We put it in the freezer and stir it often for about 130 minutes; it's usually good and cold by then.

## SPICED YOGURT SAUCE

SERVES 2 TO 4

🄖 🄕 🄐

TIME: 10 MINUTES , PLUS CHILL TIME

*This easy, quick sauce is the perfect companion to any Indian meal, authentic or otherwise. Cool and refreshing, it contrasts nicely against warm and spicy foods.*

1 teaspoon cumin seeds
1½ cups plain soy yogurt
1 teaspoon garam masala
¼ teaspoon salt
1 teaspoon freshly squeezed lemon or lime juice, or
    to taste
1 tablespoon finely chopped fresh cilantro (optional)

IN A small bowl, combine the soy yogurt, garam masala, salt, lemon juice, and cilantro.

In a small skillet, toast the cumin seeds over medium-low heat for 30 to 45 seconds, stirring constantly and taking care not burn them. Pour the seeds immediately into the yogurt mixture. Whisk to combine. Cover and chill until ready to use.

## TROPICAL AVOCADO SALSA FRESCA

MAKES A LITTLE UNDER 3 CUPS

🌀 🄖 🄕 🄸 ▱

**TIME:** 15 MINUTES

*This little fruit and avocado combo is culinary magic. It will turn plain old rice and beans into "I've never had such kick-ass rice and beans!" It's especially yummy with the spaghetti squash recipe on page 178.*

> 1 cup chopped tomato (½-inch chunks)
> 1 cup chopped pineapple, mango, or papaya (½-inch chunks)
> 1 avocado, peeled, pitted, and cut into ½-inch chunks
> ¼ cup lightly packed chopped fresh cilantro
> Juice of 1 lime

MIX ALL ingredients together in a mixing bowl. Refrigerate until ready to use.

## CRANBERRY-CHILE DIPPING SAUCE

MAKES 2 CUPS SAUCE

🌀 🄖 🄕 🄸 ▱

**TIME:** 25 MINUTES

*Pretty, red, sweet, tart, and hot. This lovely sauce is a nice low-sodium alternative to the soy-based dipping sauces that are typically served alongside steamed or fried Asian appetizers. It's also the ideal dipping sauce to serve with Butternut Squash Rolls (page 50).*

> 1 cup whole, fresh cranberries
> 1½ cups cold water
> ½ cup sugar
> 2 large serrano chiles, seeded and finely minced
> 2 tablespoons fresh lime juice
> Curls of lime zest (optional)

---

**tip**

> ➤ For a more intensely hot sauce, don't remove the seeds from the chile. Conversely, if you want a less spicy sauce, use just one chile.

COMBINE THE cranberries, water, and sugar in a medium-size saucepan. Cover and bring to a boil. When the cranberries start to pop, reduce the heat to medium and simmer, partially covered, for about 5 minutes. Add the minced chiles and lime juice, bring to a boil again, and then lower the heat to medium-low. Stir the sauce occasionally, using the back of a wooden spoon to mash some of the cranberries against the sides of the pot. Simmer the sauce, uncovered, for an additional 10 to 12 minutes, until the sauce has reduced by about less than one-fourth and looks syrupy.

Remove from the heat. The sauce will thicken up more as it cools. Store in an airtight container in the refrigerator.

## HOLIDAY CRANBERRY SAUCE

MAKES ABOUT 5 CUPS

🌀 🄖 🄕

**TIME:** 35 MINUTES, PLUS TIME TO CHILL

*Does cranberry sauce really need an introduction? You know what to do with it! We use agar to make this a little firm and the ingredients are kept simple—no orange rind or sneaky flavorings. But apple cider is the secret ingredient that keeps things interesting.*

> 1½ cups apple cider
> 2 tablespoons agar flakes (if you have agar powder, 2 teaspoons would be the equivalent)
> ¾ cup sugar
> 12 ounces fresh cranberries (a little over 3 cups)

POUR THE apple cider into a small pot and stir in the agar. Let soak for 10 minutes to soften up the agar and make it easier to dissolve. Skip the soaking step if using agar powder.

Cover and bring to a boil. Once the cider is boiling, add the cranberries and sugar. Lower the heat to medium; the mixture should be at a steady simmer. Cover, leaving a little gap for the steam to escape, and cook for about 10 minutes. At this point, the cranberries should be popping and the juice should be red. Use your mixing utensil to crush some of the cranberries and help them along. Cook, uncovered, for about 5 more minutes. The cranberries should be mostly popped and crushed, and the juice should be thick and red.

Transfer to a container and refrigerate. Let cool until it mostly stops steaming, then cover tightly with plastic wrap and place in the refrigerator until completely cooled and slightly jelled, about 3 hours.

## BASIL-CILANTRO PESTO

MAKES ABOUT 1 CUP

Ⓢ Ⓕ ㊺ ▭

TIME: 10 MINUTES

*This is our cheapskate pesto that uses almonds, which also have the benefit of making the pesto very bright and creamy.*

2 cups loosely packed fresh basil leaves
1 cup loosely packed fresh cilantro
⅓ cup slivered or sliced almonds
2 cloves garlic, crushed
2 tablespoons fresh lemon juice (from about ½ lemon)
½ teaspoon salt
¼ cup olive oil

Place the basil, cilantro, almonds, garlic, lemon, juice, and salt in a food processor and blend until pasty, scraping down the sides occasionally. With the food processor on, slowly drizzle in the olive oil. Blend until relatively smooth and no large chunks of almonds are left. If you don't have a food processor and are using a blender, then just add the olive oil at the end, since many blenders aren't equipped with an opening to drizzle into.

## CHEEZY SAUCE

MAKES ABOUT 3 CUPS

Ⓢ Ⓕ ㊺

TIME: 15 MINUTES

*This is the nooch (our shorthand for nutritional yeast) sauce that we use whenever we need a melty cheesy topping for a meal. It's quick, tangy, and flavorful. So many sauces like this call for a stick (gasp) of margarine—this recipe needs a measly tablespoon of olive oil, which makes you wonder if some cookbook authors are just being hateful. We use this on nachos, pastas, brunch things (see Tofu Florentine, page 72), or just to dip raw veggies in.*

2 cups vegetable broth or water
¼ cup all-purpose flour
1 tablespoon olive oil
3 cloves garlic, minced
Pinch of dried thyme (crumbled in your fingers)
¼ teaspoon salt
Several pinches of freshly ground black pepper
⅛ teaspoon turmeric
¾ cup nutritional yeast flakes
1 tablespoon fresh lemon juice
1 teaspoon prepared yellow mustard

COMBINE THE broth and flour in a measuring cup and whisk with a fork until dissolved (a couple of lumps are okay).

Preheat a small saucepan over medium-low heat. Place the oil and garlic in the pan and gently cook for about 2 minutes, stirring often and being careful not to burn the garlic.

Add the thyme, salt, and pepper, and cook for about 15 seconds. Add the broth, turmeric, and nutrition yeast, and raise the heat to medium. Use a whisk to stir constantly. The mixture should start bubbling and thickening in about 3 minutes; if it doesn't, turn the heat a bit higher.

Once the mixture is bubbling and thickening, stir and cook for about 2 more minutes. Add the lemon juice and mustard. The mixture should resemble a thick, melty cheese. Taste for salt (you may need more, depending on how salty your vegetable broth is), turn off the heat, and cover the pan to keep it warm until ready to use. The top might thicken a bit while it sits, but you can just stir it and it will be fine. Serve warm.

## DILL-TAHINI SAUCE

MAKES 1½ CUPS

TIME: 5 MINUTES

*A great dressing for a Mediterranean salad or just to serve with steamed veggies, greens, sautéed veggies, roasted veggies . . . you get the idea. It has a vibrant and tangy flavor, so it isn't recommended for anything that is already strongly flavored. It's definitely one of those things that will have you licking the spoon after you ladle it out.*

½ cup tahini, at room temperature

½ cup water, at room temperature

1 clove garlic, chopped coarsely

¼ cup fresh lemon juice (juice of 1 lemon)

2 tablespoons olive oil

1 tablespoon balsamic vinegar

½ teaspoon paprika (Hungarian, if you've got it)

¼ teaspoon salt

1 cup lightly packed fresh dill

COMBINE ALL the ingredients but the dill in a blender or food processor. Blend until smooth. Add the dill and pulse a few times until the dill is just small green flecks. You can serve immediately or refrigerate until ready to use, then bring back to room temperature because it will thicken a lot when cold.

## CITRUS-DATE-SESAME SAUCE

MAKES 2 CUPS SAUCE

TIME: 10 MINUTES, PLUS 2 HOURS FOR SOAKING DATES

*This sweet, tangy complex sauce pairs perfectly with kale, collards, and other bitter greens. Serve either at room temperature, or cold in warmer weather. Try it also on roasted green beans or steamed, sliced kabocha squash.*

1¼ cups fresh-squeezed orange juice

½ cup soft pitted dates, chopped

½ cup tahini

2 tablespoons sesame seeds

2 tablespoons sweet miso

¼ teaspoon ground cardamom

Salt and freshly ground pepper

**tip**

➤ Look for "sweet" or "white" miso at natural and health food stores. Chickpea miso can also be substituted.

➤ The sauce will thicken when refrigerated. Feel free to thin it out slightly with additional teaspoons of juice or water until the desired consistency is reached.

SOAK THE dates in the orange juice in the refrigerator for a minimum of 2 hours or overnight. Put in a food processor or blender, add the remaining ingredients except the salt and pepper, and blend until smooth and creamy. Taste the sauce, then season with salt and pepper to taste. Serve over steamed greens or vegetables. Sprinkle the top of sauce with additional sesame seeds for garnish if desired.

## JALAPEÑO-CORN GRAVY

MAKES ABOUT 3 CUPS

*Kids these days, they'll make a gravy outta anything. We like this gravy on mashed potatoes for a change of pace. It's yummy and corn-y with a little kick for ya.*

1 cup vegetable broth

1 tablespoon cornstarch

1 tablespoon olive oil

1 medium-size onion, chopped coarsely

2 jalapeños, seeded and chopped

3 cloves garlic, chopped

Generous pinch of dried rubbed sage

2 cups fresh or frozen corn  (thaw partially if frozen)

¼ cup plain soy milk

¼ teaspoon salt

Juice of ½ lemon

PREHEAT A saucepan over medium-high heat. In a measuring cup, mix the cornstarch with the vegetable broth and set aside.

Sauté the onion and jalapeños in the oil for about 5 minutes, until the onions are translucent. Add the garlic and sage, and sauté for 1 more minute.

Add the corn and cook for about 5 minutes, until the corn is slightly browned.

Add the vegetable broth, soy milk, and salt. Stir often and let thicken for 3 or 4 minutes. Remove from the heat and let cool a bit, just so that it's not steaming very much. Transfer to a blender or food processor and puree. Add the lemon juice to taste and puree again, then taste for salt. Gently heat before serving if not serving immediately.

## SWEET VIDALIA ONION SAUCE

MAKES A LITTLE LESS THAN 2 CUPS

**TIME:** 40 MINUTES

*Perfect over portobellos (page 28) or Chickpea Cutlets (page 133) or even just to dress up your veggie burger. You want the onions to caramelize, not crisp up, so it's important that you keep a close eye and keep the heat low.*

2 tablespoons olive oil

2 large Vidalia onions, quartered and sliced thinly (about 2 cups once sliced)

¼ cup mirin or white wine

2 tablespoons pure maple syrup

1 teaspoon white balsamic or red wine vinegar

1 teaspoon Dijon mustard (not the whole-grain kind)

Pinch of salt

PREHEAT A large, nonstick pan over medium-low heat. Sauté the onions in the oil for about 20 minutes, turning often so that they don't burn. If it looks like they are getting crisp, lower the heat. They should be very soft and honey brown. Add the remaining ingredients and stir for about 30 seconds. Turn off the heat and cover to keep warm until you're ready to serve.

# BREADS, MUFFINS, AND SCONES

BAKING IS DIFFERENT enough from cooking that it's tempting to divide the world into "bakers" and "cookers." Tempting indeed, but don't go labeling yourself just yet . . . we believe that knowing how to do both well is not only possible but essential to being the best vegan home chef you can be. So, here we have a sampling of tasty things to make when the mood hits you.

True, baking takes a slightly different mind-set: it's somewhat scientific and takes a little more practice, even a little more intuition, than does boiling pasta or simmering a soup. But at least a baking disaster is interesting and messy in a fun way, like a ninth grade chemistry project. And no matter how much you may try to get people (as in those people sitting on your couch and hogging the remote) excited about tempeh burgers, a loaf of warm banana bread will always get their attention.

Our top favorite things to bake are muffins and scones—especially on weekend mornings or for spontaneous late-night treats. They require little mixing, use the most basic ingredients that any decently-stocked pantry should have, and require 35 minutes or less from mixing bowl to cooling rack. They also take readily to healthy additions such as whole grains, fruits, spices, and nuts. Bake a batch of scones or muffins on Sunday morning and enjoy them toasted the next morning, or as a high-energy snack that afternoon.

In addition, we've including a few recipes for simple, everyday yeasted breads and quick breads. Hearty whole-grain soda bread makes an ideal treat at breakfast, and a moist cranberry-nut bread is seriously awesome when paired with (organic, fair-trade) coffee. Cinnamon pinwheels thrill guests at any brunch and an easy herbed focaccia makes any old soup a complete meal. Last but not least, unleavened flatbreads are a different and delicious alternative to rice or other starches. Flatbreads can be mixed, rolled, and then baked—without additional oil—on a hot griddle in about the same time it takes a curry or stew to simmer on the stove top.

## HOME-STYLE POTATO ROLLS

MAKES 24 ROLLS

**TIME:** ABOUT 45 MINUTES, NOT INCLUDING RISING TIME

*These golden, puffy rolls dotted with poppy seeds are just like soft, homey hugs from the oven. Great with soup, or for breakfast, or just as an after-school snack, even if you haven't been to school for decades. For the best color, be sure to use yellow potatoes such as Yukon gold.*

1½ cups warm water

1 cup soy milk

2 tablespoons nonhydrogenated vegan margarine

1 (¼-ounce) package yeast

5–5½ cups all-purpose flour, or a blend of white whole wheat and all-purpose flour

2 tablespoons brown sugar

2¼ teaspoons salt

1¼ cups cold, moist mashed potatoes, preferably Yukon gold

Glaze:

⅓ cup soy milk

1½ teaspoons potato starch or cornstarch

Poppy seeds for sprinkling

COMBINE 1 cup of the warm water with the soy milk in a medium-size saucepan, then drop in the margarine. Heat over medium heat until the margarine is melted and the soy milk mixture has slightly scalded. Remove from the heat and allow to cool until lukewarm.

In a measuring cup, mix together remaining ½ cup of the warm water and the yeast. Set aside for a few minutes until the yeast is foamy.

In a large mixing bowl, sift together the flour, sugar, and salt. Using your hands, mix the mashed potatoes into the flour to form a crumbly mixture, as if you were making a pastry dough. Stir in the yeast mixture and the soy milk mixture to form a soft dough; if the dough is very sticky, add a little flour, a few tablespoons at a time, until a firm, smooth dough forms. It's okay if there's bits of potato poking through the dough.

Turn out the dough onto a lightly floured board and knead until elastic. Return the dough to the bowl, cover with a kitchen towel, and let rise for 2 hours or until doubled in size. When pressed with a finger, the dough should spring back slowly.

*Right before the dough is ready to be punched down, prepare the glaze:*

Whisk together the soy milk and potato starch in a small saucepan. Cook over a medium-low heat, stirring constantly, until the mixture thickens slightly. Remove from the heat and cool before using.

Preheat the oven to 400°F. While the oven is preheating, lightly grease two 12-cup muffin tins. Punch down the dough, knead briefly on a floured board, and roll into two thick 14- to 16-inch ropes. Use kitchen shears or a sharp knife to slice the ropes into 1½- to 2-inch pieces. Lightly floured your hands and roll each piece into a ball the size of a walnut.

Place three balls of dough together in each muffin cup. Brush with glaze , sprinkle with poppy seeds, and very loosely cover with plastic wrap. Set aside for 25 to 35 minutes, until rolls have doubled in bulk.

Bake for 20 to 25 minutes, until the tops are shiny and browned. When the rolls are cool enough to touch, transfer from the pans to wire racks to complete cooling.

## WHOLE WHEAT SODA BREAD WITH MILLET AND CURRANTS

MAKES 1 LARGE LOAF

**TIME:** 1 HOUR 30 MINUTES

*Our whole-grain soda bread is a little like a giant scone—not too sweet, with a dense, chewy texture and slight crunch from a little cooked millet worked into the dough. The Zante currants plump up by being cooked along with the millet, in one amazing feat of culinary dexterity. This is not a traditional soda bread (even with the caraway seeds) in the slightest, but whatever! It's Terry's most favorite thing in whole world, sliced thinly and lightly toasted for breakfast or tea.*

ZANTE currants are actually cute little seedless grapes, completely different from black currants. Zantes are still referred to as currants for some mysterious reason, are commonly used as such, and are a typically a lot cheaper. Look for them in your supermarket right next to the raisins. They have a zippy, intense flavor that can satisfy any yearning for "real" currants.

**Millet:**

1 teaspoon canola oil

½ cup millet, uncooked

1 cup boiling water

1½ cups Zante currants

**Dough:**

2 cups whole wheat flour (white whole wheat flour is best)

1½ cups all-purpose flour

1 tablespoon baking powder

2 teaspoons baking soda

¾ teaspoon salt

⅓ cup sugar

1 heaping tablespoon caraway seeds

½ cup nonhydrogenated vegan margarine, cold

1¼ cups plain soy milk, plus additional soy milk for brushing top of loaf

1½ teaspoons apple cider vinegar

PREHEAT THE oven to 375°F for at least 20 minutes. Grease a 9-inch round cake pan.

*Prepare the millet:*

In a saucepan, heat the canola oil over medium heat and add the millet. Stir constantly to toast the millet for 2 to 3 minutes, until golden and fragrant. Pour in the boiling water, stir in the currants, and cover. Cook for 18 to 20 minutes, until the liquid is absorbed and the millet is plump. Remove from the heat and fluff with a fork. Partially cover the millet and allow to cool to about room temperature.

*Prepare the dough:*

In a large bowl, sift together the whole wheat flour, all-purpose flour, baking powder, baking soda, and salt. Stir in the sugar and caraway seeds, then cut in the cold margarine with either a pastry cutter or two knives held together, until a crumbly mixture forms.

Combine 1¼ cups of the soy milk and the vinegar in a measuring cup, and allow it to sit for a minute or so to curdle. Stir the curdled soy milk and the cooled millet mixture into the flour mixture. When a dough starts to form, knead it a few times in the bowl to form a dense ball of dough (if it's too moist, knead in more flour, 1 tablespoon at a time). Don't overwork the dough.

## tip

➤ This bread keeps fresh for days longer than the average quick bread. Even so, loosely wrap it in foil or store in a resealable plastic bag.

➤ Bake this bread the old-fashioned way: Place a well-seasoned, 4-quart round cast-iron pot in the oven while it preheats and leave the pot there to get hot for about 30 minutes. Use oven mitts to lift the hot pot out of the oven and onto a burner on the stove. Dust the bottom of your loaf of dough with plenty of whole-grain flour, a little wheat bran, or even a touch of cornmeal. Very carefully, lower the shaped, scored, uncooked loaf into the pot (don't burn your fingers. If necessary, just let the loaf drop into the pot). Quickly return the pot, uncovered, to the oven and bake as directed. The dough will not stick to a hot, well-seasoned pot.

Pat the ball of dough into the prepared cake pan, allowing a ½-inch space all around from the edge of the pan, to form a round loaf. With a thin, sharp knife, cut a cross into the top of the loaf. Brush the top of loaf with soy milk, and brush it a few more times during the baking process. Bake for 45 to 50 minutes until it is well browned and a knife inserted into the center comes out clean.

## FRESH ROSEMARY FOCACCIA

MAKES 1 LARGE, FLAT LOAF

**TIME:** 2 HOURS, INCLUDING RISING TIME

*This big, soft, yeasted flatbread goes well with just about any entrée or soup. We make it when we want fresh bread without too much fuss. It's very basic, so try experimenting with different fresh herbs and chopped olives, and serving this with Hummus (page 67) or any spread in the Dips section (page 62–69). If you want to be the most annoying person at the pizza party, keep reminding people that the singular of focaccia is* focacce.

> **SAMMICHES (a.k.a. sandwiches) loaded with lots of fresh or grilled veggies are even better if stuffed into sliced, fresh focaccia. Try toasting or even grilling them, maybe with a slap of Sweet Basil Pesto Tapenade (page 65) or Sun-dried Tomato Dip (page 64), used as a spread. Just sayin'.**

1 (¼-ounce) package active dry yeast
1¼ cups warm water
3 tablespoons olive oil
3 tablespoons chopped fresh rosemary, plus extra whole leaves for garnish

3 cups all-purpose flour, or 1½ cups each
   all-purpose and whole wheat

1 teaspoon salt

Olive oil for brushing

Coarse salt for garnish

Optional stuff to knead into the dough: chopped
   kalamata olives, sautéed shallots, cracked black
   pepper, chopped fresh sage, parsley, or oregano

COMBINE THE yeast and warm water in a large bowl. Stir in the olive oil, chopped rosemary, and flour, and knead to form a soft dough. If the dough is sticky, work in a little flour, 1 tablespoon at a time. Turn the dough onto a floured surface and knead for 5 to 6 minutes, until smooth. Pour a little olive oil in the original bowl, add the kneaded dough, and turn a few times to coat the dough with oil. Cover with a clean dish towel and let rise 1 hour, or until a hole poked into the side of the risen dough fills up slowly.

Punch down the dough, return it to the floured surface, and knead a few times. Then, using a floured rolling pin, roll the dough into a large circle about 1½ inches thick. Transfer the dough to a lightly greased cookie sheet. Poke several holes into the dough with a fork, sprinkle with coarse salt and rosemary leaves, and brush with a little oil (or even soy milk, for a matte finish). Cover again with dish towel and let rise for 20 minutes.

While the dough is rising for the second time, preheat the oven to 350°F. Bake for 30 to 35 minutes until the bread is lightly browned and firm. Remove from the oven and let cool for 10 minutes before slicing.

## POPPY SEED-CORNMEAL ROTI

MAKES 8 SMALL ROTI

TIME: 30 MINUTES

*Tasty alongside either East or West Indian cuisine, these little roti are not nearly as big as traditional the West*

*Indian—style flatbread but still a good size for dipping and scooping chunky stews. The addition of poppy seeds makes them crunchy, munchy good, and leftovers are fabulous for breakfast. Rolling and folding the dough maybe gets a little tedious, but with practice you can have soft, flaky, "buttery" flatbread in under 30 minutes. Make these while that curry or soup is simmering on the stove.*

*tip*

> For even more tender roti, use 1½ cups whole wheat pastry flour and 1½ cups regular whole wheat flour for the dough.
>    As a variation, add ½ cup pepitas (pumpkin seeds) to the dough while kneading.

### Roti dough:

3 cups whole wheat flour

½ cup cornmeal

2 tablespoons poppy seeds

1 teaspoon cumin seeds

1¼ teaspoon salt

1½ cups warm water

### Crumbs:

¼ cup whole wheat pastry flour

¼ cup cornmeal

2 tablespoons corn or peanut oil, plus additional oil
   for brushing

¼ teaspoon salt

**Prepare the dough:** In a large bowl, combine the whole wheat flour, cornmeal, poppy and cumin seeds, and salt. Stir in the water and mix to form a soft dough. Knead the dough in the bowl for 5 to 6 minutes; the dough will be soft and slightly moist. If the dough is very sticky, knead in a little extra flour, 1 tablespoon at a time. Coat the dough in a little oil by pouring a tablespoon of oil onto the dough and turning it several times in the bowl. Cover with a damp, clean dish towel and let it rest for at least 10 minutes.

In a small separate bowl, make the crumbs: Combine the flour, cornmeal, oil, and salt. Mix with fingers or a fork until a dry, crumbly mixture forms.

After the dough has rested, divide into six to eight balls on a surface dusted with flour. Flatten a ball into as thin a circle as possible and brush with oil. Fold the circle in half, brush with more oil, and fold again. Stretch the folded circle into a round shape, roll it out again into a flat circle, and brush with more oil. This time, sprinkle on some crumbs. Repeat folding in half, brushing with oil, and sprinkling with crumbs. Then fold it in half again and pull and roll one last time into a thin round.

Repeat with the remaining dough. Be sure to sprinkle extra flour on top of the dough circles when stacking, or use pieces of waxed paper to separate.

Preheat a cast-iron pan or heavy-bottomed nonstick skillet over medium heat. Gently place a dough circle on the hot pan and bake on each side for 3 to 4 minutes, using tongs or a large wooden spatula to turn it. The dough will bubble and brown spots will form; pressing down on cooked parts of the roti can cause bubbles to grow. Stack the cooked roti on top of one another and keep warm by wrapping in a clean, damp dish towel until ready to serve.

To reheat wrap tightly in foil for conventional ovens or wrap in damp paper towels for a microwave.

## SCALLION FLATBREAD

MAKES 8 FLATBREADS

TIME: 30 MINUTES

*This savory flatbread is a little like the love child between a flaky paratha (Indian grilled buttery flatbread) and a scallion pancake. Instead of deep-frying, we grill it on an iron skillet and serve with a sharp and savory soy dipping sauce. Include these in any Asian meal as an appetizer, in place of rice or as a side with thick curries.*

*tip*

> If you've already cut your teeth on making the Poppy Seed–Cornmeal Roti (page 221), then you know the deal with folding and rolling flatbread. If not, well then, what are you waiting for? Here's a good place to start.

**Flatbread:**

- 1 cup all-purpose flour
- 1 cup whole wheat flour
- ¾ teaspoon salt
- 2 teaspoons sugar
- 2 tablespoons peanut oil
- 2 teaspoons toasted sesame oil
- 5 scallions, green parts only, sliced into ½-inch lengths
- ¾ cup warm water
- ½ cup additional peanut oil for brushing

**Dipping sauce:**

- 3 tablespoons soy sauce
- 2 tablespoons rice vinegar
- 2 teaspoons sugar
- ½ teaspoon finely grated ginger (use a microplane grater; it should resemble almost pureed ginger)
- 1 teaspoon sesame seeds, lightly crushed or left whole

IN A large bowl, sift together the flours, sugar, and salt. Pour in the peanut and sesame oils, and mix until slightly crumbly. Add the chopped scallions and stir in ½ cup of the warm water, then add the remaining water 1 tablespoon at a time until a soft, nonsticky dough forms (add more water very gradually if necessary).

Turn the dough onto a lightly floured surface, kneading until smooth. Roll the dough into a thick rope and slice into eight equal pieces. Roll each piece into a ball. Pour about a tablespoon of peanut oil into the bowl where you made the dough and coat each ball with oil. Leave them in the bowl and cover with a clean, slightly damp dish towel. Allow the dough to rest for at least 10 minutes before proceeding.

Prepare a lightly floured surface and have ready a rolling pin, more peanut oil in a bowl, and a pastry brush. Roll a ball of dough into as thin a circle as possible, brush with oil, and fold in half. Brush the half-circle with oil, fold into a triangle shape, then pull and stretch the triangle back into a circle. Roll out this circle as thinly as possible (about ⅛-inch thick or slightly less), place on a lightly floured dish or waxed paper, and repeat with remaining dough (use waxed paper between each stacked circle to prevent sticking).

Heat a heavy-bottomed pan (preferably cast iron) over medium-high heat. Lightly brush the dough circles with peanut oil on each side, place on the heated skillet, and cook until the dough bubbles and rises, about 2 minutes. Flip once, pressing down with a spatula when it starts to bubble, and cook for another 1 to 2 minutes, until the bread is slightly puffed but not too hard. Some dark browned spots are good.

Place the hot flatbread in a large bowl lined with a clean, slightly damp dish towel, folding the dishcloth over bread. Stack the cooked flatbreads on top of one another, covered with the dish towel. This will help keep the breads warm and soft. To serve, slice into triangles and serve with dipping sauce. The breads will toughen when cooled; to soften, wrap in a moist paper towel and microwave, or wrap the breads tightly in foil and warm in a conventional oven.

*Prepare the dipping sauce:*

Combine all ingredients and serve with the hot scallion flatbreads.

# SKILLET CORN BREAD

MAKES 8 BIG SLICES

**TIME:** 35 MINUTES

*This tender and moist bread is packed with corn-y goodness to maximum capacity. It's yummy plain but even better with a savory topping or sautéed corn in the batter; see variation below. Chili, beans, and barbecued things seem a little naked when not accessorized with this corn bread. We bake it in a cast-iron skillet, but if you don't have an oven-safe skillet, use a 9 × 13-inch baking pan.*

Basic corn bread:

    **2 cups plain soy milk**

    **2 teaspoons apple cider vinegar**

    **2 cups cornmeal**

    **1 cup all-purpose flour**

    **¼ cup sugar**

    **2 teaspoons baking powder**

    **½ teaspoon salt**

    **⅓ cup oil**

Jalapeño-onion variation:

    **1 tablespoon canola oil**

    **1 medium-size yellow onion, sliced into 1 x ½-inch slices**

    **3 jalapeños, seeded and sliced thinly**

    **¼ teaspoon salt**

Double-corn variation:

    **1 cup fresh or frozen and partially thawed corn kernels**

    **1 tablespoon oil**

PREHEAT THE oven to 350°F. If making plain corn bread, lightly grease the bottom and sides of the cast-iron pan and place it in the oven to warm while the oven preheats, then proceed to prepare corn bread. If using a variation, read the following first.

### Jalapeño-Onion Variation:

Preheat a cast-iron skillet over medium heat. Sauté the onion and jalapeño in oil for about 5 minutes, until the onions are softened. Add the salt and mix well. Transfer to a bowl. Don't wash the pan; you'll pour the batter right into it in a bit.

### Double-Corn Variation:

Preheat a cast-iron skillet over medium heat. Sauté the corn kernels in oil for about 7 minutes, until the corn is slightly browned. Transfer to a bowl. Don't wash the pan; you'll pour the batter right into it in a bit.

### Prepare the Corn Bread:

Combine the soy milk and vinegar in a measuring cup and set aside to curdle as you prepare everything else.

In a large mixing bowl, sift together the cornmeal, flour, sugar, baking powder, and salt. Create a well in the center and add the soy milk mixture and oil. Use a wooden spoon to mix together until just combined; some lumps are okay. If using the double-corn variation, fold the corn into the batter.

Pour the batter into prepared cast-iron skillet. If using the jalapeño-onion variation, scatter the topping over the batter in the pan. Bake for 30 to 32 minutes, until a toothpick or butter knife inserted through the middle comes out clean. Remove from the oven and let cool just a bit before serving.

> **tip**
>
> ➤ This recipe makes large, drop-style scones but you can make them to smaller by using an ice-cream scoop and reducing the cooking time by about 5 minutes.

## BANANA-DATE SCONES

MAKES 8 LARGE SCONES

**TIME:** 40 MINUTES

*Scones can't really be health food, maybe, but if they were they would be these chewy, flavorful babies sweetened only by ripe bananas, dates, and a touch of brown rice syrup. We crave these scones on weekday mornings, for their flavor without the huge dose of sugar that most scones too often deliver. These are also moister than most, thanks to finely chopped dates that fill every bite. If any remain the next day, split, toast, and live a little by spreading them with a shmear of vegan margarine and your favorite jam.*

> 8 ounces dates
> 1 tablespoon all-purpose flour
> 1 cup mashed, very ripe banana
>   (about 3–4 bananas; their skin should
>   be almost black)
> 2 tablespoons ground flaxseeds
> ⅓ cup rice milk
> ⅓ cup canola oil
> ¼ cup brown rice syrup
> 1 cup all-purpose flour
> 1 ¼ cup whole wheat pastry flour
> 2 teaspoons baking powder
> 1 teaspoon ground cinnamon
> ¼ teaspoon ground nutmeg
> ½ teaspoon salt
> ½ cup chopped walnuts

PREHEAT THE oven to 350°F and lightly grease two medium-size baking sheets.

Finely chop the dates, place in a small bowl, and sprinkle with 1 tablespoon of flour. Toss the dates to thoroughly coat with the flour, breaking apart any clumps. Set aside.

In a large bowl, whisk together the flaxseeds and rice milk. Whisk in the mashed banana, canola oil, and brown rice syrup. In a separate bowl, sift together the all-purpose flour, whole wheat pastry flour, baking powder, cinnamon, and nutmeg. Stir into the banana mixture until the ingredients are just moistened; the dough will be thick yet sticky. Fold in the chopped dates and walnuts.

Lightly oil a ½-cup measuring cup and scoop generous half-cupfuls of dough onto a baking sheet, leaving about 3 inches of space between the scones. Gently pat down the tops of the scones and dab with a little rice milk if desired. Bake for 32 to 34 minutes, until browned and firm. Transfer from the baking sheets to a cooling rack to complete cooling.

## PUMPKIN-CRANBERRY SCONES

MAKES 12 LARGE SCONES

**TIME:** 45 MINUTES

*More scones! These large pumpkin and spice-rich treats are almost cakelike, different from your typical scone. Enjoy them hot out of the oven, or try them the next day toasted, buttered and served with a pot of strong black tea. This recipe makes plenty, so we think they would make a great addition to a Thanksgiving brunch or any fall festivity.*

2 cups all-purpose flour

1 cup whole wheat pastry flour

1⅓ cups sugar

4 teaspoons baking powder

1 teaspoon baking soda

2 teaspoons ground cinnamon

1 teaspoon ground ginger

1 teaspoon ground cardamom

¼ teaspoon ground cloves

¼ teaspoon ground nutmeg

1¼ teaspoons salt

½ cup nonhydrogenated vegan margarine, cold

¾ cup soy creamer or rice milk

4 teaspoons ground flaxseeds

1½ cups pumpkin puree

3 tablespoons molasses

1 tablespoon freshly grated lemon zest

1 cup fresh cranberries, chopped coarsely

3 tablespoons shelled pepitas (pumpkin seeds) for garnish

> *tip*
>
> ➤ If using homemade pumpkin puree and it's very watery, strain it before using for these scones. Over a small bowl, fit a double layer of cheesecloth and secure with a large rubber band. Pour in the pumpkin puree and allow to strain for a few hours. Discard the excess liquid. If this sounds like too much work, then just use a good quality—maybe organic—canned pumpkin. We won't judge you. Much.

PREHEAT THE oven to 350°F and lightly grease two baking sheets.

In a large bowl, sift together all-purpose flour, pastry flour, baking powder, baking soda, sugar, cinnamon, ginger, cardamom, cloves, nutmeg, and salt. Chop the margarine into chunks, toss in the flour mixture, and cut into the flour with a pastry cutter or a heavy fork until the mixture looks slightly crumbly.

In a medium-size bowl, whisk together the ground flaxseeds and soy creamer. Add the pumpkin puree, molasses, and lemon zest, and stir until completely incorporated.

Make a well in the flour mixture. Fold in the pumpkin mixture, then add the cranberries. Stir until a soft dough forms; take care not to overmix.

Divide the dough into two portions. Place each on a

separate baking sheet and flatten into a large circle just over 1 inch thick. With a large sharp knife, cut each round all the way through into six to eight wedges. Brush the tops of the rounds with soy creamer and press 1 tablespoon of pepitas onto each scone.

Bake for 30 to 34 minutes until a sharp knife inserted into the center comes out clean and the edges are lightly browned. If less moist scones are desired, go for the longer baking time. Let cool for 10 minutes before reslicing into wedges. Transfer from the baking sheet to wire racks to complete cooling.

## BANANA–WHEAT GERM MUFFINS

MAKES 12 MUFFINS

**TIME:** ABOUT 40 MINUTES

*Wheat germ: not just for your grandma's oatmeal anymore! In the spirit of "muffins are not desserts," we present this no-nonsense, whole-grain muffin. They have lots of big banana flavor and a little bit of crunch provided by our friend wheat germ. A big scoop of cinnamon gives these guys what for.*

> **tip**
>
> ➤ If you want high-rise muffins, fill the tins all the way to the top and bake for five extra minutes. This method will make ten muffins instead of twelve.
>
> ➤ To keep wheat germ fresher longer, store it in the fridge once opened.

1 cup plain soy milk
1 teaspoon apple cider vinegar
2 very ripe bananas
⅓ cup canola oil

⅓ cup sugar
1 teaspoon pure vanilla extract
1¼ cups whole wheat pastry flour or all-purpose flour
¾ cup wheat germ
1 tablespoon ground cinnamon
2 teaspoon baking powder
½ teaspoon salt

PREHEAT THE oven to 375°F. Lightly grease a 12-cup muffin tin with cooking spray.

Pour the soy milk into a measuring cup and add the vinegar to it. Set it aside to curdle.

Meanwhile, mash the bananas in a large mixing bowl. Add the soy milk mixture to the bowl along with the oil, sugar, and vanilla, and mix well.

In a separate bowl, mix together the flour, wheat germ, cinnamon, baking powder, and salt. Add this to the banana mixture and use a wooden spoon to gently stir the ingredients, until all the dry ingredients are just moistened.

Fill the muffin cups three-quarters full and bake for 22 minutes. Remove from the oven and, once cool enough to handle, transfer to a cooling rack to cool the rest of the way. You can also serve them warm, if you like!

## CARROT-PINEAPPLE SUNSHINE MUFFINS

MAKES 12 MUFFINS

**TIME:** ABOUT 40 MINUTES

*Bring some happy-fun-time-pineapple-carrot joy to your dismal-gray-sad morning with these tender widdle muffins. They really are like a burst of sunshine!*

½ cup vanilla soy yogurt (or any flavored yogurt, such as lemon or peach)
½ cup plain or vanilla soy milk
1 tablespoons ground flaxseed
¼ cup canola oil

½ cup brown sugar

½ cup crushed pineapple, well drained (use canned only; reserve juice)

⅓ cup pineapple juice, reserved from crushed canned pineapple

½ cup finely shredded carrot (about 1 large carrot)

1 heaping teaspoon finely grated orange zest (from 1 large orange)

½ cup Thompson or golden raisins

1⅓ cups whole wheat pastry flour or all-purpose flour, or a combination of both

1½ teaspoons baking powder

½ teaspoon baking soda

1 teaspoon ground ginger

½ teaspoon ground cinnamon

½ teaspoon salt

*tip*

➤ These muffins don't rise very high, preferring to have a flat, crisp top instead. So don't be afraid to fill each muffin cup to the top, or even a little bit past that.

➤ Fresh pineapple doesn't work so well in this recipe, so be sure to use only canned, crushed pineapple. The enzymes in fresh pineapple can interfere with the leavening process and cause uneven baking.

PREHEAT THE oven to 350°F and lightly grease a non-stick 12-cup muffin tin.

In a large bowl, whisk together the soy yogurt, soy milk, and ground flaxseed. Whisk in the canola oil and brown sugar.

Squeeze the crushed pineapple to remove as much excess juice as possible and add to the bowl, along with the reserved pineapple juice, carrot, orange zest, and raisins, and thoroughly mix. Sift in the flour, baking powder, baking soda, ginger, cinnamon, and salt. Stir only just enough to moisten the dry ingredients.

Scoop into the muffin tin, filling to the top of each cup or a little bit above (the batter is chunky and these muffins don't rise very much). Bake for 24 to 26 minutes, until a toothpick or a thin, sharp knife inserted into the center of a muffin comes out clean. Allow to cool for 5 minutes in the tin before transferring the muffins to a cooling rack.

## ALMOND-QUINOA MUFFINS

MAKES 12 MUFFINS

**TIME:** 35 MINUTES

*Another healthy muffin, surprise! Don't ever say we don't want you eating a whole grain. With that, adding cooked grains is a convenient and interesting way to boost the fiber and protein content of everyday baked goods. In these tender muffins, cooked quinoa creates a unique crunchy texture. Next time you're cooking up a batch of plain quinoa for dinner, set aside some to make these muffins the next day. The new red-hued varieties of quinoa available in some areas look particularly charming here.*

1 cup vanilla soy milk

1 tablespoon ground flaxseeds

¼ cup canola oil

¼ cup agave nectar or pure maple syrup

½ tsp vanilla extract

1¼ cups all-purpose or whole wheat pastry flour

¼ cup almond meal or almond flour

1½ teaspoons baking powder

½ teaspoons salt

½ teaspoon ground cinnamon

½ teaspoon ground cardamom

1¼ cups cooked quinoa

½ cup finely chopped dried apricots or currants

PREHEAT THE oven to 350°F and lightly grease a non-stick 12-cup muffin tin.

In a medium-size bowl, whisk together the soy milk and ground flaxseed. Allow to sit for 1 minute, then whisk in oil, agave nectar and vanilla.

In a separate large bowl, sift together flour, almond meal, baking soda, baking powder, salt, and spices. Add the wet ingredients to the dry, mixing until just incorporated. Gently fold in the cooked quinoa and the apricots and mix until only the large lumps are gone.

Pour into the prepared muffin tin and bake for 20 to 22 minutes until a toothpick inserted into the center of a muffin comes out clean.

## CRANBERRY-ORANGE-NUT BREAD

MAKES ONE LOAF

**TIME:** 1 HOUR 20 MINUTES, NOT INCLUDING COOLING TIME

*This is Isa mom's recipe, but we think it was originally from a Fannie Farmer cookbook from the '60s and been tampered with over the years. This is a bake sale favorite. It smells just as lovely as it tastes!*

½ cup soy milk

¼ cup fresh orange juice

¼ cup canola oil

1 cup sugar

1 teaspoon pure vanilla extract

2 cups all-purpose flour

1¼ teaspoons baking powder

½ teaspoon baking soda

½ teaspoon salt

¼ teaspoon ground allspice

1 tablespoon grated orange zest

1 cup chopped fresh cranberries

½ cup chopped walnuts

PREHEAT THE oven to 325°F. Lightly grease a 9 × 5-inch loaf pan.

In a large mixing bowl, mix together the soy milk, orange juice, canola oil, sugar and vanilla.

Sift in the flour, baking powder, baking soda, salt, and allspice. Mix just until smooth. The batter will be thicker than a normal cake batter, so don't be alarmed!

Fold in the orange zest, cranberries, and walnuts. Spoon the batter into the prepared loaf pan.

Bake for about 1 hour. Let the bread cool for about 15 minutes before inverting it onto a cooling rack. Flip it right side up to cool further.

## LOWER-FAT BANANA BREAD

MAKES ONE LOAF

**TIME:** 1 HOUR 20 MINUTES, NOT INCLUDING COOLING TIME

*This bread is pure, unadulterated banana goodness. No one will know it's lower in fat, swear to God. We've made this with two large or three small bananas, but don't stress about the exact measurement; it always comes out really yummy.*

*Never use a hand mixer for banana bread because it makes it gummy; treat it like a muffin batter and mix with a wooden spoon just until the wet and dry ingredients are combined. In fact, if you would like to turn these into muffins, pour the batter into a greased muffin tin and bake for eighteen minutes.*

2 large or 3 small very ripe bananas

¼ cup applesauce

¼ cup canola oil

½ cup sugar

2 tablespoons molasses

2 cups all-purpose flour

¾ teaspoon baking soda

1 teaspoon ground cinnamon

¼ teaspoon ground nutmeg (or grated fresh)

½ teaspoon salt

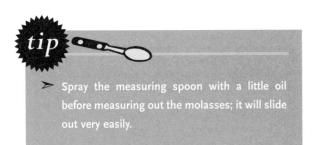

> Spray the measuring spoon with a little oil before measuring out the molasses; it will slide out very easily.

PREHEAT THE oven to 350°F. Lightly grease a 9 × 5-inch loaf pan.

In a large mixing bowl, mash the bananas really, really well. Add the sugar, applesauce, oil, and molasses, and whisk briskly to incorporate.

Sift in the flour, baking soda, spices, and salt. Use a wooden spoon to mix until the wet and dry ingredients are just combined. Fold in the chocolate chips, if using.

Transfer the batter to the prepared pan and bake for 45 to 50 minutes. The top should be lightly browned and a knife inserted through the center should come out clean. (If you're using the chips then of course some chocolate will come out on your knife.)

Remove from the oven and invert onto a cooling rack; flip the bread right side up and let cool.

## APPLESAUCE–OAT BRAN MUFFINS

MAKES 12 MUFFINS

**TIME:** 45 MINUTES

*Apples and oat bran are as honest as a muffin can get. These may be our favorite in this triptych of well-behaved baked goods. These little muffins have a special moist texture and a distinctive applesauce aroma and oat bran's hearty texture. Oat bran can be found in the cereals section; it's sold as a hot cereal but also leads a secret double life of lending plenty of heart-healthy fiber to baked goods.*

¾ cup soy or rice milk
½ teaspoon apple cider vinegar

1 cup unsweetened natural applesauce
3 tablespoons canola oil
½ cup brown sugar, packed
1½ cups all-purpose or whole wheat pastry flour
¾ cup oat bran
2 teaspoons baking powder
½ teaspoon baking soda
1 teaspoon ground cinnamon
1 teaspoon ground cardamom
½ teaspoon ground nutmeg
½ teaspoon salt
½ cup raisins or dried cranberries or dried apple pieces

PREHEAT THE oven to 350°F and lightly grease a 12-cup nonstick muffin tin.

In a large bowl, whisk together the soy milk and apple cider vinegar; allow it to rest for 1 minute to curdle. Add the applesauce, canola oil, and brown sugar, and whisk to completely incorporate them.

In a separate, smaller bowl, sift together the flour, oat bran, baking powder, baking soda, spices, and salt. Fold the dry ingredients into the wet; stir only to moisten and don't overmix. Fold in the raisins. Use an ice-cream scoop or measuring cup to scoop the batter into the muffin cups.

Bake for 28 to 30 minutes, until a toothpick inserted into the middle of a muffin comes out clean. Allow the muffins to cool in the tin for 10 minutes, then transfer to a wire rack to complete cooling.

## MAPLE AND BROWN SUGAR PINWHEELS

MAKES 12 TO 14 ROLLS

**TIME:** ABOUT 2 HOURS

*Brown sugar swirls with a touch of spice and orange zest are sure to please for brunch or an afternoon snack. We think these are sweet enough on their own, but we've included an orange icing for fancy occasions. Make these rolls with white whole wheat flour and feel virtuous when you're going for seconds.*

**tip**

➤ If you like, flip over the buns when hot, right out of the oven, so that the gooey stuff on the bottom is transferred to the top.

**Dough:**

1¼ cups soy milk

¼ cup nonhydrogenated vegan margarine

⅓ cup warm water

1 (¼-ounce) package active dry yeast

4–4¼ cups all-purpose flour, whole wheat white flour or a combo of the two

⅓ cup granulated sugar

¾ teaspoon salt

1 teaspoon grated orange zest (about 1 large orange)

1 teaspoon ground cardamom

¼ teaspoon ground allspice

**Filling:**

2 tablespoons nonhydrogenated vegan margarine, melted

2 tablespoons pure maple syrup

1 cup brown sugar, packed

2 tablespoons grated orange rind (about 2 large oranges)

½ cup raisins, coarsely chopped (optional)

**Orange icing:**

1 cup confectioners' sugar, sifted

2 tablespoons nonhydrogenated vegan margarine

1 teaspoon grated orange rind

1 tablespoon orange juice

1 tablespoon soy milk

**Prepare the dough:** Heat the soy milk and margarine in a small saucepan over medium heat, stirring until the margarine is just about melted. Remove from the heat and allow to cool until tepid (don't add the hot soy milk to the dough or it could kill the yeast cells).

In a measuring cup, mix together the warm water and the yeast, setting aside for a few minutes until the yeast begins to foam. In a large mixing bowl, stir together the flour, granulated sugar, salt, cardamom, and allspice, and form a well in the center. Pour in the soy milk mixture and the yeast, then stir until a firm dough forms. If it's sticky, add extra flour a few tablespoons at a time.

Turn out the dough onto a lightly floured surface and knead until smooth, 6 to 8 minutes, and form into a ball. Pour less than a teaspoon of any light-flavored oil into the mixing bowl; add the kneaded dough, and turn the dough in bowl to coat the surface with oil. Cover the bowl lightly with plastic wrap, cover with a clean dish towel, and set in a warm, draft-free place to rise for about an hour. The dough should double in size. When you press its surface and the indentation fills in slowly, it's ready to shape.

While is the dough rises, line two large baking sheets with lightly greased baking parchment.

When the dough is ready, punch it down and knead it a few times on a lightly floured surface. Use a rolling pin to flatten the dough and roll it into a 11 × 18-inch rectangle ¼ inch thick. It helps to use your hands to very gently stretch and pull the dough to shape.

Fill the dough: Combine the melted margarine and maple syrup in a small bowl or measuring cup. Brush the mixture over the dough, leaving about 2 inches unbrushed unbrushed along one of the long edges. In another small bowl, combine the brown sugar, orange zest, and raisins; sprinkle this on top of the area that's been brushed with the maple mixture.

Grease two baking sheets. Roll the dough fairly tightly, starting from the filled long edge to other bare edge (like rolling sushi or a jelly roll). If desired, seal the seam of the roll with a little soy milk and place roll seam side down on a cutting board. With a sharp, thin, serrated knife, slice the roll into 1½-inch pieces and place about 2 inches apart on the prepared baking sheets. Cover the slices loosely with plastic wrap and then a kitchen towel, and let rise another 30 to 40 minutes.

While the rolls are rising, preheat the oven to 350°F. If desired, brush the tops of the rolls with a little soy milk just before baking. Bake rolls for 25 to 30 minutes, until golden brown. Turn out onto a rack to cool.

Prepare the icing: In a medium-size bowl, cut the confectioners' sugar into the margarine to form crumbs. Whisk in the soy milk, orange rind, and orange juice. Ice the cooled buns.

*tip*

➤ Line baking sheets with parchment paper to avoid any sticking issues.

# COOKIES AND BARS

EVEN THE MOST jaded vegan can get behind (and into his or her mouth) a perfectly chewy, crunchy, sweet, nutty, chocolaty, or spicy cookie without the addition of dairy products.

We use flaxseeds and starches to create chewy or crispy textures, and sometimes both, so you can toss out that dusty old box of "egg replacing powder." Instead, invest in the best-quality flours, oils, chocolate, and spices you can buy. Go organic if you can. Of key importance is to get your hands on high-budget, real vanilla extract. Without butter or eggs to get in the way, you'll really taste every glorious note in these wholesome confections. On that note, why not replace some all-purpose flour with a little whole wheat pastry and boost the fiber content? We love the rich color; light, nutty flavor; and delicate texture that whole-grain flours add to cookies and other baked goods. But if you'd rather keep things traditional, we won't hold it against you either.

And who can resist the charm of a plateful of bar cookies? This chapter also includes our famous fudgy wudgy blueberry brownies, which is surely the taste combination to usher us into the next decade. We've also finally created the perfect lemon bar that shines like a citrus-colored jewel. Meanwhile, apple lovers and peanut butter lovers can finally come to an agreement and end their thousand years' war once and for all, with our apple bars topped with peanut butter caramel.

## tip

### COOKIE TIPS

➤ Cooling racks are great for perfectly textured cookies; this way they won't brown too much on the bottom. But if, for whatever reason, you refuse to get cooling racks, you can turn the cookies upside down on a plate to cool completely.

➤ Store completely cooled cookies in a tightly covered container and they should last for 3 to 5 days.

➤ Silpat is a silicone baking surface that you can place over your cookie sheet, making greasing the sheet or baking parchment obsolete.

➤ When we direct you to lightly grease the cookie sheet, you can spread a very thin layer of shortening on it or spray with a light coating of cooking spray.

## PISTACHIO-ROSE WATER COOKIES

MAKES 32 COOKIES

45

TIME: 35 MINUTES

*Pretty as a picture, these delectable disks are studded with jadelike pistachio nuts and are delicately scented with rose water. These cookies are a miracle of science, really; delicately flavored and somehow light and airy, chewy and crispy all at once. Lime juice and zest add a little citrus kick. A perfect end to your Persian feast, or even just some Middle Eastern takeout.*

1¼ cups sugar

½ cup canola oil

3 tablespoons rice milk (soy is okay, too)

1 tablespoon rose water

2 teaspoons pure vanilla extract

1 tablespoon fresh lime juice

1 teaspoon finely grated lime zest

¼ cup cornstarch

1¾ cups all-purpose flour

1 teaspoon baking powder

½ teaspoon salt

¼ teaspoon ground cardamom

½ cup shelled pistachios, coarsely chopped

## tip

➤ The easiest way to chop pistachios is to pulse them in a food processor about twenty times. Otherwise, use a chef's knife on a cutting board and be gentle so that they don't shoot all over the place.

➤ If you are aching to try these cookies but can't afford pistachios at the moment, replace them with chopped almonds.

PREHEAT THE oven to 350°F. Lightly grease two cookie sheets.

In a mixing bowl, whisk together the sugar, oil, rice milk, rose water, vanilla, lime juice, and zest. Add the cornstarch and whisk until dissolved.

Add the flour, baking powder, salt, and cardamom. Mix well.

Roll the dough into balls about 2 teaspoons in size (a bit smaller than a walnut) and dip the tops into the chopped pistachios. Press down with two fingers; the dough will flatten a bit and pistachios will collect on the bottom.

Place the cookies, nut side up, about 2 inches apart on the baking sheets. You should be able to fit sixteen on a standard baking sheet. Bake for 13 minutes; they will be soft but that's okay, they will firm up as they cool.

Remove from the oven and let cool on the cookie sheets for about 5 minutes. Transfer to a cooling rack to cool completely.

## CHEWY CHOCOLATE-RASPBERRY COOKIES

MAKES 2 DOZEN

TIME: 35 MINUTES

*It's official—everyone loves the combination of chocolate and raspberry. These cookies are soft, dense, chewy, and just a little puffy. They're wonderful as ice-cream sandwich cookies.*

½ cup raspberry preserves

1 cup sugar

⅓ cup canola oil

1 teaspoon pure vanilla extract

1 teaspoon almond extract

½ cup plus 2 tablespoons unsweetened cocoa powder (sifted if clumpy)

1½ cups all-purpose flour

¾ teaspoon baking soda

¼ teaspoon salt

PREHEAT THE oven to 350°F. Lightly grease cookie sheet.

In a large mixing bowl, stir together the raspberry preserves, sugar, canola oil, vanilla, and almond extract.

In a separate mixing bowl, sift together the other ingredients. Add the dry to the wet in three batches, mixing well with a fork after each addition. When you get to the last batch, you may need to use your hands to work the batter into a soft and pliable dough.

Roll the dough into walnut-size balls and then flatten them with your hands into 2½-inch-diameter disks. Place on a cookie sheet (they need be only ½ inch apart because they don't spread out when baking). Bake for 10 minutes.

Remove from the oven and let cool for 5 minutes. Transfer to a cooling rack to cool completely. You can also serve these cookies still warm over a scoop of ice cream. Or three.

## FIG SMUSHED-ANISE-ALMOND COOKIES

MAKES 24 COOKIES

TIME: 40 MINUTES

*You could call these Koala Noses because that's what they look like. Using demerara sugar adds a slight brown-sugar taste and a little crunch because the crystals are bigger than normal sugar, but you can use turbinado sugar (as available in supermarkets as Sugar in the Raw) or even regular old granulated if that's what you have; just cut back on it by two tablespoons or so. These cookies are crispy outside, chewy inside, and the anise pairs beautifully with the fruity figs. Plus, they will have your kitchen smelling like an Italian bakery.*

¼ cup soy milk

2 teaspoons ground flaxseed, or 1½ teaspoons whole flaxseeds

1¼ cups demerara sugar

⅔ cup canola oil

1 teaspoon pure vanilla extract

2 cups all-purpose flour

½ teaspoon anise extract

1 teaspoon baking powder

½ teaspoon salt

½ cup finely chopped almonds (start with slivers or sliced to make your life easier)

12 dried black mission figs, rough stem removed, cut in half lengthwise

PREHEAT THE oven to 350°F. Lightly grease two baking sheets.

If using preground flaxseeds, place in a mixing bowl and beat vigorously with the soy milk. If using whole flaxseeds, grind them up in a blender and then add the soy milk. Blend until frothy. Add to the mixing bowl and proceed with the recipe.

Add the sugar and oil to the mixing bowl and beat until emulsified. Mix in the vanilla.

Add about 1 cup of the flour along with the baking powder and salt. Mix well. Add the remaining flour and mix. Fold in the chopped almonds. At this point a hand blender might not work, so use a wooden spoon or your hands.

Loosely roll the dough into golf ball–size balls, then flatten them with your hands into 2-inch-diameter cookies. Place on a cookie sheet and gently but firmly smush a fig half, cut side down, into the center of each cookie.

Bake for 12 to 14 minutes. The fig should be soft and the cookies should be golden brown on the bottom. The tops don't brown much.

Remove from the oven and let sit on the sheets for about 5 minutes, then transfer to a cooling rack to cool completely.

## TERRY'S FAVORITE ALMOND COOKIE

MAKES 24 COOKIES

**TIME:** 35 MINUTES

*Terry says, "Calling this cookie 'my favorite' makes it sound like I've been searching far and wide for the ultimate almond cookie. Which is sort of true; almonds usually find their way into my favorite desserts and snacks. These crisp cookies are inspired by the kind one might find in their local Chinatown; flat, crunchy, with a distinctive almond aroma but without the obvious texture of chopped almonds. They rely on the subtle presence of almond meal and almond extract to give them that special flavor."*

**tip**

➤ This recipe makes large cookies (good for sandwiches). Make smaller cookies by using just 1 tablespoon of dough per cookie and reducing the baking time by 2 minutes.

2¼ cups all-purpose flour

½ cup almond meal or ground almonds

1¼ teaspoons baking soda

½ teaspoon salt

½ cup canola or peanut oil, or a mixture of the two

¼ cup brown rice syrup

¼ cup rice or soy milk

1 cup granulated sugar

1½ teaspoons almond extract

½ teaspoon vanilla extract

1 teaspoon toasted sesame oil

⅓ cup sliced, blanched almonds

PREHEAT THE oven to 350°F. Grease two large cookie sheets.

Sift together the flour, almond meal, baking soda, and salt, and set aside. In a large bowl, beat together the oil, brown rice syrup, rice milk, sugar, extracts, and sesame oil. Add the flour mixture and mix until a firm dough forms.

Roll the dough into balls, using about 2 tablespoons of dough apiece. Press one side of each ball into the sliced almonds and place at least 2 inches apart, almond side up, on a cookie sheet. Flatten each ball to about an inch thick (a flat-bottomed 1-cup measuring cup works great for this). Bake for 12 to 15 minutes, until slightly golden brown on edges.

Allow to cool for at least 10 minutes before removing from the sheets; the cookies will be very soft when first out of the oven but will firm up while cooling. Let cool on the cookie sheets for 5 minutes and then transfer to a cooling rack to cool completely.

## CHOCOLATE-CHOCOLATE CHIP-WALNUT COOKIES

MAKES 36 COOKIES

**TIME:** 30 MINUTES

*Deep, dark, chocolaty and nutty, this is a perfect (soy)milk and cookies cookie for chocolate lovers. The recipe is incredibly versatile, so check out some of the variations.*

➤ If you don't have flaxseeds, you can leave them out of the recipe. The cookies will be a bit less chewy but still yummy!

**2 cups all-purpose flour**
**⅔ cup unsweetened Dutch-processed cocoa powder**
**1 teaspoon baking soda**

**½ teaspoon salt**
**⅔ cup canola oil**
**1½ cups sugar**
**4 teaspoons ground flaxseeds**
**½ cup soy milk**
**2 teaspoons pure vanilla extract**
**½ teaspoon almond extract**
**¾ cup vegan chocolate chips**
**¾ cup walnuts, chopped small**

PREHEAT THE oven to 350°F.

In a large bowl, sift together the flour, cocoa, baking soda, and salt.

In a separate large bowl, mix together the oil and sugar. Add the flaxseeds, soy milk, and vanilla, and mix well.

Fold in the dry ingredients in batches. When the batter starts to get too stiff to mix with a fork, use your hands until a nice stiff dough forms. Add the chocolate chips and walnuts, and mix with your hands again. Your hands will get covered in chocolate, but worse things have happened.

Wash your hands and line two baking sheets with baking parchment. Roll the dough into 1-inch balls and flatten into disks about 1½ inches in diameter. Place about an inch apart on the lined cookie sheets.

Bake for 10 minutes. Remove from the oven and let cool for about 5 minutes, then transfer to a wire rack to cool completely.

*Variations:*

You can do so much with these!

**White Chocolate Chip–Cherry–Chocolate Cookies:** Replace the chocolate chips with white chocolate chips and replace the walnuts with dried cherries.

**Orange–Chocolate–Chocolate Chip Cookies:**

Omit the walnuts. Add 3 teaspoons of finely grated orange zest to the liquid ingredients.

Chocolate-Hazelnut Cookies: Omit the chocolate chips. Replace ¼ cup of the soy milk with hazelnut liqueur. Replace the walnuts with chopped, toasted hazelnuts.

## WHEAT-FREE CHOCOLATE CHIP COOKIES

MAKES 18 COOKIES

TIME: 45 MINUTES

*These cookies couldn't be any easier to make, unless you had someone else make them for you. Oat flour makes a dense and crumbly style of cookie that is perfect for all cookie monsters, not just those avoiding wheat. Note: Although oats do not contain gluten, some people with wheat allergies still avoid them. If you're making these for a celiac friend, ask if they eat oats first.*

**tip**

➤ Oat flour is available in many supermarkets, but if you can't find it or don't think you'll be using it much, you can make your own by whizzing rolled oats in a blender or food processor until it resembles flour.

1¾ cups oat flour
½ teaspoon baking soda
¼ teaspoon salt
¼ cup brown sugar
½ cup granulated sugar
⅓ cup canola oil
1 tablespoon ground flaxseeds
¼ cup soy milk
1 teaspoon vanilla
¾ cup chocolate chips

PREHEAT THE oven to 375°F.

Sift together the oat flour, baking soda, and salt.

In a small mixing bowl, whisk together the flaxseeds and soy milk. Add the brown and granulated sugars and stir, add the oil and vanilla, and whisk vigorously until all ingredients are emulsified (about a minute).

Mix the wet ingredients into the dry; fold in the chocolate chips.

Drop the batter by the tablespoon onto an ungreased baking sheet, leaving 1½ inches of space between the cookies. Bake for 10 to 12 minutes.

Remove from the oven and let cool for 5 minutes. Transfer to a cooling rack to cool the rest of the way.

## PEANUT-GINGER-SESAME COOKIES

MAKES 42 COOKIES

TIME: 35 MINUTES

*This chewy, shortbreadlike cookie is the perfect, light finale to any Asian meal. Or just great paired with a dark and smoky black or oolong tea. The peanut butter flavor in these dense little morsels is subtle, while chunks of candied ginger and a coating of crunchy sesame seeds make a big, bold statement.*

2¼ cups flour, either all-purpose, whole wheat pastry, white whole wheat, or a combination of these

½ teaspoon baking powder

½ teaspoon baking soda

½ teaspoon salt

½ teaspoon ground ginger

¼ teaspoon ground cinnamon

½ cup nonhydrogenated vegan shortening, softened

½ cup chunky peanut butter

¼ cup brown rice syrup

1¼ cups sugar, plus additional sugar for rolling

½ cup soy milk

1 teaspoon vanilla extract

½ teaspoon almond extract

5 ounces candied ginger, diced finely

⅓ cup each white sesame seeds and black sesame seeds, or ⅔ cup of just one kind

PREHEAT THE oven to 350°F and lightly grease two cookie sheets.

Sift together the flour, baking powder, soda, salt, ground ginger, and cinnamon, and set aside.

In a large bowl, use electric beaters to cream the shortening until light and fluffy, about 3 minutes. Add the peanut butter, rice syrup, sugar, soy milk, and extracts, and continue to beat until creamy, 4 to 5 minutes. Using a rubber spatula or wooden spoon, stir in the flour mixture, then add chopped candied ginger and stir until a very firm dough forms. You can use your hands toward the end to mix the dough.

Roll scant tablespoons of the dough into walnut-size balls. Roll each ball in either white or black sesame seeds (or a little of both), then roll in a little sugar and place on a prepared cookie sheet, leaving about 1½ inches of space between each cookie.

Flatten the balls just slightly (optional) and bake for 10 to 11 minutes for chewy cookies, up to 14 minutes for firmer, crunchier cookies.

Remove from the oven and allow the cookies to remain on the baking sheets for a few minutes before transferring to wire racks to cool.

## RUMNOG PECAN COOKIES

MAKES 24 COOKIES

TIME: 45 MINUTES

*This grown-up holiday cookie spiked with rum and nutmeg still retains a sense of good old-fashioned fun, with its topping of lots of frosting and sprinkles. Before baking, the dough is rolled in crunchy pecans, and after cooling they're topped with creamy, rum-infused icing. The flavor improves after a few hours and the icing firms up, making them ideal for gift giving.*

Cookies:

⅓ cup canola oil

¼ cup soy or rice milk

1 cup plus 2 tablespoons granulated sugar

1 tablespoon molasses

2 tablespoons dark rum

1½ teaspoons vanilla extract

1½ cups all-purpose flour

¼ cup cornstarch

1½ teaspoons baking powder

¼ teaspoon baking soda

½ teaspoon grated nutmeg

½ teaspoon ground cinnamon

½ teaspoon salt

1½ cups coarsely chopped pecans

Frosting:

2 tablespoons nonhydrogenated vegan margarine,
softened

2 tablespoons soy milk, soy creamer, or rice milk

2 tablespoons dark rum

¼ teaspoon vanilla extract

2 cups confectioners' sugar

Optional decoration:

Freshly grated nutmeg

Colored sugar sprinkles

PREHEAT THE oven to 350°F and lightly grease two baking sheets.

*Prepare the cookies:*

In a large bowl, combine the oil, soy milk, granulated sugar, molasses, rum, and vanilla, and beat until slightly foamy. Sift in the flour, cornstarch, baking powder, baking soda, nutmeg, cinnamon, and salt, and mix until a soft dough forms.

Roll the dough into walnut-size balls (about 1 heaping tablespoon), roll in the chopped pecans, and place about 2 inches apart on the baking sheets. Bake for 10 to 12 minutes, until the cookies have puffed.

Remove from the oven and allow to cool on the baking sheets for 5 minutes before transferring to a wire rack.

*Prepare the frosting:*

Use electric beaters to cream the margarine until light and creamy. Add the confectioners' sugar and stir with a fork until crumbs form, then beat in the soy milk, rum, and vanilla. The frosting should have a consistency similar to that of buttercream frosting. If it's too thin, beat in more confectioners' sugar, 1 tablespoon at a time, until the desired consistency is reached. Spread 1 teaspoon or more frosting on each cooled cookie. Sprinkle with nutmeg and colored sugar, if desired, while the frosting is still moist.

These are best when allowed to sit for a few hours so that frosting becomes firm.

## CHEWY OATMEAL-RAISIN COOKIES

MAKES 30 COOKIES

**COOKING TIME:** 30 MINUTES

*Terry loves the chewy texture these cookies deliver from their caramellike brown rice syrup, nutty whole-grain flours, and plenty of raisins. This recipe is as basic as a pair of jeans and, we suppose, could be doctored with a handful of chocolate chips or shredded coconut, but why mess with perfection? These cookies are equally at home packed into lunchboxes or served with cold soy milk or a steaming cup of tea or hot apple cider.*

½ cup canola or safflower oil

⅓ cup brown rice syrup

⅓ cup rice or soy milk

¾ cup light brown sugar

1 teaspoon vanilla extract

2⅓ cups whole wheat pastry flour or all-purpose flour

¾ teaspoon baking soda

½ teaspoon baking powder

2 teaspoons ground cinnamon

½ teaspoon ground nutmeg

½ teaspoon allspice

½ teaspoon salt

2 cups rolled or instant oats

1½ cups Thompson raisins

PREHEAT THE oven to 350°F and lightly grease two baking sheets.

➤ If you have any issues with cookies' sticking to the baking sheets, line sheets with either baking parchment or Silpats.

In a large bowl, combine the oil, brown rice syrup, soy milk, brown sugar, and vanilla, and beat until smooth. Sift in the flour, baking powder, baking soda, cinnamon, nutmeg, allspice, and salt, and combine to beat just until a dough begins to form. Fold in the oats and raisins.

Roll the dough into walnut-size balls (about 1 heaping tablespoon) and place about 2 inches apart on the baking sheets. Press the cookies down lightly with your fingers or the bottoms of a glass dipped in water (to prevent sticking). Bake for 10 to 12 minutes, until the cookies have spread and are lightly browned.

Remove from the oven and allow to cool on their baking sheets for about 2 minutes before transferring to a wire rack. Cool the cookies completely before storing in a tightly covered container.

## ALMOND-ANISE BISCOTTI

MAKE 18 COOKIES
TIME: ABOUT AN HOUR

*This is the classic twice-baked Italian cookie—not overly sweet, bursting with toasted almonds or chocolate or spices, with a definite cookie crunch. These biscotti are ideal treats for midafternoon snacks or packing into lunch boxes, especially lunch boxes for grown ups. And of course, these hold up perfectly when dipped into tea or a soy latte. Try some of the variations as well, such as the Orange-Chocolate Chip and Cranberry-Pistachio.*

⅓ cup almond or soy milk
2 tablespoons ground flaxseeds
¾ cup sugar

½ cup canola oil
½ teaspoon vanilla extract
½ teaspoon almond extract
1⅔ cups all-purpose flour or whole wheat pastry flour
2 tablespoons arrowroot powder
2 teaspoons baking powder
2 teaspoons aniseeds
½ teaspoon salt
1 cup whole, raw almonds

➤ It's not necessary to flip these biscotti during the baking. However, if you feel confident in your biscotti-making ability and want really crisp, firm cookies, try flipping them once during the middle of the second baking. Our fingers are made of asbestos so we use those, but most normal people just use a small spatula.

PREHEAT THE oven to 350°F. Lightly grease a large cookie sheet.

In a large bowl, whisk together the almond milk and flaxseeds for about 30 seconds. Add the sugar, oil, and extracts, and mix until smooth. Sift in the flour, arrowroot, baking powder, aniseeds, and salt.

Stir to mix all the ingredients and, just as a firm dough starts to form, knead in almonds. Knead the dough only briefly. Some of the almonds might pop out; just push them back in.

On the baking sheet, form the dough into a rectangle about 12 inches long and 3 to 4 inches wide. Bake for 28 minutes until lightly puffed; the top may also be slightly crackled, which is okay.

Remove from the oven and allow to cool for 30 minutes, until very firm.

Turn up the oven heat to 375°F. Carefully transfer the baked dough to a cutting board. With a heavy, very sharp knife, slice the dough into ½-inch-thick slices.

The best way to do this is in one motion, pushing down; don't saw the slices off (or use a serrated knife) or the slices could crumble. Be gentle when handling the biscotti at this time, as they are delicate.

Set the slices on the cookie sheet on their cut sides, and bake for 12 to 15 minutes, until your desired level of brownness and crispness is achieved.

Cool for a few minutes on the baking sheet before transferring the slices to a cooling rack. When completely cool, store in an airtight container.

## Variations:

**Orange-Chocolate Chip:** Substitute fresh orange juice for the almond milk. Omit aniseed and almond extract, and increase the vanilla to 1 teaspoon. Omit the almonds and add 2 tablespoons of packed, grated orange zest and ½ cup of vegan chocolate chips.

**Cranberry-Pistachio:** Omit the aniseeds and almonds. Add ½ cup each dried cranberries and shelled green pistachios

**Hazelnut:** Omit the almonds and use hazelnuts.

## CHOCOLATE-HAZELNUT BISCOTTI

MAKE 18 COOKIES
**TIME:** ABOUT AN HOUR

*These are mouth-watering, dark chocolate biscotti chock full of crunchy hazelnuts. Make a double batch of these because they're sure to disappear fast.*

⅓ cup almond or soy milk
2 tablespoons ground flaxseeds
¾ cup plus 2 tablespoons sugar
½ cup canola oil
½ teaspoon vanilla extract
½ teaspoon almond extract
1½ cups all-purpose flour or whole wheat pastry flour

⅓ cup unsweetened Dutch-processed cocoa powder or regular unsweetened cocoa powder
2 tablespoons arrowroot powder or cornstarch
2 teaspoons baking powder
½ teaspoon salt
1 cup whole, raw hazelnuts

PREHEAT THE oven to 350°F. Lightly grease a large cookie sheet.

In a large bowl, whisk together almond milk and flaxseeds, mixing for about 30 seconds. Add the sugar, oil, and extracts, and stir until smooth. Sift in the flour, cocoa powder, arrowroot, baking powder, and salt. Stir to mix and, just as the dough starts to come together, knead in hazelnuts. Knead very briefly to form a stiff dough; if some of the nuts pop out, just push them back in.

On the baking sheet, form the dough into a rectangle about 12 inches long and 3 to 4 inches wide. Bake for 28 minutes, until lightly puffed; the top may also be slightly crackled.

Remove from the oven, allow to cool for 30 minutes, until very firm.

Turn up the oven heat to 375°F. Carefully transfer the baked dough to a cutting board. With a heavy, very sharp knife (or use a serrated knife), slice ½-inch-thick slices. The best way to do this is in one pushing-down motion; don't saw the slices off or the slices could crumble. Be gentle when handling the biscotti at this time, as they are delicate.

Set the slices on the cookie sheet cut side down and bake for 12 to 15 minutes until your desired level of brownness and crispness is achieved.

Remove from the oven and cool for a few minutes on the baking sheet before transferring the slices to a cooling rack. When completely cool, store in an airtight container.

## Variation:

**Chocolate-Hazelnut-Espresso:** Whisk 1 tablespoon of instant espresso powder into the liquid ingredients before adding the dry ingredients.

## APPLE-PEANUT BUTTER-CARAMEL BARS

MAKES 12 BARS

TIME: 1 HOUR 15 MINUTES, PLUS COOLING TIME

*These bars were created one autumn night when we were sitting around with our friend Paula, thinking about apples and peanut butter. Everyone loves peanut butter on apples, so why aren't there any treats dedicated to this combination? Could all the world's problems be solved if only we would take hold of our innermost desires? To the kitchen we went. The result is this bar; an apple pie filling inside a graham cracker crust, with a crumb topping and ribbons of luscious peanut butter caramel.*

> **tip**
>
> ➤ If you can't find vegan graham crackers, vegan vanilla cookies make a good substitution.

### Crust:

**3 cups graham cracker crumbs**

**⅓ cup canola oil or 5⅓ tablespoons nonhydrogenated vegan margarine, melted and cooled**

**3 tablespoons plain soy milk**

**1 teaspoon vanilla extract**

### Crumb topping:

**½ cup all-purpose flour**

**3 tablespoons sugar**

**2–3 tablespoons canola oil**

**Pinch each of ground cinnamon, ginger, and allspice**

### Apple filling:

**3 pounds Granny Smith apples (about 6), cored and sliced thinly (peeling is optional)**

**1 tablespoon canola oil**

**⅓ cup sugar**

**3 tablespoons all-purpose flour**

**1 tablespoon water**

**Pinch each of ground cinnamon, ginger, and allspice**

### Peanut butter caramel:

**⅔ cup chunky peanut butter (the no-stir kind, not the kind that separates)**

**¼ cup pure maple syrup**

**3 tablespoons brown rice syrup**

PREHEAT THE oven to 350°F. Grease a 9 × 13-inch baking pan.

### *Prepare the crust:*

Place the graham cracker crumbs in a mixing bowl. Drizzle with the oil and mix until moistened. Add the soy milk and mix with your fingers; the crumbs should hold together if pinched. Press the crumbs firmly into the prepared baking pan to form a crust.

### *Prepare the topping:*

Place the flour, sugar, and spices in a mixing bowl. Drizzle 2 tablespoons of oil into the flour and mix with your fingertips until crumbs start to form. Keep tossing the mixture with your fingers; you want the crumbs to be fairly large for crumbs. Add more oil if necessary.

### *Prepare the apple filling:*

Combine all the ingredients in a bowl, coating all the apples.

Layer the apples onto the crust and sprinkle with the crumb topping. The topping won't solidly cover the entire pan; just sprinkle it randomly over the top so that the apples are peeking through in places.

Bake for 40 to 45 minutes, until the apples are tender.

When the bars are almost done baking (at the 35-minute point), start preparing the peanut butter caramel: Mix all the ingredients very well with a fork, in a small saucepan. Heat over medium heat for about 3 minutes. The mixture should soften and slide off the fork in ribbons.

When the bars are done baking, drizzle the caramel in ribbons all over the top. Let cool completely before serving; you can place the pan in the fridge to hasten the cooling process. Slice into bars and serve.

## FUDGY WUDGY BLUEBERRY BROWNIES

MAKES 16 BROWNIES
**TIME:** 50 MINUTES

*These brownies are ridiculously fudgy. They better be, they're called fudgy wudgies. They have triple chocolate power—in the form of melted chocolate, cocoa powder, and then chocolate chips. And they have double blueberry power—in the form of blueberry spreadable fruit and plump, fresh blueberries, adding a tangy contrast to each sweet bite. The blueberry-chocolate combo is not the most popular one, but it should be! For a variation, try raspberry-chocolate by replacing the blueberry ingredients with raspberry ones.*

**tip**

➤ The highest-quality vegan chocolate chips will produce the highest-quality brownie. The only ingredients should be chocolate liqueur, sugar, cocoa butter, vanilla, and possibly lecithin. Avoid chips with high-fructose corn syrup as an ingredient.

➤ Since the consistency of spreadable fruit varies from brand to brand, we used the kind that had no whole blueberries visible. If yours looks like it does have whole fruit, no worries! Just pulse it in a blender a few times until smooth. You can add the recipe's measure of soy milk to it, if necessary, to make the blending easier.

**⅔ cup plus ½ cup semisweet chocolate chips**
**10 ounces blueberry spreadable fruit**
**¼ cup soy milk**
**¾ cup sugar**
**½ cup canola oil**
**2 teaspoons pure vanilla extract**
**½ teaspoon almond extract**
**1½ cups all-purpose flour**
**¼ cup unsweetened cocoa powder**
**¼ teaspoon baking powder**
**½ teaspoon baking soda**
**¼ teaspoon salt**
**1 cup fresh blueberries**

PREHEAT THE oven to 325°F. Grease a 9 × 13-inch baking pan.

Melt the ⅔ cup of chocolate chips, reserving the other ½ cup as whole chips. To melt, create your own double boiler: Heat a small pan of water over high heat until boiling. Place another small pan on top of that and place the chips in that one. Use a rubber spatula to stir until melted. Remove from the heat and let cool just a bit while you prepare everything else. Or, if you want to melt the chips in a microwave instead, place them in a microwave-safe bowl (obviously) on high heat for 1 minute. Stir the partially melted chips and microwave again for another 30 seconds.

In a large mixing bowl, combine the blueberry spreadable fruit, soy milk, sugar, canola oil, and extracts. Mix on high speed (if using an electric hand mixer) until no large clumps of the spreadable fruit are visible. This could take 2 to 3 minutes.

Sift in the flour, cocoa powder, baking powder, baking soda, and salt. Stir until well mixed; we use a fork here because the batter is very thick and can clump up in a whisk or mixer. Mix in the melted chocolate as well.

Fold in the remaining ½ cup of chocolate chips and the fresh blueberries. Spread the batter in the baking pan (don't worry if it doesn't come to the very corners of the pan because the batter will spread while baking and it will all work out).

Bake for 45 minutes. You can't really do a toothpick test here because the chocolate chips will make the pick look wet and the top will appear soft and crinkly and not done when, we promise you, it is done.

Remove from the oven and let cool. Slice into sixteen squares (or whatever size you want). If you want to serve it warm, wait about 30 minutes, so it is still warm but not hot. For true decadence, serve with vanilla ice cream (page 260) and a little bit of blueberry syrup, plus some fresh blueberries for good measure.

## LEMON BARS

MAKES 12 BARS
**TIME:** 4 HOURS (MOST OF THAT FOR CHILLING)

*Bet you thought you'd never have a lemon bar again in the land of vegan culinaria. Well, turn that frown upside down—café-style lemon bars are here! Lots and lots of tangy, creamy, jelled lemon topping blankets a shortbread crust. And with a sprinkling of confectioners' sugar, these are as pretty as can be.*

Crust:

1¾ cups all-purpose flour
⅔ cup confectioners' sugar, plus additional to decorate the finished bars
¼ cup cornstarch
1 cup nonhydrogenated vegan margarine

Filling:

1⅓ cups water
3 tablespoons agar flakes
1¼ cups granulated sugar
⅛ teaspoon turmeric
⅔ cup fresh lemon juice
3 tablespoons arrowroot powder

1 tablespoon finely grated lemon zest (from 2 large lemons)
¼ cup soy milk

LIGHTLY GREASE a 9 × 13-inch baking pan.

*Prepare the crust:*

Pulse the flour, confectioners' sugar, and cornstarch in a food processor. Add the margarine in spoonfuls and blend 8 to 10 seconds, and then pulse until the mixture resembles coarse meal. Sprinkle the mixture into the prepared baking pan and press firmly into an even layer with slightly raised sides, so that it can hold in the filling. Refrigerate for about 30 minutes and preheat the oven to 350°F. Bake the unfilled crust for 25 minutes. remove from the oven, and let cool.

*Meanwhile, prepare the filling:*

In a saucepot, soak the agar in the water for 15 minutes. Use the time while it soaks to zest your lemons and squeeze your lemon juice. Mix the arrowroot into the lemon juice to dissolve.

When the agar has been soaked for 15 minutes, turn on the heat and bring the mixture to a boil. Boil for about 10 minutes, or until the agar is completely dissolved. Add the granulated sugar and turmeric, and boil until they have dissolved, about 3 minutes. Turn down the heat to medium and add the arrow root mixture, then add the lemon zest and soy milk. Whisk constantly until the mixture thickens, about 5 minutes. It should not be rapidly boiling, but low bubbling is okay.

Pour the mixture into the prepared crust. Let cool for 20 minutes and then refrigerate for at least 3 hours, until the filling is only slightly jiggly and has set. Use a sifter or a fine-mesh strainer for sprinkle the bars with confectioners' sugar. Slice into squares and serve.

# DESSERTS

DESSERTS ARE USUALLY listed at the end of a cookbook but we suspect that you've snuck a peek and this is the first thing you are seeing. So, hi! Welcome to our cookbook! We talk a lot about how wonderful broccoli is but, at the end of the day, we know what really wins people over is a chocolate pie smothered in caramel and pecans.

Coming down from a sugar high from our last cookbook, *Vegan Cupcakes Take Over the World*, we really needed to take a break from cake batter and instead set our sights on luscious desserts featuring nature's bounty of fruits. Good old-fashioned crisps become interesting again when spiked with aniseed, and juicy pears are poached in tea and, because we couldn't resist, placed in a pool of chocolate sauce.

Of course, we also couldn't resist adding a few cupcakes into the mix.

## TEA-POACHED PEARS
## IN CHOCOLATE SAUCE

SERVES 4

TIME: LESS THAN AN HOUR, PLUS CHILL TIME

*This dessert may seem like it should be served by your butler, but give him the day off and make it yourself— it's incredibly easy. Pear halves are poached in strong black tea and then the tea is used to make a soupy pool of chocolate sauce for the pears. A little orange peel gives these a subtle citrus kick. It's an especially good dessert after an Italian meal.*

**tip**

➤ To easily core the pears, slice them in half and use a melon baller or a round measuring spoon to scoop out the seeds in one fell swoop.

3 cups water

4 tea bags black tea

¼ cup sugar

4 firm Bosc pears, peeled, sliced in half lengthwise, and cored

Zest from ½ navel orange

1 teaspoon pure vanilla extract

8 ounces bitter or semisweet vegan chocolate, chopped (½ cup or so)

Vanilla ice cream (page 260) (optional)

Mint sprigs for prettiness (optional)

BOIL THE water in a medium-size saucepan. Once the water is boiling, turn off the heat, add the tea bags and sugar, and steep for 15 minutes. Remove the tea bags and stir to make sure the sugar is dissolved.

Bring the tea to a boil and add the pears, orange peel, and vanilla. Turn down the heat to simmer and

cover. Let simmer; remove the orange peel after about 15 minutes because it can get bitter. Simmer for another 20 minutes until the pears are tender.

Transfer the pears and liquid to a large bowl to cool. Remove a cup of the liquid from the bowl and place it back in the pot. Bring it to a simmer, then turn off the heat and add the chocolate. Whisk until completely dissolved. Let the sauce cool for the same amount of time as the pears, about an hour altogether. It tastes really good at room temperature.

*To assemble:*

Ladle a good amount of the chocolate sauce, about half a cup, into small dessert bowl. Place one pear, cored side down, in the sauce, and another, cored, side down, perpendicular to it and overlapping. If desired, place a scoop of vegan ice cream on one side and garnish with a sprig of mint.

## STRAWBERRY-ROSE WATER COBBLER
## WITH LEMON-POPPY SEED PASTRY

SERVES 6 TO 8

TIME: 50 MINUTES

*For this dessert, juicy strawberries are made even more fragrant with a little rose water. The lemon-scented crust isn't plopped on as it is on most cobblers; here it's placed in lattice strips, to add a little down-home sophistication. It's so pretty and cheery that if you aren't already donning a '50s-style apron, you'll feel as if you should be.*

**tip**

➤ If you don't want to braid your lattice, just place some strips one way and others overlapping them the other way. Still cute!

## How to Make a Lattice Crust

GENTLY lay four strips of dough in parallel across the cobbler with some space between them. Then lift the second strip and lay a new strip perpendicularly across underneath it. Lift the fourth strip and tuck your cross strip under that one, too. So now you have a kind of weave. Repeat with the next strip, this time lifting the first and third original strips. When all the strips are used, tuck in the edges around the strawberries.

### Filling:

3 pounds strawberries, hulled and cut into quarters
½ cup sugar
2 tablespoons tapioca flour
1 tablespoon water
2 tablespoons rose water

### Pastry:

½ cup soy milk
1 tablespoon lemon juice
1 tablespoon lemon zest
1 teaspoon vanilla extract
1 cup all-purpose flour
3 tablespoons sugar
2 teaspoons poppy seeds
1½ teaspoons baking powder
Generous pinch of salt
¼ cup canola oil

PREHEAT THE oven to 375°F. Have ready an 8-inch square baking dish or pan.

Mix together all the filling ingredients in a large mixing bowl. Stir to coat the strawberries and set aside.

*Prepare the lattice pastry:*

In a measuring cup, combine the soy milk, lemon juice, zest, and vanilla. In a separate bowl, stir together the flour, 2 tablespoons of the sugar, and the poppy seeds, baking powder, and salt. Sift together with a fork. Drizzle the canola oil into the flour mixture and stir with a fork until the mixture is crumbly. Add the soy milk mixture and mix with a wooden spoon just until the dough holds together.

Flour a flat work surface and your hands. Give the dough a quick knead in the bowl (like five times or so) and then turn it onto the work surface. If it feels very sticky, add a bit more flour. Gently flatten the dough into roughly the size of the baking dish you are using. With a floured pizza cutter or a knife, create seven or eight strips of dough, each about an inch or so wide.

Give the strawberry mixture another stir, and transfer to the baking dish.

Now make a lattice on top of the cobbler. You don't know how to make a lattice? See the sidebar.

Sprinkle the top with the remaining tablespoon of sugar and bake for 35 minutes, until the cobbler is bubbly and the dough is slightly browned.

Remove from the oven and let cool a bit before serving. You'll need to cut the cobbler with a serving spoon to get all the juices. For optimum presentation, serve each slice into a bowl, then lift the crust to preserve the lattice and spoon more strawberries and juice into the bowl. Don't forget the vegan ice cream!

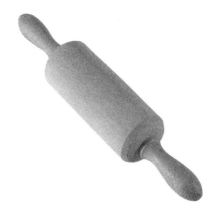

## BERRY-COCONUT CRISP

SERVES 4

TIME: LESS THAN AN HOUR

*This warm, fruity dessert topped with a crumbly coconut topping could be easily summarized by that popular bumper sticker "Berries ♥ Coconut." Never saw that one? Oh well, at least here's a recipe that's way more fun than reading bumper stickers. Quick to make and not too sweet, this crisp is also gluten free, to boot. If you don't want to make it gluten free, go ahead and substitute ¾ cup of flour for the quinoa and rice flours. We used blueberries and raspberries but you can use whatever kind of berries you have on hand.*

Topping:

    ½ cup quinoa flour

    ¼ cup white rice flour

    ¾ cup shredded unsweetened coconut

    ¼ cup sugar

    ½ teaspoon ground nutmeg

    5 tablespoons cold, nonhydrogenated vegan
        margarine

Filling:

    2 cups frozen blueberries, partially thawed

    2 cups frozen raspberries, partially thawed

    1 tablespoon tapioca flour

    1 tablespoon cold water

    ¼ cup sugar

    ½ teaspoon coconut extract

    ½ teaspoon pure vanilla extract

PREHEAT THE oven to 350°F.

*Prepare the topping:*

Mix together the flours, coconut, sugar and nutmeg. Add the margarine in small pieces and use a pastry knife to cut the butter into the flours until coarse crumbs form. Set aside.

*Prepare the filling:*

Place the berries, tapioca, and cold water in an 8-inch square baking dish. Mix together to dissolve the tapioca. Add the sugar and extracts; mix to combine. Sprinkle the topping over the berries. Bake for 45 minutes; the filling should be bubbly and yummy looking.

Remove from the oven and let cool for about 10 minutes. Serve in bowls with scoops of vegan vanilla ice cream.

## STRAWBERRY-PLUM CRISP

SERVES 6

TIME: ABOUT AN HOUR

*Who ever thought that strawberries and plums could be such good buddies in this heavenly crisp? Tart, sweet, juicy plums are the star here, with a few strawberries in a supporting role. The oat topping is spiked with licorice-y aniseeds. A scoop of Vanilla Ice Cream (page 260) on top would be pretty awesome right about now, wouldn't it? Serve on a summer's night when plums and strawberries are in abundance.*

Filling:

    2 pounds black plums (about 10)

    1 cup strawberries, hulled, sliced in half

    1 tablespoon tapioca flour or arrowroot powder

    ¼ cup sugar

    1 teaspoon pure vanilla extract

    ½ teaspoon ground cinnamon

    ½ teaspoon ground ginger

    ⅛ teaspoon ground cloves

**Topping:**

- ¾ cup rolled oats
- ½ cup all-purpose flour
- ¼ cup sugar
- 1½ teaspoons aniseeds
- ½ teaspoon ground cinnamon
- Pinch of salt
- 3–4 tablespoons canola oil

PREHEAT THE oven to 375°F.

*Prepare the filling:*

Chop the plums by cutting around the seed (this gets a bit messy). Cut them into slices that are between ¼ and ½ inch thick. Place in an 8-inch square baking pan. Add the rest of the filling ingredients and stir to dissolve the starch. Set aside.

*Prepare the topping:*

Toss all the topping ingredients except the canola oil into a mixing bowl and mix together with a fork. Drizzle in the oil by the tablespoon while tossing with fork until the topping becomes crumbly and doesn't look too dry. If you've got it by 3 tablespoons of oil, more power to you; but you may need to add another few teaspoons up to a tablespoon, to get the right consistency. Sprinkle relatively evenly over the plum mixture.

Place in the oven and bake for 45 minutes; the filling should be bubbly.

Remove from the oven and let cool for about 10 minutes. Scoop into bowls. Top with vegan vanilla ice cream.

## INDIVIDUAL HEART-SHAPED APPLE GALETTES

MAKES 6 INDIVIDUAL GALETTES

**TIME:** 1 HOUR 30 MINUTES

*A galette is a thin, freeform pie. Although here we have forced them into the shape of hearts, so they are no longer free. A thin layer of sweet, tangy apricot preserves is spread onto each crust before baking. A little sugar and cinnamon are sprinkled on top of the apple, making a lovely, simple fruit dessert with a crisp, melt-in-your mouth crust for you and those you love. Or just you, six times.*

**Crust:**

- 2 cups all-purpose flour, or ½ cup whole wheat pastry flour and ½ cup whole wheat flour
- 1 tablespoon granulated sugar
- 1 teaspoon salt
- ½ cup nonhydrogenated vegan shortening
- 1 teaspoon apple cider vinegar
- ½–¾ cup very cold water

**Apple filling:**

- 2 Granny Smith apples, peeled, cored and sliced very thinly (⅛ inch or less)
- 2 tablespoons light brown sugar
- ¼ teaspoon ground cinnamon
- 6 teaspoons apricot preserves
- Canola oil spray

*Prepare the dough:*

IN A large mixing bowl, combine the flour, granulated sugar, and salt. Add the shortening in three batches by the teaspoon, but you don't need to be precise about this; you just want to add it in small chunks. Cut the shortening into the flour with each addition, until the dough is crumbly and pebbly.

In a measuring cup, combine the vinegar with ½

cup of cold water. Add the diluted vinegar to the flour mixture in three batches, gently mixing it into the dough with a fork, until the dough holds together when pinched. If need be, add up to ¼ cup more water.

Gather the dough into a ball and knead gently a few times until it holds together. Form again into a ball and flatten just a bit into a disk. Refrigerate for about 30 minutes. If you refrigerate it longer, that is fine; but in that case you may need to leave it out for 15 minutes or so until you can easily roll it.

Fifteen minutes before you are ready to prepare the galette, preheat the oven to 425°F and slice your apples. Also, in a small bowl, mix together the brown sugar and cinnamon and lightly grease a baking sheet.

On a clean, lightly floured surface, roll out the dough into a 12 × 15-inch rectangle that is ¼ inch thick. It helps if you flour the rolling pin as well, so the dough doesn't stick. Use a butter knife to cut four 8-inch hearts from the dough. When you have done four hearts, place them on the prepared baking sheet, roll out your dough scraps, and create two more hearts. Place those on the baking sheet as well.

Roll in the edges of each heart to create a rimmed crust. You will have to do some pulling on top where the two curves meet, but it doesn't have to be too precise, as long as you get the general heart shape. Now take a butter knife and score the rolled edges on a slight diagonal to create a pretty design. "Score" just means to press gently with the knife's edge. This not only makes the crust pretty, it also secures the rim in place.

**tip**

➤ If you don't want to make hearts or are just scared of them (scared of love?), eight-inch circles will work, too!

➤ If you don't have a pastry cutter, cut the shortening into the flour with two knives held together.

Spread a teaspoon of apricot preserves in each crust. Starting from the top, place four apple slices on both sides of the heart, slightly overlapping, to create a fan effect. You might have to press them into the edges if there doesn't seem to be room; that is perfectly fine. The curved side of the apple slices should go along with the curve at the top of the heart.

Spray with a bit of canola spray, to keep the apples from drying out, and sprinkle with the brown sugar mixture. Bake for 25 to 30 minutes, until the edges of the crusts are golden brown.

Serve warm, with a scoop of vegan ice cream, if desired.

## MANGO PEAR PANDOWDY

**TIME:** 1 HOUR 15 MINUTES

*Pandowdy is an old-fashioned American dessert that doesn't get much play these days. The concept reminds us of the kind of thing a child might decide to do to their food, if they were industrious enough to roll out a pastry. It's simply a pie whose crust has been smashed into the fruit halfway through cooking. The appeal is in the texture; the top of the pastry stays flaky and crispy and the bottom is mushy and soggy with fruit. We love the sloppy beauty of it. This version is mango and pear with just a hint of ginger and cinnamon, but try the method with any pie you make.*

**2 mangoes, peeled and cut into ½ inch dice**
**2 pounds Bartlett pears, cut into ½ inch dice**
**½ cup sugar**
**2 tablespoons arrowroot or tapioca flour**
**1 teaspoon ground ginger**
**1 teaspoon ground cinnamon**

**1 tablespoon sugar for sprinkling on top of crust.**

1 single pie crust (page 262)

PREHEAT oven to 350 F. Have your pie crust rolled out and ready.

Combine all filling ingredients in a pie plate. Mix until the arrowroot or tapioca is dissolved. Cover with the pie crust, and tuck the edges around the filling and sprinkle with the tablespoon of sugar. Bake for 30 minutes, then remove from the oven.

Slice the crust into roughly ones inch pieces, then use a spoon to smush the crust into the pie. Return to the oven to finish baking for 20 more minutes to half an hour. The filling should be bubbling over and the crust should be browned.

Serve warm, with a scoop of ice cream if you are so inclined.

## BANANA-CHOCOLATE CHIP BREAD PUDDING

SERVES 6 TO 8

**TIME:** ABOUT AN HOUR

*Bread pudding is something of a miracle: stale bread and a few unassuming ingredients transform into an irresistible, old-fashioned treat that tastes great on a cold winter's night (or morning for a very naughty breakfast). This version is unapologetically decadent, packing in plenty of deep, dark chocolate; creamy, sweet bananas; and a warming hint of cinnamon. This pudding makes the best use of leftover Homestyle Potato Rolls (page 218), or any rustic bread.*

6 cups (1-inch cubed) stale bread (about 1 pound)

2 ¼ cups rice, almond, or soy milk

3 tablespoons arrowroot powder or tapioca flour

½ cup pure maple syrup

1 teaspoon vanilla extract

½ teaspoon ground cinnamon

¼ teaspoon ground nutmeg

1 cup vegan chocolate chips

3 large, ripe bananas, sliced ½-inch thick

**tip**

➢ Try using an ice-cream scoop to scoop the pudding out from the pan and serve as pretty mounds.

➢ Impatient types can make bread stale a little quicker by cutting it into cubes, spreading them on baking sheets, and let them dry in a 300°F oven for 30 minutes, until the cubes are firm and rather dry. More patient types don't bother with the oven step and let that bread sit out on the counter for a few hours.

PREHEAT THE oven to 350°F. Lightly grease a 9 × 5-inch loaf pan. Place the cubed bread in a large bowl.

In a small bowl, whisk together ½ cup of the soy milk and the arrowroot powder until no lumps remain. Add the remaining 1½ cups soy milk, maple syrup, vanilla, cinnamon, and nutmeg, and whisk to mix thoroughly. Pour over the cubed bread and stir to coat every piece.

Allow the mixture to sit for at least 15 minutes, for the liquid to soak into the bread. Depending on what kind of bread you use and how stale the bread is, add more soy milk (¼ cup at a time) and allow more soaking time until every piece of bread is saturated and there's a little bit of extra liquid in the bowl. The mixture should look mushy and wet.

Fold in the chocolate chips and bananas (using your hands is the easiest for this), mashing the bananas slightly. Pour the mixture into the loaf pan, patting down to make an even top.

Bake for 30 to 35 minutes, until the top is puffed, slightly browned, and feels firm.

Remove from the oven and allow to cool slightly before slicing and serving.

# CARAMEL-APPLE-SPICE CUPCAKES

MAKES 12 CUPCAKES

**TIME:** ABOUT AN HOUR

*This is a tender cupcake, bursting with caramelized apple chunks, with just the right amount of spice and old-fashioned, fun-to-say penuche frosting with a light caramel flavor. Have a few extra cupcake liners handy as there can be some leftover batter, or enjoy a shot of apple batter with a friend.*

2 tart, firm cooking apples, such as Granny Smith or Northern Spy
2 tablespoons brown sugar
1 tablespoon nonhydrogenated vegan margarine
1 cup soy milk
1 tablespoon lemon juice
⅓ cup canola oil
¾ cup granulated sugar
1 teaspoon grated lemon zest
1 teaspoon vanilla extract
1½ cups all-purpose flour
1½ teaspoons baking soda
½ teaspoons baking powder
¼ teaspoon salt
1 teaspoon ground cinnamon
¼ teaspoon ground nutmeg

### Caramel-penuche frosting:

½ cup granulated sugar
3 tablespoons nonhydrogenated vegan margarine
1 tablespoon molasses
⅓ cup soy creamer or soy milk
2 tablespoons plain or vanilla soy milk powder
Pinch of salt
2½ cups confectioners' sugar
1 teaspoon vanilla extract
½ cup chopped, roasted peanuts for sprinkling

## Penuche

**WHAT** is penuche and why would anyone put it on a cupcake? Penuche is actually a really old-fashioned American fudge candy, so old school in fact there's no chocolate or cocoa in it. Its deep, caramel flavor is achieved primarily by boiling brown sugar (along with butter and maybe a little vanilla). We skip to the chase in this recipe and use a combination of white sugar and molasses, because that's all that brown sugar really is. The texture of the frosting does indeed have a dense, smooth homemade fudgy quality that really delivers.

PREHEAT THE oven to 350°F and line a 12-cup muffin tin with paper cupcake liners.

Leaving the skins on the apples, core and dice them into small pieces (about ¼-inch cubes), for about 1⅔ cups of diced apple.

Heat the brown sugar and margarine in a heavy skillet over medium heat, stirring, until the mixture begins to bubble. Add the apple pieces and stir to coat. Cook the apples, stirring occasionally, until almost all of the water has evaporated and the apples are lightly caramelized, about 12 minutes. Remove from the heat and allow to cool before proceeding.

In a large bowl, whisk together the soy milk and lemon juice, and allow to sit for a minute to curdle. Add the canola oil, granulated sugar, lemon zest, and vanilla, and beat well. Sift in the flour, baking powder, baking soda, salt, cinnamon, and nutmeg the and stir only until the dry ingredients are moistened. Fold in the sautéed apples along with any remaining juices.

Fill the cupcake liners three-quarters of the way with batter, and bake for 20 to 22 minutes, until a toothpick inserted into the center of a cupcake comes out clean.

When the cupcakes are done, remove them from the oven and cool on wire racks.

While they cool, prepare the Caramel-Penuche Frosting: Combine the sugar, margarine, molasses, soy milk, powdered soy milk, and salt in a heavy-bottomed saucepan over medium heat. Stir and bring to a boil. Allow the mixture to boil and foam for 7 to 8 minutes, stirring occasionally. Remove from the heat.

When the frosting mixture has cooled slightly and is still a little warm, stir in half the confectioners' sugar and the vanilla, then beat with electric beaters for 2 to 3 minutes, until creamy. Slowly beat in remaining confectioners' sugar until a thick, smooth, fudgelike frosting forms. (The frosting can be spread warm or slightly cooled, but too much cooling will make the frosting too stiff to spread. If this happens, just let it warm to room temperature.)

Frost the cupcakes and sprinkle with chopped peanuts.

## JELLY DONUT CUPCAKES

MAKES 12 CUPCAKES

TIME: ABOUT 40 MINUTES

*Here is a treat that defies all logic: it's both a tender cupcake and sugared jelly donut at the same time. They're cute, yummy, and deceptively easy to make, too. No need to use a pastry bag to fill the cupcake in order to create its amazing jelly donut effect; the jam bakes right into it, doing all the work for you. Add a sprinkle of confectioners' sugar and you have yourself one heck of a cupcake moonlighting as a jelly donut.*

1 cup soy or rice milk

1 teaspoon apple cider vinegar

2 tablespoons cornstarch

1½ cups all-purpose flour

¾ teaspoon baking powder

½ teaspoon baking soda

½ teaspoon ground nutmeg

½ teaspoon salt

⅓ cup canola oil

¾ cup plus 2 tablespoons granulated sugar

2 teaspoons pure vanilla extract

About ⅓ cup raspberry jam or preserves (you can use strawberry or grape if you prefer)

2 tablespoons confectioners' sugar

PREHEAT THE oven to 350°F. Pour the soy milk, vinegar, and cornstarch into a measuring cup and set aside. Line a 12-cup muffin pan with paper cupcake liners.

In a large mixing bowl, sift together the flour, baking powder, baking soda, nutmeg, and salt. Create a well in the center of the flour to pour your wet ingredients into.

Stir the soy milk mixture with a fork to dissolve the cornstarch, then pour into the flour mixture. Add the oil, granulated sugar, and vanilla. Stir until well combined.

Fill the cupcake liners about three-quarters full with batter. Place a heaping teaspoonful of jam on the center of each cupcake. You don't need to press down on the jam or do anything else; the baking will take care of all of that and it will sink in.

Bake for 21 to 23 minutes. You can't really do a toothpick test here because of the jelly filling, but the

**tip**

➤ The cheaper your jam, the more authentic your donut will taste, so skip the organic spreadable fruit stuff here and go for the bright red, ambiguously "berry"-flavored supermarket brand. The cops down at the station will thank you for it.

➤ The trick to these cupcakes is to leave them out in a cool place overnight, so make these a day ahead if you can, although it's fine if you can't wait.

cupcakes should be done by this point. The tops should be firm.

Remove from the oven and let cool completely on wire racks.

Once cooled, set them someplace cool and dry, and leave uncovered. If it's winter, leave them in your coldest room. If it's summer, leave them somewhere air-conditioned, if possible. If it's not possible, don't sweat it—just don't leave them anywhere very warm. Let them sit overnight and preferably up to 24 hours. This will make the tops dry and a little bit crispy and more donutlike.

Sprinkle with confectioners' sugar (using a sifter if you have one). Serve with coffee.

## VANILLA-YOGURT POUND CAKE

MAKES 1 LOAF

**TIME:** ABOUT 1 HOUR 30 MINUTES

*Pound cake should be simple: just sweet enough, with a hint of vanilla, citrus, or other aromatic flavors. Densely textured yet moist. Lovingly delivers abundant calories directly to your thighs and waist with each meltingly tender bite. Without the usual pound of butter and eggs, in this recipe we've made good use of vanilla soy yogurt and silken tofu to get the job done. The flavor and texture of this cake develops as it cools, so be sure to allow the loaf to cool to room temperature before slicing. And don't forget that pound cake loves to be adorned with fresh berries, or sliced and lightly toasted with a little dab of your favorite vegan margarine.*

½ cup vanilla soy yogurt
½ cup blended silken tofu (blend the tofu first, then
  measure it out)
¾ cup vanilla or plain soy milk
1¼ cups sugar
½ cup canola oil

2 teaspoons vanilla extract
½ teaspoon lemon extract, or ½ teaspoon grated
  lemon zest
½ teaspoon orange extract, or ½ teaspoon grated
  orange zest
2 cups all-purpose flour
3 tablespoons arrowroot powder
1 ½ teaspoons baking powder
½ teaspoons baking soda
½ teaspoon salt

PREHEAT THE oven to 325°F. Lightly grease and flour a 9 × 5-inch loaf pan. A metal pan with a dark finish is the best choice for this cake.

In a large bowl, combine the soy yogurt, blended silken tofu, soy milk, sugar, oil, and extracts. Use an electric mixture to beat until everything is smooth, about 2 minutes.

Sift in the flour, arrowroot powder, baking powder, baking soda, and salt. Stir with a rubber spatula to combine, then beat with electric beaters for 1½ to 2 minutes, until a very thick batter forms. Don't overmix.

Pour the batter into the prepared loaf pan. Use the rubber spatula to scrape all of the batter out of the bowl and smooth the top of the loaf. Bake for 60 to 65 minutes, until a toothpick or thin sharp knife inserted into the center comes out clean (a little moisture is okay). Don't open the oven to peek for at least the first 45 minutes of baking!

**tip**

➤ This cake has a very thick batter and requires a well-preheated oven at just the right temp to rise properly. Allow the oven to heat for at least 20 minutes and, as always, use an oven thermometer.

➤ For best results, use a pan that's no bigger than 9 x 5-inches. Using an 8 x 4-inch pan also works great.

Remove from the oven and let cool in the pan 10 minutes, then carefully transfer the loaf to a wire rack to cool completely before slicing. Store the cake in an airtight container.

## Variations:

**Nut, Chocolate Chip, and/or Fruited Pound Cake:** Stir in ½ to 1 cup of any of the following: toasted chopped walnuts, chocolate chips, raisins, dried sweetened cranberries, dried chopped cherries (if using cherries, omit the citrus extracts and use 1 teaspoon of almond extract instead).

**Lemon Pound Cake:** Use lemon yogurt and up the lemon extract to a full teaspoon. Reduce the vanilla extract to 1 teaspoon.

**Rose Water Pound Cake:** Omit the orange and lemon extracts. Reduce the vanilla extract to 1 teaspoon. Add 1½ teaspoons of rose water.

# PUMPKIN CRUMB CAKE WITH PECAN STREUSEL

MAKES 16 SQUARES

**TIME:** 1 HOUR 10 MINUTES

*How does moist, sublime, spiced pumpkin cake get better? A crummy mess of pecan streusel topping would get our vote any day. Perfect for autumn high tea.*

## Pecan streusel:

¼ cup all-purpose flour
3 tablespoons brown sugar
   (granulated sugar is okay, too)
¼ teaspoon ground cinnamon
¼ teaspoon ground allspice
1 tablespoon canola oil
1 cup coarsely chopped pecans

## Cake:

1 (15-ounce) can pureed pumpkin (not pumpkin pie mix)
¾ cups soy milk
¾ cups canola oil
1½ cups granulated sugar
3 tablespoons light molasses
2 teaspoons pure vanilla extract
2⅔ cups all-purpose flour
1 tablespoon baking powder
1 teaspoon salt
1½ teaspoons ground cinnamon
¾ teaspoon ground nutmeg
¾ teaspoon ground ginger
½ teaspoon ground allspice
⅛ teaspoon ground cloves

PREHEAT THE oven to 350°F. Lightly grease a 9 × 13-inch baking pan.

## Prepare the streusel:

In a small bowl, mix together the flour, brown sugar, and spices. Drizzle in the canola oil and mix with your fingertips until crumbs form. Add the chopped pecans and mix.

## Prepare the cake:

In a large mixing bowl, combine the pumpkin, soy milk, oil, granulated sugar, molasses and vanilla. Mix well. Add roughly half the flour, the baking powder, salt, and spices, and use a fork to fold everything together. Add the remaining flour and mix gently until combined. Don't use a hand blender for this, as pumpkin can get gummy if it's mixed too aggressively. Blending with a fork helps maintain the texture.

Pour batter into the prepared baking pan and spread it out with a spatula. Scatter the streusel on top as evenly as possible. Bake for 45 to 50 minutes, until a knife inserted through the center comes out clean.

Remove from the oven, let cool, and cut into squares.

## COCONUT-LEMON BUNDT CAKE

SERVES 10

**TIME:** 1 HOUR 30 MINUTES

*Bundt is a hilarious name for this variety of cake. Get past the silliness with the enticing combination of tangy, bright lemon and irresistible chewy shredded coconut, made extra moist with plenty of coconut milk. No need for an icing on this cake, which is bursting with extreme flavor. It's so simple and good—just "slice and go"—but sprinkle with a little powdered sugar to dress it up.*

1⅔ cups granulated sugar

⅔ cup canola oil

1 (14-ounce can) coconut milk

¼ cup rice or soy milk

¼ cup lemon juice

3 tablespoons finely grated lemon zest

2 teaspoons pure vanilla extract

3 cups all-purpose flour

2 teaspoons baking powder

1 teaspoons baking soda

1 teaspoon salt

1½ cups shredded unsweetened coconut

A few tablespoons confectioners' sugar for sprinkling

PREHEAT THE oven to 350°F. Lightly grease an 8- or 10-inch Bundt pan.

In a large mixing bowl, combine the granulated sugar, oil, coconut milk, rice milk, lemon juice and zest, and vanilla. Stir to combine.

Sift the flour, baking powder, baking soda, and salt into the wet ingredients in batches, mixing well after each addition. Fold in the coconut.

Pour the batter into the Bundt pan. Bake for 1 hour, or until a knife inserted through the cake comes out clean.

Remove from the oven and let cool for about 10 minutes, then place a cutting board over the cake pan,

gently flip over, and release the cake from the pan. Let cool completely. One cooled, sift a sprinkling of confectioners' sugar over the top. Slice and serve.

## LOWER-FAT DEEP CHOCOLATE BUNDT CAKE

SERVES 12

**TIME:** 70 MINUTES

*This is a wonderfully rich chocolate Bundt with a delicate crumb. And it delivers big chocolate flavor without a whole lot of fat. Fresh brewed coffee and almond extract heighten all that chocolate, and applesauce stands in beautifully for most of the oil. This cake doesn't need a glaze or frosting, just a simple sprinkling of confectioners' sugar.*

**tip**

> Whole wheat pastry flour leaves the fiber of the wheat intact without sacrificing any of the texture, but if you can't find whole wheat pastry flour then regular all-purpose flour will do the trick. But don't substitute *regular* whole wheat flour, it is different from pastry flour and will result in a rough and chewy texture.

1¾ cups fresh brewed coffee

⅔ cup unsweetened Dutch-processed cocoa powder

1½ cups granulated sugar

⅓ cup canola oil

⅓ cup applesauce

¼ cup cornstarch

2 teaspoons vanilla extract

1 teaspoon almond extract

2 cups whole wheat pastry flour or all-purpose white flour

1 teaspoon baking soda

1½ teaspoons baking powder

½ teaspoon salt

2 teaspoons confectioners' sugar

PREHEAT THE oven to 325°F. Lightly grease an 8- or 10-inch Bundt pan.

Bring the coffee to a simmer in a saucepan over medium heat. Once it is simmering, turn down the heat and whisk in the cocoa powder until it has dissolved. Remove from the heat and set aside to bring to room temperature.

In a mixing bowl, whisk together the granulated sugar, canola oil, applesauce, and cornstarch until the sugar and cornstarch are dissolved, about 2 minutes. Mix in the extracts. Once the chocolate has cooled a bit, mix that in as well.

Sift in the flour, baking powder, baking soda, and salt. Beat until relatively smooth, about 1 minute with a hand mixer or 2 minutes with a whisk.

Pour the batter into the prepared Bundt pan and bake for about 45 minutes, until a toothpick or butter knife inserted through its center comes out clean. If your pan is on the smaller side, it could take up to 55 minutes.

Remove from the oven and let cool for about 20 minutes, then invert onto a serving plate to cool completely. Once cool, sift confectioners' sugar over the top and enjoy.

## SMLOVE PIE

SERVES 8

TIME: 1 HOUR PLUS 3 HOURS FOR CHILLING

*This pie was inspired by the question "What would Paula Deen bake if she were vegan?" It's a rich yet airy chocolate pie, smothered in peanut butter caramel, studded with maple candied pecans, and finished off with a chocolate drizzle for good measure. We use a graham cracker crust but a chocolate cookie crust would be nice and decadent, too. The pie filling is gluten free, so if you*

*have a recipe for a gluten-free crust, you celiacs are good to go. If you don't want to go through the trouble of making the toppings, the pie by itself is pretty yummy, too! Top it with soy whipped cream if you've got it.*

Graham cracker crust:

12 graham crackers, or 1¾ cups graham cracker crumbs

¼ cup canola oil

1 tablespoon soy milk

Chocolate pie filling:

1 pound silken tofu (not the vacuum-packed kind), drained

¼ cup hazelnut liqueur (other liqueurs would work, too, such as coffee or chocolate, or just use rice or soy milk)

2 teaspoons pure vanilla extract

2 tablespoons arrowroot powder

12 ounces bittersweet vegan chocolate, melted (see tip on page 243 for melting chocolate)

Maple candied pecans:

1 cup pecans

2 teaspoons canola oil

⅛ teaspoon salt

2 tablespoons pure maple syrup

Peanut butter caramel:

⅓ cup natural peanut butter, smooth or chunky, at room temperature

3 tablespoons pure maple syrup

2 tablespoons brown rice syrup

Chocolate drizzle:

4 ounces bittersweet vegan chocolate, chopped, or ¼ cup vegan chocolate chips

¼ cup soy or rice milk

PREHEAT THE oven to 350°F. Spray a 10-inch pie plate with cooking spray.

### Prepare the crust:

Process the grahams into fine crumbs. Place them in a bowl and drizzle the oil on them. Use your fingertips or a fork to mix in the oil until all crumbs are moistened; sprinkle in the soy milk and mix again. Pour the crumbs into the pie plate and firmly press them to the bottom and sides of the plate. Set aside.

### Prepare the filling:

First, melt your chocolate. Crumble the tofu into a blender or food processor. Add the liqueur, vanilla, and arrowroot to the tofu and blend until completely smooth. Scrape down the sides to make sure you get everything. Add the melted chocolate and blend again until completely mixed. Pour the filling into the pie crust and bake for 40 minutes. The center may still be jiggly, but that's fine.

Remove from the oven and let cool on a rack on the countertop for 10 minutes, then chill in the fridge for at least 3 hours. The top of the pie should be firm to the touch.

Meanwhile, prepare your candied pecans: Cover a large plate with baking parchment. Preheat a heavy-bottomed skillet over medium heat. Add the pecans and stir them very frequently for 3 minutes, until they start to brown. Stir constantly for 2 more minutes, until they are a few shades darker and relatively uniformly toasted. (If a few don't look toasted, don't worry about it. That's better than having them burn.)

Add the oil and salt, and stir for another minute. Add the maple syrup, stirring constantly for about a minute. The maple syrup should get bubbly and dry. Use a spatula to transfer the pecans to a plate and spread them out as much as you can; it's best if they aren't touching. Place in the fridge until ready to use.

Once the pie has been chilling for at least 3 hours, prepare the peanut butter caramel and chocolate drizzle. Have your pie out and ready to be assembled.

### To prepare the peanut butter caramel:

Stir all the ingredients together in a small saucepan. Gently heat everything over low heat, stirring constantly with a fork, just until smooth and heated through. It should fall from your fork in ribbons. If it seems stiff, turn off the heat immediately and add a little extra brown rice syrup, until it's fluid again. (This happens because different peanut butters have different amounts of moisture.)

Pour the peanut butter over the center of the pie, leaving an inch or two bare at the edges because it spreads. Get your pecans and place them on top of the caramel, pressing them in firmly. You may have to break the pecans apart from one another if they cooled touching.

### Prepare the chocolate drizzle:

In a small saucepan, heat the soy milk to boiling, then add the chocolate and turn down the heat. Use a fork to stir until completely blended. Turn off the heat and let cool for 5 minutes, stirring occasionally.

You can drizzle the chocolate over the pie with a spoon, but we like to put it in a pastry bag fitted with a wide writing tip and drizzle it that way, in stripes. Chill the pie for at least 10 minutes before serving, so that the chocolate firms up a bit.

## LOST COCONUT CUSTARD PIE

SERVES 6 TO 8

**TIME:** ABOUT 45 MINUTES, PLUS CHILLING TIME

*Lost, literally. That is, the recipe for this pie (which once appeared in an episode of* The Post Punk Kitchen, *our public-access cooking show) melted into the shadows soon after that episode was filmed and hasn't been seen for years. Yeah, we could have actually just rewatched the show and maybe paid attention to how the pie was made, but where's the fun in that?*

*But, whatever. This new and improved version of the recipe is better than ever: more fresh coconut flavor from more luscious coconut milk. Not to mention it's now soy-free, with the inclusion of rice milk. Because this pie originated as a dessert for Passover, we've included its "traditional" matzo crust. But swap graham cracker crumbs (or prepare a prebaked pastry crust) for matzo meal and this cool, sweet, and creamy dessert is the perfect finish to any summertime BBQ or Caribbean-themed meal. Serve it up with slices of fresh pineapple, mango, kiwi, or your favorite seasonal fresh berries.*

## Crust:

1 recipe Basic Single Pastry (page 262), rolled, shaped, and baked, or Crumb Crust (recipe below), prepared with matzo meal or graham cracker crumbs

## Filling:

1 cup rice or soy milk

2 tablespoons arrowroot powder or cornstarch

½ teaspoon agar powder, or 1½ teaspoons flakes

1 (14-ounce) can coconut milk, regular or lite

1 tablespoon lemon juice

1 cup sugar

1½ teaspoons vanilla extract

1 teaspoon coconut extract (optional but good)

Pinch of salt

¾ cup shredded, unsweetened coconut

Optional garnishes: additional shredded coconut or slices of fresh mango, pineapple, sliced strawberries (sprinkle with lemon juice first before topping), or any fresh, sliced fruit or berry.

PREPARE ANY of the crusts, bake it, and set aside.

In a small bowl or measuring cup, whisk together ½ cup of the rice milk with the arrowroot powder. Set aside.

In a large, heavy-bottomed saucepan, whisk together the remaining ½ cup of the rice milk with the

agar power. Over medium-high heat, bring the mixture to a boil, stirring constantly. Allow it to boil for about 1 minute, then turn down the heat to medium-low. In a slow, steady stream, pour in arrowroot mixture (you might need to give it a brief stir before pouring), stirring this mixture constantly.

Pour in the coconut milk, lemon juice, and sugar. Using a wire whisk, stir constantly and cook until the mixture has thickened, 3 to 5 minutes. Remove from the heat and stir in vanilla extract, coconut extract if using, salt, and shredded coconut. Immediately pour into the pie crust. If you have any leftover filling, pour that into a small serving dish and there you go, bonus coconut custard! Allow the pie to cool on a countertop for 15 minutes, then carefully transfer to the refrigerator and allow to chill for at least 2 hours. Cover tightly in plastic wrap until ready to serve.

## CRUMB CRUST

*If using graham cracker crumbs, for best results purchase whole crackers and smash them up yourself. This will give you coarser crumbs with a more interesting texture than premade graham crumbs. Why not do the same if using matzo, too?*

½ cup unsweetened, shredded coconut

1¾ cups matzo meal or coarse graham cracker crumbs, or vanilla cookie crumbs

2 tablespoons sugar

3 tablespoons nonhydrogenated vegan margarine, melted, or unrefined coconut oil

3–5 tablespoons soy or rice milk

PREHEAT THE oven to 350°F.

Combine the shredded coconut, matzo meal, and sugar in a large bowl. Pour in the melted margarine and toss to create soft crumbs. Add the soy milk, a tablespoon at a time, until the mixture is moist and holds together if squeezed. Gently but firmly pat the mixture into a 9- or 10-inch deep pie plate, pressing the mixture up the sides, and form a slight lip if desired. Bake for 12 to 15 minutes until the coconut and matzo are lightly toasted and the crust is firm. Remove from the oven and allow to cool on a rack before filling.

## VANILLA ICE CREAM

MAKES 1½ PINTS ICE CREAM

**TIME:** 10 MINUTES FOR PREPPING AND OVERNIGHT FOR CHILLING

*Making your own ice cream gives you such a feeling of accomplishment, like you just passed the bar exam or climbed a mountain. But it also gives you something even more important . . . ice cream! Coconut milk and pureed silken tofu make this ice cream extra thick and super creamy, like it should be. Because ice-cream makers vary by manufacturer, our directions basically say to follow the directions your ice-cream maker came with. Basically, you add the ice cream to the container of your ice-cream maker, and then it churns away to keep your ice cream from forming ice crystals. Remember to make* sure all your ingredients are cold by keeping them refrigerated overnight the day before your big ice-cream event. Also, prep your ice-cream bowl by keeping in the freezer overnight. You want everything as cold as can be.

½ cup cream of coconut milk (see tip)
1 cup soy milk
¾ cup sugar
6 ounces silken tofu
1 tablespoon vanilla extract

PUREE ALL ingredients in a blender or food processor until smooth. Pour into your ice-cream maker and follow the machine manufacturer's instructions.

### Variations:

**Green Tea Ice Cream:** Add 2 tablespoons of matcha green tea powder when blending.

**Any Berry Ice Cream:** Try raspberry, blueberry, cherry, or blackberry, coarsely chopped. If using strawberries hull and slice them thinly.

You will need ¾ pound of berries. Place half of them in a saucepan with ¼ cup of water, 1 tablespoon of arrowroot powder, and 2 tablespoons of sugar. Bring to a boil, then turn down the heat to low and simmer. Simmer for about 7 minutes until slightly thickened, stirring often, then let cool completely.

Once cooled, proceed with the Vanilla Ice Cream recipe adding your cooled mixture to the blender. Once you pour into the ice-cream maker, add the remainder of sliced berries and stir. You can also add a cup of chocolate chunks at this point.

**Banana Ice Cream:** Place two large ripe bananas in the blender with the Vanilla Ice Cream ingredients and proceed with the recipe. If you like, mix in ½ cup of chopped walnuts and ½ cup of chocolate chips when you transfer the mixture to the ice-cream maker.

> **tip**
>
> ➤ We actually just used the cream from a can of coconut milk. Place the can in fridge overnight and the cream will rise to the top. Open the can carefully and scoop out half a cup of the cream. Freeze the rest for use in a soup or another recipe some other time.
>
> ➤ If you are not even considering making your own ice cream, we recommend trying Temptation Ice Cream, from a vegan-owned and -operated company in Chicago.

# Ice Cream Sandwiches

WHAT'S better than a sandwich? A sandwich made of homemade ice cream smooshed between two freshly baked cookies. Okay, you might have a few other suggestions, but really what is better on a warm summer evening while you're walking around the city in your new flip flops?

Here's a quick and snappy list of some suggestions featuring some of the cookies in this book stuffed with ice creamy favorites. Use the basic Vanilla Ice Cream (page 260) recipe and create any of the variations listed. Or, revel in your laziness and buy your favorite extra decadent non-dairy ice cream.

For best results, allow ice cream sandwiches to freeze for a minimum two hours (or until frozen completely solid) before serving. Anything less and the ice cream won't have time to freeze firm and biting into a sammie will likely result in half-melted ice cream dripping all over your toes.

For maximum prettiness and decadence, roll the edges of your ice cream sandwiches in pretty shredded coconut, chopped nuts, or shaved chocolate. Place your rolling ingredients on a plate and roll the sammich like a tire across the plate before freezing.

THE GREEN TEA: Terry's favorite almond cookie with Green Tea Ice Cream

BLACK FOREST: Chocolate-Chocolate Chip-Walnut Cookies with Cherry Ice Cream rolled in shredded coconut

THE MOCHA: Chocolate-Chocolate Chip-Walnut Cookies with Coffee Ice Cream rolled in chocolate sprinkles

CHUNKY MONKEY: Spread Chocolate-Chocolate Chip-Walnut Cookies with Peanut Butter Caramel and fill with Banana Ice Cream. Tuck in a few thin slices of ripe banana for kicks before smooshing halves together.

THE PERSIAN: Add a tablespoon of rose water to Vanilla Ice Cream, scoop into Pistachio Rose Water cookies and roll in finely chopped pistachios.

OPEN SESAME: Peanut-Ginger-Sesame Cookies filled with Peanut Butter Ice Cream and rolled in toasted sesame seeds. These make cute little tea sandwiches.

THE PIRATE: Skip the frosting on Rumnog Pecan Cookies, spike Vanilla Ice Cream with rum or a tablespoon of rum extract, fold in raisins and roll in finely chopped pecans.

THE CLASSIC: Wheat-Free Chocolate Chip Cookies filled with Vanilla Ice Cream and rolled in shaved chocolate.

COCOA RASPBERRY: Chewy Chocolate-Raspberry Cookies filled with Raspberry Ice Cream.

Coffee Ice Cream: Replace ½ cup of the soy milk with ½ cup of strong, cold espresso, or add 2 tablespoons of coffee extract to the blender.

Chocolate Ice Cream: Reduce the sugar by ¼ cup. Add 8 ounces of cooled, melted semisweet chocolate to the blender.

**Peanut Butter Ice Cream:** Increase the sugar to 1 cup and stir ½ cup of your favorite creamy or chunky all-natural peanut butter into the blender.

**Pistachio-Anise Ice Cream:** Stir in 1 teaspoon of almond extract, ⅔ cup of coarsely chopped, roasted pistachios, and ½ teaspoon of anise extract into the blender.

## BASIC SINGLE PASTRY CRUST

MAKES 1 PASTRY CRUST

**TIME:** 20 MINUTES, PLUS CHILL TIME

*This recipe produces a flaky, all-purpose, unsweetened pie crust. We used to get incredibly frustrated with pastry crusts because they are so temperamental—but now we know the secret. Make sure all of your ingredients are cold as can be—you should even refrigerate the flour. This way, the pockets of fat will stay pockets of fat and provide you with the flakiness you so desire. Baking powder and a touch of vinegar tenderize the flour for even more flakiness. Finally, a humble piece of baking parchment keeps the pastry from sticking and also makes a handy vehicle for flipping your pastry into the pie plate.*

1½ cups all-purpose flour
1 tablespoon sugar
½ teaspoon salt
¼ teaspoon baking powder
⅓ cup cold nonhydrogenated vegan shortening
¼ cup cold water, plus 2 tablespoons if needed
2 teaspoons apple cider vinegar

IN A large mixing bowl, combine the flour, sugar, salt and baking powder. Add the shortening by the teaspoon, but you don't need to be precise about this. You just want to add it in small chunks in three batches and then cut it into flour with each addition.

Cut the shortening in until the dough is crumbly and pebbly.

Combine the vinegar with ¼ cup of the water. Add the mixture to the dough in three batches, gently mixing it into the dough with a fork, until the dough holds together when pinched. If need be, add up to 2 tablespoons more water.

Gather the dough into a ball and knead gently a few times, just until it holds together. Sprinkle a clean work surface with flour, then flatten the ball into a disk. Wrap in plastic wrap and refrigerate for about an hour.

When ready to roll out the crust, place a large piece of baking parchment on your work surface. Unwrap the dough and place it on the parchment. Sprinkle your rolling pin with flour and roll the dough into a 12-inch circle. It may slip around a bit from the parchment, but that's okay, just work steadily and gently. Your crust is now ready to use.

If using as a bottom crust, lift the parchment and flip the crust into the pie plate. Tuck in and trim the edges.

If using as a top crust, lift the parchment and flip the crust onto the filling. Trim the edges and press with the tines of a fork to get pretty edges, or pinch the circumference with your thumb and forefinger.

## NOT-TELLA

MAKES ABOUT 1½ CUPS

**PREPARATION TIME:** UNDER 30 MINUTES

*There's a certain commercially prepared chocolate-hazelnut spread that often makes an appearance spread on cookies or slathered in crepes, which is both sorely missed and lamented by vegans and those looking to eat just a little bit healthier. The name brand we're thinking of contains hydrogenated oils and artificial flavors, among other undesirable ingredients, which we think such a wonderful combination of chocolate and hazelnut (in a great spreadable form!) could well do without.*

*This homemade version is far from being health food (yes, that's ten tablespoons of oil you see). However, you can be certain of its wholesomeness since it's made at home (try using organic ingredients). It's a little less sweet than the commercially prepared stuff, which allows the cocoa and toasted hazelnut flavors to really shine. While it won't fool a die-hard fan of the original, ours has a thick, fudgelike texture—like a luxurious nut butter—and a deep, distinctively nutty flavor and aroma.*

*This is best used as a spread (as it doesn't really melt), such as on crepes, scones, toast, or sandwiched between oatmeal cookies or gingersnaps. It would be wonderful gently dabbed onto sliced bananas or fresh, ripe strawberries, or stuffed into dates. And of course, the simplest and best vehicle of all is a thick slice of crusty French bread. The flavor develops even more when it's allowed to sit overnight.*

1 generous cup (about 5 ounces) toasted, skinned hazelnuts (see tip)

2 tablespoons hazelnut liquor (such as Frangelico), or 1½ teaspoons hazelnut extract

¼ teaspoon vanilla extract

¾ cup confectioners' sugar

¼ cup unsweetened cocoa powder, regular or Dutch-processed

2 tablespoons plain soy milk powder

8–10 tablespoons peanut or hazelnut oil, or a combination of both

EMPTY THE hazelnuts into your food processor bowl. Set the food processor to "pulse" and process the hazelnuts into crumbs. Continue to pulse the hazelnuts until an oily paste forms, stopping often to scrape the sides of the bowl with a rubber spatula.

When the hazelnuts form a thick, glossy, and oily mass (similar to a moist marzipan), add the hazelnut liquor, vanilla extract, confectioners' sugar, and cocoa. Blend until a crumbly mixture forms, again scraping the sides of the bowl often. Add the powdered soy milk and 4 to 5 tablespoons of oil. Continue to pulse and scrape as before. The mixture will resemble very thick fudge. Now, drizzle in a tablespoon of oil at a time and pulse/scrape. Add oil until a thick, spreadable mixture is achieved, or a desired consistency is reached. If not sweet enough, sprinkle in 1 to 2 additional tablespoons of confectioners' sugar.

Store in the refrigerator in an airtight container. The mixture will firm up as it chills; let it sit on the counter for about 20 minutes to warm up a little before spreading. Stir if the oils have separated.

**tip**

➤ This recipe makes a "milk" chocolate–style hazelnut spread. For a dark chocolate, spread leave out the soy milk powder. Increase the confectioners' sugar by a tablespoon or two, if desired.

➤ The easiest way to toast hazelnuts: Preheat the oven to 300°F. Place the raw hazelnuts on a baking sheet and roast for 8 to 10 minutes, until the skins are peeling and the nuts start to smell and appear toasted; be careful not to burn. Remove from the oven. Immediately pour the hot hazelnuts into the center of a large, rough kitchen towel. Twist the ends of the towel tightly around the nuts to form a sack. Agitate the sack vigorously for a few minutes to remove the skins. Some skin might still stick to hazelnuts, but this is okay. Pick the hazelnuts out of the crumbled skins and set aside in a bowl to cool. The quickest way to clean the towel of hazelnut skins is to shake it outside.

➤ If you're using hazelnut oil, try using a little bit of peanut oil in addition to the hazelnut oil. It lends an authentic, full flavor.

➤ This recipe will really give your food processor a workout. Be kind to your machine and use the "pulse" setting, stopping to rest the motor (and scraping the sides of the bowl) frequently.

# THE
# MENUS

# MENUS
# FOR THE MASSES

GENERALLY, WE DON'T like to fuss over planning a big menu. Menu planning should really be cooking what makes sense to you, with foods that are in season and foods that you know your guests enjoy. (Obviously, if your Great-Aunt Frimmie hates broccoli rabe, Thanksgiving may not be the time to try to make her like it!)

But sometimes it's useful to have a menu on hand, so in this section we suggest plenty of dishes that go well together. Hosting a dinner party can be stressful for anyone (even certain cookbook authors) and the host is usually worrying the whole time. It can be even more daunting for the vegan host, because we folks have the additional task of representing veganism. It's useful to keep in mind that we are often our own worst critics. But on a more practical level, if you're cooking for a crowd, you should give the dishes that you plan to serve a test run a week or two beforehand; that always helps make the big event go a bit more smoothly.

The following are dishes from this cookbook that make great plates to serve as "whenever meals." Or you can use our additional suggestions to create a multicourse menu for a special occasion.

### MY OWN PRIVATE INDIA MENU

Tamarind Lentils • Basmati Rice • Curried Tofu • Cornmeal Masala Brussels Sprouts

**SUGGESTED SOUP:** Roasted Yellow Pepper and Corn Bisque
**SUGGESTED DESSERT:** Mango-Peach Pandowdy

### SOUTH BY SOUTHEATS MENU

Southwestern Corn Pudding • Chile Cornmeal-Crusted Tofu • Green Pumpkin-Seed Mole • Steamed Broccoli

**SUGGESTED SOUP:** Smoky Red Pepper n' Beans Gumbo
**SUGGESTED DESSERT:** Smlove Pie

### CHINESE TAKE-OUT-EAT-IN MENU

Baby Bok Choy with Crispy Shallots • Marinated Asian Tofu (baked) • Brown Rice

**SUGGESTED SOUP:** Hot and Sour Soup (leave out the tofu)
**SUGGESTED DESSERT:** Green Tea Ice Cream Sammiches

### MARDI GRAS–ANYTIME MENU

Creole Stuffed Peppers • Messy Rice • Hot Sauce–Glazed Tempeh
**SUGGESTED SOUP:** Baked Potato and Greens Soup with Potato Wedge Croutons
**SUGGESTED DESSERT:** Strawberry-Rose Water Cobbler with Lemon–Poppy Seed Pastry

### MEDITERRANEAN COMFORT MENU

Tomato and Roasted Eggplant Stew with Chickpeas • Soft Poppy-Seed Polenta • Roasted Cauliflower

**SUGGESTED SALAD:** Portobello Salad in Spicy Mustard Dressing
**SUGGESTED DESSERT:** Tea-Poached Pears in Chocolate Sauce

### DOWN-HOME GOURMET MENU

Cheater Baked Beans • Smoky Grilled Tempeh • Sautéed Collards

**SUGGESTED SOUP:** Creamy Tomato Soup
**SUGGESTED DESSERT:** Fudgy Wudgy Blueberry Brownies with Vanilla Ice Cream

### FANCY-SHMANCY MENU

Chickpea Cutlets • Mustard Sauce • Roasted Asparagus

> **SUGGESTED SALAD:** Roasted Fennel and Hazelnut Salad with Shallot Dressing
> **SUGGESTED DESSERT:** Sweet Crepes with Not-Tella

### GREEK TO ME AND YOU MENU

Mediterranean-Style Baked Lima Beans • Lemony Roasted Potatoes • Easy Stir-Fried Leafy Greens (made with a blend of dandelion and kale)

> **SUGGESTED SOUP:** French Lentil Soup with Tarragon and Thyme
> **SUGGESTED DESSERT:** Lemon Bars

### LAZY INDIAN GOURMET

Samosa Stuffed Potatoes • Sautéed Spinach and Tomatoes • Five-Minute Mango Chutney • Jasmine Rice

> **SUGGESTED SALAD:** Garden Salad with Curried Vinaigrette
> **SUGGESTED DESSERT:** Vanilla Yogurt Pound Cake with Fresh Fruit

### THE VEGAN GHOST OF JULIA CHILD MENU

Sautéed Seitan with Mushrooms and Spinach • Herb-Scalloped Potatoes

> **SUGGESTED SALAD:** Bulgur, Arugula, and Cannellini Salad
> **SUGGESTED DESSERT:** Heart-Shaped Apple Galettes

### PICNIC MENU

Apricot Baked BBQ Tofu • Prospect Park Potato Salad • Grilled Corn

> **SUGGESTED DESSERT:** Lower-Fat Banana Bread

### SMASH YOUR TV DINNER MENU

Mac Daddy • Roasted Zucchini • Roasted Butternut Squash with Coriander Seeds

> **SUGGESTED SOUP:** Tomato-Rice Soup
> **SUGGESTED DESSERT:** Pumpkin Crumb Cake with Pecan Streusel

### MEXICAN, NOT MEXICAN'T MENU

Black Beans with Chipotle Adobo Sauce • Guacamole • Mexican Millet

**SUGGESTED SALAD:** Jicama-Watercress-Avocado Salad with Spicy Citrus Vinaigrette

**SUGGESTED DESSERT:** Banana–Chocolate Chip Bread Pudding

### ROMAN GODDESS MENU

Chickpeas Romanesco • Saffron-Garlic Rice • Roasted Green Beans

**SUGGESTED SALAD:** Caesar Salad with Roasted Garlic Croutons

**SUGGESTED DESSERT:** Biscotti and Espresso

### RUSTIC GODDESS MENU

Tomato Couscous with Capers • Rustic White Beans with Mushrooms

**SUGGESTED SOUP:** Broccoli-Potato Soup with Fresh Herbs

**SUGGESTED DESSERT:** Berry-Coconut Crisp

# Timing Is Everything!

SMARTY-PANTS cooks prepare as much as possible a day or two in advance and store it in airtight containers. Use the following guide to plan out your next major event and you'll have plenty of procrastination time on your hands as a present to yourself.

### UP TO TWO DAYS IN ADVANCE:

Any soup, dip, most sauces, and baked goods such as cookies and pie crusts can be made up to two days in advance.

### THE DAY OR NIGHT BEFORE:

Homemade seitan, stuffings, or other grain dishes; marinated overnight tofu/tempeh; sandwich fillings; and any casserole can be assembled a day before and cooked the day of. Prepare and shape bean balls, burgers, and patties, and keep tightly covered in the refrigerator. Bake and wrap any cakes, cupcakes, or muffins.

### TWO HOURS (AND COUNTING) BEFORE:

A few hours before serving the big meal is the ideal time to wash and dry salad greens, and prepare the dressing and store it in the fridge. Cut any fresh fruit, and assemble the appetizers. Also, bake or reheat the preassembled casseroles, wrap them tightly in foil, and keep them warm in the oven at 200°F (or the "warm" setting) until mealtime. Pasta, however, should be boiled and served as close to serving time as possible. For things that need to be served right away, give yourself an extra half hour to relax before cooking them. It also allows you some additional time to get everything together and check that there's no spinach between your teeth before your guests start rolling in.

Because your mother isn't here, we might as well remind you that this is the time to set the table, arrange glassware and stuff for drinks, fold some napkins, set the stereo on some soft rock/black metal or whatever floats your boat, and maybe light a candle for ambiance. Take a shower if time permits. We spare nothing when it comes to being classy.

# ACKNOWLEDGMENTS

**Terry and Isa would like to thank:**

Katie McHugh, our beautiful and patient editor at Perseus

Matthew Lore, our publisher at Perseus who took a chance on us in the first place

Christine Marra, our other editor at Perseus, for calling us every 5 minutes

Pauline Neuwirth, our book designer superhero.

Marc Gerald, our super-agent at the Agency Group

Julia Moskin at the NY times, who made us famous

The Nerd NYC community

**Isa would like to thank:**

Justin Field, for building me shelves and keeping the cats at bay.

My mom, Marlene Stewart, for transitioning to veganism and loving tempeh.

Josh Hooten for finally admitting that I am the new face of veganism and he is a washed up old man who listens to Les Savy Five and wonders what might have been. And his beautiful wife Michelle for publishing *Herbivore Magazine*.

Amy Sims, for being muh guh, (lylas!)

The Post Punk Kitchen forum mods; Paula, Eppy, Angela, Katie and Brian, for deleting spam and threads about honey and dating omnis, thus freeing up my time to play scrabble and write cookbooks.

Erica Levine because I have to thank her in every book or else she headbutts me (someone please help!)

Michelle Moskowitz-Brown for being my sister, even if she doesn't name the new baby after me. Also, Max for being cute and Aaron Brown for having good genes. (There is still time to name the baby after me)

Gorilla Coffee in Brooklyn, for having free wi-fi and keeping the soy milk out in a thermos. I spent many, many hours there doing most of the writing and editing for *Veganomicon*.

The Brooklyn Public Library at Grand Army Plaza for being a glorious place with air conditioning free wifi and, oh yes, so many books! Also, for being around the corner.

**Terry would like to thank:**

John Stavropoulos, my wonderful husband. Who gives great hugs, isn't afraid to tell me if he doesn't like something and breaks for seitan.

My parents, Teresa and Nerio, who will make every recipe in this book (even if they don't know this yet).

My sweetie mother-in-law Eleni for bringing me oregano from Greece that she picked herself from the side of a mountain in Sparta. Now that's hardcore.

The Forest Hills crew for keeping me company in the kitchen and being awesome: Erica, Keren, Evelyn, Paula, Frank, Jim and Jason.

Drozdal for his evil insight (the title of this tome you hold in your hands).

My boss Mark, my co-workers and my job for being understanding and really nice during my manic months spent making this book (yes, this was the reason I was furiously typing away in my cubicle-cave).

Our recipe testers guided our way throughout this cookbook. Not only did they tirelessly test our recipes, find our typos, help us clarify directions and hold our hands, they also let us know what foods they were craving and gave us endless ideas and inspiration. They let us know what they wanted in a cookbook, so while we would love to take full credit for being psychic culinary geniuses, we'll pull back the curtain and give them big fat hugs. Thank you guys so much, we love you all!

Pictured: Amanda Sacco tested over 100 recipes. No sooner did we post something than Amanda had tested it. We think she might be a vegan robot. But aren't all robots vegan?

Erica Johnson
Lisa Coulson
Raelene Coburn
Jayne Ott, Nadia and Brigit Wendt
Webly Bowles
Megan Duke
Julie Farson
Anna Hood
Abby Wohl

Andrea Zeh
Michelle Gardinier
Carrie Lynn Morse
Rachel Bavolar
Keren Form
Allicia Cormier
Mike Desert
Connie Leonard
Kim Cannard
Jessica DeNoto
Katie Marggraf
Molly Tanzer
Eryn Hiscock
Amanda Sacco
Mike Crooker & Liz Bujack
Shanell Dawn Williams
Lauren Ulm
Deborah Diamant
Jenna Mari Brooks
Lucy Allbaugh
Joanna Vaught
Kim Carpenter
Paula Gross
Karla E. Nolt
Jordan Faulds
Mat Winser
Michele Thompson
Terri Kruse
Jessica Scoles
Val Head
Erica Manney
Jill Murray
Angelene Gaal
Drew Blood
Cassondra Herman-Zajac
Elizabeth Ryan

# APPENDIX
## RECIPES BY ICON

## GLUTEN FREE RECIPES

# LOW FAT/REDUCED FAT RECIPES

## ⓸⓹ RECIPES UNDER 45 MINUTES

## 🍴 SUPERMARKET FRIENDLY RECIPES

### SNACKS, APPETIZERS, LITTLE MEALS, DIPS AND SPREADS

### BRUNCH — 70

### SALADS AND DRESSINGS — 80

### DRESSINGS — 92

### SAMMICHES — 95

### MIX AND MATCH — 104
### VEGETABLES — 105

# INDEX

Sushi rolling mat, 47, 48
"Sweat" defined, 18, 20
Sweet Basil Pesto Tapenade, 65
Sweet Crepes, 78
Sweet Orange or Lemon Crepes, 78
Sweet potatoes
  Jamaican Yuca Shepherd's Pie
    with Sweet Potato, Kidney
    Beans, and Plantains, 157–158
  Mashed Spiced Sweet Potatoes,
    111–112
  roasting, 34
  Sweet Potato–Black Bean Tortillas,
    50
  Sweet Potato–Pear Tzimmes with
    Pecans and Raisins, 156
Sweet Squash in Mole Sauce, 185
Sweet Vidalia Onion Sauce, 216

**T**
Tacos, Baja–Style Grilled Tempeh
  Tacos, 96–97
Taco salad, 96
Taco slaw, 96–97
Tahini
  Dill–Tahini Sauce, 215
  Miso Tahini Dressing, 93–94
Tamales
  Everyday Chipotle–Vegetable
    Tamales, 59–60
  freezing/reheating, 59
Tamarind Lentils, 123
Tangerine Baked Tofu, 126–127
Tapenade, Sweet Basil Pesto
  Tapenade, 65
Tapioca flour, 7
Tarragon
  Asparagus Quiche with Tomatoes
    and Tarragon, 153–154
  French Lentil Soup with Tarragon
    and Thyme, 141–142
Tea–Poached Pears in Chocolate
  Sauce, 246
Tempeh
  Baja–Style Grilled Tempeh Tacos,
    96–97
  broiling, 130, 131
  Creamy Asian Pear and Tempeh
    Salad with Wasabi Dressing,
    90
  grilling, 130, 131
  Hot Sauce–Glazed Tempeh,
    129–130

panfrying, 130, 131
pantry stocking of, 4
Pear and Tempeh Roll, 48
"sautéing," 22
Smoky Grilled Tempeh, 130–131
Spicy Tempeh and Broccoli Rabe
  with Rotelle, 190–191
Spicy Tempeh Nori Rolls,
  47–48
Tempeh Shepherdess Pie,
  167–168
Temptation Ice Cream, 260
Terminology of cooking/prepping,
  18–20
Terry's Favorite Almond Cookie, 235–
  236
Thousand Island Dressing, 93
Thyme
  cooking with, 170
  French Lentil Soup with Tarragon
    and Thyme, 141–142
Timing major event preparations, 270
Toasted sesame oil, 8
Toasting
  hazelnuts, 263
  sesame seeds, 57
Tofu
  Baked BBQ Tofu, 128
  baking, 126, 129
  Basic Broiled Tofu, 126
  Chile Cornmeal–Crusted Tofu,
    125–126
  Chile Cornmeal–Crusted Tofu Po'
    Boy, 99
  Curried Tofu, 127
  Greek Tofu Benedict, 74
  grilling, 128–129
  Marinated Asian Tofu, 129
  Marinated Italian Tofu, 128–129
  Mushroom and Spinach Strata,
    72–73
  panfrying, 125
  pantry stocking of, 4
  "sautéing," 22
  Silken Mayo Dressing and
    variations, 92–93
  Tangerine Baked Tofu, 126–127
  Tofu Florentine, 72
  Tofu Ricotta, 206
Tomatillos, about, 210
Tomatoes
  Asparagus Quiche with Tomatoes
    and Tarragon, 153–154

Creamy Tomato Soup, 148
Greek–Style Tomato–Zucchini
  Fritters with Fresh Herbs,
  52–53
grilling, 29
Midsummer Corn Chowder with
  Basil, Tomato, and Fennel, 144
pantry stocking of, 3
roasting, 34
Sautéed Spinach and Tomatoes,
  106–107
Tomato and Roasted Eggplant
  Stew with Chickpeas, 179–180
Tomato–Basil Soup, 148
Tomato Couscous with Capers,
  117–118
Tomato–Rice Soup with Roasted
  Garlic and Navy Beans, 137
Tomato Sauce, 164–165
See also Sun–dried tomatoes
Tongs, 16
Tools
  for outdoor grilling, 25
  See also Kitchen equipment
Tortillas
  Grilled Yuca Tortillas, 49–50
  Spinach–Cilantro Tortillas, 50
  Sweet Potato–Black Bean Tortillas,
    50
Tropical Avocado Salsa Fresca, 213
Tubers and root vegetables. See Root
  vegetables and tubers
Turbinado sugar, 7
Turnip Puree, 111
Turnips, roasting, 34
Tzimmes, Sweet Potato–Pear
  Tzimmes with Pecans and
  Raisins, 156

**U**
Udon with Shiitake Mushrooms and
  Kale in Miso Broth, 201–202
"Under 45 minutes" definition/icon, 1
Utensils, 16

**V**
Vanilla extract, 6
Vanilla Ice Cream, 260
Vanilla–Yogurt Pound Cake, 254–255
Vegan bacon, 146
Vegan chocolate chips, 243
Vegan Ghost of Julia Child Menu, 268
Vegan graham crackers, 242

297

• INDEX

# ABOUT THE AUTHORS

PHOTO COURTESY OF EVAN MCGRAW

**ISA CHANDRA MOSKOWITZ** is America's most popular vegan chef. She is the author of *Vegan with a Vengeance*, which won PETA's Proggy Award for Best Cookbook 2006. She has done vegan cooking demonstrations around the country and has been featured in dozens of print and online publications. She and **TERRY HOPE ROMERO** are the authors of *Vegan Cupcakes Take Over the World*, winner of *VegNews'* Veggie Award for Best New Cookbook. Since 2003, Isa and Terry have hosted the public access/podcast vegan cooking show The Post Punk Kitchen. They can be found online at www.theppk.com and linked on countless blogs.